3000

FROM REVOLUTION TO POWER IN BRAZIL

RECENT TITLES FROM THE HELEN KELLOGG INSTITUTE SERIES
ON DEMOCRACY AND DEVELOPMENT

Paolo G. Carozza and Aníbal Pérez-Liñan, series editors

The University of Notre Dame Press gratefully thanks the Helen Kellogg Institute for International Studies for its support in the publication of titles in this series.

Ignacio Walker
Democracy in Latin America: Between Hope and Despair (2013)

Laura Gómez-Mera
Power and Regionalism in Latin America: The Politics of MERCOSUR (2013)

Rosario Queirolo
The Success of the Left in Latin America: Untainted Parties, Market Reforms, and Voting Behavior (2013)

Erik Ching
Authoritarian el Salvador: Politics and the Origins of the Military Regimes, 1880–1940 (2013)

Brian Wampler
Activating Democracy in Brazil: Popular Participation, Social Justice, and Interlocking Institutions (2015)

J. Ricardo Tranjan
Participatory Democracy in Brazil: Socioeconomic and Political Origins (2016)

Tracy Beck Fenwick
Avoiding Governors: Federalism, Democracy, and Poverty Alleviation in Brazil and Argentina (2016)

Alexander Wilde
Religious Responses to Violence: Human Rights in Latin America Past and Present (2016)

Pedro Meira Monteiro
The Other Roots: Wandering Origins in Roots of Brazil *and the Impasses of Modernity in Ibero–America* (2017)

John Aerni-Flessner
Dreams for Lesotho: Independence, Foreign Assistance, and Development (2018)

Roxana Barbulescu
Migrant Integration in a Changing Europe: Migrants, European Citizens, and Co-ethnics in Italy and Spain (2019)

Matthew C. Ingram and Diana Kapiszewski
Beyond High Courts: The Justice Complex in Latin America (2019)

For a complete list of titles from the Helen Kellogg Institute for International Studies, see http://www.undpress.nd.edu.

FROM REVOLUTION TO POWER IN BRAZIL

How Radical Leftists
Embraced Capitalism and
Struggled with Leadership

KENNETH P. SERBIN

University of Notre Dame Press
Notre Dame, Indiana

University of Notre Dame Press
Notre Dame, Indiana 46556
undpress.nd.edu

Cover images: shutterstock // Front cover images: (*top*) Police in São Paulo detain a man during a street protest in São Paulo, October 1968. Iconographia; (*bottom*) In 1971, President Médici visited the National Steel Factory in Volta Redonda, an area of national security and hotbed of political activism. Iconographia. // Back cover image: Former National Liberating Action militant Paulo de Tarso Vannuchi, Minister of the Special Secretariat for Human Rights (left), with President Luiz Inácio Lula da Silva, August 2006. Photo by Ricardo Stuckert.

Library of Congress Cataloging-in-Publication Data
Names: Serbin, Ken, author.
Title: From revolution to power in Brazil : how radical leftists embraced
   capitalism and struggled with leadership / Kenneth P. Serbin.
Description: Notre Dame, Indiana : University of Notre Dame Press, [2019] |
   Series: Helen Kellogg Institute series on democracy and development | Includes
   bibliographical references and index. | Identifiers: LCCN 2019017145 (print) |
   LCCN 2019020350 (ebook) | ISBN 9780268105884 (pdf) |
   ISBN 9780268105877 (epub) | ISBN 9780268105853 (hardback : alk. paper)
Subjects: LCSH: Brazil—Politics and government—1964–1985. | Brazil—Politics and
   government—1985–2002. | Ação Libertadora Nacional (Organization : Brazil)—
   History. | Revolutionaries—Brazil—History—20th century. |
   Military government—Brazil—History—20th century. |
   Terrorism—Brazil—History—20th century. | Capitalism—Brazil—
   History—20th century. | Brazil—Economic conditions—1985–
Classification: LCC F2538.25 (ebook) | LCC F2538.25.S465   2019 (print) | DDC
   981.06—dc23
LC record available at https://lccn.loc.gov/2019017145

∞ *This book is printed on acid-free paper.*

For my parents, whose souls are at rest

For the Huntington's disease community

For Regina and Bianca

CONTENTS

LIST OF ILLUSTRATIONS

KEY HISTORICAL FIGURES

Nine Former ALN (National Liberating Action) Militants, the Main Subjects of This Book

Adriano—Adriano Diogo, a São Paulo politician active in the Workers' Party and social and environmental causes.

Aloysio—Aloysio Nunes Ferreira Filho, a senator and three-time cabinet minister for the Brazilian Social Democratic Party.

Arlete—Arlete Diogo, a teacher, São Paulo Workers' Party activist, and key assistant to Adriano Diogo.

Carlos Eugênio—Carlos Eugênio Sarmento Coêlho da Paz, public enemy number one of the Brazilian dictatorship, political activist, and musician.

Colombo—Colombo Vieira de Souza, a convicted hijacker, political prisoner, and political advisor in the Democratic Labor Party.

Jessie—Jessie Jane Vieira de Souza, a convicted hijacker, political prisoner, political activist, and historian.

Manoel—Manoel Cyrillo de Oliveira Netto, the man who wounded the U.S. ambassador, political prisoner, and successful public relations specialist.

Márcio—Márcio Araújo de Lacerda, a leading telecommunications entrepreneur who became mayor of Brazil's fourth largest city.

Paulo—Paulo de Tarso Vannuchi, one of the militants most tortured during the dictatorship and later a presidential advisor and minister of the Special Secretariat for Human Rights.

OTHER IMPORTANT FIGURES

Aécio—Aécio Neves da Cunha, a senator of the Brazilian Social Democratic Party and presidential candidate in 2014.

Brizola—Leonel Brizola, the brother-in-law of deposed President João Goulart and one of Brazil's leading nationalist politicians.

Che—Che Guevara, a leader of the Cuban Revolution of 1959.

Dirceu—José Dirceu de Oliveira e Silva, a former student leader, revolutionary, cabinet minister, and top leader of the Workers' Party.

Dom Paulo—Dom Paulo Evaristo Arns, the cardinal-archbishop of São Paulo and outspoken defender of human rights.

Elbrick—Charles Burke Elbrick, the U.S. ambassador to Brazil kidnapped in September 1969.

Figueiredo—Gen. João Baptista de Oliveira Figueiredo, the fifth and final military president (1979–85), who, struggling with an economic crisis, oversaw the return to civilian rule.

Geisel—Gen. Ernesto Geisel, the fourth military president (1974–79) and initiator of the political liberalization and relaxation of censorship.

Goulart—João Goulart, democratically elected president (1961–64) overthrown in the U.S.-backed military coup of 1964.

Juarez—José Juarez Antunes, the most prominent labor leader of the 1980s in the steel town of Volta Redonda and politician with independent views.

Kubitschek—Juscelino Kubitschek de Oliveira, president from 1956 to 1961, the builder of Brasília, and one of Brazil's most popular leaders.

Maluf—Paulo Maluf, a right-wing politician in São Paulo and the military's favorite for president in the 1985 indirect presidential election.

Marighella—Carlos Marighella, the founder of the ALN, lead proponent of guerrilla warfare, and assassinated by the repressive forces in 1969.

Médici—Gen. Emílio Garrastazu Médici, the third military president (1969–74) and overseer of Brazil's "economic miracle" and torture chambers.

Prestes—Luiz Carlos Prestes, the leader of the Brazilian Communist Party and proponent of peaceful coexistence with the United States and capitalism.

Vargas—Getúlio Vargas, dictator and president of Brazil (1930–45, 1951–54), the architect of Brazil's state-led capitalist model.

ABBREVIATIONS AND GLOSSARY

ALN	Ação Libertadora Nacional (National Liberating Action)
Bandeirantes	Backwoodsmen of colonial Brazil who explored the hinterland and enslaved natives
BNM	"Brasil: Nunca Mais" ("Brazil: Never Again"), antitorture project
Bolsa Escola	Bolsa Escola, a scholarship program aimed at encouraging needy families to send their children to school regularly instead of having them work to support the household
Centro Acadêmico	A university student council
cortiços	Crowded tenements where people from Brazil's impoverished Northeast region settled in São Paulo.
CSN	Companhia Siderúrgica Nacional (National Steel Factory)
DEOPS	Departamento Estadual de Ordem Política e Social (State Department of Political and Social Order), the political police in São Paulo state during the dictatorship
desaparecido	A missing person "disappeared" (i.e., murdered) by the repressive forces
diretas já	"Direct Presidential Elections *Now*," a national campaign against the dictatorship in 1983–84
DOI-CODI	Destacamento de Operações de Informações do Centro de Operações de Defesa Interna (Intelligence Operations Detachment of the Center for Internal Defense

	Operations), the interrogation units of the Brazilian army during the dictatorship. The model was the OBAN (see below).
IA-5	Institutional Act No. 5, decreed on December 13, 1968, closed the Congress and severely restricted civil liberties
justiçamento	The assassination by guerrillas of supporters of the military regime or of suspected traitors
MDB	Movimento Democrático Brasileiro (MDB, or Brazilian Democratic Movement), one of two political parties created by the dictatorship after the abolition of all other parties
mensalão	"Big fat monthly payment," bribes paid to congressional representatives in return for political support
MOLIPO	Movimento de Libertação Popular (Movement for Popular Liberation), an offshoot of the ALN
movimento popular	Popular movement, best translated as "Power to the People," Brazilian-style, a wide variety of grassroots pressure groups and organizations opposed to the dictatorship and seeking a more just society
MR-8	Movimento Revolucionário 8 de Outubro (October 8 Revolutionary Movement), a Brazilian revolutionary organization whose name evoked the capture of Che Guevara on that date
OBAN	Operação Bandeirantes (Operation Bandeirantes), a multiforce investigative unit established by the dictatorship in 1969 to hunt down revolutionaries. It gave way to the DOI-CODI units (see above). See also "Bandeirantes," above.
PCB	Partido Comunista Brasileiro (Brazilian Communist Party)
PC do B	Partido Comunista do Brasil (the Communist Party of Brazil, a Maoist offshoot of the PCB)
PDS	Partido Democrático Social (Democratic Social Party), the right-wing party succeeding the official proregime party of the military era
PDT	Partido Democrático Trabalhista (Democratic Labor Party)

PMDB	Partido do Movimento Democrático Brasileiro (Party of the Brazilian Democratic Movement), the successor to the MDB created in 1980. In 2017 the party changed its name back to MDB.
Ponto	Regular, prearranged, secure meetings of usually two or three leftist militants, who shared information and checked on each other. A missed meeting indicated that a comrade had been captured.
PSB	Partido Socialista Brasileiro (Brazilian Socialist Party)
PSDB	Partido da Social Democracia Brasileira (Brazilian Social Democratic Party)
PT	Partido dos Trabalhadores (Workers' Party)
PTB	Partido Trabalhista Brasileiro (Brazilian Labor Party)
SEDH	Secretaria Especial de Direitos Humanos da Presidência da República (or Special Secretariat for Human Rights of the President of the Republic), created by President Fernando Henrique Cardoso in 1997 and raised to a cabinet-level position by President Luiz Inácio Lula da Silva in 2003
Telebrás	Telecomunicações Brasileiras (Brazilian Telecommunications), a federal holding company set up in 1972 to oversee public and private telecommunications initiatives
USP	Universidade de São Paulo (University of São Paulo)
VPR	Vanguarda Popular Revolucionária (People's Revolutionary Vanguard)

TIMELINE OF IMPORTANT EVENTS

March 31–April 1, 1964	Overthrow of democratically elected President João Goulart by the Brazilian military
April 15, 1964	General Castello Branco becomes president
March 15, 1967	General Costa e Silva becomes president
Late 1967	Foundation of the guerrilla organization ALN (National Liberating Action)
December 13, 1968	Decree of Institutional Act No. 5 (IA-5), suspending civil liberties and freedom of the press
July 1969	Operação Bandeirantes (OBAN) created in São Paulo to hunt down subversives
August 1969	Costa e Silva suffers a stroke and is replaced by a military junta
September 4–7, 1969	Kidnapping of U.S. ambassador by ALN and MR-8 revolutionaries, including Manoel Cyrillo de Oliveira Netto, Virgílio Gomes da Silva, Joaquim Câmara Ferreira, Paulo de Tarso Venceslau, Fernando Gabeira, and Franklin de Souza Martins
October 30, 1969	General Médici becomes president
November 4, 1969	Assassination of ALN leader Carlos Marighella
March 30, 1973	Three thousand people attend a memorial/protest Mass for Alexandre Vannucchi Leme at the cathedral in downtown São Paulo
March 15, 1974	General Geisel becomes president and initiates the political liberalization
March 15, 1979	General Figueiredo becomes president
August 28, 1979	President Figueiredo promulgates the Amnesty Law, permitting return of exiled Brazilians and release of

	political prisoners but also preventing prosecution of human rights violations
March 15, 1985	Brazil returns to civilian rule after twenty-one years of military dictatorship; after death of president-elect Tancredo Neves, chosen by an electoral college without a popular vote, Vice President José Sarney takes office on April 21
October 5, 1988	Promulgation of the Constitution of 1988
March 15, 1990	Fernando Collor de Mello takes office as the first democratically elected president since 1960
December 29, 1992	Impeached by the Chamber of Deputies, President Collor resigns as the Senate votes to convict him of corruption charges; Vice President Itamar Franco assumes the presidency
January 1, 1995	Fernando Henrique Cardoso of the Brazilian Social Democratic Party takes office as president and stabilizes the Brazilian currency after decades of inflation
January 1, 2003	Luiz Inácio Lula da Silva of the Workers' Party takes office as the first president of working-class origin in Latin American history
January 1, 2011	Former political prisoner and torture victim Dilma Rousseff of the Workers' Party takes office as the first female and ex-revolutionary president in Brazilian history
August 31, 2016	After her impeachment by the Chamber of Deputies, President Dilma is convicted by the Senate and removed from office; Vice President Michel Temer assumes the presidency
October 28, 2018	Election to the presidency of Jair Bolsonaro, a prodictatorship congressman and former army captain

MAP OF BRAZIL

AC -Acre
AL - Alagoas
AP - Amapá
AM - Amazonas
BA - Bahia
CE - Ceará
DF - Distrito Federal (Brasília)
ES - Espírito Santo
GO - Goiás
MA - Maranhão
MT - Mato Grosso
MS - Mato Grosso do Sul
MG - Minas Gerais
PA - Pará
PB - Paraíba
PR - Paraná
PE - Pernambuco
PI - Piauí
RN - Rio Grande do Norte
RS - Rio Grande do Sul
RJ - Rio de Janeiro
RO - Rondônia
RR - Roraima
SC - Santa Catarina
SP - São Paulo
SE - Sergipe
TO - Tocantins

PROLOGUE

I went to Brazil to write about the dead, but the Brazilians convinced me to focus on the living.

On September 11, 1996—exactly five years before al-Qaeda crashed jetliners into the towers of the World Trade Center and the Pentagon—I conducted my first interview with a member of the leading organization of the armed resistance to the military dictatorship that ruled Brazil from 1964 to 1985. I belonged to a generation of "Brazilianists"—foreigners specializing in the history, society, and culture of Brazil—who had not personally witnessed the dictatorship. Aiming to improve my Portuguese and get a basic introduction to the world's fifth-largest country, I had first traveled to Brazil in mid-1986. Brazilians were then euphoric about the first good economic times in years. They were also preparing to choose a National Constituent Assembly—which would draft a new constitution to replace the one imposed by the dictators in 1967—in the first fully free national election after the military era. That trip fueled my Ph.D. dissertation on liberationist Catholicism in Brazil[1] and my interest in the history of the dictatorship.[2] During my doctoral research in Rio de Janeiro (1988–91), I met a Brazilian woman who later became my wife and the mother of our daughter. Brazil became my second home.

My studies brought me into contact with many adversaries of the dictatorship—individuals now working to overcome the legacies of military rule, whom I interviewed extensively over a period of years, from 1996 to 2015. The military had come to power in 1964 with U.S. support. Dubbed the "country of the future" by Austrian writer Stefan Zweig in 1941, Brazil was a major U.S. ally. Brazilian iron ore helped support U.S. manufacturing during World War II, and the country's troops battled alongside G.I.'s in Italy, the only unit from Latin America to join in the ground war. After the war, guided by national security concerns, Brazil's

1

leaders and military wanted to transform it into a world power.[3] Under the Kennedy and Johnson administrations, the United States made Brazil a pawn in the Cold War, the geopolitical chess game it played with the Soviet Union, with each side fomenting surrogate conflicts in Third World countries. However, from former presidents to people in the streets, a substantial portion of Brazilians opposed their country's dictatorship. In many nations with anti-Communist Cold War regimes, leftist revolutionaries arose to combat their governments. In Brazil, militants formed more than three dozen groups—"terrorists" in the eyes of the military—aiming to overthrow the generals and implant socialism. I wanted to learn more about these revolutionaries. Paulo de Tarso Vannuchi, my initial interviewee in September 1996, had fought for Ação Libertadora Nacional (ALN, or National Liberating Action), the largest of the guerrilla organizations. The ALN formed in late 1967 in response to the repression and the refusal of the Partido Comunista Brasileiro (PCB, or Brazilian Communist Party) to resist the military.

During the revolutionaries' childhood years, presidents Getúlio Vargas (1930–45, 1951–54) and Juscelino Kubitschek de Oliveira (1956–61) had led the country into a new era of industrialization—supported by many in the military—that introduced Brazilians to consumer goods and fed the drive for economic power. Seizing the presidency in the violent, modernizing Revolution of 1930 and acting as a dictator from 1937 to 1945, Vargas adapted to Brazil's new democratic system after the war, winning election to his second term as a populist in 1950. Vargas veered to the left, carrying out a nationalistic platform that included the nationalization of the country's oil and the creation of Petrobras, a state-owned petroleum firm, in 1953. Conservatives attacked Vargas as a radical. In 1954, accused of corruption and facing military intervention, Vargas committed suicide. Under his successor Kubitschek, Brazil regained political stability. Kubitschek oversaw the construction of Brasília, a new capital in the interior that replaced Rio and, in parallel with the United States, stimulated the construction of interstate highways and the rapid expansion of the automobile industry.[4] Industrialization and the vast movement of people from the countryside into the burgeoning cities transformed the country's image as an agricultural producer into one of a bustling, evermore urban nation. Progress generated optimism and a nationalistic ethos. For the 1950 World Cup, Rio inaugurated its Maracanã soccer stadium, the world's largest, and Brazil won the cup in 1958 and 1962 thanks

to the young phenomenon Pelé. In 1958 emerged another Brazilian phenomenon, the music known as bossa nova, which, by the early 1960s, had
migrated to the United States thanks to João Gilberto, Antônio Carlos
(Tom) Jobim, and others and was embraced by such American musical
giants as Stan Getz and Frank Sinatra.

Brazilians' expectations rose, but poverty and a host of other problems
held the nation back. The revolutionaries, who are at the heart of this
book, had grown up in a country with a feeling of inferiority about its past.
Brazil had imported more African slaves than any other country in the
hemisphere, nearly eight times more than the United States. That heritage, combined with the traditions of the Portuguese colonists, the natives,
and numerous other ethnic groups descended from immigrants, had produced an exuberant people symbolized in Rio's pulsating Carnival. But—
especially in the eyes of the revolutionaries—the people were oppressed by
the economic elite. Slavery had bequeathed to Brazil a steep social pyramid,
with poor people, often of darker skin, at the lower levels always expected
to act with great deference toward their superiors, usually of lighter skin.
Mainly from privileged families, the guerrillas were painfully aware of
Brazil's historic, subordinate role in the global system as an exporter of
sugar, gold, diamonds, coffee, and rubber—all categories in which it had
once led the world. Brazil's natural bounty was epitomized in the stunning
scenery of Rio, where the mountains met the sea, the Sugar Loaf mountain stood guard at the entrance to the lovely Guanabara Bay, and the
Christ the Redeemer statue's providential arms stretched out from atop
the unique Corcovado peak, symbolizing Brazil's status as the world's
largest Catholic country. In stark contrast, however, massive favelas
(shantytowns) stood out like sores on Rio's picturesque hillsides, revealing
the country's deep inequalities.

Restless for change, a generation of idealistic young Brazilians felt a
strong urge to achieve social justice in Brazil immediately. As their counterparts struggled and sometimes died for the defense of civil rights in the
United States, they sought to transform society by taking their music,
theater, and politics to the deprived of the favelas and the poor eking out
an existence in the countryside.

Paulo[5] was born in 1950 in the small rural town of São Joaquim da
Barra, located 220 miles from São Paulo, Brazil's largest city, in the state
of São Paulo. The son of a teacher who had studied for the Catholic priest-
hood, Paulo grew up in an extended family with strong Christian values

and a desire for social justice. Like many of his generation, Paulo was deeply impressed by the progressive reforms proposed by President João Goulart (1961–64). A Vargas protégé and Kubitschek's vice president, Goulart swung further to the left. A growing tide of left-wing grassroots movements, union leaders, student groups, and radical politicians supported his plans to carry out redistribution of land and defend the poor. Politically precocious, Paulo was swept up in the wave of hope for a more equitable society.[6]

Brazil's growing leftist tendencies angered the Kennedy and Johnson administrations and also Brazil's pro-U.S. generals. Many of those officers had trained in the United States and helped lead the Brazilian Expeditionary Force in Italy. They believed that their country had a special relationship with the United States in fighting Communism and promoting economic development. With the U.S. anti-Communist war escalating in Vietnam, U.S. leaders feared that Brazil would follow the lead of Fidel Castro and Che Guevara's 1959 Cuban Revolution and become the next domino to fall into the Communist system. Conservative generals and civilians in Brazil believed that Goulart had opened the door to Communism. Together with Goulart's civilian opponents, and answering the appeal for intervention by the large segment of anti-Communists, they conspired against the president. Meanwhile, Goulart struggled to manage an economy that had sputtered after the Kubitschek boom.

On the night of March 31, 1964, anti-Goulart generals in the neighboring state of Minas Gerais led troops toward Rio, where Goulart and the federal government still maintained many operations because the move to Brasília, inaugurated in 1960, was still in progress. The invading force entered Rio the morning of April 1. President Johnson immediately congratulated the military junta that took charge of the government. The pro-Goulart faction within the military was too weak and indecisive to counterattack. Goulart also feared that resistance might spark a civil war. He fled to Brasília to get his family, then to his home state of Rio Grande do Sul in the south of the country, and then into exile in Uruguay. However, even before Goulart left the country, Brazil's Congress declared the office of the presidency vacant. With the coup leaders in control of the country, on April 11 it voted the staunchly pro-U.S. Gen. Humberto de Alencar Castello Branco in as president. At least five opponents of the coup died in the immediate aftermath.[7] In the ensuing months, military and police personnel arrested tens of thousands of leftists, union leaders,

Catholic radicals, and others. Scores of individuals were brutally tortured. The antileftist witch hunt had begun. Dejected by the news of the coup, Paulo locked himself in a bathroom at home and cried. The police arrested two teachers in his town for their support of the Goulart reforms. Paulo's uncle, an outspoken priest accused of Communism, spent several days in jail.[8]

Because of the U.S.-backed coup, Goulart knew he had little chance of staying in power.[9] The Johnson administration had directed the CIA, the FBI, and the diplomatic corps to carry out covert political operations and furnish assurances of support and potential logistical backup. Secretly, a U.S. Navy task force sailed for Brazil in order to intervene in support of the coup, if necessary, but it was recalled after the anti-Goulart forces had effectively taken control. Brazil's leftists suspected U.S. involvement but lacked proof at the time. After emboldening the coup plotters, U.S. ambassador Lincoln Gordon helped lead the campaign of denial regarding U.S. support. However, in a speech at Brazil's National War College, he put the ouster of Goulart on a par with "the Marshall Plan, the end of the Berlin blockade, the defeat of Communist aggression in Korea, and the solution of the missile crisis in Cuba as one of the critical moments in world history at the mid-century."[10]

Previous military interventions in twentieth-century Brazil had ended in a return to civilian rule. Many politicians expected General Castello Branco to confirm the 1965 presidential election, with the participation of civilians. However, Cold War fears, distrust of civilians' capability to govern and manage the economy, and pressure from hard-line officers led to long-term control of the country. Castello Branco was succeeded by Gen. Artur da Costa e Silva (1967–69), Gen. Emílio Garrastazu Médici (1969–74), Gen. Ernesto Geisel (1974–79), and Gen. João Baptista de Oliveira Figueiredo (1979–85)—all chosen secretly by top-level officers. To consolidate military rule, Castello Branco and his successors issued "institutional acts" and other decrees that severely hampered or destroyed Brazil's relatively new democratic institutions. The Castello Branco government abolished the political parties formed after 1945, shunting politicians into two newly created official parties, the proregime Aliança Renovadora Nacional (National Renovating Alliance, 1966–79) and the opposition Movimento Democrático Brasileiro (MDB, or Brazilian Democratic Movement, 1966–79). The regime also banned disfavored politicians from public activity. Goulart died in exile in 1976, and Kubitschek only occasionally reentered Brazil, where he died the same year. The government seized control of unions by arresting pro-Goulart leaders and appointing figureheads. Strikes were prohibited. The regime granted the president extraordinary powers, turning Congress and the courts into puppets. In 1967, the regime issued a new constitution focused on national security and the elimination of dissent. The dictators interfered in the universities, even sending troops to some campuses.

Already in 1966, thousands of student protestors took to the streets throughout the country, demanding an end to the dictatorship. In São Joaquim da Barra, the sixteen-year-old Paulo and his friends resisted the dictatorship with public, collective readings of left-wing poems. In late 1967, he moved to São Paulo to prepare for the entrance exam for the medical school at the Universidade de São Paulo (USP), Brazil's most prestigious university. São Paulo was becoming a hub of the resistance, led by students, labor organizers, and revolutionaries. Paulo met with some of the organizers.[11] The student movement reached a crescendo in 1968, with one protest in Rio attracting 100,000 people. That year, Brazil's guerrilla groups, including the ALN, sprang into action. The ALN acted primarily in São Paulo and Rio, also a center of the struggle against the government. On September 2, 1968, MDB congressman Márcio Moreira Alves, a journalist who had denounced the use of torture, urged the populace to boycott the traditional military parade on September 7, Independence Day. He also suggested that Brazilian women should not sleep with officers who took part in or failed to condemn the abuses. The speech deepened the political crisis. On December 13, the regime responded to the growing unrest by decreeing Institutional Act No. 5 (IA-5), which suspended civil liberties and freedom of the press. Referred to as the "coup within the coup," IA-5 represented the undisputed dominance of the hard-liners within the Costa e Silva administration. Under IA-5, Costa e Silva shut down the Congress, turning Brazil into a full dictatorship. IA-5 gave the military and the police carte blanche against the revolutionaries. The armed forces ran security, establishing special units for capturing, interrogating, and torturing suspected militants.

Under President Médici, the economy completed its recovery from the Goulart-era stagnation, producing massive growth, known as the "Brazilian miracle," which heightened national pride. Médici also allowed the security forces to mercilessly pursue the guerrillas and quell any hint of protest. Under him the regime systematized torture. It also adopted an

Figure 1. Police in São Paulo detain a man during a street protest in São Paulo, October 1968. Iconographia.

informal, secret policy of executing many captured guerrillas.[12] Future presidents Geisel and Figueiredo knew of and approved this policy, as documented in a 1974 CIA memorandum.[13]

In 1969, during his first year at USP medical school, Paulo joined the ALN, first in a supporting, nonviolent role. As the need for guerrilla recruits grew, he graduated to armed actions. Paulo ultimately fell victim to the security steamroller. In February 1971, he was imprisoned in São Paulo. In March 1973, his cousin Alexandre Vannucchi Leme,[14] an ALN activist and popular student leader at the USP, was arrested in an antiterrorist dragnet and taken to the same intelligence center where Paulo had been held. Twenty-four hours later, brutalized by interrogators bent on revenge after the ALN had assassinated a particularly vicious torturer near Copacabana beach in Rio, Alexandre died from the abuses.

I hoped to write a book about Alexandre to personify the horrors of dictatorship in South America. In targeting him, Brazil's dictators had eliminated yet another young idealist, one on track to join the country's political and economic elite. In a typical cover-up, the government claimed he had tried to escape from the police and had been run over by a motorist as he ran into the street. The Catholic cardinal of São Paulo, Dom Paulo Evaristo Arns, defied the dictators by organizing a memorial Mass for Alexandre. Three thousand people crowded into the city's cathedral. The security forces sent in infiltrators and patrolled the nearby streets. Many organizers of the Mass were arrested. A leading regime official accused Cardinal Arns of provoking a potential bloodbath. But the Mass, and the civic energy it liberated, helped Brazil turn the corner on the dictatorship.

I later published the first detailed historical account of Alexandre's death and its aftermath within my book on the Catholic Church and the dictatorship.[15] Later, prominent Brazilian journalist Caio Túlio Costa wrote a moving, book-length account of the episode.[16]

During our 1996 interview, Paulo relived his time in prison and the events surrounding Alexandre's death. Paulo was one of the most tortured of the dictatorship' political prisoners. At one point, to show me the force of the electric shocks applied by torturers, he gripped the arms of his chair and shook it furiously, causing his entire body to tremble.

Despite the trauma, Paulo had survived. Like thousands of other revolutionaries and leftists repressed by the government, he had not only rebuilt his personal life but was thriving professionally. Paulo's office in the São Paulo megalopolis was very close to power. He worked in the inner sanctum of the think tank set up by the Partido dos Trabalhadores (PT, or Workers' Party). It was planning for a potential government led by the PT's popular two-time candidate for president, Luiz Inácio Lula da Silva (known as Lula). He later won election to two terms (2003–11).

The stark contrast between Paulo's past and present suggested that Brazil was overcoming the dark years of the dictatorship. So I concluded that, rather than focusing solely on the guerrillas' feats and the regime's abuses, as had a plethora of revolutionary memoirs and scholarly and journalistic books, I should tell the largely ignored story of how individual Brazilians and the nation had fared *after* that period. That story was equally significant if not more so, my interviewees would suggest. For example, Jessie Jane Vieira de Souza, along with her husband, Colombo, and two other ALN militants, had attempted to hijack a Cruzeiro Airlines flight in July 1970 in order to force the military to release forty political prisoners. For their crimes, Jessie and Colombo spent ten difficult years as political prisoners. Nevertheless, Jessie affirmed that the next step posed an even bigger challenge: "After getting out of prison, it was very difficult to put our lives back together. I believe it was more difficult than being in prison."[17]

Thus, from 1996 to 2016, I researched the lives of Paulo, Jessie, Colombo, and about two dozen other ex-militants, mainly from the ALN. In all, I conducted around 300 hours of detailed interviews with a select group of militants, and many additional hours with others. I also followed their careers through press reports and other sources. In addition, I accumulated information on twenty-six more former ALN militants (seventeen men, nine women) who responded to a biographical questionnaire.

Delving into their life stories was like entering another dimension. I grew up in Ohio, the heartland of America, the world's capitalist center. I had no experience as a combatant or protestor, but I was deeply troubled by the 1970 killing of four unarmed students by the National Guard during a demonstration against the Vietnam War at nearby Kent State University. Initially, I perceived my interviewees as part of a very alien social grouping, given their profound revolutionary experience and set of values. I also had no familiarity with the type of physical and psychological cruelty that many of them had endured or of the deep sense of fear and anguish they had felt either in prison or in exile.

Relying on my experience as a researcher of the Brazilian Catholic Church, I gained access to interviewees by tapping into activist networks. Many interviews involved typical Brazilian socializing and hospitality. I watched Brazil play in the World Cup on TV in the living room of one former revolutionary in São Paulo, ate steak cooked by another at his apartment in Rio, and, as a guest of his parents, slept in Alexandre's bedroom in Sorocaba, the city about fifty-five miles west of São Paulo where he grew up. Threaded through all of the interviews was discussion of the former militants' professional development, their personal lives, and their spouses, children, and grandchildren. I met most of the ex-revolutionaries' families and, in some cases, became privy to their personal travails. All were forthcoming and extremely generous with their time.

The former militants revealed how they tried to overcome the personal consequences of the dictatorship and, with hindsight, to comprehend their experiences. We explored violent actions and the resultant psychological consequences. They shared with me the devastation of torture and the loss of comrades and loved ones. In a few instances, I became the first nonfamily member to whom these individuals confided difficult memories of the revolutionary era and their struggles to find meaning and solace.

We probed many topics relevant to their fight against the dictatorship and its aftermath: the evolution of Brazil's human rights movement, the strengths and weaknesses of Brazilian democracy, and the performance of the country's presidential administrations. We discussed economic policy and the environment.

We also focused on the armed resistance to the dictatorship and their views of revolution, violence, and terrorism. At its base, revolutionary action spoke to the deep human desire for improvement. History has demonstrated that revolutions are far from linear and often result in immense carnage, as occurred in the twentieth century in the Soviet Union under Joseph Stalin and in China under Mao Zedong. Both Stalin and Mao were complex individuals shaped by history. Their ideas, though they became gospel for many leftists around the world, were not a given but evolved over a lifetime and in response to circumstances.[18]

In the post–World War II era, revolutions took on varied forms, ranging from anticolonial movements in Africa and Asia (including the Vietnam War) to the struggle against apartheid in South Africa. On the periphery of global power, revolutionaries in Latin America resisted the international capitalist order. A large segment of the Brazilian population created a culture of the Left involving Marxist political ideas, admiration for the Soviet Union, Communist China, and the Cuban Revolution, and resistance to U.S. influence. The arts—music, theater, and cinema—amplified these and related themes.

In Brazil, leftist culture flourished thanks in large part to the activities of the PCB, founded in 1922 as the Partido Comunista do Brasil and in 1958 renamed Partido Comunista Brasileiro. In 1935, the pro-Soviet PCB attempted a violent revolt against the government of Vargas. Suppressed by the military, the rebellion stiffened anti-Communist resolve in Brazil. Antileftist military officers later saw it as a turning point in the country's history. The Vargas regime imprisoned PCB leader Luiz Carlos Prestes and thousands of party members and sympathizers for years. Some were barbarously tortured. The PCB, following the violent Soviet line, executed several suspected traitors in the 1930s. Despite Vargas's repression, the PCB survived underground. After Vargas's overthrow in 1945, when Brazil embarked on its first democracy, the PCB participated in electoral politics as a legal party until 1947, when membership reached 220,000. The important port city of Santos had so many Communists that it was dubbed "Little Moscow." The large number of PCB members was important in a country seeking to jump-start modern, representative parties and expand the electorate beyond a privileged minority.[19]

However, with the Cold War underway, in 1947 the government proscribed the PCB and ended diplomatic relations with the Soviet Union. The PCB returned to the underground. Even so, it remained highly influential. Prestes and the party supported the nationalistic platform of Vargas's second term (1951–54). More than any other party in Brazil, the PCB attracted intellectuals, artists, and entertainers. Students and journalists also entered or collaborated with the party, as did large numbers of workers. In the 1950s, one Communist sympathizer even had his son baptized in the Catholic Church with the name "Lenin," the atheist first leader of the Soviet Union. That same decade, the PCB covertly organized strikes of hundreds of thousands of workers. After the death of Stalin in 1953, the PCB continued to support the Soviet Union as the center of world socialism—but it also embraced the new, post-Stalin notion of peaceful coexistence with capitalism and a peaceful transition to socialism in Brazil. It rejected the idea of exporting revolution, a priority of the brash leaders of the Cuban Revolution.[20] Association with the PCB exposed Brazil's intellectuals to the risk of persecution, but it also provided them with mutual support and validation as the vanguard of world revolution. The PCB-dominated culture of the Left nourished the powerful, albeit not practically defined, idea of a Brazilian revolution that would allow the nation to overcome its underdeveloped status and help individuals reach their full potential.[21] The party backed President Goulart's progressive agenda and, in the quest for socialism, an alliance with democratic politicians, labor unions, and nationalistic business leaders, the so-called national bourgeoisie. However, by the mid-1960s revolutionaries would consider the PCB conservative. Caught off guard, Prestes and the party did not resist the coup. At a party congress in 1967, the PCB officially reaffirmed its opposition to armed struggle, a stance it maintained throughout the dictatorship. Nevertheless, the PCB's history and culture seeded the rise of the armed resistance.

Brazilians' revolutionary efforts in the late 1960s and early 1970s sprung from numerous theories and strategies of how to fight and to bring about social and political progress. For this and other reasons, they lacked a united front. Thus, as the generals solidified power and increased repression, the militants essentially abandoned revolution and focused on resisting the dictatorship.[22] Like revolutionaries throughout Latin America, Brazil's guerrillas were partially motivated by the Cuban Revolution, even if they did not agree with all of its tactics or outcomes. However, they also responded to the authoritarian coup of 1964 that inaugurated a wave of such regimes, which dominated Latin America from the 1960s to the 1980s. These regimes were encouraged by U.S. Cold War policies.

Authoritarian leaders or dictators would also come to rule in Argentina, Bolivia, Chile, Ecuador, El Salvador, Guatemala, Honduras, Panama, Paraguay, Peru, and Uruguay. Government repression led to more than three thousand deaths and disappearances in Chile and more than fifteen thousand in Argentina. Civil wars between governments and guerrillas resulted in 75,000 dead in El Salvador and 200,000 in Guatemala. In Brazil, the repressive forces killed or disappeared 475 individuals. In the countryside, gunmen hired by landowners allied with the military government murdered more than one thousand poor people. The guerrillas caused more than one hundred casualties.[23]

In Brazil, nonviolent resistance ultimately played a larger role in ending the dictatorship than the revolutionaries. Initially rejected by the revolutionaries, the heterogeneous MDB served as a pole of attraction and key reference point for the legal opposition. Starting in the mid-1960s, the underground PCB had encouraged its members to join the MDB. The PCB continued its support of the MDB throughout the dictatorship. The MDB also received backing from other left-wing organizations, the Catholic Church, lawyers, journalists, politicians, labor unions, artists and musicians, students, and others. Numerically, the guerrillas were weaker, with fewer than a thousand actual fighters, but thousands participated in their support network, and many sympathized with their fight. However, the booming economy, the threat of repression, and the elite, intellectualized leadership of the revolution discouraged the masses from taking part. Although some revolutionaries came from rough backgrounds steeped in the country's patchwork of violence, a majority were whites of the middle and upper-middle classes. Alarmed, the military sought to counteract revolutionary influence in the high schools and universities where the guerrilla organizations recruited such individuals. At the same time, the guerrilla threat allowed the military to justify its grip on the country. By 1975, the military had suppressed the armed resistance, but it continued the fight against alleged "subversion" into the early 1980s. Abandoning combat as a strategy, the radical Left joined the peaceful opposition. It thus secured a role in the transition to civilian rule—accomplished in 1985 with the indirect, negotiated assumption of power by President José Sarney (1985–90)—and the future governance of the country.

"Was the dictatorship in Brazil overthrown?" Paulo asked rhetorically in an interview during Lula's first year in office, referring to the gradual, peaceful return to civilian rule. "No, it wasn't. What happened was that there was a political process, a controlled transition in which they won the confrontation with the Left. They destroyed us. And, paradoxically, we won out in the long run."[24] A number of the main interviewees echoed Paulo, but others criticized the transition to democracy as incomplete and highly flawed. Regardless, the ex-revolutionaries came to play an important part in the life of the nation.

Because of the heavy repression, resistance fighters, radicals, and nonviolent defenders of democracy in Latin America paid a much higher price for their actions than did contemporary opponents of the status quo in the United States and other developed nations. Their struggle echoed resistance against tyranny stretching back millennia and epitomized by prisoners of conscience, such as Dietrich Bonhoeffer, a German Protestant minister and theologian who conspired with others to assassinate Adolph Hitler. "In the face of Hitler's atrocities, the way of nonviolence would bring inevitable guilt—both for the 'uncontested' injustices and for the innocent lives that might have been saved," Bonhoeffer biographer Charles Marsh wrote of the pastor's rationale. "To act responsibly in these circumstances meant killing the madman if one could, even though such action violated God's commandment not to kill." Bonhoeffer was hanged in a Nazi concentration camp in April 1945.[25]

In the attempt to topple the dictatorship, Brazil's revolutionaries committed terrorist acts: bombings, kidnappings, hijackings, killings, and executions of suspected traitors. Terrorism provokes apocalyptic feelings in many. It has frequently dominated the news and shaped countries' political agendas—from hijackings and the kidnapping and killing of the Israeli Olympic athletes in 1972, to the Iranian hostage crisis of 1979–81, to the 9/11 attacks. However, the phenomenon of terrorism stretched back to antiquity and has been open to widely different interpretations.[26] Furthermore, because it has taken on diverse forms, with even governments as offenders, terrorism lacks a concise meaning. Terrorism expert Bruce Hoffman suggested a very broad working definition: the deliberate creation and exploitation of fear through violence or the threat of violence for political objectives.[27]

But were the Brazilian militants really terrorists? Or were they, as they preferred, revolutionaries? In the minds of the historical actors, both defining terrorism and justifying its use are clearly matters of perspective. A key example from U.S. history drives home this point. Antislavery crusader John Brown helped spark the Civil War and laid the basis for the civil rights movement by carrying out terrorist attacks. He was hanged in 1859. Historian David Reynolds points out that Brown's contemporaries were divided in their opinion, "with many seeing him as a bloodthirsty terrorist and others viewing him as a saintly liberator." Referring to British novelist Doris Lessing's notion of "good terrorism," Reynolds concluded that Brown was justified to the extent that he aimed to combat "obvious social injustice."[28] In Brazil, the revolutionaries resisted a violent military government that abolished freedoms and used torture. The regime referred to the resistance as terrorism, but the revolutionaries usually sought to avoid harming innocent bystanders. Walter Laqueur, a historian of terrorism, classified the Brazilian case as "defensive" terrorism.[29]

The Brazilian record challenges the idea of "terrorists" as naturally brutish and violent. On the contrary, the Brazilian revolutionaries were reacting to circumstances. After the defeat of the armed resistance, they came to appreciate the necessity and efficacy of peaceful politics. Thus, it's important to study these individuals not just as perpetrators or supporters of violence but as people with lives. We need to view their actions from *their* perspective. We must understand their multiple transitions, which were fraught with complexities and contradictions. Situations of terror and violence can be steered into more hopeful scenarios. In Brazil, the ex-revolutionaries' willingness to reassimilate into society helps explain how the country became politically stable. I have aimed to transcend the predictable storyline portraying Brazil's ex-guerrillas as heroes (as in revolutionary memoirs) or villains (as in military accounts).[30]

In the vast literature on terrorism, violence, and peacemaking, few scholars have focused on the long-term effects of the transition to nonviolence, notably militants becoming peaceful politicians.[31] For example, in South Africa, the tactically violent, antiapartheid, prosocialist African National Congress (ANC) abandoned more than three decades of revolutionary struggle to embrace liberal democracy, leading to the historic election of ANC leader and former political prisoner Nelson Mandela as president (1994–99). The ANC's multiracial leaders transformed the formerly white-controlled government. The compromises wrought earlier in Latin America, including Brazil, served as a key model for South Africa.[32]

I was especially intrigued by a supreme irony: how these radicals adapted to and then came to build, manage, and improve the capitalist system that they had tried to topple. I examined their participation in politics and government and their rise to positions of leadership. My investigation took me to all levels of Brazilian society—from the halls of the Palácio do Planalto, the presidential executive palace in Brasília, to slums in São Paulo echoing with the beat of young Afro-Brazilian protest rappers. I observed the former militants as they performed their duties as public officials or pressed the flesh as candidates. Throughout this process, I gauged how these former revolutionaries faced the challenges of running Brazil. The final interviews took place in July 2015, during the second term of Lula's successor, Dilma Rousseff, Brazil's first female and first ex-revolutionary president (2011–16). She was the quintessential revolutionary turned ruler.

Employing oral history, I have constructed a collective biography largely presented in my subjects' own words but also framed with documentary sources and scholarly writings. To keep the narrative manageable for the reader, I have decided to focus on nine individuals representing a spectrum of experiences, outlooks, and adaptations to life and politics in a capitalist democracy: Adriano Diogo, Arlete Diogo, Aloysio Nunes Ferreira Filho, Márcio Araújo de Lacerda, Manoel Cyrillo de Oliveira Netto, Carlos Eugênio Sarmento Coêlho da Paz, Colombo Vieira de Souza, Jessie Jane Vieira de Souza, and Paulo de Tarso Vannuchi.

On one level, to paraphrase Brazilian journalist and author Zuenir Ventura, this book answers the question: What happened to the generation of young 1960s idealists that wanted to rule and transform a society?[33] On a deeper level, the narrative presents a history of Brazil of the last five decades, a period dominated by the dictatorship, the global competition between capitalism and Communism, the struggle for democracy in Brazil, and the quest to build a more productive and just society.

As Antonio Delfim Netto, a leading conservative economist and holder of three cabinet positions during the dictatorship, has observed, capitalism is not a "thing" but "only a transitory moment" in humanity's long quest to build a civilization aimed at maximizing individual fulfillment.[34] Capitalism, just as nuclear potential, can be used for constructive or destructive purposes. Between 1900 and 1973, during both democratic and authoritarian rule, Brazil's per capita GDP grew at an annual rate of 2.5 percent, exceeded only by Finland and Japan.[35] Starting under President Vargas, Brazil adopted a state-led capitalist model that enhanced economic growth through support for numerous industries. Later, it also developed a world-class agribusiness sector. The flagship of this model was Petrobras, the state-owned oil company. The government started many other enterprises and also backed selected private firms with loans and other benefits. These enterprises and firms were the "national champions" of Brazil's economy.[36] In simple terms, this was crony capitalism. To suit its own goals, the dictatorship reinforced this model, spurring further growth and development of infrastructure, but it also created an inefficient, noncompetitive economy.

Brazil's economy also generated deep inequality and vast environmental destruction. Many Brazilians called it "savage capitalism." With a legacy of slavery, the democratic rule of law really started to take root only after the promulgation of the postdictatorial Constitution of 1988, a detailed, 125-page document outlining citizens' rights and responsibilities. It guaranteed the vote to all citizens, including the millions of illiterate individuals historically disenfranchised. "Brazil never was a classical liberal country because the historic tasks of the bourgeoisie (agrarian reform, democracy, public education, etc.) were left undone and ended up in the PT's [Workers' Party's] hands, therefore becoming socialist demands," observed historian Lincoln Secco.[37] Brazil was a classic Third World country, called in the 1970s "Belindia" by economist Edmar Bacha, a combination of developed Belgium and impoverished India. Brazil consistently ranked among the world's most unequal countries.

In the late 1970s and early 1980s, as they pushed for the return to democracy, Lula and the PT advocated socialism. Adding to the prosocialist chorus, many former militants from the ALN and other extinct revolutionary organizations joined the PT—but many opted for other left and center-left parties. On November 9, 1989, as Lula ran in the first presidential election of the postdictatorial era, he and leftists around the globe watched the fall of the Berlin Wall, the monolith of socialism. Later that month, Lula lost in the second round to free-market candidate Fernando Collor de Mello. In 1991, the Soviet Union collapsed. Left-leaning political leaders around the globe moved toward the center. Abandoning many of their parties' left-leaning stances, U.S. president Bill Clinton (a Democrat) and British prime minister Tony Blair (of the Labour Party) developed the "Third Way," which emphasized capitalism and limited government. The "Washington Consensus" of free-market reforms deeply influenced policymakers throughout the developing world. Similarly, in Brazil politicians headed toward the center and built a new macroeconomic consensus.[38] Continuing a trend begun under President Collor, the country's leaders shifted toward free-market capitalism, believing it could both reduce cronyism and lift living standards. They rejected the anti-

American, antibusiness policies desired by the remnants of the extreme Left and central to the hard-left regime in Cuba.

The main architect of this reform was not a conservative, but a long-time leftist and enemy of the dictators, President Fernando Henrique Cardoso (1995–2003) of the Partido da Social Democracia Brasileira (PSDB, the Brazilian Social Democratic Party), an originally center-left party that shifted to the center and built alliances with the Right. In the 1970s, right-wing terrorists had bombed his think tank in São Paulo. Fernando Henrique beat Lula in 1994 and 1998, relying mainly on his defeat of hyperinflation. For more than two decades, Brazilians had seen prices rise inexorably, stemming in large part from the military government's policies. In 1989, the rate reached 2,000 percent. Throughout this period people rushed to spend their paychecks before the value eroded. Inflation especially hit the poor, who lacked access to the financial hedges available to the middle and moneyed classes. In the mid-1990s, Fernando Henrique's new economic strategy and the creation of a new currency, the *real*, dramatically lowered annual inflation to just a few percentage points. Many more poor people became consumers. Deeply underestimated by many on the left, this represented a major, lasting accomplishment for Fernando Henrique and for Brazil.

In the 2002 election, as Fernando Henrique termed out, Lula turned sharply to the center, abandoning socialism and pledging a smooth transition from his predecessor. Admiring Lula's working-class origins and political rise, during the campaign U.S. ambassador Donna Hrinak in effect endorsed Lula, calling him "the personification of the American dream." (She could have added that the United States and Brazil shared key similarities, such as a multiethnic society with slaveholding roots. The two countries have maintained good relations throughout much of their history, including, as noted, close cooperation during World War II.)

After taking office in 2003, Lula extended Fernando Henrique's policies, which had laid the groundwork for higher economic growth. "We transform ourselves by taking the middle road," Lula declared after his 2006 reelection victory. "That's the road that must be followed by society."[39] Lula encouraged greater consumption and the growth of the historically anemic domestic market by increasing welfare payments and launching other initiatives bolstering the poor. On his watch, Brazil created its own version of the American way: it became one of the first developing countries to achieve a majority middle-class society. A nation of have-nots was becoming a nation of haves and leaving the Third World. During the "inclusionary decade" of the 2000s, inequality fell to record low levels, with the incomes of the poor growing at triple the rates of those of the rich.[40] The United States had become a majority middle-class society in the late 1960s, but, in a cautionary development for Brazil and the world, lost that status in 2015 because of its own inattention to inequality.[41] In 2010, Lula's last year in office, GDP growth reached 7.5 percent.

Under Fernando Henrique, Lula, and then President Dilma, Brazil's image changed dramatically as it rose from regional actor to world economic power. Seeking to implement the Constitution of 1988, Brazil strove to become a social democracy that stimulated political participation (including obligatory voting), provided welfare for the poor, and granted universal access to health care.[42] Brazil became a world leader in the fight against AIDS. Illiteracy diminished; the number of people with college degrees rose. Brazilians became among the most digitally savvy people in the world, with even people in the favelas acquiring computers and cell phones.[43] As an economic giant, Brazil produced orange juice and beef, autos and airplanes, genome codes and software. From a classical liberal standpoint, Brazil had moved toward a competitive market economy. Even from a traditional Marxist perspective, the changes were also positive because they suggested the mastering of capitalism as a necessary precondition for socialism. Meanwhile, because of technological and scientific advances, the very nature of capitalism—which Marx wisely perceived as a constantly innovative, self-destructive process—was changing globally. The capitalism attacked by 1960s leftists was not the capitalism of the twenty-first century. By endorsing capitalism and successfully steering it, Brazil's Left stole political thunder from the Right. Ultimately, Brazilians sought a universal aspiration: economic prosperity, stability, and social inclusion.

Along with most of Brazilian society, the former revolutionaries embraced Western-style democracy. Brazil's politicians were committed to free elections and a free press. In 1992, a vigorous press helped to bring about the impeachment of President Collor. Some in the military voiced concerns about Lula during his 1989 run, but he took office in 2003 without interference.

Brazilian democracy allowed the full participation of ex-revolutionaries. Indeed, some of my interviewees rose to national prominence, while others became leaders at the state and local level. Each in his or her own way contributed to the governing of Brazil. A number ran for public office or served in other government posts, as exemplified by President Dilma. Aloysio Nunes Ferreira Filho served in two cabinet positions under Fernando Henrique and in 2010 won the most votes ever in a Brazilian senatorial election. After earning millions in the telecommunications business, Márcio Lacerda worked in Lula's government and then became mayor of Belo Horizonte, the country's fourth-largest city. Manoel Cyrillo de Oliveira Netto built a successful career in public relations, ultimately working for Petrobras. Adriano Diogo served in the São Paulo City Council and State Assembly. Arlete Diogo became a key player in São Paulo municipal politics as Adriano's top aide during his time on the council. Carlos Eugênio Sarmento Coêlho da Paz, whom the dictatorship in the early 1970s considered "public enemy number one," became an ombudsman representing working-class interests at the Secretariat for Labor of the state of Rio de Janeiro in the early 2000s. He asserted: "We knew not only how to destroy the state, but also to construct it."[44] The ex-revolutionaries had entered the political and social mainstream.[45]

In the early twenty-first century, a "pink tide" took place in South America with the rise of leftist leaders such as Venezuela's Hugo Chávez (1999–2013) and Bolivia's Evo Morales (2006–), who criticized the U.S. role in the region. In Chile, Michelle Bachelet, a socialist and opponent of that country's dictatorship, became its first female president (2006–10, 2014–18). Lula's election seemingly formed part of this tide. But despite occasional pink rhetoric, Lula and many other Brazilian leaders acted pragmatically. In Brazil, former left-wing radicals adapted well to capitalism as they took charge of the system.

Like China, India, and Russia, Brazil's importance in the world grew in the twenty-first century. China and Russia ran revolutions in reverse, from Communism to capitalism, but very differently. After the start of China's shift toward capitalism in 1979, few would have predicted that the world's largest Communist country would become a major partner—and threat—in the world system dominated by the United States. In Brazil, too, the Left mainly embraced capitalism. However, as the world's third-largest democracy, Brazil avoided the repression, censorship, and social turmoil (such as frequent strikes and protests) that plagued the Chinese economic boom. With free elections and peaceful transitions of power, Brazil is relatively stable among developing nations. As a result, Brazil appeared on the scene as a cooperative competitor in the style of capitalist fair play, not as the kind of menace that many feared with the rise of China.

However, as all of the interviewees pointed out, full democracy in Brazil still faced many barriers. Despite the economic progress, it remained one of the world's most unequal countries. As the former militants gained power and influence, they had to address this and other ills that they long denounced. As a Lula advisor and secretary for human rights, Paulo devised programs to attack inequality, fought to improve the country's difficult human rights record and make human rights a central item on the societal agenda, and dealt with the politically knotty problem of seeking justice for the victims of the dictatorial repression. Adriano, appointed São Paulo's secretary of the environment, tackled improving the ecosystem of one of the world's largest and most congested cities, an enormous challenge. Working as public administrators, Jessie, Colombo, and Márcio encountered the formidable obstacles of nepotism, gross inefficiency, and special interests within government agencies. Also, Brazil was still hampered by fascist-inspired government institutions from the Vargas era, such as special labor-relations courts.

The special-interest-laden bureaucracy reflected the history of Brazil's patrimonial state, one not dedicated to the public good but to the special interests of the bureaucracy and the elite. "There is no such thing as a public servant," Jessie maintained. "There are only public enemies. Defining what's public and private in a patrimonial country like ours is very complicated."[46] The federal government reduced this tendency somewhat by requiring more upper-level employees to take civil service exams and exercise greater professionalism, but the old patterns remained strong at the lower federal echelons, at the municipal level, and in people's perceptions of government.[47] The newly empowered Left's success rested on how well it could make government more responsive by becoming more efficient, more accountable, and less bound by the country's culture and history.[48] Recent reforms in public management globally have helped developing nations improve public service, and Brazil took note. It outperformed much of Latin America but lagged behind developed and middle-income nations outside the region.[49] Márcio's story especially illustrated the contribution of the private sector to Brazilian development and the potential for business culture to improve government and its delivery of services such as transportation, education, and health care.

Brazil encountered new challenges, such as widespread urban violence and violent, overcrowded prisons controlled by criminal gangs—both reflections of inequality and corrupt, inefficient, and underpaid police forces. Brazilian society was cordial yet violent, with great potential, yet, according to Brazilians, still badly administered. In 2013, massive protests erupted echoing this discontent. The shortcomings meant that for many Brazilians life was often difficult, even precarious, thus hampering efforts to improve democracy, reduce inequality, and make capitalism function efficiently.

Brazil's leftist rulers had a mixed record when struggling with another of Brazil's historic problems, one they had not considered in their revolutionary days: corruption. Under the Workers' Party administrations, this problem became exacerbated. Brazil was proud to be a global leader in several categories: sugar and coffee production, World Cup soccer titles, the number of Catholic and Pentecostal religious believers. But it gained a dubious record in 2016: in conjunction with investigators in Brazil and Switzerland, the U.S. Department of Justice revealed that a multibillion-dollar corruption scandal involving Petrobras, the Brazilian government, and the Brazilian construction conglomerate Odebrecht S.A. had become the world's largest bribery case. The investigation of this scandal became known as Operation Car Wash. Along with a deep recession and massive public protests, the scandal undermined the administration of President Dilma, resulting in her impeachment and eventual removal from office. It occurred on August 31 while Rio hosted the Olympic Games. As an opposition leader, Aloysio played a critical role in Dilma's downfall: he was the PSDB vice presidential candidate in 2014 and a member of the Senate's impeachment committee. Staunchly defending Brazil's institutional integrity, he criticized Dilma's mismanagement of the government, but he and other PSDB politicians themselves—including presidential candidate Aécio Neves—came under suspicion of corruption. Paulo continued to advise Lula as the PT strove to rebuild itself. Originally perceived as an honest, good-government party, it became as corrupt as—if not more so—than the parties it had vociferously criticized. In July 2017, Lula was also convicted on corruption and money-laundering charges. In April 2018, he started serving a twelve-year sentence. In the end, some of the ex-revolutionary leaders of the party became what they had loathed. Not only did these leaders compromise their ideals, but their human frailties and greed impeded the national transformation that they had long sought. An astounding yet enigmatic protest of the Left and corruption came with the

October 2018 election to the presidency of Jair Messias Bolsonaro, an ultraright-wing congressman and former army captain who praised the dictatorship and approved of torture. Many referred to the outspoken Bolsonaro as a "Brazilian Donald Trump."

How and why the nine former ALN militants evolved politically—and interpreted their lives—involved multiple factors. During the 1970s, they were defeated militarily, in part because they failed to draw the masses into the fight. Starting then, they reflected profoundly on the use of political violence, the value of democracy, and politics in general. They were also influenced by tendencies in European democracy and Eurocommunism, which accepted democracy.

Like many other former comrades, the ex-militants' diverse post-revolutionary paths highlighted human flexibility.[50] A key factor was the ALN's pluralism. Primarily concerned with "national liberation," postponing the transition to socialism, the ALN attracted people of distinct political stripes and backgrounds, including nationalists, socialists, Communists, business people, and even Catholic clergymen. It rejected Marxist-Leninist dogmas and sought to build a uniquely Brazilian socialism. Significantly, even though it was anti-imperialist and opposed U.S. interventions, it expressed no hatred for everyday Americans. "You notice that I always talk about the American government, the American administration, and I keep the American people out of it," Manoel insisted. "I separate one thing from the other."[51]

At least nominally, much of the Brazilian revolutionary Left was Marxist and socialist, and analysts have emphasized its antidemocratic character.[52] The dictators and many of the revolutionaries were obviously authoritarian. Still, democracy was a key reference point of the era because of Brazil's brief but significant pre-1964 experience with a vigorous, albeit flawed, democracy.[53] Indeed, after the dictatorship, many of the revolutionaries rewrote their political biographies to appear as champions of democracy.[54] However, because of its pluralism, the ALN did include democrats in its ranks. Moreover, the dictators retained some democratic institutions, including regular elections for many offices. Though the regime manipulated the elections, it respected the results. Voters and the opposition could thus express at least some disagreement via the ballot box. Brazilians lived through the dictatorship hoping for a return to democracy. Even the dictators stated that was their aim.[55]

Ultimately, the fall of so-called real socialism after 1989 left former Brazilian revolutionaries—indeed, most of the world—with no choice. Jessie described what this meant for her and Colombo: "The idea that there is nothing but capitalism, not even the capitalism of the nineteenth century or the mid-twentieth century, but the capitalism of the 1990s. That created a lack of perspectives: either you join the club or you're out."[56]

The former militants' lives were shaped by new circumstances in Brazil and the world, the emergence of new ideas, the accumulation of personal experience, the raising of children, and the passage of time. All asserted that they had maintained their basic values and not compromised them in any way under Brazil's capitalist system. Most continued to defend their initial choice to join or support the ALN, but many admitted that the strategies of guerrilla warfare—and, for some, even the decision to engage in it—were mistaken. However, although the fight against the dictatorship dominated a large portion of their lives and memories, postrevolutionary life meant constant changes, including the need to learn a living. "Everything in life is dynamic," Manoel reflected. "Everything is moving: the universe, nature."[57] Thus, the former militants should not be seen as ideological automatons (as revolutionary dogma viewed people) or, in the present, as speaking for the ALN. It represented one historical moment. They had moved on.

Ultimately, they acquired maturity and wisdom. To Paulo, his personal and intellectual evolution had made him more "eclectic" in his political outlook and analysis of Brazil's situation. He had gained a more realistic and more humanistic attitude toward politics and life.[58] Flexibility could lead to previously unimaginable alliances and the adoption of new political and economic strategies. Changes in the political system did not require the former militants to abandon politics but to adapt to them. Their diverse party affiliations resulted not just from ideology but also other factors, such as personal connections and regional differences. Depending on the situation, sometimes they acted radically, sometimes moderately, sometimes even conservatively.[59]

Moreover, interpreting people primarily through the lens of "left" versus "right" fails to account for their multiple motivations.[60] "I became a much more mature person," Adriano recalled. "For example, I was the type who had the idea that being a good public administrator meant saying 'no.' And that is entirely not the case. . . . 'No. I won't talk with business people,' for example. That's absurd. . . . The world is not divided between the good and the bad. That division is much more complex."[61] Even those who still vehemently opposed capitalism recognized that they had to work within the system and make it more just. The desire to use power played a key role: instead of idealistically rejecting a system that did not meet all of their political criteria, they chose to participate in it, with the hopes of improving it.

Before the fall of the Berlin Wall, Brazilian leftists spoke dogmatically. Once in power, those leftists acted far more pragmatically than the ideologies of the 1960s and 1970s suggested. The paths taken by Fernando Henrique, Lula, and Dilma between 1994 and 2016 relied heavily on that pragmatism, a long-term tendency in Brazil's policymaking and bureaucracy.[62] As rulers, they governed not just their left-wing followers but all of Brazil with its diverse population and political outlooks. They needed not just to think politics but to play politics, too. This included bargaining—and even sharing power—with the Right.

Over the past half century, the nine former ALN militants had witnessed immense progress in Brazil. Although in the final interviews for this book they remained frustrated about many aspects of Brazilian society, they and their generation had come a very long way. In the late 1960s, after all, the ALN sought to turn Latin America into a massive Vietnam and dislodge the United States from its dominant position in the world. Thus, our story begins in 1969—fifty years before the publication of this book—with an episode that shocked the people of both countries and that would forever tie Brazil's revolutionaries to U.S. history.

PART I

REVOLUTION AND REPRESSION

CHAPTER 1

The Surprise of the Century

Manoel had to make a split-second decision.

Minutes earlier, on the afternoon of September 4, 1969, he and three fellow revolutionaries had commandeered the Cadillac limousine carrying U.S. ambassador Charles Burke Elbrick from his residence to the embassy in downtown Rio de Janeiro after their comrades in other vehicles had surrounded and halted the limousine. Manoel had abandoned plans for college and a budding career as a publicity agent to fight against Brazil's military dictatorship. Within the ALN, he quickly became one of Brazil's most active guerrillas. The tall and wiry Manoel participated in robbing a dozen banks and other businesses, stealing explosives, and blowing up police and military targets.[1] In one bank robbery, a policeman died from a guerrilla's gunshot, but it was unclear who hit the officer.[2] In a firefight with two policemen, one of Manoel's accomplices took five bullets in the abdomen, while another killed one of the officers.[3] Just twenty-three, Manoel was flush with the adrenaline, ambition, idealism, and hubris of a new generation of Latin American youths. They had come of age between the 1959 Cuban Revolution and 1968, the year that marked a high point of a global revolution in politics, customs, religion, and gender relations. They needed such bravado to challenge the highly repressive government that had seized power in 1964 with U.S. support.

Virgílio Gomes da Silva, the tough leader of the abduction team whose nom de guerre was Jonas, and Manoel, the second-in-command, flanked Ambassador Elbrick in the back of the limo with their revolvers ready. In the front seat, two other armed comrades forced the chauffeur to sit between them. One car in front of the limousine and another behind carried other plainclothes guerrillas, who gave cover as the guerrilla driver, wearing the chauffeur's cap, negotiated the ambassador's vehicle through the streets of one of Rio's busiest residential neighborhoods. Minutes later they ascended a secluded street that wound up a heavily forested hillside. Soon they reached a vacant lot, where a getaway van was waiting.

Manoel and Jonas removed Elbrick from the limo and ordered him to close his eyes. But Elbrick kept them open.

In August 1968, the U.S. ambassador to Guatemala, John Gordon Mein, had been shot to death as he attempted to flee guerrillas attempting to kidnap him—the first U.S. ambassador killed in the line of duty. In October 1968, the ALN carried out its first *justiçamento*, an execution in the name of revolutionary justice, killing an American. Marco Antônio Braz de Carvalho, the first commander of the ALN's armed operations, and members of another revolutionary organization shot U.S. Army captain and Vietnam veteran Charles Rodney Chandler, believing he had come to Brazil to spy for the CIA and teach methods of torture. In June 1969, less than three months before accosting Elbrick, Manoel and other ALN members bombed the building in São Paulo housing the U.S. Chamber of Commerce shortly before New York governor Nelson Rockefeller was scheduled to appear.

Fearing that he was about to be executed, Elbrick tried to deflect Jonas's gun. Manoel believed the ambassador wanted to grab the weapon. He viscerally knew how easily an operation could spin out of control. If Jonas, Elbrick, or anybody else were shot, this high-stakes gamble could end disastrously.

Grasping his own revolver, Manoel struck the ambassador's forehead with the cylinder just hard enough to stun him. Only then did Elbrick, now bleeding, begin to understand that his abductors did not want to kill him—at least not yet.[4]

"'I've got to stop this guy,'" Manoel remembered thinking at the time. "'I've got to show him that he'll come to an inglorious end, that his desperate attempt at self-defense will get him nowhere. I've got to bring him to his senses and back to reality.' That's why I thought of hitting him with my gun. He was shocked, and it hurt. He got scared, and that allowed us to achieve our objective.... He apologized, not me. I shouted, 'No, I'm the

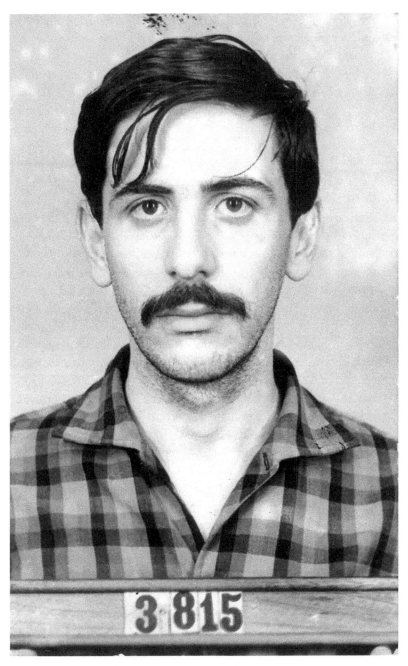

Figure 2. A police photo of Manoel Cyrillo de Oliveira Netto. Manoel Cyrillo de Oliveira Netto collection.

one who should apologize. I was the violent one. You didn't do anything to blow the violence out of proportion. I'm the one who acted violently, but it was for your safety and ours too.'"[5]

Manoel exemplified the guerrillas' complicated attitude toward violence. They had no qualms about killing military targets such as Chandler, but they wanted to avoid harming innocent civilians. "Hurting the ambassador was horrible for all of us, especially for the comrade who hit him," accomplice Fernando Gabeira, an October 8 Revolutionary Movement (MR-8) militant and journalist, would write of Elbrick's injury in his memoir. "Every chance he got, he [Manoel] wanted to know how he was doing, whether he was feeling pain, whether he was still bleeding."[6] However, Elbrick was a politically valuable prisoner who represented the U.S. government. After releasing the chauffeur, the guerrillas left a threatening manifesto in the limousine. Twenty-one-year-old revolutionary Franklin Martins wrote the 850-word document in the moralistic, uncompromising, direct style typical of Brazil's armed militants. It demanded a costly political ransom and left no doubts as to Elbrick's fate if it were not met:

> Today revolutionary organizations detained Mr. Charles Burke Elbrick, the United States ambassador, and, taking him to a location within Brazil, are keeping him in custody. This is not an isolated episode. It is one in a series of revolutionary acts already carried out: bank robberies, committed in order to collect money for the revolution and to recover what the bankers have taken from the people and from bank employees; attacks on barracks and police stations, in order to obtain arms and ammunition for the struggle to overthrow the dictatorship; attacks on prisons, in order to liberate revolutionaries and to return them to the people's struggle; explosions of buildings that symbolize oppression; and the execution of killers and torturers. . . .

> Mr. Elbrick represents within our country the interests of imperialism, which, allied with the leaders of big business, large landowners and wealthy Brazilian bankers, prop up a regime of oppression and exploitation. . . .

> The life and death of the ambassador is in the hands of the dictatorship. If it complies with two demands, Mr. Elbrick will be freed. If it does not, we will be obliged to carry out revolutionary justice. Our two demands are:

(a) The release of fifteen political prisoners. The fifteen revolutionaries are among the thousands who suffer torture in military prisons throughout the country, who are beaten, mistreated and who
endure the humiliations imposed by the military. We are not asking
the impossible. We are not demanding that innumerable combatants
killed in the prisons be brought back to life. They, of course, cannot
be freed. Someday they will be avenged. We demand only the freedom of these fifteen men, leaders of the struggle against the dictatorship. From the standpoint of the people, each of them is worth one
hundred ambassadors. But from the standpoint of the dictatorship
and its exploitation, a U.S. ambassador is also worth a lot.

(b) The publication and reading of this message, in its entirety,
by the principal newspapers, radio stations and television outlets
throughout the country.

The fifteen prisoners must be transported on a non-commercial
flight to a specific country—Algeria, Chile or Mexico—where they
will be granted political asylum. No reprisals must be taken against
them, or else there will be retaliation.

The dictatorship has forty-eight hours to respond publicly
whether it accepts or rejects our proposal. If the response is positive,
we will release the list of fifteen revolutionary leaders and wait twenty-
four hours for their transport to a safe country. If the response is negative, or if no response is given by the deadline, Mr. Elbrick will be
executed. . . .

Finally, we want to warn those who torture, beat, and kill our
comrades: we will no longer allow this to continue. We are giving our
last warning. Whoever continues to torture, beat, and kill had better
be ready. Now it is an eye for an eye, a tooth for a tooth.

National Liberating Action (ALN)
October 8 Revolutionary Movement (MR-8)

They had taken an enormous risk. Shocking even fellow revolutionaries, the kidnappers had transgressed an unspoken international norm.
Political kidnappings had a history reaching back to at least the early nineteenth century. But this was the first time anywhere that someone had
kidnapped a U.S. diplomat.[7] In Washington, DC, President Nixon received news of the abduction from his assistant for national security affairs,

Henry Kissinger, and was said to personally follow the situation.[8] The kidnapping made international headlines. "Gunmen Kidnap U.S. Envoy in Brazil," stated a three-column, front-page headline in the September 5, 1969, edition of the *New York Times*. In an editorial the next day, the paper warned of the "escalating urban terrorism of revolutionary left-wing groups in Latin America," but also criticized Brazil's military rulers for "oppressive policies" that allowed terrorism to flourish. The paper also published an English translation of the revolutionary manifesto.[9] "It was just unheard of to touch a diplomat," Valerie Elbrick, the ambassador's adult daughter, who was in Yugoslavia when she received the news of the abduction, recalled four decades later. "That kidnapping was the surprise of the century to the Brazilian government."[10] It also caught the State Department's Office of Security completely off guard, prompting extensive new efforts to safeguard U.S. overseas posts, including an increase in the use of "follow cars" to protect ambassadors in transit and the adoption of armored vehicles in high-risk capitals.[11]

Elbrick held great importance not only because of his country's superpower status. He had a long, distinguished career, rising to the rarely awarded rank of career ambassador, the highest in the U.S. Foreign Service. Though he was under discussion for the ambassadorship in Moscow, Elbrick preferred Brazil because of its importance for the United States and his lifelong curiosity about the country, Valerie recalled.[12] In September 1969, he had been in Rio less than two months, but with his fluent Portuguese (from service in Portugal) he communicated easily with the kidnappers. If Elbrick were harmed, political leaders and diplomats everywhere would be further shocked, and U.S.–Brazilian relations would be jeopardized.

IN 1969, THE generals' drive to make Brazil a geopolitical player seemed within reach. As the "Brazilian miracle" boosted growth, the country's GDP approached the top ten in the West. It was now the world's ninth-largest automaker. However, the suffocation of democracy, the growing use of torture and intimidation, and the desire for revolution prompted the guerrilla groups to step up their actions.

One of the most important guerrilla leaders was fifty-five-year-old Carlos Marighella, the founder of the ALN. A former congressman and high-level PCB leader, Marighella dissented strongly from the party's official refusal to take up arms. As it became clear that the military would not return the government to civilians, Marighella focused on not just restoring democratic liberties, but also on overthrowing the institutions that hampered the achievement of social justice. He went to Cuba in 1967 to obtain support for guerrilla activity in Brazil. During an interview on Cuban radio, Marighella declared that Brazilian revolutionaries needed to "seize power violently and destroy the bureaucratic-military apparatus of the state, replacing it with a people's army."[13] He soon quit the PCB, as would half of its 55,000 members that year, ending the party's half-century hegemony on the Brazilian Left. Also, that month Che Guevara exhorted revolutionaries in Latin America to create "many Vietnams" to end U.S. domination and help destroy the international capitalist system. Inspired by the variety of revolutionary theories circulating in Latin America, the ex-PCB members and other prorevolution Brazilians formed more than three dozen organizations to resist the government.

Marighella started the ALN in 1967. As its name indicated, the ALN fought mainly for "national liberation" from imperialism and U.S. dominance. The much smaller MR-8, operating mainly in Rio, aimed to immediately establish a socialist regime. Other organizations adopted their own strategies. They all sought to overthrow the dictatorship, but they often diverged over obscure ideological points and engaged in geographical and political factionalism. Within the ALN itself, the college-age guerrillas from São Paulo developed an air of superiority toward their high-school-age ALN counterparts in Rio. Marighella hailed from Bahia, the state with the country's deepest African heritage. He was a mulatto—his father an Italian immigrant, his mother a descendant of slaves. A poet and passionate devotee of Brazilian culture, Marighella tried to stand above the many divisions within the resistance. A survivor of torture, imprisonment, and bullet wounds suffered in a clash with the police after the coup, he became the armed Left's most famous and most charismatic leader.[14]

Che was captured on October 8, 1967—a date that inspired MR-8's name—while trying to start a revolution in Bolivia. Bolivian soldiers executed him the following day. Despite Che's demise, his ideas continued to exercise powerful influence over young people throughout Latin America. He became practically a saint of the Latin American radical Left. Radicals such as the Weathermen in the United States and guerrillas in Latin America and other Third World countries adopted violence to foment political and social change. However, Guevara's ominous rhetoric belied a huge miscalculation in terms of inspiring guerrilla action: Latin America was *not* another potential Vietnam because, other than the failed Bay of Pigs paramilitary operation in Cuba in 1961 and a small-scale intervention in the Dominican Republic by U.S. (and Brazilian) troops in 1965, no U.S. forces had invaded the region in the 1960s.[15] It would be tougher to inspire anti-imperialist guerrilla action.

For the ALN, the dictatorship embodied U.S. interests in Brazil. The ALN was the largest guerrilla organization, with about three hundred fighters and a total of six thousand collaborators throughout the country and contacts in Cuba, Europe, and Asia.[16] (Probably thousands of collaborators supported the numerous other clandestine groups.[17]) As long as collaborators could contribute in some way to the fight—with fighting ability, skills, money, logistical support, connections—Marighella showed little concern about background or ideology. His supporters ranged from the working class to professionals, from Communists to Catholics—including the priests and brothers of the Dominican Order and other clergymen. Catholic doctrine recognized the right of people to rise up violently against unjust governments.[18] Marighella espoused an eclectic strategy to fight what he knew was an asymmetrical war against the military government, whose army had 300,000 men. Adapting the Cuban model, he proposed small cells of militants who could commit revolutionary acts on their own. Marighella liked to cite phrases from the Cuban Revolution, such as "Action is the revolutionary vanguard" and "Permission is not required to practice revolution."[19]

Marighella spurned fundamental notions of the Communist movement as defined by Marx and the first Soviet leader, Vladimir Lenin. Still calling himself a Communist after exiting the PCB, he nevertheless disdained the formation of a political party. Focusing on the countryside, he rejected the notion of the urban working class as the vanguard of the revolution. Nor did he embrace the idea of a dictatorship of the proletariat. His rural approach reflected the revolutionary history of not just Cuba but also of China. Marighella also studied the ideas of Gen. Vo Nguyen Giap, the leader of the North Vietnamese army. Marighella agreed with Che that to defeat the United States, revolutionaries around the globe needed to rise up simultaneously to provoke numerous U.S. interventions. In Marighella's plans, Brazil itself could become a Vietnam. First, the ALN would have to defeat or at least sufficiently harass the Brazilian armed forces. This ultimately required establishing highly mobile columns of guerrilla fighters in the heart of the country, drawing the military away from its strongholds in Rio, São Paulo, and other coastal cities.[20] Urban operations such as the Elbrick kidnapping were a mere preamble.

Like the other revolutionary organizations, with its intense focus on the overthrow of the dictatorship, Marighella's ALN had no actual blueprint for government or model of society in the event of victory.[21] Marighella harbored no illusions about the enormous challenge faced by the revolutionaries. "I'm not fooling anyone," he told one young guer-rilla recruit. "I'll imitate [Winston] Churchill: I promise you blood, sweat, tears . . . and prison, torture, and death."[22]

The kidnappers' audacity was magnified by the heady idealism of the times. The year 1968 unleashed a worldwide avalanche of cultural experi-mentation and questioning of the status quo, producing a "generation gap" between youths and their elders. People in the United States, Brazil, and other parts of the world experimented with mind-altering drugs, free sex, the hippy lifestyle, novel music, and other forms of alternative culture. In the United States, students and radicals protested the Vietnam War. Assassins killed two liberal leaders, Martin Luther King Jr. and Robert F. Kennedy. Just days before the opening of the Mexico City Olympics, the authoritarian Mexican regime gunned down scores of antigovernment demonstrators and innocent bystanders. During the Olympics, two cham-pion African American athletes from the United States raised their fists in the Black Power salute as the U.S. national anthem played during the medal ceremony.[23] In Brazil, the decision to fight the generals involved "a certain romanticism," ALN guerrilla Takao Amano recalled in his memoir of the period. "So, in those days the myth of the guerrilla was something comparable to that of the Beatles. It was commonplace, even as a part of political marketing. I believe it was our hearts, and not our heads, that moved us. To fight for your country, against the dictatorship, you could only do by grabbing a gun."[24]

Brazil, too, faced upheaval. In March 1968, protestors throughout the country poured into the streets after police killed a student in Rio, and in June 100,000 marchers in Rio demanded an end to the dictatorship. Some of Elbrick's kidnappers-to-be took part in these protests. In October, the police broke up a clandestine meeting of hundreds of student leaders from around the country held at a farm outside the town of Ibiúna, not far from São Paulo. To obtain funds to support its growing organization and pre-pare for guerrilla warfare, the ALN robbed banks and carried out other assaults. Other guerrilla groups carried out similar operations. On November 20, the minister of justice declared Marighella "public enemy number one."[25] On December 13, the regime responded to the growing turmoil by decreeing IA-5 (Institutional Act No. 5).

A secret CIA memorandum produced ten days later expressed deep skepticism about the effects of IA-5 on Brazilian society.[26] In his telegram analyzing the situation, the U.S. embassy's charge d'affaires wrote that "perhaps greatest beneficiary of IA-5 today is Marighella. Imposition of dictatorship favors those already operating outside law. Hopelessness of legal opposition can be expected to increase flow of recruits to terrorist organizations."[27] The Brazilian military understood this. IA-5 allowed the security forces to counter both violent and nonviolent opponents, detaining individuals for days and even weeks without having to respect habeas corpus. To aid in the fight against the guerrillas, the dictators set up interrogation centers, where torturers plied their malicious craft with impunity. Shortly after his arrival in Rio in March 1969, Ambassador Elbrick told the foreign minister that the military government needed to improve its human rights record. Elbrick cabled the U.S. State Department about the military government's surprise at domestic and international criticism of the political purges resulting from IA-5.[28] The U.S. government stood in the difficult and embarrassing position of having supported the coup but now having ties with a highly repressive regime.[29]

Despite the repression, the "economic miracle" made it harder for the armed opposition to obtain popular support. In a country of 90 million, the guerrillas were having a minuscule effect. In 1969, they had not yet perceived that economic growth benefited a growing middle class and helped the generals score political points.[30] They did not have the means to counteract the successes of the military government, and they could not attack prisons to rescue political prisoners. Also, not everybody in the ALN agreed with Marighella. Some members believed that violence needed to be joined by political work. Others worried about how society would view guerrilla actions that most people would interpret as everyday criminal acts. "For a Communist proletarian, robbing a bank is horrible, it's theft," militant José Luiz Del Roio stated in late 1968. "They don't steal. They prefer to die while on strike at a factory." Criticizing "bureaucrats," Marighella responded with a letter widely circulated within the ALN: "On the guerrilla front you have carte blanche to take action." The ALN leader remained confident. "In essence, we owe our success to acts of revolutionary terrorism and to guerrilla operations and tactics," he wrote in an internal ALN document. "For the first time ever in Brazil, terrorist acts have come to play a role in political conflict." Even so, the ALN needed something spectacular to catch the government off guard, seize the attention of the nation, and advance to the ultimate goal of taking the fight into Brazil's vast countryside. With strict censorship after IA-5, the public remained in the dark about the guerrillas' activities, including stunning incidents, such as the anti-Rockefeller bombing. The ALN put a number of possibilities on the table, including dynamiting bridges, attacking a Shell oil refinery, sabotaging the electrical grid, and hijacking aircraft. It vetoed ideas that it considered beyond its capabilities, such as downing Rockefeller's plane.[31]

The ALN and MR-8 put aside their ideological differences to collaborate in seizing Ambassador Elbrick. The ALN provided ample operational experience, the MR-8 a dedicated group of militants in Rio. Deliberately planning the action for the middle of Brazil's 1969 Independence Week celebrations, the guerrillas aimed to contrast their plan for a Brazil free of oppression with the military's stodginess and maintenance of the U.S.-backed status quo. Marighella had chosen 1969 as the "year of rural guerrilla warfare."[32] If all went as they hoped, the people would rise up and join the guerrillas to overthrow the dictatorship.

The time seemed providential. The kidnapping came at an extremely delicate moment for the generals. President Costa e Silva had suffered a stroke eight days before the kidnapping—a crisis kept from the public eye by military censors. Unable to speak, Costa e Silva was replaced by a three-man junta on August 31, 1969. Authority and cohesion within the armed forces threatened to disintegrate.

THE KIDNAPPERS MADE Elbrick lie on the floor of the getaway van and covered him with a tarp. Then they drove to a safe house near downtown Rio, in the Santa Teresa neighborhood. They forced Elbrick to sit inside the van several hours in a detached garage. He still wore the sunglasses given him by the kidnappers, who forced him to look straight ahead. His face still bloodied from Manoel's blow, Elbrick asked for water to cleanse himself. The guerrillas granted his wish. At dusk they transferred him to the interior of the house.

Emotions ran high as the guerrillas celebrated: they had just captured the U.S. ambassador! Cláudio Torres, who had donned a suit to assume the role of limousine driver, demanded that Elbrick reveal the names of the CIA officers stationed in Brazil. He threatened the ambassador with further interrogations, but, he added, unlike the way the Brazilian regime treated political prisoners, they would not torture Elbrick. Joaquim Câmara Ferreira, the senior leader of the operation known by his revolutionary code name Toledo, also questioned Elbrick. Embarrassed and irritated at Cláudio's emotional and improvised grilling of their captive, some of the other guerrillas decided to keep him away from Elbrick. Manoel, Jonas, and another comrade took turns discreetly keeping watch at the door of the bedroom holding the ambassador.

The government mobilized 4,200 agents in a citywide search for Elbrick, including roadblocks and the detention of 1,800 people during the seventy-nine hours of his captivity. The armed forces put numerous houses under surveillance, including the one where Elbrick was held, but they were unable to locate him. During one tense moment, two military intelligence officers in plain clothes knocked at the door and had a brief conversation with Gabeira.[33] In the bedroom upstairs Jonas held a gun to Elbrick's head, ready to shoot if the military came crashing in.

However, most of the interaction between the ambassador and his kidnappers remained calm. Elbrick worked to keep it so. He represented his country, but, outnumbered by heavily armed abductors, he wanted to avoid antagonizing them. To that end, he debated U.S. politics with them. "They seemed to ascribe all the troubles and difficulties in Brazil to what they called North American imperialism," Elbrick later reflected. "I told them that that reflected a colonial mentality on their part."[34] Gabeira, who lived in the safe house and had a turn keeping guard over Elbrick, admired the Black Panthers. As he pointed his gun at the ambassador, Gabeira told Elbrick that the Panthers could help improve democracy in the United States. Elbrick disagreed, stating that the Panthers were too radical and "had not the least chance of success."[35]

Elbrick was a conservative and, unbeknownst to the kidnappers and even his own family, a contributor to the Republican Party.[36] Despite the concern he expressed to the foreign minister about human rights violations, Elbrick also later stated in internal diplomatic communications that ruthless "terrorist" violence also provoked repression.[37] Claiming to be a member of the Democratic Party, he told the guerrillas that he opposed the Vietnam War and did not approve of the Brazilian dictatorship and of the Republican Nixon's policy of collaboration with it.[38] This, too, was likely a ruse: Elbrick was extremely loyal to Nixon, even supporting him throughout the Watergate scandal of 1973–74.[39]

The ambassador came to understand that the guerrillas had "legitimate grievances," he later reflected, but affirmed that "violence never solves anything." Elbrick perceived his captors as "audacious, intelligent, courteous, and dedicated" to their cause.[40]

For their part, the kidnappers maintained the famed Brazilian cordiality. Prepared to kill the ambassador at any moment, they nevertheless treated him kindly. They even washed Elbrick's shirt. For a military action, it was an extremely polite affair. It was also a meeting of Brazilian and U.S. elites. Like the majority of Brazil's revolutionaries, many of the kidnappers had middle- and even upper-class origins. For example, Martins was the son of a senator.

In Elbrick's briefcase the guerrillas found papers from the CIA stamped "Top Secret." The documents detailed alternative political scenarios for Brazil—including a return to civilian rule. According to the documents and Elbrick, the CIA had identified Dom Hélder Câmara, the archbishop of Olinda and Recife and a founder of Brazil's liberation theology movement, as the best person to lead a civilian government and unify the country. Prior to 1964, Dom Hélder had served as an auxiliary bishop in Rio, where he became an influential national figure with access to presidents. His advocacy of socialism and human rights earned him the wrath of the regime; in May 1969, a right-wing death squad had murdered one of his priests. Elbrick complied with the guerrillas' request to make a tape recording of his comments about the archbishop. In June, Manoel and another team of armed revolutionaries had taken control of a radio transmitter of Rádio Nacional, a highly popular station based in São Paulo. They broadcast a taped revolutionary message from Marighella, a rare break through the wall of censorship. The kidnappers planned to do the same with the Elbrick tape.[41] The explosive revelation about the CIA and Dom Hélder would further demoralize the regime and embarrass the U.S. government.

The Brazilian government immediately condemned the kidnapping as an "act of pure and simple terrorism."[42] But within the government, tensions mounted between hard-liners and moderates. Rejecting the guerrillas' demands, some military commanders wanted to storm a location where they believed Elbrick was being held or publicly execute jailed revolutionaries—even if such actions led to Elbrick's death. The Nixon administration largely avoided public comment, avoiding use of the term "terrorist." However, it applied diplomatic pressure for Elbrick's safe return. In the end, the Brazilian moderates prevailed. They included Mozart Gurgel Valente, the Brazilian ambassador to Yugoslavia during Elbrick's tenure there and a close friend of the family. Valente occupied the No. 2 position in the Ministry of Foreign Relations, where government officials had gathered to address the crisis. He explained the gravity of the matter. "At issue is the life of the United States ambassador," Valente told his fellow officials. "As a government we are responsible for his life, for his safe return to his family and to his official duties here in Rio. We are responsible to our ally the United States and to the diplomatic corps in Brazil. The rest can be dealt with later—this band of thugs, as you say."[43]

Within a few hours the generals acceded to the guerrillas' demands. The night of the kidnapping, September 4, the revolutionary manifesto was broadcast widely. Newspapers also published it along with extensive reports of the kidnapping and the efforts to save the ambassador. However, because the dictatorship stringently censored the press, no editorials or letters to the editor offered comment, and no article or opinion assessed the reaction of everyday citizens. Even so, Brazilians were abuzz about the kidnapping.[44]

Inside the safe house, the guerrillas' euphoria heightened. On the afternoon of Independence Day, Sunday, September 7, the kidnappers received the news that the fifteen political prisoners designated by the guerrillas had safely landed in Mexico City aboard a Brazilian air force plane. Jonas then escorted Elbrick out of the safe house to a waiting getaway car. Manoel and two other comrades occupied a second car that would trail and give cover to the ambassador's vehicle.

A car filled with armed officers on the lookout for the ambassador chased the two guerrilla vehicles. For a few harrowing moments, the two sides prepared to start shooting at each other. However, the agents were unable to stop the kidnappers as they drove toward the Maracanã stadium. As the revolutionaries had hoped, the streets around the Maracanã that afternoon filled with people streaming out of the exits after a soccer match. They dropped Elbrick off in the midst of the crowd and slipped away. By day's end, all of the guerrillas had successfully eluded the security forces.[45]

Figure 3. Ambassador Charles Burke Elbrick shortly after his release on September 7, 1969. Iconographia.

MARIGHELLA, IN HIS highly influential *Minimanual of the Urban Guerrilla*, wrote that "to engage in acts of violence, to be a 'terrorist,' ennobles any decent person because it is an act of a revolutionary engaged in the armed struggle against the shameful military dictatorship and its atrocities."[46] Manoel and other members of the ALN's São Paulo Armed Tactical Group contributed substantially to the document. Perhaps inspired by the French anarchist Georges Sorel, the *Minimanual* was more a thunderous propaganda piece calling for armed struggle than an actual guide to fighting. Marighella completed it in September, the same month as the Elbrick operation. At that point, the ALN clandestinely produced one hundred secret mimeographed copies. A few weeks later, Radio Havana quoted it on the air. In March 1970, ignoring a prohibition by their government, a large group of French publishers banded together to publish the pamphlet.[47] A State Department official in Washington called in a representative from the Soviet embassy to complain about the Cuban government's apparent endorsement of the *Minimanual*, which, he pointed out, recommended political executions, kidnappings, and aircraft hijacking.[48] *Time* magazine reported that the Black Panthers and other U.S.-based left-wing groups had put out their own editions of the *Minimanual*.[49]

In contrast with Che, who warned against the harm terrorism could bring to revolutionary movements, Marighella explicitly advocated left-wing terrorism against specific enemies. "Each revolutionary act is a tactical operation having as its objectives the demoralization of the authorities, the encirclement of the repressive forces, the interruption of their communications, damage to the property of the state and of the big capitalists and landowners," he wrote in a late 1969 publication. However, Marighella clearly distanced himself and the ALN from terrorism as a method of mass murder or instilling panic in the general populace: "Acts of revolutionary terror and sabotage do not aim to disturb, frighten, or kill the common people."[50] Marighella's wholehearted embrace of revolutionary violence and terror made it crystal clear what the ALN leadership expected of its young recruits, but individual guerrillas and ALN supporters interpreted the need for violence as circumstances and the resistance evolved. Later, most abandoned violence. How and why they did so is one of the main themes of this book.

So, what did these former militants think about violence and revolution? Some of the Elbrick kidnappers became famous. Gabeira ran for president in 1989 and served in the Congress from 1998 to 2010. (As in the United States, the Congress has both a senate [with three members from each state] and a house of representatives, known as the Chamber of Deputies, whose members are elected not from districts but through a system of proportional representation within each state.) Gabeira's memoir inspired the controversial 1997 Brazilian-American film about the Elbrick episode, *O que é isso, companheiro?* (*Four Days in September* in the U.S.), literally translated as "What the heck's going on, comrade?" Martins became a prominent journalist and spokesperson for President Lula. Manoel's story was less known. I was deeply curious to learn more about the man who had wounded the U.S. ambassador. What motivated him? What did he think, then and now, about terrorism and armed resistance? After reaching Manoel through other former ALN militants, we arranged to meet on June 19, 2006.

That evening, I had in mind not just Manoel's blow to Elbrick, but also other kinds of violence. I feared getting mugged or hit by a stray bullet from the virtual war between drug traffickers and policemen in the favelas interspersed among the city's middle- and upper-middle-class neighborhoods. Arriving at the building where Manoel lived in Rio's Leme district, near Copacabana, I rode the elevator to his eleventh-floor apartment. Manoel opened the door with a smile and shook my hand. He was dressed informally and was wearing glasses. From his window, we could see a favela, located just a few hundred yards away. Between 1979, when Brazil's federal government began keeping statistics, and the time of the interview, the country had almost 1 million murders.[51] Over this period, the Brazilian murder rate averaged 33,000 per year, nearly four times the per capita rate in the United States (for murder and nonnegligent manslaughter).[52] I was relieved to conduct the interview in an inner room, out of sight of the favela.

Manoel the public relations man effectively defended the legitimacy of Brazil's revolutionary movement of the late 1960s and early 1970s. Accomplished guerrillas understood the need for good propaganda. "Throughout our fight, we moved to develop other types of much more effective propaganda," Manoel observed in a later interview. "Taking over a radio station is an example, isn't it? The Elbrick action itself was, too."[53]

In numerous scholarly writings on the dictatorship, the revolutionaries are portrayed as primarily socialists or Communists and opponents of liberal democracy, which suggests that a "democratic resistance" was a myth.[54] Manoel did not fit this mold. He explained that concerns for de-mocracy *did* play a role in his decision to resist. Manoel's father staunchly supported ex-president Juscelino Kubitschek. Kubitschek had presided over a peaceful transition of power to a new president after the 1960 elec-tion and had aimed to run for the presidency again in 1965 before the dic-tatorship canceled the election. "My father was the most pro-Juscelino guy in the world, 'JK in '65,'" Manoel affirmed in our June 21, 2006, interview. "I remember the candidate songs we had at home. Our country, our laws, our constitution, all of our norms of democratic coexistence—they all came tumbling down and were attacked and taken apart by them!"[55] Un-like many other revolutionaries, many of whom had belonged to the PCB or acted in the student movement, Manoel had no political experience before entering the ALN. He gained political consciousness by discuss-ing the deteriorating situation in Brazil with a young uncle, João Carlos Cavalcanti Reis, and a few friends he had grown up with in São Paulo, to which his family had moved from their home state of Bahia. Marxist ideas rarely entered their conversations.

As they saw freedoms destroyed, the group decided to join a revolu-tionary organization. They especially admired Marighella and read his book *Porque Resisti à Prisão* (*Why I Resisted Arrest*), which reflected on the Communist leader's violent encounter with the police after the coup and his determination that Brazilians should fight the dictators. Both before and after the coup, Marighella had defended classic democratic liberties. However, he also recognized that Brazil's political institutions might need to be replaced in order to bring about social reform.[56] João, the mentor of Manoel's group, became the first among them to join the ALN. He stud-ied at the Universidade de São Paulo (USP), which was becoming an ALN stronghold. João recruited Manoel and two other friends. "We had a ro-mantic vision of guerrilla warfare," Manoel recalled. "For example, we went to Água Branca Park to take a course in tanning hides, because it could be useful for a guerrilla to capture an animal and prepare the hide [laughter]." In Manoel's understanding, "the ALN proposed to create a democratic and popular political model that broke with all of the practices of the dic-tatorship and its unbridled repression." Once Brazil returned to a demo-cratic system, all political interests could compete freely, and Communists and socialists could attempt to transform Brazil into a socialist country, "if it were the wish of everybody, or the majority. But it wouldn't neces-sarily be imposed. This was the outlook of the ALN: to open the road to socialism."[57]

When I asked about the "kidnapping," Manoel immediately objected to my use of that term. We discussed this again in a follow-up interview in 2007. In both instances, I sometimes thought that we were playing semantic games. Upon further reflection, I came to appreciate how our discussion went to the root of the debate over the legitimate use of violence for political ends. Were Manoel and his comrades "terrorists," as Marighella had hoped and as their enemies had labeled them in the 1960s and 1970s? Indeed, the term "terrorism" became a powerful propaganda tool of the regime, with the government posting "Terrorists Wanted" signs showing pictures of the hunted revolutionaries. Manoel and his comrades referred to themselves as "revolutionaries," "combatants," "guerrillas," or "militants."

Then and thereafter, participants in the Elbrick action and others connected to the incident could not agree on precisely how to define it. In 1969, it had caught many around the world off guard. In their manifesto, the revolutionaries used the word *rapto* (abduction) and *detiveram* (detained). Publicly, the Brazilian government used "kidnapping," but in secret documents it referred to the *rapto* and *expropriação* (expropriation) of the ambassador.[58] An assistant to the ambassador referred to the kidnapping as a "theft."[59] In a 2005 roundtable discussion including Manoel and four other participants in the Elbrick incident, the men used four different terms in Portuguese to refer to the action: *sequestro* (kidnapping), *captura* (capture), *rapto* (abduction), and *abdução* (abduction). Edited by a former MR-8 member sympathetic to the operation, the very book in which the roundtable transcript appeared employs the word "kidnapping" in its subtitle.[60]

In his recollections, Manoel insisted that he had helped "capture" (*capturar*) the ambassador in the context of an international conflict:

> I had taken part in the capture of the ambassador of a state that was the enemy of our people. It was an enemy because it was a state that provided incentives, that spent millions and millions of dollars here during the country's fully democratic governments, starting in the 1950s, in order to create a coup mentality, to transform the military outlook of the Brazilian army ... to create a Brazilian geopolitical outlook, a geopolitics that was aggressive and favoring a coup, a totalitarian geopolitics. So it was a representative of that state that we captured. . . . We would give up our prisoner, the ambassador, while the dictatorship would also free our imprisoned comrades.[61]

Figure 4. Clockwise, from upper left: the author with Manoel in 2009 at the former ambassadorial residence in Rio (a), at the corner of Elbrick's capture (b), and at the safe house (c). In the final photo, Manoel at the former embassy building (d). Marcelo Ulisses Machado.

As noted in the prologue, more than one hundred innocent civilians died in guerrilla operations. However, Manoel insisted that he and other ALN combatants were not terrorists, because they scrupulously attempted to avoid harming bystanders.[62] When the ALN exploded its bomb to protest Rockefeller's visit, it had no intention of hurting the visiting dignitary and sought to prevent harm to others. Manoel recalled:

We occupied the building . . . at 4 a.m. We occupied the building where the American Chamber of Commerce functioned in São Paulo, where he was to give a speech the next day. We got everybody out of the building, from the top floor to the ground floor. We set up a bomb made of fifty or sixty kilos of dynamite. We used the elevator so that it would explode in the middle of the building, about the fifteenth floor. . . . Nobody was hurt. We stood by at the door of the building until the explosion took place and blocked pedestrians from passing in front of the lobby, because there the draft from the blast would probably come through. In short, we took all the precautions necessary to avoid hurting someone, no innocent bystanders, to not commit an act of terrorism, something we never did.[63]

Despite Manoel's justification, this type of operation matched Marighella's prescription for terrorist acts.

Although he himself claimed that he had not taken anyone's life, Manoel believed that the revolutionaries had the right to kill agents of the state. That was the nature of guerrilla warfare. He further affirmed that the assassinated Captain Chandler had deserved to die. Officially, Chandler had temporarily moved to São Paulo with his family to take a sociology course and study Portuguese. He gave interviews to the local press and spoke on the Vietnam War to a group of Brazilian military personnel. He caught the attention of revolutionaries, and a small group of them ordered his death after trying him in absentia in a revolutionary tribunal. They believed that Chandler had tortured members of the Vietnamese Viet Cong.[64] The members of the tribunal thought they had sufficient evidence that Chandler was working for the CIA.[65] But nobody ever proved the allegations against the captain—or found proof of any other suspicion of U.S. involvement in teaching or participating in torture. In reality, the revolutionaries killed Chandler because he was an American and a military officer. Using distorted logic, they viewed his assassination (and others) as successful propaganda for their movement. For Marighella, the execution of the alleged CIA spy demonstrated that the revolution was advancing.[66]

Despite the evidence, Manoel fervently defended the execution. "From my point of view, it wasn't terrorism for us to execute a Charles Chandler, an American instructor of torture who came here with the mission of teaching torture to our military," Manoel affirmed. "It was a direct action against an individual who was completely guilty. We didn't need to judge him formally. It wasn't necessary. It was sufficient to just execute him and be done with it."[67] Proof was irrelevant, as was the question of whether Chandler actually worked for the CIA, Manoel stated. "To the extent that the information we had was that he was an [instructor], he had to be executed," he stated, noting that documents of the U.S. government itself have confirmed the country's involvement in the repression carried out by the region's dictatorships.[68] Kidnapping Chandler was not an option. "He was just a despicable instructor of torture, a totally disposable cog in the system, a useless leftover," he concluded. "Nobody would exchange him for anybody. His life wasn't worth a single penny. . . . A torturer has no exchange value."[69]

Manoel rejected the equation of political violence with terrorism. In Brazil the revolutionaries killed or harmed civilians only by accident, he maintained. Manoel pointed out that terrorism has a sociological definition based on specific historical incidents and contexts. "Not everybody who takes up arms is a terrorist," Manoel stated. "How do you explain the fight for independence in the United States of America? What would the British crown have said? Wasn't that terrorism? England sent troops to repress the American revolutionaries." Manoel reflected on the al-Qaeda attacks of 9/11. Too many questions about that incident remained unanswered, he said, for final conclusions about the motives and actions of Osama bin Laden, the George W. Bush administration, and the other players in the Middle East conflicts. Only history would render a verdict, Manoel asserted. "What I know is that every twenty years or so the American government releases CIA documents that demonstrate aberrations, where anything becomes possible," he stated. Recalling the Elbrick operation, he added, "I myself held an ambassador's folder that spoke about a civilian solution for Brazil." However, he considered unacceptable the kind of mass attack against civilians carried out by bin Laden. "That is something I would never, ever do." The accusations of terrorism against Brazil's revolutionaries were "slanderous." "Nobody was a terrorist," Manoel stated. "Everybody was a political activist. . . . We were doing politics in the way we found possible. If all the doors are shut, the Congress is closed, the parties are banned, how were we supposed to act politically? By taking up arms. That's what we did. But that was political."[70]

Manoel's explanation of the Brazilian resistance made it sound more like self-defense than terrorism. Some might put it in the vein of Doris Lessing's "good terrorism," the combat of obvious social injustice. Historian Walter Laqueur classified the Brazilian case "defensive" terrorism.[71] Indeed, the government (and its right-wing allies) committed many acts of terror, burning theaters, exploding newsstands, and destroying the headquarters of the Rio newspaper *Correio da Manhã*. One of the most notorious plans emerged in 1968, when air force general João Paulo Moreira Burnier tried to get paratroopers in Rio to assassinate key opposition leaders; to blow up a Sears outlet, a Citibank branch, and the U.S. embassy; and to dynamite a large natural gas storage facility. In the ensuing mass panic, the armed forces would hold Communists responsible and embark on an anti-Communist killing spree. A key subordinate refused to follow Burnier's orders, and the plan was never carried out.[72] In 1981, in the infamous Riocentro incident, officers linked to the intelligence services tried but failed to explode a bomb at a packed convention center.

BRAZILIAN GUERRILLAS' MOST spectacular operation, the Elbrick abduction marked the high point of their attempt to topple the dictatorship and move toward a socialist regime. Indeed, immediately after Elbrick's release, the young, politically inexperienced guerrillas realized that they could have dealt an even more devastating blow to the regime by demanding the freedom of *all* political prisoners—who totaled as many as several hundred people (but not the thousands claimed in the revolutionary manifesto).[73] If the people answered their call to arms and the Brazilian revolution succeeded, Latin America's biggest domino would fall into the socialist camp and could swing the balance of the Cold War in favor of the Communist bloc.[74]

Above all, for the guerrillas the Elbrick operation was about redeeming national pride.

"Our action . . . allowed the people to avenge themselves," Manoel remembered with great emotion. The kidnapping was a "patriotic statement" against a country that had aided the 1964 coup. "I think that it was one of the most crushing defeats for American imperialism. . . . The documents subsequently released prove it: the coup was the initiative of the United States. It wasn't our initiative. It was the U.S. government. And Brazilians knew it; they figured it out. . . . And after the kidnapping, all of the indications I had, even while fleeing from the police, were feelings of excitement, euphoria, of 'finally we did something!'"

The historical record shows that Manoel both downplayed the Brazilian military (and its civilian allies' role in the 1964 coup) and exaggerated the U.S. participation. Nevertheless, his interpretation and recollections reflected the anger that many Brazilians had toward the United States because of its support for the overthrow. Censorship and the repression had forced most Brazilians to express their opposition to the regime only in private. Manoel continued:

> But not at the moment of the kidnapping. All of the Brazilian media, the radio and televisions stations, started reading our manifesto. . . . In my opinion, that demand was the most painful for the dictatorship to comply with—to allow us speak, to allow us to tell our story, to allow us to talk about what was happening at that moment in our country. . . . Everybody ignored the censorship. Everybody lost fear, and people spoke openly, on the streets, in the bars, on the buses, at the newsstands, where the news was stamped in the headlines. Everybody was talking about it. . . . In Rio nobody talked about anything else. People had the kind of outpouring of national pride rarely seen in Brazil.[75]

Those were Manoel's perceptions as a guerrilla fighting in the heat of the moment, and as a defender of the action five decades later. However, that riveting moment would be short-lived.

CHAPTER 2

The Wrath of the Dictators

Many Brazilians cheered on Ambassador Elbrick's kidnappers during the four-day national drama that the typically rigorous military censors could not keep out of the news. However, practically nobody answered the call to violent resistance. In their manifesto, the ALN and MR-8 envisaged the opening of a rural guerrilla front by year's end—the formula for success in the Chinese and Cuban revolutions and seen by Brazil's revolutionaries as essential for seizing power. But they failed to do so. The mainly middle- and upper-class guerrillas failed to inspire the poor masses. With its clandestine structure, the guerrilla movement was incapable of recruiting more people. Furthermore, already struggling for survival, everyday Brazilians were not interested in risking their lives. Revolutionary theories were beyond most people's intellectual reach, in large part because the guerrillas themselves had sharp disagreements. A brilliant but fleeting stroke of propaganda, the kidnapping was also an act of desperation: it was the only way to free captive comrades. As soon became clear, the abduction amounted to little more than a defensive tactic aimed at the groups' basic survival.[1]

The attention-grabbing operation exposed the guerrillas to the authorities, inviting harsher repression. Manoel and his fellow kidnappers won a major short-term victory in the crucial battle for international sympathy, but they also inflamed the military's wrath.[2] The kidnapping confirmed the military's emphasis on internal security.[3] The day after Elbrick's release, the junta officially banished the fifteen freed prisoners from Brazil, in effect stripping them of their rights as citizens. That night the junta broadcast a message on radio and TV affirming that the country had begun a war against subversives. It was the "duty of all citizens to take a responsible part in the measures necessary for confronting subversion."[4] Breaking with Brazil's tradition of relatively lenient criminal punishment, on September 19, 1969, the regime instituted the death penalty and life imprisonment for political crimes involving killing—a clear message to revolutionary groups. Nine days later, the government put into effect a tough new national security law that removed the last remnants of civil liberties and press freedoms, making journalists criminally responsible for articles unfavorable to the dictatorship. Three weeks later, it issued a massive constitutional amendment—in effect, a new constitution—further facilitating repression.[5]

Those were the legal, public measures. Behind the scenes, in the shadowy world of the regime's security forces, the soldiers and police officers who did the generals' dirty work cracked down ever harder against the revolutionary organizations. The day before the abduction, officers had arrested a militant near Ambassador Elbrick's residence. After the kidnapping, they immediately suspected him of knowing details of the operation. Army policemen beat him to death after three hours of interrogation. They later determined he was innocent. They reported his death as a suicide.[6]

The night of Elbrick's release, September 7, Jonas, Manoel, and two other men from the operation stayed in an apartment near downtown Rio used by revolutionaries as a safe house. Jonas and Manoel taught their comrades how to take apart and clean a machine gun kept in the apartment. They pulled the trigger of the unloaded gun twice to demonstrate its operation. The noise likely attracted someone's attention, because the next morning a man they believed to be a cop knocked at the door asking to enter the apartment to check on a supposed plumbing leak. Jonas and Manoel figured that the police would soon arrive. They decided to spend the day on the streets pretending to be tourists. That evening they met up with their two comrades, who reported that they had jumped out the back window of the apartment and fled, one of them in his underwear, after looking through the keyhole and seeing a man holding a machine gun. As planned, Jonas and Manoel took the 270-mile bus ride back to their base of operations in São Paulo. The next day the newspapers published pictures of the items found in the apartment, including a wig used by Jonas as a disguise. Furthermore, the police dealt the guerrillas a huge loss by seizing Elbrick's documents and the sensitive tape recordings of the ambassador's interrogation, which the guerrillas had hoped to use to disparage the dictatorship.[7]

In São Paulo, Manoel and the ALN leadership took stock of the Elbrick episode. Marighella believed that the ALN and MR-8 had gone too far. He had no foreknowledge of the kidnapping. Neither did the members of the ALN in Rio; Jonas, Manoel, and Toledo had come from São Paulo without notifying their comrades. Just a few days after the operation, Marighella privately dressed down Toledo for what he considered to be a precipitous operation that would surely provoke the military regime to increase the repression. Toledo listened without saying a word.[8] Meeting with Manoel and other ALN kidnappers and leaders, Marighella repeated his concerns and criticized the failure to warn about the operation as highly risky for comrades in Rio, where the police and the military had stepped up the repression significantly. When Manoel and the others countered with Marighella's own statements about revolutionary autonomy, the leader changed his opinion. But they did recognize their errors. "We didn't need to say what we were up to in any detail, but somehow we should have communicated that something was up," Manoel recalled.[9] During the same meeting, Marighella ended up praising the operation and wrote a welcoming message to the fifteen released prisoners. He soon announced in a revolutionary circular that more abductions would follow.[10] However, in private he remained furious.[11]

In mid-September 1969, Jonas, Manoel, and the rest of the São Paulo ALN prepared for a mega-operation against the regime: a group of guerrillas would simultaneously rob four banks on the same street and temporarily occupy an entire city block. For the first time, all São Paulo ALN guerrillas would act in unison. "We needed superior firepower and military superiority for that moment," Manoel recalled. "We started to realize that, if we took just a few more comrades than normal to take part in that action, we could achieve a much larger political victory from the expropriation."[12] Brazil's guerrillas always referred to robberies and thefts as "expropriations" carried out in favor of the people, the victims of exploitation by businesses and the U.S.-backed military regime. Immediately after the mega-operation, the ALN guerrillas would head for the Amazon region to launch the crucial rural front. Marighella planned to reinforce them with a small force of guerrillas freshly trained in Cuba.

But the mega-operation never took place. To secure transportation for their operations, the guerrillas routinely stole cars and tagged them with stolen license plates. On September 24, an ALN guerrilla preparing for the big event put a plate taken from a white Volkswagen on another white Volkswagen stolen by another ALN member. The incorrect plate caught the attention of the police. A contingent of about 100 officers, led by Sérgio Paranhos Fleury, one of Brazil's most infamous torturers, prepared an ambush on the block where the Volkswagens were parked. At about 3 p.m., Manoel and Luiz Fogaça Balboni approached one of the cars on a side street near the Avenida Paulista, the bustling financial center of São Paulo and a symbol of the military regime's "economic miracle." Without warning or attempting to make an arrest, the police opened fire with machine guns and other weapons from numerous vantage points. Unable to return fire, the two revolutionaries ran. The officers fired at them and missed, but two policemen blocking Manoel's and Balboni's path were killed by friendly crossfire. "That was crazy!" Manoel remembered of the "absurd" tactics of the police. "There was no way they should have done that. What could have led them to put one group of armed men shooting in the direction of another directly across from them?" But then Balboni was hit. Manoel tried to carry him for several yards while running and shooting. Balboni was rapidly losing blood and drooped. "If I had insisted on taking him with me, both of us would have died," Manoel recounted. "So I had to abandon him."[13] The police tortured the twenty-four-year-old Balboni for several hours before taking him to the hospital.[14]

Under fire and with police cars chasing him the wrong way on a one-way street, Manoel jumped in front of an oncoming car, a large Chevy from the 1950s, and threateningly waved his pistol in the air, causing the motorist to crash into another vehicle. The accident caused a traffic jam at the nearby intersection and slowed the police pursuit. Manoel raced to the next corner, where he violently opened the door of another car and forced the male driver into the lap of his female companion. Manoel ordered the couple out of the car and sped down the median strip of the two-lane street between the two lines of traffic, banging into other cars as he could hear the police officers' gunshots.[15]

Unable to get through the next intersection, Manoel abandoned the vehicle and muscled his way into the Ford Corcel of an elderly woman, Maria Helena de Souza, and made her move to the passenger's seat. "And just as I was getting ready to take off, the car stalled," Manoel recalled. "As I was starting the car up again, somebody opened my door. The only thing I could do was shoot him in the stomach. I don't know if he was trying to help. Don't ask me if he was a pedestrian or driver, or whether he was a civilian or policeman. I don't know, because the police did not open an official investigation into what happened. [The press revealed that the victim was hospitalized; he apparently survived.] . . . I closed the door and took off. The woman was very scared."

Having eluded the police, Manoel drove a good distance until he could safely drop off Maria Helena on a street named, ironically enough, Nebraska in an area crisscrossed by streets with many other U.S. names. Along the way, Manoel explained that he was a revolutionary and recounted what had just happened near the Avenida Paulista, including his failed attempt to save Balboni. "I told the whole story, and she changed her opinion. She calmed down and started saying, 'Don't worry. There is no way I'm going to report you to the police.' And so my conversation with her took on a different aspect. I insisted that she should report me. Otherwise she would fall into the hands of the security forces. She would get hurt." Manoel and Maria Helena agreed on a plan. She would request a tranquilizer from her family physician and pretend to use it or, in case of increased anxiety, actually take it. Meanwhile, her husband would report the incident at the local police station but state that his wife was too nervous to be interviewed. The next day, however, she would recover from her anxiety and tell the whole story. By then Manoel would be back in hiding. "And she did exactly that. She was great! . . . The next day the *Jornal da Tarde* and the Estadão group interviewed her about the incident, and she told the story that I suggested she tell. She behaved fantastically! Very interesting indeed!" Whereas many critics of the guerrillas—including regime opponents—thought that the fighters were isolated from everyday Brazilians, Manoel believed that Maria Helena's sympathetic attitude proved otherwise. "It goes to show that we were not so out of touch as people say," he said.

Manoel made his way to a main thoroughfare and caught the first available bus. Still armed, he discreetly left his revolver on the bus before getting off. "It was better to go about unarmed rather than armed on a night such as that in São Paulo," Manoel explained. "It was a night when lots could be happening as a result of the gun battle. The repressive forces were undoubtedly extremely agitated." Manoel got off near the Hospital das Clínicas, the USP's teaching hospital. He saw policemen at the entrance. "So I thought that I acted correctly in getting rid of my gun, because a gun can always cause a problem," Manoel said. "A gun will protect you, but it can also attract attention. . . . I had no way of hiding it on myself. And we used guns only after planning, and during a planned action. We did not walk the streets casually carrying guns."[16] Little did Manoel know that the police would later take Balboni to the Hospital das Clínicas after working him over. He died there shortly after midnight.[17]

Near the hospital, Manoel caught a bus to another part of town. "I took all the necessary precautions to avoid any possibility of being followed," he recalled. "I did an incredible and very meticulous zigzag across the city. I planned it all as best as I could, despite being very tense about all that had happened."[18] Sure that he was free of any tails, Manoel returned to his ALN hideout.

According to Manoel, ALN militants and sympathizers in the area of the Avenida Paulista ambush claimed that about twenty innocent bystanders died in the shooting. "People died," he stated. "And I mean lots of people. So many people, in fact, that they did not file a report. I'm speaking of a gun battle, but this was not a classic gun battle with people on two sides. It was hot pursuit."[19] Subject to regime censorship, the press did not report any civilian deaths, so it is difficult to verify Manoel's assertion. Regardless, as a result of the September 24 attack and the torture of captured militants, agents solved thirty crimes committed by the revolutionaries, shut down thirteen safe houses, and made twenty-six arrests.[20]

These agents worked for the Operação Bandeirantes (OBAN, or Operation Bandeirantes), Brazil's most notorious guerrilla-hunting outfit, including a horrific torture chamber. OBAN was named for the rugged backwoods pioneers, the *bandeirantes*, who helped establish São Paulo during the frontier-like conditions of sixteenth-century Brazil and hunted and enslaved indigenous peoples. OBAN soon came under the control of the military security hierarchy and, like similar units in other cities, became known as DOI-CODI.[21]

On September 27, still less than three weeks after Ambassador Elbrick's release, an OBAN team arrested Jonas. This was a prize catch. A former factory worker and boxer, Jonas exemplified the type of working-class revolutionary the ALN and other organizations hoped to recruit but who constituted a minority of the membership. He entered the OBAN headquarters surrounded by about fifteen men kicking and spitting at him. Although his hands were cuffed behind his back, Jonas kicked and spit back ferociously until one man wounded him seriously with a kick to the head, a prelude to the more violent treatment that would end his life.[22] Manoel remembered:

> Jonas was a very courageous person and, above all, physically very strong. He was a boxer his entire life. . . . In the culture of the factories and unions of that time boxing was a very popular sport. . . . He threw himself into things and did so with political and ideological resolute-ness. He was extremely aware and mentally tough, and he probably did not bend an inch before the repressive personnel. He refused to speak with them. He resisted with every last ounce of strength all that they were trying to do. And that probably provoked them to great anger, even to the point of total lack of control. At that point in history they were not killing people. His death happened as a result of their having lost control. They had not planned to kill him. But with Jonas they were playing with fire.[23]

The OBAN officers carried Jonas into the torture chamber. For ten hours, they brutalized him with electric shocks, drowning, beatings, burn-ing, and hanging him hog-tied upside down on the infamous parrot's perch, a metal bar suspended above the floor. That position left a prisoner completely vulnerable to torturers. When the agents dragged Jonas out of the chamber, they beat his head on the floor. At that point Jonas was likely dead. On September 29, the OBAN officers got rid of his body. Jonas thus became Brazil's first political prisoner to become a *desaparecido*, a disap-peared person. Inside the OBAN, the prisoners were told that Jonas had escaped. The false stories of "escapes," "suicides," and "shootouts with the police" became routine under military rule in Brazil and other Latin American countries—a way for agents to boast of their power, demoralize the militants, and avoid potential future prosecution. Continuing the farce, a year later the regime convicted Jonas in absentia and sentenced him to thirty years in prison.[24] In 2004, nearly twenty years after the return to de-mocracy, a Brazilian journalist, researching in police archives, discovered the coroner's report of Jonas's death and a photograph of his badly beaten face. The examiner noted more than a dozen different injuries and concluded that Jonas died of a skull fracture.[25] His remains have not been found.[26]

Manoel was still free. The events of September 24—the shootout, the escape, and the taking of a hostage—had left him traumatized, and they undoubtedly further incensed the security forces. He received orders from the ALN to go into hiding to rest from the many months of intensive operations. He recalled: "I completely lost touch with the organization. I had no more *pontos*. I had absolutely nothing." *Pontos* were regular, prearranged, secure meetings of two militants, who shared information and checked on each other. If one missed a meeting and didn't notify anybody within twenty-four hours, the others knew that a comrade had been captured. The militants quickly warned comrades about an arrest or disappearance and frequently abandoned safe houses, because the torturers sought information leading them to the revolutionaries' support networks. Thus, torturers knew they had to break revolutionaries within twenty-four hours. The ALN intended to prepare a forged passport for Manoel to go to Cuba for intensive training in rural guerrilla warfare. Manoel headed to São Sebastião, a small beach town on the road between São Paulo and Rio, far from the security police. He stayed in a house sometimes used by the organization. Jonas's wife and three of his four children were also there, awaiting a chance to leave the country. The ALN thought that they should exit Brazil to avoid possible capture: before he died, Jonas was supposed to help to lead the rural guerrilla front. The São Sebastião residence was isolated, so distant from both São Paulo and Rio that the ALN did not even use it as a safe house. They did not carry out armed operations in São Sebastião. As with several other homes in the town, it was used mainly for summer vacation, which, in the Southern Hemisphere, was still months off. The presence of children obliged Manoel to arrive unarmed. Late into the night he read Shakespeare and other classics while lying on the top part of a bunk bed.[27]

But the police were on his trail. One prisoner taken after the September 24 ambush did what militants commonly did under torture: he made up facts to confuse or throw off the police. In this case—not knowing that Manoel and Jonas's family were in São Sebastião—he told fantastic lies about the house there. Thus, in the minds of the police, the simple vacation home had become a massive underground fort with barracks and conference rooms. The OBAN sent a major force to attack. At 5 a.m. on September 30, Manoel was knocked off the bunk bed and awoke on the floor with a gun to his head and men kicking him. They demanded to know the entrance to the "secret tunnels," which, of course, did not exist.

The next stop for Manoel was the OBAN. He recalled:

On the way there, they forced a hood over my head. I wasn't able to see anything. I was in the back of the police wagon. So I hardly had any communication. I saw nothing. I knew nothing, not even where I was being taken. . . . I calculated that I was being taken to the DOI-CODI [OBAN]. I knew about that place. And when I arrived it was terrible, because they've got everything ready for you. The ritual of torture is very difficult. It's a crushing experience. Shouting, hysteria. A horrible, frenetic thing. Beatings, clubbing, lots of hate. All of these things together. It's all mixed together and staged with purpose. They've got every technique. And you start to get confused. They want it that way. It was really hard. I was taken in very quickly with them punching and pushing me through the door. They were beating the hell out of me from all sides. They took me right to the parrot's perch, ripping my clothes off on the way. It was horrible. . . . I was in the same room where they had killed Jonas. And as I hung on the parrot's perch, I could see the blood. I was beside the wall where his blood was, where his brains were. And they bellowed at me: "Ah! You see? That's from Jonas. It's all over, son-of-a-bitch. You've lost the war." And they showered me with blows. It was extremely violent, with electric shocks, something that is very difficult.

Despite the passing of thirty-seven years, Manoel recounted these horrific details as if they had occurred the day before. I asked if the torturers shocked him in the first session. Manoel recalled:

Yes, in my case they did, because when I arrived there, they knew that I was a guy from the Elbrick operation. I was "Sérgio" from São Paulo. Or "Bené," or however it was that I presented myself. They knew who I was. I was the guy from the police sketch. They knew everything that I had done. I believe that I survived because I ended up admitting things. Talking always gets you some protection during a torture session like that one. And I talked. I found the best way I could and kept with it. And also at that stage of the political repression they still hadn't given the directive to exterminate people. . . . I lost, I don't have several of my teeth because of the electric shocks, because . . . in those days they used lots of metal fillings and all of them would come out. The human organism expels those things as a result of the shocks. They also broke people's teeth by beating and clubbing people. I know that I lost many teeth. You also defecate. You urinate during a torture session. Because of that, because of the fact that you are defecating . . ., some of them tortured you with a perfumed handkerchief covering their noses. . . . They tortured the whole body. You turn purple all over. Your balls get burned. My God! It's terrible! It was totally absurd! Incredible!

The police had snagged one of the ALN's top leaders. And he was providing information, as opposed to some prisoners, such as Jonas, who refused to give up anything and, as a result, paid the consequences with more brutal torture or even death. Manoel explained how the MR-8, based in Rio, had come to seek an alliance with the ALN in São Paulo to kidnap Elbrick because it lacked sufficient manpower and resources to do the job alone. Manoel drew for the police a detailed geographical sketch of how the kidnapping had taken place, including the position of each person in the operation.[28] He also told the police about the other operations he had taken part in.

Manoel opened up to the police to preserve not only himself but also his political mentor and uncle João and two childhood friends who had also entered the ALN. On the one hand, his revelations demonstrated the cooperation that the police desired. On the other hand, he strategically omitted facts and fabricated others to avoid mentioning the involvement of the three comrades, because the police, who had no knowledge of them, would have immediately sought to arrest them. In his recollection, Manoel recognized that he had violated the revolutionary obligation to never break under interrogation—a security measure rooted in the Communist ethos, Brazilian machismo, youthful idealism, and loyalty and propagated by Marighella and other senior leaders of the resistance. In 1951, Marighella had written *Se fores preso, camarada* . . . (If you're arrested, comrade . . .), a guide to resisting torture that reduced the predicament to a question of mere choice, fortitude, and loyalty. As leader of the ALN, he carried poison to ingest to avoid being captured alive.[29] Manoel recalled:

> They already knew, when I arrived at the Operação Bandeirantes, that I had taken part in that action [the kidnapping]. Imagine that level of torture, and the level of risk. And that's what led me to reveal all that I had done. I turned into an important prisoner for them. They were satisfied with those actions because I was a key element, and with me they were clearing a series of cases. That was my behavioral tactic. And it was wrong, especially at that moment, which was the beginning of the political repression. The armed organizations, especially mine—I should not have done that. I supplied their database with information. I ended up implicating many of the comrades who took part in those actions.... But it was the strategy that I adopted in order to preserve the three comrades that I could have identified perfectly.[30]

To further distance himself from his uncle and friends, Manoel mixed lies with facts. He remembered:

> How had I entered the ALN? If I had told that story, I would have put at risk the lives of those comrades, and also my own. I would have fallen apart completely. I could not tell that story. So I had to find a way not to tell it. So I made up things.... On the other hand, torture is something that is so absurd, bestial, inhuman. It's terrible. You have to open up to them about some things. You break down and you end up talking. You say a few things and as you say them, the torturer, who believes so much in torture, solemnly believes everything said. They didn't even check my information. So I made up, for example, that I was an architecture student. You can see in all of the documents that I identify myself as "architecture student, the PAU, Program in Architecture and Urban Design, Universidade de São Paulo." I never set foot near the PAU. That small episode is a terrific example of how torture worked under the dictatorship. And how absurd it was.

Manoel spent sixteen long, painful days at the OBAN. On October 16, 1969, he was transferred to the jail of the political police, the Departamento Estadual de Ordem Política e Social (DEOPS, State Department of Political and Social Order) and placed in a cell with other captured revolutionaries. The OBAN was an extralegal unit, so it fell to the DEOPS to convert Manoel's testimony under torture into an official, signed interrogation to be filed with the courts. Manoel had thus passed from the shadowy world of the security forces to the status of a formal prisoner. He soon would have access to a lawyer. Although the regime could return prisoners to the OBAN for further interrogation and torture, once they had seen lawyers, and therefore had contact with the outside world, it became politically riskier.

Manoel had survived the wrath of the dictators—but only barely and at significant cost to himself and the revolution. After the Elbrick kidnapping, the massive counterattack by the dictatorship had destroyed the ALN's capacity to take the battle into the countryside.[31]

CHAPTER 3

Decapitating the Revolutionary Leadership

The morning of November 4, 1969, the DEOPS police suddenly transferred all but one of the ALN militants to São Paulo's Tiradentes Presídio, a prison named for a national hero, the martyr of a failed revolt for independence against Portugal in 1789. Something big was afoot. The remaining ALN member, Paulo de Tarso Venceslau, had taken part in the Elbrick abduction and was captured by the police following the September 24 ambush near the Avenida Paulista. DEOPS torturers working over Venceslau had discovered among his belongings a checkbook with a phone number and the name "Osvaldo" written on it.[1]

Osvaldo was a code name for Marighella. The telephone number belonged to the residence of the Dominican friars, one of Brazil's most progressive Catholic religious orders. Marighella had sought the Dominicans' help. Eager to resist the dictatorship, the Dominicans aided the ALN by storing weapons in their São Paulo convent. They also mapped out a region near another convent in the distant Amazon region where the rural front might launch. The friars assisted with logistics in the Amazon and elsewhere. At Brazil's southern border, Carlos Alberto Libânio Christo, a journalist-turned-friar known as Frei Betto, helped pursue ALN guerrilla operatives, including deputy leader Toledo, slip into Uruguay.[2]

The police quickly uncovered the Marighella–Dominican connection. DEOPS officers invaded the São Paulo convent and arrested numerous friars and seminarians. They picked up two other friars in Rio, torturing them brutally until they revealed the procedure for contacting Marighella. On the evening of November 4, Officer Fleury and twenty-eight other officers set up another stakeout near the Avenida Paulista just blocks from where they had tried to corner Manoel on September 24. They forced the two tortured Dominicans to sit in the Volkswagen Beetle in which Marighella usually met the friars. When the unarmed Marighella arrived and sat down in the backseat, the two friars jumped out, as prearranged by the police. Fleury and other officers emerged from the darkness. Fleury ordered Marighella to surrender. When the revolutionary leader tried to open a portfolio containing cyanide pills kept for committing suicide, Fleury and the officers opened fire. Five bullets hit Marighella, all shot from point-blank range. Two months to the day after the Elbrick capture, the police had killed the dictatorship's public enemy number one. Though they claimed publicly that they had wanted him alive for interrogation, in reality they executed him. The military was euphoric. Brazil's most admired revolutionary was dead.[3] The regime had decapitated the ALN.

The news of Marighella's death traveled like a shockwave through Brazil's guerrilla organizations. In Paris, a contingent of ALN militants received the news of their leader's death and debated future strategy.[4]

The group included Aloysio Nunes Ferreira Filho. Aloysio had taken a highly unusual path to the ALN that involved time in the bosom of the imperialist enemy. The son of a former São Paulo state assemblyman and student at the prestigious USP law school, in mid-1965 Aloysio won a spot in a three-week exchange program in the United States sponsored by the Inter-American University Association of São Paulo. The association, initiated under President Kennedy, and continued under President Johnson, was funded mainly by the American business community in Brazil, but also by the U.S. State Department. The program sought to identify and cultivate rising young leaders in Brazil, especially those considered left-wing, and introduce them to American society and government. In July 1962, President Kennedy met briefly with the delegation of seventy-six Brazilian students during a White House visit.[5] After the coup, both the military and sectors of the Left viewed the program unfavorably—the regime because of the students' leftist tendencies, the Left because it thought that Brazilian students had nothing to learn from the United States, an antisocialist country.[6]

On his visa application for his 1965 trip, Aloysio omitted his membership in the PCB. His group stayed with American families in the Boston area and attended classes on U.S. institutions organized by Henry Kissinger, then teaching at Harvard University. The visitors took part in a Harvard sit-in against the Vietnam War that included musical performances by folk singer Joan Baez and the Dave Brubeck Quartet. They visited New York City and in Washington, D.C., met Sen. Robert Kennedy and National Security Advisor Walt Rostow. Aloysio spoke enough English to communicate well during the trip. "I was chosen to speak in the name of the Brazilians," he recalled of the Rostow meeting, transmitted on the Voice of America government radio broadcast. "I gave an extremely violent speech against the invasion of the Dominican Republic. The aggression, the idea of self-determination, the fact that Brazil had acted as a lackey of American imperialism." Rostow listened politely.[7]

Most of the students opposed the Brazilian dictatorship. "We asked everybody we could to support us in our denunciations of what was taking place, which would get even worse later on," Aloysio recounted. Later, upon joining the ALN, he felt no contradiction between his esteem for the United States and membership in the anti-imperialist resistance. "I was never anti-American, because I always admired American institutions, the American constitution, American history, the American Revolution," he observed. "That defense of individual liberty, of the respect for individual rights. . . . I was against U.S. involvement in our country." Despite his time in the United States, nobody in the ALN questioned Aloysio's loyalty. "They knew that I was someone without any connection whatsoever to espionage," he explained. "And the program had nothing to do whatsoever with U.S. national security bureaucracy or espionage or the CIA. And many leftists went on that trip."[8]

At the USP law school, Aloysio became the president of the Centro Acadêmico XI de Agosto, a prestigious leadership position that had been a launching pad into national politics. He obtained his degree in late 1967. An early ALN comrade, Aloysio stored arms and ammunition in his apartment, served as Marighella's chauffeur, and drove a getaway car during a spectacular ALN train robbery. He managed to leave Brazil for Paris just hours before a court issued a warrant for his arrest on a previous charge of political agitation. Marighella had decided that Aloysio would then proceed to Cuba for further guerrilla training to prepare for an eventual return to the front in Brazil. Aloysio's departure for Cuba was delayed because his girlfriend, Vera Maria Tude de Souza, an ALN collaborator, was carrying twins and had a difficult pregnancy. After Marighella's death,

Figure 5. Aloysio Nunes Ferreira Filho, front and center, at the Universidade de São Paulo law school in the 1960s. Aloysio Nunes Ferreira Filho collection.

Figure 6. Typical in dictatorial Brazil, this "Wanted: Murderous Terrorists" sign included a picture of Aloysio, second row, third from left. Aloysio Nunes Ferreira Filho collection.

however, Toledo—who had led the Elbrick operation, escaped to Uruguay, and then gone to Paris—immediately started to rethink the revolution. "I spoke to Câmara [Toledo] and he thought I should not go to Cuba," Aloysio remembered of their meeting in Paris. "He really thought nobody else should go to Cuba . . . and looked for a way to get out those who were already there, and eventually even reformulating the ALN's politics into some other type of activity. . . . Our plans collapsed with Marighella's death."[9]

In the ensuing months, the security forces continued to round up other guerrilla leaders and many of their hard-core followers. In the process, they picked up most of the rest of Elbrick's abductors.

The evisceration of the organizations created tensions within the revolutionary movement. At Tiradentes, Manoel awaited trial on a dozen charges of violating the regime's national security legislation. Brazil's system of military justice tribunals took many months to bring an individual to trial. Manoel and other imprisoned ALN members debated their organization's actions and norms, including how militants should behave behind bars. Despite the enormous pain they had experienced, the prisoners argued bitterly about revelations made under torture. They especially wanted to figure out how the police had discovered the Marighella–Dominican connection. Nobody wanted to take the blame for his death—a controversy that would linger for decades.[10] Some of Marighella's followers came to speculate that the CIA had a role in luring him into the ambush, but no proof for this hypothesis ever emerged.[11] The blame, of course, lay with the police torturers. However, a combination of denial, machismo, inexperience, and unrealistic expectations about the ability to withstand torture often led the victims to lash out at themselves and their comrades. Only after months of intense, organized criticism and self-criticism did the prisoners sort out all of the actions in which they had taken part and all that had been confessed under torture, leading them to a clearer understanding of their military failure. That process allowed the ALN men to overcome the pain suffered under torture and the sorrow at Marighella's death, leading them to unite as a political force within the prison.[12]

On the outside, the remaining guerrillas from the ALN and other groups fought increasingly less for the revolution and more for mere organizational survival. On March 12, 1970, the Vanguarda Popular Revolucionária (VPR, or People's Revolutionary Vanguard) kidnapped the Japanese consul in São Paulo and obtained the release of just five prisoners. On April 5, another group tried to kidnap Curtis Cutter, the U.S. consul in Porto Alegre. Driving a large car, Cutter was able to bump away the Volkswagen Beetle chasing him, but not before the guerrillas wounded him with a gunshot to the shoulder. On June 11, a joint team of ALN and VPR guerrillas abducted the West German ambassador, killing one of his Brazilian bodyguards. The government accepted the guerrillas' demands and flew forty prisoners to Algeria.[13]

On the morning of July 1, a group of four militants boarded a Cruzeiro Airlines plane at Rio's Galeão International Airport for a flight to Buenos Aires via São Paulo. Brothers Eiraldo and Fernando de Palha Freire and a couple, Jessie Jane and Colombo, both just nineteen, sat in the front rows. The daughter of a fervent Communist, Jessie (whose name was *not* inspired by the American bandit Jesse James but by her father's reading of an unrelated novel) had joined the ALN, as had the three men. Jessie wore a maternity dress to hide a stash of weapons. Twenty minutes into the flight, with guns drawn, the four militants forced their way into the cockpit and announced that they were carrying out a revolutionary action. They demanded that the captain, Harro Cyranka, return to Rio. In exchange for the thirty-four passengers and seven crew members they wanted the release of forty political prisoners. Together with the hijackers and two Catholic cardinals to be taken on board to guarantee safe passage, the released prisoners would proceed to Cuba. Cyranka, who had thirty thousand hours of flying time, tried to convince the poorly informed militants that they should not return to Rio but instead fly with the hostages to the Amazon region, where the plane could refuel before going on to Cuba. The hijackers were unaware that the air force commander in Rio, the fanatically right-wing General Burnier, was competing with the navy and the army to repress the revolutionary organizations. "Forget the political prisoners and don't go back to Rio because you're going to fall right into the lion's mouth," Cyranka said. They refused to heed his advice. Jessie recalled, "We had no technical knowledge of what an air base was, nor about military strategy."[14]

When the airliner landed at the airport, awaiting air force troops machine-gunned the tires and threw sand on the runway. Soldiers positioned on the ground surrounded the plane. "We understood immediately that we had done something foolish," Jessie said. "Eiraldo was a very sensitive person. He asked me, 'And now what?' I said, 'Well, we're not going to have the courage to kill these people, are we? We calculated everything, except the fact that there would be people inside the plane.' That is very difficult. We grabbed people—we hurt no one."[15]

Burnier and his officers refused to negotiate, even after passengers signed a petition asking that the government guarantee their safety as Brazilian citizens. As psychological tensions rose along with the cabin temperature because of the sweltering Rio afternoon, the air force directed the operators of fire trucks stationed around the plane to spray it with white foam to facilitate officers' access. Using a blowtorch, one officer managed to open the main door. Soldiers threw large quantities of tear gas canisters inside the plane. In the ensuing panic, with air force personnel firing their weapons, Cyranka was wounded in the leg. Colombo and Fernando were captured, while Jessie and Eiraldo hid in a bathroom. When they tried to exit, the soldiers jumped on Jessie and started beating her. Eiraldo was shot and wounded in the back. Fernando, Colombo, and Jessie suffered brutal torture at the air force post and were later transferred to the army DOI-CODI. There the prisoners suffered more abuse.[16]

Because the DOI-CODI officers believed Eiraldo was Jessie's husband, on July 3 they brought her to see him in the infirmary in the hopes of destabilizing her emotionally and getting her to reveal more information about the ALN. Eiraldo died the next day in the air force hospital in Rio. Jessie's encounter with Eiraldo proved that he did not die in the way the censored press reported the incident (in two different versions): that he had committed suicide or been shot by Colombo.[17] The officers also pressured Jessie to go on television to reject the revolution, as several other revolutionaries had been forced to do. Publicly winning over a high-profile, young, attractive female would score key political points for the dictatorship. "They were saying clearly: 'Imagine the impact of putting that girl on television,'" Jessie recalled.[18] To further pressure Jessie, the security forces arrested her mother and younger sister, and one officer tortured the sister in front of her. But Jessie refused to cooperate.[19] The regime would soon exact its revenge.

Jessie later said of the attempted hijacking:

> We committed a profound mistake. We did something that was not correct in a political sense. I have no regrets, but if you analyze it from the political and military-strategic standpoint, it was a mistake. . . . We had incorrectly interpreted the revolutionary process and what

were Brazil and the dictatorship and its alliances and goals. This was an error of the Left as a whole—an error in analyzing the historical process. As a group [of organizations], we did not have the historical conditions to do what we proposed. As a result of that faulty interpretation of Brazil, the entire objective of the armed Left became inconsistent, because it wasn't based on persuasion of the masses.[20]

Meanwhile, the repression became more efficient. Just weeks after the failed hijacking, the government broke up a plot to kidnap the Japanese consul in Recife. Shortly thereafter, it foiled an ambitious plan to kidnap an ambassador, a Brazilian businessman, and a member of the president's cabinet to force the release of two hundred prisoners.[21]

The military tried revolutionaries in tribunals it had set up in 1964 to judge the large number of alleged subversives. Juries were composed of military officers. In August 1970, Manoel finally came before a tribunal. At the start of the trial, Manoel's lawyer read aloud a statement Manoel had written to protest the proceedings. "I feel pride, not because I stand in the presence of you officers, members of this court who wear the same uniform as countless torturers located in Brazil's barracks, OBs [Operações Bandeirantes] and [DOI-]CODIs, also the same uniform as our dictators," Manoel wrote. "I feel pride because I belong to a people—and by people I mean the poor and the oppressed—that is beginning to rise up and take up arms to fight for our sovereignty." The dictatorship, he stated, "sold" Brazil's independence to the United States. Manoel described the regime's propaganda efforts, which capitalized on Brazil's spectacular June victory in the 1970 World Cup of soccer, as "a false triumph of the dictatorship." Such propaganda "recalled the days of Hitler. . . . But you, sirs, having accepted this farce, this dirty game of the powerful, the circus that is this tribunal, will be deservedly convicted. And your conviction will be much harder and more severe than the one you will apply to me today: it will be the conviction of history and not that of a military dictatorship." The judge and prosecutors demanded that the attorney stop reading the statement, but he proceeded until he was arrested and removed from the courtroom. During the proceedings, Manoel denounced the torture and death of Jonas at the OBAN.[22] Manoel, as did the most audacious guerrillas, received long sentences. Convicted in September 1970, he got thirty years in prison. After guilty verdicts in two other cases, his sentence was increased to fifty-four years.

O DIA

Da esquerda para a direita, Paulo de Tarso, Antônio de Frei tas Silva, Cláudio Tôrres da Silva e Manoel Cirilo de O. Neto

Condenados os terroristas que seqüestraram Elbrick

Dos dezoito subversivos julgados on-tem, por terem participado, em setembro do ano passado, do seqüestro do Embai-xador norte-americano Charles Burke El-brick, quinze foram condenados, tendo as penas variado de dois a oito anos de reclusão. Apenas quatro compareceram ao Conselho Permanente de Justiça da 1ª Auditoria do Exército, sendo os demais julgados à revelia.

A oito anos de prisão foram condenados Manuel Cirilo de Oliveira Neto, Cláudio Tôrres da Silva, Paulo de Tarso Venceslau, Sérgio Rubens de Araújo Tôrres, Franklin de Sousa Martins, João Lopes Salgado, Joaquim Câmara Ferreira e José Sebastião Rios de Moura. Helena Bocaiúva Khair terá de cumprir três anos de cadeia, enquanto seus companheiros Antônio de Freitas Silva e Francisco Lopes de Oliveira permanecerão presos por dois anos. Fernando Paulo Nagle Gabeiro, Cid de Queirós Ben-

jamim e Vera Silvia de Araújo Maga-lhães foram banidos do País.

Acusação

A acusação coube ao Promotor Má-rio José de Carvalho Salvador, que iniciou o libelo com uma retrospectiva da ação que culminou com o seqüestro do diplomata. Rememorou alguns lances dramáticos que marcaram a captura dos implicados, e falou sôbre os diversos ma-nifestos em que os terroristas concita-vam o povo a apoiá-los em nome de uma falsa democracia. Pediu, finalmente, a condenação de todos êles, «por ter ficado a ação subversiva perfeitamente caracte-rizada nos autos».

Defesa

Funcionaram na defesa os advogados Alcione Barreto, Augusto Sussekind de Morais Rêgo e Manuel Francisco de Lima. O primeiro, patrono de Antônio de Freitas Silva, negou que o mesmo

tivesse tido qualquer ligação com o grupo terrorista, frisando:

— Meu constituinte era um simples caseiro da residência da Rua Barão de Petrópolis, 1.026, onde a Polícia estourou o aparelho.

Ao final dos trabalhos, as sentenças foram anunciadas, sendo os réus incursos nos Artigos 16 e 25 do Decreto-Lei 510, que correspondem, respectivamente, à violação das imunidades de um diplomata estrangeiro e ao seqüestro pròpriamente dito.

Desmaio

Mais tarde, na 2ª Auditoria do Exército, era julgada a estudante Maria Dal-va Leite de Castro, que sofreu um ataque de epilepsia e teve de ser socorrida, juntamente com Maria Dalva, era sub-metida a julgamento sua colega Abigail Paranhos. Por solicitação do advogado de defesa, os trabalhos foram suspensos.

Figure 7. A Rio newspaper article reporting the military tribunal convictions of the Elbrick kidnappers. In the photo, from left to right: Paulo de Tarso Venceslau, Antônio de Freitas Silva, Cláudio Tôrres da Silva, and Manoel. Edileuza Pimenta de Lima collection.

The military regime had instituted the death penalty to quell the revolution. Because of their ostensible involvement in the death of comrade Eiraldo, Jessie Jane and Colombo both received a death sentence. Their sentences were later converted to decades-long prison terms. Released after a short time in jail, Jessie's mother and sister and four other siblings went into exile. Colombo was imprisoned at a facility for political prisoners on Ilha Grande, a largely deserted island off the coast of the state of Rio de Janeiro. Jessie was sent to the Talavera Bruce Women's Penitentiary. For her refusal to renounce the revolution on TV, she received a year in solitary confinement.[23]

In October 1970, Officer Fleury dealt another major blow to the revolution by capturing Toledo, who had returned to Brazil. They acted on a tip from an ALN militant-turned-informant, José Silva Tavares. At a secret interrogation center outside São Paulo, Fleury tortured Toledo on the parrot's perch. When Toledo started gasping for air, a physician was called in to try to keep him alive so that Fleury could extract information. It was too late. Toledo died a short while later.[24]

On December 7, the VPR and another group kidnapped the Swiss ambassador in Rio. They were led by Carlos Lamarca, an army officer-turned-guerrilla, who became one of the most hunted men in Brazil after the death of Marighella. The guerrillas wanted seventy prisoners freed. President Médici refused to free prisoners who had been accused or convicted of murder, received a life sentence, or been involved in kidnapping. Thus, the VPR had to identify other militants to replace those denied by Médici. Negotiations dragged on for forty days. Among those finally flown to exile in Santiago, Chile, was Washington Alves da Silva, Jessie Jane's father. The operation was the last kidnapping of a foreign diplomat.[25]

As the military gained experience negotiating with guerrillas, kidnapping lost efficacy as a form of resistance. Taking advantage of the kidnappers' amateurism, the generals turned the tables and imposed their own conditions. "It was all so precarious, all so badly done, all so badly conducted," Manoel remembered. "The dictatorship realized that and was able to manipulate the situation very well." His name had appeared on the initial list of those to be freed in the Swiss operation. He was thus transferred from Tiradentes back to the DEOPS and prepared for possible release. The officers stripped him of his clothing and placed him alone in a small holding cell where they could secretly observe and film him for the purpose of future identification. The police required Manoel to sign a document accepting his official banishment from Brazil. He refused. "That caused a big argument," Manoel recalled. "And there was nothing they could do. They couldn't torture me. They made lots of threats and shouted a lot, but they couldn't torture me, because if I were released, and released with marks all over me, there would be a huge outrage. I was in a position that allowed me to refuse. I said: 'I do not want to be banished.' I wanted to leave prison; but if I were to leave, I wanted to go for other reasons—to go out because my comrades were fighting for something." However, in the end, Manoel was not released because of Médici's tough criteria.[26]

Resistance to the dictatorship came at a high price: not only did individuals suffer, but the revolutionaries also lost leaders and organizational strength. Of the thirteen people involved in the Elbrick operation, two (Jonas and Toledo) were tortured to death; three were sent to prison; four were jailed but sent into exile as part of an exchange after the abduction of the West German ambassador; three escaped detection and lived underground or in exile; and one would be mysteriously murdered in the 1980s.[27] The Dominican friars arrested in the operation to eliminate Marighella, including Frei Betto, all went to prison. Brazil's other revolutionary organizations suffered similar losses.

Their leaders and comrades in exile, prison, or dead, the remaining guerrillas became increasingly intimidated and demoralized.

CHAPTER 4

The Guerrilla's Lamentation

Forced onto the defensive, the guerrillas went deeper underground, isolating themselves even further from the people they purportedly fought to liberate. Some ALN members took stock of the situation and advocated a strategic retreat to consider other forms of resistance. These militants believed in striking a balance between political action and armed struggle. The hard-core guerrillas, however, saw violence as the only way to defeat the regime. In general, Brazil's guerrilla groups became divided between *massistas* (supporting action involving the masses) and *militaristas* (prioritizing military action).[1] Dominated by the hard-core guerrillas, and with the organization fading, the ALN became *militarista*, completely dependent on violence for its survival.[2] Only the Partido Comunista do Brasil (PC do B, the Communist Party of Brazil, a Maoist offshoot of the PCB) was able to open a rural front by installing guerrillas in the Amazon region. However, it was small and disorganized. Thus, the security forces could focus their efforts on hunting downing guerrillas in the major cities. This further accentuated the reliance on violence.

Militarism mirrored the dictators' own use of force. However, it also emerged from heated worldwide debates over revolutionary ideas in the late 1960s and early 1970s. In the ALN, militarism was rooted in the fundamental idea of action for action's sake, to the point where action became nearly a fetish.[3] The hard-core elements gave "military action an exaggerated, sometimes even exclusive, importance," recalled Paulo Vannuchi.

Paulo had started out in the ALN's Frente de Massas, "Front for the Masses," which did political work primarily among students.[4] Fighters often devalued the work of the ALN's unarmed support network.[5] Even Manoel, one of the most militarily active of the ALN guerrillas, admitted that the organization had experienced "a certain militarist deviation" and embraced the idea of "armed action for the sake of armed action." He observed that "whoever carries a gun suddenly has a greater propensity to see the world in that way." The guerrillas, Manoel stated, came to believe that "the force of arms could resolve and substitute for a series of other things fundamental in any revolutionary process. . . . I believe that our approach and our organization came into existence and emerged from the vast vacuum left by the Communist Party, because of the inaction of the Communist Party. But we ended up swinging to the other end of the pendulum. . . . Marighella used to say, 'Let's start the revolution. We'll theorize about it later.'"[6] Terrorist organizations in other societies degenerated because of a similar unquestioning embrace of violence. For example, for the Red Brigades in Italy—operating, admittedly, in a democracy—overreliance on violence became a virtual religion inspired by myths of arms and death.[7]

With Marighella and Toledo gone, people mainly in their twenties and even teens had to maintain the fight. So the ALN came under the leadership of the militarily superb but politically inexperienced guerrilla Clemente, the code name for Carlos Eugênio Sarmento Coêlho da Paz. Carlos Eugênio was only seventeen when he entered the ALN in 1968, and he brought into the organization other youths, including one who was just fourteen.[8] When he took control in late 1970, he was just twenty.

Carlos Eugênio "embodied better than anybody the militarism followed by the armed left," wrote Denise Rollemberg, a historian of Brazil's revolutionaries.[9] Although Marighella had insisted on autonomous revolutionary cells, the confusion following his and Toledo's deaths led to the centralization of much of the leadership under Carlos Eugênio. In meetings where decisions were ostensibly collective, he often imposed his will by shouting and swearing at his comrades.[10] From this point, Carlos Eugênio and the other members of the São Paulo Armed Tactical Group controlled the ALN and led it down an increasingly militaristic path.[11] Over the next three years, he and his team frenetically robbed banks, assaulted businesses, stole weapons from the police, and engaged in gun battles with DOI-CODI operatives, Officer Fleury, and other repressive

Figure 8. Carlos Eugênio Sarmento Coêlho da Paz. Arquivo Público do Estado de São Paulo.

units. They also killed people. Lacking any political platform or future plans, the ALN's strategy disintegrated into pure violence.

Under Marighella's wing, Carlos Eugênio received his guerrilla schooling in a Rio de Janeiro that, despite the harshness of the dictatorship, retained a remarkable cultural charm for the young militants because of its music, Carnival, cinemas, and status as the former capital.[12] The toughest—and most seductive—of the guerrillas, Carlos Eugênio could pull a trigger as easily as he could pluck guitar strings. When he wasn't on the revolutionary prowl, he made love to his girlfriends and, also displaying tenderness, acted as a guardian of the other guerrillas in the confines of ALN safe houses in São Paulo.

Carlos Eugênio replaced Marighella as public enemy number one of the dictatorship.[13] He struck fear in the police and the military with his combat skills and uncanny survival instinct. "Clemente was the champion of armed actions in Brazil," recalled Marival Chaves, a former São Paulo DOI-CODI intelligence analyst who later publicly revealed secrets of the repressive forces. "All of the armed actions carried out by the ALN in Brazil have Clemente's fingerprints on them. . . . Clemente was considered by the repressive forces to be a highly dangerous activist, because of his level of activity and his record. Because he was courageous. He acted, he killed, he made things happen." Chaves explained that, thanks to the 1979 Amnesty Law, a key element of the transition to democracy that freed political prisoners, Carlos Eugênio never faced trial or jail time. "Because if he were to be judged for the crimes he committed, he'd be serving a prison sentence of more than 100 years," he observed.[14]

MY FIRST CONTACT with Carlos Eugênio came through his memoir *Viagem à luta armada*, literally translated as *Voyage to Armed Struggle*.[15] Rarely have I read a book so gripping and disturbing. In the words of Brazilian sociologist Maria Cláudia Badan Ribeiro, who conducted a detailed analysis of Carlos Eugênio's writings, "the appearance of such a visceral and chaotic narrative necessarily reflects the resistance and suffering faced in that period."[16] The book's impression on me was multiplied because I read it while living in Rio in 1997 very near many of the places where Carlos Eugênio had acted as a guerrilla. For several nights, I read into the wee hours of the morning to finish *Viagem*. I slept fitfully and awoke with a sense of foreboding.

The book opens with Carlos Eugênio shooting heroin and smoking hashish while lying in a warm bathtub in Paris in 1974—his way of soothing his mind after years of daily threats of violence, the guilt of killing, and the loss of lovers and fellow combatants. Above all, Carlos Eugênio seeks to replace the highs and lows of the guerrilla experience: the adrenaline rushes of combat and the ever-present danger of capture. He introduces the ALN and its key figures, taking the reader into safe houses, on missions, and into the workings of his own mind. He describes making split-second life-and-death choices. Whereas many revolutionary memoirs of the period ultimately portray the guerrillas as victims of the military and downplay guerrilla actions, *Viagem* celebrates, in an impolitic way, the revolutionary Left's embrace of violence.

Upon the recommendation of a former antiregime militant and human rights activist who served as a reference, I called Carlos Eugênio. We met at his modest rented apartment in Rio's upper-class Ipanema district. We each sat in chairs from a kitchen set, the only pieces of furniture in the living room. Carlos Eugênio dressed casually and lived simply: in revolutionary style, he showed little concern for material goods. I imagined this spartan setting as the kind I would have encountered in an early 1970s safe house.

I explained that I sought information on Alexandre Vannucchi Leme, the cousin of Paulo Vannuchi, a USP student and ALN militant tortured to death in March 1973 at the São Paulo DOI-CODI. With an excellent memory, Carlos Eugênio was a fount of information.[17] For four hours he spoke passionately about the ALN as if the events of a quarter century ago had occurred the day before.

Over the next twelve years, I interviewed Carlos Eugênio ten times. In all, we spent about forty hours discussing his life, the ALN, and Brazilian politics. We also spoke on the phone, conversed informally over meals or at bakeries where he liked to drink strong Brazilian coffee, and communicated many times via e-mail and Facebook. Carlos Eugênio proved as cordial as any of the ex-ALN members I had met. In August 2007, our meeting turned into an all-day affair, with Carlos Eugênio preparing steaks in a pan while we stood in the kitchen and spoke with his girlfriend and her son. He enjoyed housework, he once said. However, like so many of his generation of radicals, Carlos Eugênio rejected traditional marriage.

During our meetings, Carlos Eugênio often seemed ready to burst into action. Full of nervous energy, he fidgeted. His face sometimes twitched. He smoked cigarettes. Once, he happily noted that he had quit, only to start again the next year. Although I found smoking repugnant and obviously unhealthy, I viewed inhaling secondhand smoke from Carlos Eugênio (and other interviewees) as a necessary occupational hazard, part of the cultural experience of Brazil, where, in the 1980s and 1990s, many people ignored smoking bans in buses and public places. In discussing the ALN's controversies, Carlos Eugênio appeared to transport himself back into the moment, cursing and speaking vociferously as if the very force of his words could determine the truth. Killing, seeing so many comrades die, running from the law, shooting heroin, suffering a heart attack after the publication of *Viagem*—despite all of this, Carlos Eugênio still had immense vitality for a man in his fifties. His strength and acute awareness of his surroundings helped make him both leader and survivor.

In a 2001 meeting, I asked Carlos Eugênio the same question a Brazilian news magazine had posed: How many people did he kill? He said that he didn't know. Some of his victims he had seen die. In some shootouts, it was more difficult to know who died and who did the killing. "I don't worry much about the number," he said. He did remember clearly the first time he knew with certainty that he had killed: a policeman and a taxi driver who was transporting the officer and his colleagues in the Vila Prudente neighborhood of São Paulo in November 1970 after Carlos Eugênio and two other ALN members had distributed revolutionary leaflets in the area. Killing for the first time profoundly shocked him.[18]

Working decades later as a guitar teacher and playing bass guitar in a bossa nova group, Carlos Eugênio became known in Rio's musical circles as "Carlinhos," Little Carlos, a nonthreatening, affectionate name associated with harmony.[19] After we finished our 2007 interview and ate his steaks, Carlos Eugênio put on a bossa nova CD he and other musicians had recorded. He let me download it onto my laptop. Whenever I hear the songs, I reflect on Carlos Eugênio's life and the meanings of violence and terrorism.

Historians and social scientists generally do not consider luck in analyzing people and events. However, in the case of Carlos Eugênio, it played a huge role. Most guerrillas were captured or killed within a year's time. Carlos Eugênio survived nearly three years in the São Paulo Armed Tactical Group. "Everybody in his circle died," Chaves observed. "In São Paulo, he left a *ponto* and was followed, and he would have been killed, but they lost him. So, I attribute that to a huge stroke of luck."[20]

THE ROOTS OF Carlos Eugênio's militarism went far deeper than the revolution, Marxism, and resistance to the dictatorship. He hailed from a region that deeply contradicted the ideas of Brazilian cordiality and nonviolence. Carlos Eugênio was born in the northeastern state of Alagoas, not far from where *bandeirantes* during the colonial era had fought and destroyed Palmares, a large colony of runaway slaves who had established an independent kingdom that threatened slaveholder dominance. Stories and incidents of violence filled Carlos Eugênio's childhood. An aunt and uncle, despite raising many children together, distrusted each other to the point where each kept a knife and revolver under the pillow. One cousin worked as a hired gun.[21] "It's a falsehood that Brazilians aren't violent," Carlos Eugênio affirmed. His region of Brazil was immersed in violence: people fiercely defended personal and familial honor. In Alagoas people took this to extremes. In Maceió, the seaside capital of Alagoas, people regularly carried arms. For a while Carlos Eugênio lived with an aunt in a backlands town, where he started primary school at age six. On the first day, two boys started fighting in class, one cutting the other's face with a razor blade. In a bar in the same town, a man tried to knife another but failed. Enraged, he struck out at one of Carlos Eugênio's relatives, an innocent bystander, and killed him. The culprit deliberately spent his life in jail for fear that a relative of the victim would exact revenge. Such family feuds were common in the region. "For that guy, bullets required" was a popular expression for describing how killing was the only way to solve a problem. In Maceió, Carlos Eugênio's father took him to see the bullet holes in the walls of the state legislature, where elected officials had once engaged in a shootout. In 1963, two Alagoas senators confronted each other on the floor of the Brazilian Senate. One fired a gun at the other but mistakenly shot dead another senator. Neither man went to prison or lost his seat—a common outcome for members of the privileged upper classes. The first senator was the father of President Collor. "Insults are washed away with blood," said Carlos Eugênio. When his family moved to cosmopolitan Rio, he was shocked that men fought only with fists.[22]

Carlos Eugênio's family was not rich, but in Rio they had sufficient income to enroll him in the Colégio Andrews, an elite primary and secondary school. His classmates made fun of his northeastern accent, calling him *paraíba*, the name of a state in that region and a pejorative term for northeasterners roughly equivalent to "hillbilly." Not surprisingly, Carlos

Eugênio got into frequent fights[23] and landed his blows and kicks on "idiot snobs."[24]

He transferred to the Colégio Pedro II, a top public high school named for Brazil's second emperor (1840–89). In a society where only a small minority attended high school and even fewer reached college, he and his classmates could have easily become successful professionals. However, renouncing material success, they thirsted for social justice. In late 1967, Carlos Eugênio participated briefly in the PCB. He and his friends were deeply attracted to the idea of revolution. One friend was Alex de Paula Xavier Pereira, whose parents, longtime PCB militants, had left the party with Marighella to form the ALN. Alex introduced Carlos Eugênio to Marighella.[25]

In 1968, Carlos Eugênio and his Colégio Pedro II friends joined the ALN. They formed a tactical team assigned to steal license plates and carry out armed robberies. They also stole mimeograph machines, used for printing revolutionary flyers and publications. Whereas Marighella's main ALN base in São Paulo consisted primarily of university students and included older members of the working class, in Rio he recruited heavily among secondary school students. The older São Paulo militants looked down on their Rio counterparts, and tensions developed between the two factions.[26] (Memories of these tensions remained strong in the twenty-first century.) Nevertheless, over time the Rio group proved itself militarily. After the São Paulo contingent lost many members following the Elbrick kidnapping, Carlos Eugênio and other Rio militants reinforced the ALN in that city.

Members of Carlos Eugênio's family also entered the resistance. His mother, Maria da Conceição Sarmento Coêlho da Paz, had close ties to the PCB and joined the ALN. As a middle-aged woman, she could more easily do surveillance before robberies.[27] She was arrested in 1974. On July 23 of that year, Officer Fleury tortured her solely because it was Carlos Eugênio's birthday. As Fleury broke her teeth, she spit blood in his face.[28] Carlos Eugênio's older sister, Valderez, participated in the student movement. Along with hundreds of other activists, she was arrested at the important 1968 clandestine national student congress in Ibiúna, São Paulo, held in defiance of the generals.[29]

Carlos Eugênio used his extraordinary energy to spring into combat. In April 1969, during a failed attempt by him and his comrades to hold up the box office at a crowded Rio movie theater, he shot and wounded a security guard who was aiming at the guerrillas. Preparedness was his creed. Typical of Brazil's guerrillas, he went about in normal clothing, expertly stuffing the pockets with two semiautomatic pistols, a .38-caliber revolver, grenades, and an ample supply of clips. He carried his machine gun in a large, commonly used shopping bag. Carlos Eugênio thrived on action and adrenaline. He challenged the police to capture him, for example, by purposely imprinting his fingerprints on car windshields. "I'm leaving my signature in order to provoke them," he told his comrades.[30] When Toledo offered him cyanide pills for use in case of capture, Carlos Eugênio scoffed at the idea. "I want to make them work until my last breath, to take with me as many as I can and hope for luck, betting that destiny will allow me to live."[31]

Whereas Marighella sent Alex and other militants to Cuba for extended guerrilla training, he ingeniously proposed that Carlos Eugênio, who had yet to fulfill his obligatory military service, enlist in the army. Marighella explained the mission:

> From this moment on you are a revolutionary infiltrator in the army. Secrecy is your only weapon. It will be important for you to learn all that you can: the handling of weapons, military discipline, obtaining an inside view of how the enemy operates, how he thinks, how he reacts. Don't let yourself be fooled by appearances. An army has its own logic, which we sometimes underestimate because we don't understand it. Let them transform you into a soldier. Don't run the risk of losing the initiative. Be aware. Learn to obey and you will learn to command with your power of leadership. You will become a fine guerrilla.... Don't get involved in politics or talk about current events, because you could give yourself up.[32]

With steely discipline, Carlos Eugênio sought to channel his personal experience with violence into becoming a revolutionary. Through a family connection he obtained an assignment at the army's historic Copacabana Fort. In 1922, a small band of young military revolutionaries had used the fort as a base to launch a rebellion against the government, which they viewed as corrupt and stagnant. In the late 1960s, the fort housed antiguerrilla specialists. "I'm going to learn how to fight against myself," Carlos Eugênio thought. "They attempt to create discipline through humiliation and intimidation. That part's not for me. A guerrilla is disciplined because he is aware of the need for a hierarchy in combat, not because they've made him a cog in the wheel."[33] He attended obligatory civics lectures where he heard the guerrillas described as "terrorists and communists . . . atheists who want to destroy the Brazilian family and do away with liberty."[34] He drilled exhaustively to become an expert marksman and model soldier. He learned to toss grenades and fire different kinds of machine guns, pistols, and rifles. He took part in army shooting competitions. A captain suggested that Carlos Eugênio enter the prestigious officers' academy at Agulhas Negras.[35]

Because most soldiers and draftees were laidback regarding their service, Carlos Eugênio's complete dedication raised the suspicions of a lieutenant. He successfully deflected the officer's questions about his motivations by professing his desire to excel and finish his service quickly before attending college. Meanwhile, Carlos Eugênio slipped out into the Rio evenings to carry out guerrilla activities. He rigorously maintained this dual existence for nearly a year. In July 1969, Valderez, mistaken for a guerrilla, was arrested and held for more than a week at the Rio DOI-CODI, thus forcing Carlos Eugênio to move out of the family home to maintain his cover. Not much later, Carlos Eugênio was decorated by Gen. Syseno Sarmento as the best soldier in the fort. As commander of the crucial Rio de Janeiro region, the hard-line Sarmento was one of the army's most powerful men. He commanded the torture chamber where Valderez was taken. As Carlos Eugênio looked into Syseno's eyes, he thought: "You tortured my sister. You knew that in military police quarters that you command political prisoners are being tortured. If you deny this, it's because you're cynical or incompetent. In either case, you don't deserve my respect. I'm part of an army that is much smaller, but that doesn't torture prisoners." Later, outside the fort, Carlos Eugênio threw his medal down a drain. He and Marighella plotted to explode a bomb in the fort to create a propaganda victory. The sudden death of Marighella on November 4, 1969, however, ended those plans and forced Carlos Eugênio to desert his post immediately. For weeks, his disappearance remained a mystery to his army superiors, who, believing he might be dead, searched the morgue for his body.[36]

With the military seeking him, Carlos Eugênio needed to escape from Rio. At the start of 1970, he transferred to São Paulo's burgeoning industrial megalopolis, the key focus of the ALN and the repression. He immediately set out to rebuild the decimated São Paulo Armed Tactical

Group and, in coordination with Toledo, obtain the resources to open the potentially decisive rural front. The Armed Tactical Group resumed bank robberies and other actions. Carlos Eugênio plunged into violence. He and his fellow guerrillas faced constant risk of confrontation with the police and the military. They had to manage fear and adrenaline rushes while maintaining internal equilibrium. That equilibrium, however, was constantly threatened by the lack of adequate intelligence, the element of surprise, the possibility of torture, and the presence of traitors and spies. At every corner, they awaited potential challenges. Still, the guerrillas celebrated violence, embracing it as the spur to political change. Action for action's sake affirmed male revolutionary masculinity and dominance within the ALN, which had had very few female leaders. As sociologist Maria Cláudia observed, Brazil's guerrillas, and especially the ALN, embellished the idea of action for action's sake with emphasis on courage, risk, and even a sports-like view of their activities. The guerrillas were euphoric about the impending revolutionary victory. For these youths, living underground and fighting the dictatorship were spectacular. They killed and died for their ideals. The ALN's slogans echoed these sentiments: "Support urban guerrilla warfare," "All power comes from the barrel of a gun," "It's time to die for Brazilian freedom!"[37]

"You're crazy if you think you can defeat the Brazilian armed forces with a handful of youngsters," Carlos Eugênio's father warned about their idealism. Carlos Eugênio responded: "I prefer a clear conscience. I'm part of my era, and I want to help change it. Whether that's a dream or some delirium, I don't know. My desire for justice overrides everything else." He later recalled that "those who opposed armed struggle could not clearly explain to us their doubts about our methods, in part because we wouldn't listen to them for more than five minutes. We had no time to lose. There was a revolution to make, a country to change, the heavens to take by assault. We were young Quijotes inflamed by the sixties and the thirst for liberty, a pure and deceiving cause." His generation of guerrillas had "the honor of participating in the most beautiful utopia of our history. . . . It was a time of excesses . . . but we gave our lives for tenderness and camaraderie." Like Manoel and others, Carlos Eugênio denied that he was a terrorist. "I'm a revolutionary fighting against the dictatorship," he said. "I'm not the bloodthirsty person they say I am."[38]

Despite his bravado, Carlos Eugênio acted as a parent to his comrades. He felt personally responsible for the security of the ALN and each militant. He helped set up the safe houses where guerrillas could eat, sleep, recover from their wounds, and experience a modicum of peace. To avoid detection of the ALN by the military, which monitored hospitals for the intake of wounded revolutionaries, he and his comrades set up a secret hospital for extracting bullets from the wounded. Carlos Eugênio patrolled the streets daily to map out escape routes from operations or surprise encounters with the enemy. He used both stolen and properly registered cars. Whenever he switched vehicles, he did so carefully to avoid notice by the police. Before entering a safe house, he first checked the surroundings for police on stakeout. In one safe house, he kept a pet dog that he walked in the evenings, thus creating familiarity with the neighbors. Inside safe houses, Carlos Eugênio insisted that guerrillas regularly clean and oil their weapons. Many a night, when threat levels were high or after a serious casualty or death, he kept vigil at the windows while everyone else slept, only to go out on patrol at the usual time the next morning. Sleeplessness became his frequent companion. "I need the counsel of insomnia," he told himself.[39]

As ALN MILITANTS were captured or killed with increasing frequency in 1970 and 1971, Carlos Eugênio "became an instinctual animal obsessed with security," he remembered in *Viagem*. "I thought about that all day long and demanded that others do the same." Even God would have to follow Carlos Eugênio's strict rules if he belonged to the ALN, he once said.[40] "I know that my first responsibility as a revolutionary is to preserve my life."[41]

The mere suspicion of a threat had led the ALN and the VPR to assassinate Captain Chandler in August 1968 (see chapter 1). The thirst for vengeance and the obsession with security ultimately led ALN guerrillas to punish suspected traitors in their own ranks. On March 26, 1971, Carlos Eugênio and three comrades would commit what he would later describe as "the most polemical act in the history of the ALN."[42]

The incident involved staunch ALN member Márcio Leite, who had grown up in the interior and come to the São Paulo metropolis in 1965 to study law and later also sociology. In 1967, he became the president of the Centro Acadêmico (the student body) at the Escola de Sociologia e Política de São Paulo. That year he participated in the same Inter-American University Association exchange program in the United States in which Aloysio had taken part in 1965.[43] Leite stepped into the student movement just in time to join the 1968 protests. He also enlisted in the student wing of the underground PCB. In mid-1968, he entered the ALN. Leite was arrested twice on suspicion of subversion but freed both times. The ALN then sent him to Cuba for intensive guerrilla training. The proposed eight-month stay extended to two years.[44] During that period Leite displayed a domineering personality.[45]

In May 1970, Leite and other ALN guerrillas reentered Brazil. After Toledo's death in October 1970, some key members of the ALN began to question the armed resistance. Unable to convince Carlos Eugênio and the leadership to strategically retreat, two men in Leite's circle of comrades decided to quit the ALN. They invited him to join them, but he declined, believing that the fight should continue. However, he also feared that the ALN was falling apart. He believed that it urgently needed to review its methods and address its lack of popular support.[46] He, too, backed a temporary retreat.[47] He opposed Carlos Eugênio's ultramilitarism.[48]

The ALN was further threatened, and riddled with new tensions, because Fleury had used the turncoat Tavares to capture Toledo. Tavares had trained in Cuba with other ALN militants. Back in Brazil, he was taken prisoner, but the police secretly released him. Tavares told his ALN comrades that he had attempted suicide and escaped from a hospital. Carlos Eugênio and other shrewd comrades immediately distrusted Tavares. If Tavares did not prove trustworthy, they wanted to execute him. However, Toledo gave him the benefit of the doubt. That mistake—and his comrades' failure to protect its leader—cost Toledo his life.[49]

Carlos Eugênio was determined to avoid another atrocious lapse in security. Though he and Leite had become friends and planned many guerrilla operations together,[50] they began to part ways after Toledo's death. Leite inexplicably disappeared for forty days. In response, Carlos Eugênio and the ALN's national leadership formally removed Leite from the inner circle. Shortly thereafter, Leite failed to open fire against the enemy during an ALN team's theft of a vehicle. The leadership punished Leite by taking him off the team, effectively removing him from future armed operations. At this point Leite saw no future in the ALN. Following revolutionary norms, he requested release from the organization and permission to join another.[51] However, Carlos Eugênio and the leadership set a severe condition: Leite must leave Brazil. He knew too much. They feared that if he betrayed them, or were captured and tortured, the police would discover all of the ALN's safe houses and security measures. "He denies it, but we know that he's shaken up by the difficulties of the struggle, which is very different from training in Cuba," Carlos Eugênio said in deliberating on the matter with two other guerrillas. "If he were captured in his current emotional state and without us being able to directly control the situation, it would be a catastrophe."[52] The ALN frequently sent people out of Brazil, and in some cases it helped arrange exile for those unwilling or unable to serve in combat, such as a married couple that established themselves in the United States and became a link to the Black Panthers.[53] Leite's father and a comrade with whom he had trained in Cuba both encouraged him to leave Brazil, offering him money.[54] Leite refused. To the ALN he declared: "Why should I leave the country? Nobody has the right to make that demand on a revolutionary!"[55]

In two meetings, with a total of eight participants, an ALN tribunal tried Leite in absentia.[56] Carlos Eugênio affirmed that the decision was unanimous. "We will execute [Leite]," Carlos Eugênio informed his three comrades in the ALN São Paulo leadership. "He is a danger to the organization. He is wavering and will not agree to leave the country. He is hiding his weaknesses behind the fact of supposed political differences. We prefer to assume this responsibility rather than see our comrades captured and killed because we were not firm in our action. We're not taking into account the rules of war. This is an act of survival. It will bring us no glory. We will never know if it was the right thing to do. Simply put, it's the times that demand that we act." Carlos Eugênio and three other militants were chosen to carry out the execution. They swore themselves to secrecy about their identities.[57]

The four guerrillas arranged a *ponto* with their comrade. Leite arrived with a document he had prepared in defense of his actions and opinions. "It's no longer possible to continue tolerating the errors and omissions of a command that also already had an opportunity to make corrections but failed to do so," Leite had written. "I will continue working for the revolution because it is my only commitment. I will seek to be effectively useful to the movement wherever I can." Leite hoped to use the document as a starting point of a conversation with his comrades.[58] However, he would not get a chance to present it. At the *ponto*, his comrades informed him immediately that he was condemned to die. He lifted his hands to protect his face. Two militants stood guard while Carlos Eugênio and another poured bullets into Leite. Next to his body they left a brief manifesto in which they accused Leite of "dishonesty" and warned that the revolution would not tolerate traitors. Márcio Leite died with his own manifesto still in his pocket.[59]

FEARING DESPERATELY FOR their survival, the ALN guerrillas had followed their violent impulses to a logical but tragic result: the *justiçamento* of a comrade. Historian and former revolutionary Jacob Gorender identified three other such incidents during the dictatorship, two of them involving the ALN.[60]

After the incident, Carlos Eugênio and the ALN militarists faced harsh criticism from other revolutionaries. For instance, shortly after the execution, the ALN in the state of Minas Gerais leveled vehement opposition.[61] Gorender later disputed Carlos Eugênio's assertion of a unanimous decision. He concluded that the execution was "unjustifiable" and that its political cost was far greater than the alternative of reorganizing ALN security so as to render useless any confessions Leite might make to the police.[62] Brazilian writer Antonio Pedroso Júnior, who conducted a detailed study of the incident, demonstrated that the execution became a propaganda victory for the military regime because it could portray the guerrillas as divided and harsh. In fact, the execution of a fellow revolutionary seemed so implausible that some militants first thought that the police had masqueraded as revolutionaries and killed Leite to denigrate the cause.[63] The execution had a chilling effect on other ALN militants. Because of their own doubts about the ALN, some feared that they, too, might be executed.[64] In retrospect, former militant José Carlos Giannini believed that the execution helped provoke the formation of the ALN offshoot known as Movimento de Libertação Popular (MOLIPO, Movement for Popular Liberation), which sought to reinvest in politics along with armed struggle. Giannini termed the execution "criminal." According to him, Carlos Eugênio and the remnants of Brazil's guerrilla organizations lacked political astuteness. However, another militant, Arthur Scavone, downplayed the incident's importance for MOLIPO.[65] Pedroso Júnior and others even asserted that Carlos Eugênio had schemed to kill Leite to ensure his predominance in the organization.[66] According to Leite's friend and fellow militant Renato Martinelli, the execution was "the most insane act in the history of the ALN."[67]

However, Carlos Eugênio, the only person still alive from the operation, consistently defended the action as the only way to preserve the ALN from Leite's potential cooperation with the police. In 1971, nobody discussed whether the *justiçamento* violated Leite's human rights. "The logic of the moment was the logic of the clandestine," he said in July 2001. "It was a wartime decision."[68] In an interview with a Brazilian journalist, Carlos Eugênio stated that "there's no such thing as a clean war. We were living a situation that could only have led to that conclusion. If you accept violent methods, you must accept the dirty side that comes with it."[69] In an interview with sociologist Maria Cláudia, Carlos Eugênio invoked the summary executions carried out by the French and Yugoslav resistance movements during World War II: "The Márcio [Leite] case was one of those, a summary execution decided in wartime by people who had set up a court-martial just as in any army in the world, . . . so in that case we were a clandestine army that was being surrounded and needed to defend the organization. If we had done that with [José Silva Tavares], [Toledo] would not have been killed."[70]

The death of any comrade was lamentable but nevertheless preferable to treason, Carlos Eugênio affirmed, recalling the episode of the notorious Cabo Anselmo, a sailor and leftist militant whose collaboration with the security forces led to the death of numerous revolutionaries, including Anselmo's own girlfriend.[71] Anselmo assisted Officer Fleury in the attempt to track down Carlos Eugênio and other ALN members. In one intense shootout with Fleury and the police, Carlos Eugênio saw Anselmo at the officer's side.[72] According to Carlos Eugênio, nobody can today affirm that Leite might not have become a traitor. If he and his comrades had not killed Leite, "today I would be held responsible for the death of others," Carlos Eugênio said.[73]

The abstract decision to resist the regime was easy. However, the decisions to engage in actual acts of violence were wrenching.

Carlos Eugênio reflected on Leite's execution as if living in two moments with two, contradictory sets of emotions. In one moment, he is the tough, twenty-one-year-old guerrilla preoccupied with survival in the wake of his organization's devastating infiltration by the repressive forces. In another moment, he is the older, wiser man who struggles with guilt and—true to the ideal of revolutionary responsibility, and perhaps as a way of expiating that guilt—engages in harsh self-criticism.[74] In *Viagem*, he wrote that he felt the need to "confess" what he had done. "Már[c]io is at the end of the tunnel, and behind him, the light," he wrote. "Már[c]io is hurting in all of our consciences. Each of us has his or her way of assuming this. Denial and affirmation are both part of the same reality, the same dynamic."[75] Two pages later, he reveals the depth of his remorse: "There are moments so decisive that we should have eternity to choose their outcomes."[76]

In the next passage, he describes his ultimate commitment to the cause as revealed in a 1986 newspaper article disclosing his role in Leite's death: "Már[c]io must not be seen as a traitor, and the comrades who made the decision must not be seen as cold-blooded murderers who killed for control of the organization," he wrote. "I will not assume the role of the victim. We fought for a just cause. . . . We fought against violence, oppression, and torture. We used the violence of the oppressed, and we were defeated. We committed errors. We must admit them and learn from them. To deny that is a sin that I will never commit, because it would make me a traitor."[77]

If the ALN could execute its own comrades, to what extent would revolutionary justice have been applied if the guerrillas had taken over Brazil? Carlos Eugênio in power in 1971 might have continued to use violence to transform the country.

However, the older and wiser Carlos Eugênio also seemed to shy away from violence: "To come face-to-face with violence and our sinful and inglorious errors is the eternal dilemma of all of those who live and no privilege of mine," he wrote in *Viagem*. "To determine someone's moment of death is a terrible power that should be given to nobody, whatever the reason for that power." In his final reference to Leite, near the book's end, Carlos Eugênio states that there was only one way "to make amends for such an extreme act," and that was for him to make a personal plea: "I hope that all of you readers reflect profoundly on the use of violence in history and in everyday life."[78]

IN APRIL 1971, Carlos Eugênio carried out another *justiçamento*, one of the most daring acts of the revolution: a public assassination in São Paulo of Henning Boilesen, the Danish-born president of Ultragás, a large energy company. A leading fundraiser for the São Paulo DOI-CODI, Boilesen drew the ire of the revolutionaries. He personified the shady side of the "Brazilian miracle," where unchecked corporate, military, and government interests came together to support the repression in the name of national security. With Carlos Eugênio commanding the assassination team, which included militants from the Tiradentes Revolutionary Movement, the guerrillas started shooting at Boilesen as he left for work in his car. (It was very near the spot where the police had killed Marighella.) The wounded Boilesen tried to flee but fell to the ground. Carlos Eugênio caught up with him, touched his head with the barrel of his gun, and, pulling the weapon back a few inches to allow the bullet space for maximum velocity, delivered the coup de grace. The revolutionaries' gunfire sprayed into an open-air food market, wounding two people. The gunmen quickly distributed revolutionary flyers denouncing Boilesen and declaring to the shocked onlookers, "We have condemned and executed him [Boilesen] because of the torture and murders he sponsored, because of the cowardly acts he carried out against defenseless revolutionaries in the dictatorship's dungeons."[79]

Carlos Eugênio's agitated state and dedication to the revolution ultimately cost him the love of his life, the guerrilla Ana Maria Nacinovic. She believed that he put too much stock in security. "You want to be the super-guerrilla, to win the war, to enter history," she told him with a mixture of love and anger. "And you expect the same from all of us." Carlos Eugênio thought that it was necessary to end their relationship. Their passion diverted his attention from the guerrilla effort. But he later lamented this loss, describing her as his "first wife, first loss, unforgettable love aborted by my weakness and obsession with putting survival above all else. . . . I learned to survive. It does me no good. I don't know how to live."[80]

In June 1972, Ana Maria was executed along with two other ALN militants taken to the São Paulo DOI-CODI.[81] For Carlos Eugênio, Ana Maria was just one in "the entire rosary of dead people, my dead people."[82] In just the ALN, Carlos Eugênio knew well over a dozen individuals shot or tortured to death, including Marighella, Toledo, and Eduardo Collen Leite (no relation to Márcio Leite). Officer Fleury and others tortured and mutilated Collen Leite for 109 days, poking out his eyes in the process. As an ALN leader, Carlos Eugênio carried a heavy burden of guilt about these deaths, once asking himself: "Mirror, mirror on the wall, am I the most guilty of all?"[83] The death of a lover, friends, and comrades deprived Carlos Eugênio of "almost every bit of affection that had remained."[84]

Carlos Eugênio embodied the history of the ALN. The only military commander to survive the armed resistance, he had a unique vantage point. Yet in many ways Carlos Eugênio was the exception that proved the rule: a lone survivor among the many killed in combat, murdered, or tortured to death. Most guerrillas expected to live a year or two, but with his combat kills, acute survival instincts, and a huge dose of luck, Carlos Eugênio escaped capture by the security forces. Unlike most militants, he did not once go to jail, nor was he forced into exile or officially banished.[85] As the de facto leader of the ALN after Toledo's death, he had the complete loyalty of other young militants, some of whom refused to reveal his whereabouts despite extremely brutal torture.[86] Carlos Eugênio himself never experienced torture. He had indeed been lucky. But that luck could run out. In late 1972, at the suggestion of his comrades, Carlos Eugênio traveled clandestinely to Cuba to obtain additional training and aid in the attempt to restructure the organization.[87]

However, militants reacting nonviolently to the death of another ALN militant would start to transform the character of the resistance.

CHAPTER 5

The Resistance Becomes Nonviolent

Although Carlos Eugênio was ensconced in Communist Cuba, his lieutenants continued to pursue revolutionary vengeance. On February 21, 1973, three ALN guerrillas gunned down a São Paulo restaurant owner whom they blamed for the death of Ana Maria and her two comrades because he had called the police to his establishment after recognizing them on "Wanted" posters.[1] Four days later, three ALN gunmen and two guerrillas from other organizations lying in wait in Rio's Copacabana district shot dead Octávio Gonçalves Moreira Junior (known as Otavinho), an extremely cruel DOI-CODI torturer with ties to the ultraright-wing group Communist Pursuit Command.[2] Retaliation came quickly. On March 15, security officers killed the three guerrillas who had shot the restaurant owner.[3]

In the search for Otavinho's killers, the DOI-CODI cracked down once again on a long-standing focus of antiregime sentiment, the USP. DOI-CODI officers arrested numerous student militants denounced by an ALN turncoat. On March 16, they picked up Alexandre Vannucchi Leme, the ALN's key campus political coordinator. Alexandre studied in the geology program, known for its opposition to the dictatorship because of its students' nationalistic critique of the regime's exploitation of Brazil's natural resources.[4] A nationalist, Alexandre criticized foreign involvement in Brazil's economy.[5]

Alexandre entered the USP in 1970. As an activist, he criticized the government's Transamazon Highway project, a new road through the world's largest and (one of its most pristine) rainforests. In contrast with the regime's plan to simply plow through the forest, Alexandre believed that a multidisciplinary team of geologists, biologists, engineers, and ecologists should manage the project. In an article for a university bulletin, he predicted dire consequences for the Amazon from the project: the spread of illnesses, the destruction of the Amazon River's headwaters, and climate change.[6]

The Transamazon and other massive public works projects embodied the ethos of the "Brazilian miracle." In 1973, growth reached a phenomenal 14 percent. Brazilian agribusiness, including exporters of soy and soy products, gained a significant boost in this period. Economic growth vastly increased access to consumer goods such as cars, televisions, and appliances for the expanding middle class. Many middle-class families purchased units in high-rise condos. To support the new consumer lifestyle and the industries that furnished it, the government made huge investments in steel, electric energy, telecommunications, petroleum products, and public works, including numerous bridges and highways. In addition to the Transamazon, the Médici administration built other massive symbols of development, such as the 8-mile, 236-foot-high bridge over Guanabara Bay connecting Rio to Niterói. It also planned the Itaipú hydroelectric dam, at the time the world's largest. The administration began to develop a nuclear energy program. Among other factors, the economic expansion prevented Brazil's revolutionaries from attracting more followers.

Despite such growth, Brazil became a more unequal country, with the upper classes gaining a greater share of national income. Numerous public works projects were bungled, in part because of few checks and balances, given that the dictators concentrated decision-making at the top.[7] Along with the large-scale, precarious colonization of the jungle, the Transamazon in particular stimulated massive deforestation and other forms of environmental devastation. It also harmed native peoples. The government hoped that the highway and settlers would act as a counterweight to guerrilla groups, such as the PC do B, active in the Amazon.[8] The atmosphere in the Amazon became choked with smoke as people cut and burned trees to fuel progress in the growing cities. As Brazil's industrial hub, São Paulo especially suffered enormous ecological consequences.

Alexandre's activism led to a friendship with Adriano Diogo, another geology student, campus leader, and staunch ALN supporter. In late 1970, they produced a play titled *Transa-Amazônica*, a satire about the Transamazon. They called their theater group Teatro Jornal (News Theater). For the Amazon play, they received guidance from Augusto Boal, the founder of the *teatro de guerrilha* (street theater) movement and a member of the ALN's support network. Alexandre wrote the play. On campus, Adriano had earned the nickname "Mug," the name of a popular toy doll that, like the five-foot-four, 212-pound Adriano, was plump. He played the role of Antônio Delfim Neto, the rotund minister of finance who helped guide the economic miracle.[9] "It was a kind of engaged theater, also known, inappropriately, as Guerrilla Theater," Adriano recalled.

> We interpreted the news items of the day. So, when somebody died mysteriously and we thought it could have been the result of torture but was presented as someone having been run over by a car, we interpreted the news item by acting out the different roles. Or it might be something very simple, very easy to interpret, like the text from the actual newspaper article. And the characters were the torturers, the coroners, the workers, the arrested students. The story about the construction of the Transamazon was amazing, with me playing the role of Delfim Neto. It was a kind of parody of gangsters who showed up to build a road, and we talked about Herman Kahn, that idea of Herman Kahn's Amazonian lake. [An American conservative futurist, Kahn had proposed transforming the Amazon into five large lakes.] We debated that idea by presenting in front of the students at lunchtime, which is when they would get together to converse.[10]

In mid-1972, Alexandre met with Carlos Eugênio to discuss ALN political strategy. They conversed in a car used for combat. For the increasingly isolated revolutionaries, Alexandre provided a crucial link to the outer world. He brought in new, badly needed campus recruits. Alexandre knew Ronaldo Mouth Queiroz, a geology student who had gone underground to become an ALN guerrilla. In addition, Alexandre had strong ties to the Catholic Church. His uncle Aldo Vannucchi was a progressive priest, and three aunts were nuns. After losing the now imprisoned or exiled Dominican friars, the ALN relied on Alexandre to revive links to

Figure 9. Adriano Diogo, far left, at a street protest in São Paulo, July 1968. Iconographia.

Catholic progressives, who were becoming increasingly critical of the regime.[11] Alexandre rejected traditional Catholicism but embraced the progressive Church. In February 1973, he met some of the leading progressive bishops at an event at the Pontifícia Universidade Católica de São Paulo.[12] "He was a true ALN combatant, albeit not a military cadre," Carlos Eugênio later observed.[13]

At the USP, Alexandre worked to revitalize the student governing bodies for each major, the "Centros Acadêmicos." The centers had been officially shut down by the dictatorship and replaced with regime-controlled Central Student Directorates. However, the traditional centers were allowed to continue at the USP because of its prestige. Although a student activist and ALN militant, Alexandre chiefly exercised leadership via his intellectual capacity. "He always worked on the big picture of the movement, the ideas," Adriano remembered.[14]

Alexandre also had professional ambitions as a future geologist. After graduation, he hoped to work as a geologist for Petrobras. However, in early 1973 he received an offer to work for a mineralogical firm.[15]

The night before his arrest, Alexandre and another USP student leader had met with Honestino Guimarães, the president of the National Union of Students, a politically influential organization whose leadership went underground after the dictatorship banned it. The three leaders talked into the morning hours regarding their doubts about the effectiveness of the armed resistance and the future of the student movement.[16]

In opposing the regime, Alexandre echoed a sentiment widespread at USP in early 1973. "The climate was very much one of questioning things," recalled fellow geology student Fernando Antonio Rodrigues de Oliveira. "Alexandre was not apart from the rest of the students like some Communist agent. Not at all. He was someone who was part of the historic political situation and the situation at the university." The regime and its repressive forces reached deeply into campus life: "The logic of that period is not the logic of today. It's difficult to explain some aspects that sometimes get lost with time. The climate at the university was very tense. The police really had a strong presence within the university. But I mean really conspicuous." Fernando himself had several encounters with the police, but was not arrested. "They infiltrated all kinds of people into the university," he continued. "It was not a joking matter. There was constant pressure from them. Imagine yourself as a student back then, with a fucking swarm of student movements. I wasn't even a guerrilla or anything at all. And *I* was experiencing all that tension. . . . There was always a consensus that we were living under a dictatorship and that it was necessary to fight against that kind of thing. After all, a university is supposed to be a place of thought, isn't it? It's a place where you're supposed to learn to influence society and contribute to it."[17]

THE VANNUCCHI/VANNUCHI CLAN was no stranger to the authorities. Several of its members had clashed with the regime. In the postcoup, anti-Communist witch hunt of 1964, the police in the city of Sorocaba, São Paulo, detained Alexandre's uncle, Father Aldo, on a suspicion of subversion.[18] Two of Alexandre's cousins, revolutionaries José Ivo and Paulo Vannuchi, had been arrested and tortured. José Ivo was a member of the Armed Forces for National Liberation, a small organization primarily active in the interior of São Paulo state. He was imprisoned at Tiradentes. Paulo joined the ALN in 1969, his first year as a student at the USP school of medicine. At first, he did not fully comprehend the ALN's political platform. He initially supported the cause by collecting items for the care of the wounded and injured: sample prescription medications from fellow medical students, antibiotics, stitching material, and IV packs. In early 1970, Paulo became deeply involved in setting up the organization's student wing. He thus identified with the *massistas*, those emphasizing mass participation and the political side of the revolution. With minimal tactical training, he also began participating in actions requiring weapons, including the theft of license plates and autos and distribution of illegal propaganda flyers, primarily to students. He also prepared to take part in bank robberies. With the death of Toledo in October 1970, the need to involve Paulo and other recent recruits in armed actions grew, but he still emphasized balancing violence with political strategy. Learning that the police were searching for him, in January 1971 Paulo went underground. On the morning of February 18, as Paulo started driving along with a comrade to a locale to distribute flyers, DOI-CODI officers hiding nearby opened fire on the vehicle. Losing control, Paulo crashed the car into a tree. Despite the rain of bullets and the accident, Paulo escaped serious injury. He was taken immediately to the DOI-CODI. Over the next ten days the torturers brutalized him frequently.[19]

At first, because Paulo had successfully denied belonging to the ALN, they employed standard, less barbarous techniques. However, after another prisoner inadvertently linked Paulo to the organization, they responded with a vengeance. Paulo recalled how agents tortured him as he sat in the "dragon's chair," an electric chair:

> It's an unrestrained torture. That day I learned what was the kind of torture that kills. . . . It's not that meticulous thing where the guy gets the device and follows the routine. It's the kind where the guy comes at you all angry. I was tied up on the dragon's chair. . . .
>
> And it got to my breaking point and that's what I was trying to explain: blood is a problem—the right torture shouldn't have any blood. And then comes the shocks to the penis, on the tongue. And you bite down. A lot of blood starts coming out of your mouth. One nut started to throw something on me. Because when you receive lots of shocks, you start losing your ability to withstand things and you are almost fainting. So, to keep you awake, they pour a little bottle of ammonia into one of your nostrils. You wake up. One time I did not wake up. The guy pulled my head back and put the bottle of ammonia into

my nose. You have the sensation of drowning, because what that guy did could very well have killed me. I mean, it takes a long time to take effect. I spent more than a minute without breathing, and in those circumstances, you can faint. A crust formed on my nose and wouldn't go away for weeks. Ammonia is corrosive. At that point, to get them to stop torturing, I made up a *ponto* that I really didn't have any more. Or there were the *pontos*, for example, that you have every first day of the month for six months. But I made up a *ponto* with the intention of finding a way to kill myself. That was a way people knew of for handling certain moments. . . .

Suicide is also a legitimate weapon of the revolutionary. I made up a *ponto*. I don't remember with whom, at the corner of Iguatemi and Tabapuã Streets. At a very busy bakery. A bakery that I had previously used for a *ponto*. . . .

Looking back on that moment, if my decision to kill myself had been firmer, I would have thrown myself in front of a bus because that would have been definitive. You can throw yourself in front of the bus. Buses ran down that street frequently. I attempted a form of suicide that implied a weak desire to die. The bakery was full of people, around six or seven in the evening. People were drinking beer. I walked up to the counter. To make sure you don't run away from the *ponto* the police tie your scrotum to your thigh, so that you have to walk very slowly. They take you to the *ponto* with two or three cars. They put me in the bakery alone and several of them spread out about ten yards away. At the counter, I got a bottle of beer. I broke the bottle on the counter and put it to my throat to try to cut my jugular. And one of the cops, who later actually became a friend, jumped on me the minute I put that thing to my throat. . . . It was Sergeant Carlão. He jumped me and hit me on the back. He started shouting to the others: "I knew this *ponto* was a lie." They were shocked by what I had done. It caused quite a scene. Nobody in the bakery understood what was going on. My neck was bleeding badly. Lots of blood. They put me in a car. They took me back to the DOI-CODI. It wasn't that serious an injury. They even gave me stitches right then and there. They put in the stitches without using any anesthetics.[20]

In all, Paulo spent three months at the DOI-CODI. Following routine, the police then transferred him to the DEOPS for legal processing.

Convicted of belonging to the ALN, Paulo entered Tiradentes prison to serve out a twelve-year sentence. Once in prison, political prisoners rarely returned to the DOI-CODI. Paulo became a stark exception, returning on seven occasions over the next year. The most harrowing one involved a trip to the torture chamber because of a political prisoners' hunger strike in which Paulo took part in May 1972. They were protesting the dictators' decision to transfer them out of Tiradentes to several different prisons in order to divide them geographically and undermine their ongoing resistance while in custody.[21] "During the hunger strike they chose two prisoners to be taken to the DOI-CODI and dissuaded from striking with the threat of torture," Paulo recalled. "I was one of the two. . . . They wanted us to stop the hunger strike. . . . They used a straightjacket. . . . Their approach was: 'Look here, the strike is over.' No fucking way. So they tie you up and try to force milk down your throat. They put the funnel in your mouth and start pouring in the milk." The commander of the DOI-CODI, Major Carlos Alberto Brilhante Ustra, took part in the torture. "There was one time when I was yelling at him," Paulo remembered. "I called him a coward, a torturer, a piece of scum. . . . I was really angry. I lost control. I started to yell. I think nobody had ever done that before. And I think I did it because I was already in prison for more than a year. . . . And he turns to me and says something like: 'You came here like some kid, saying you were innocent and didn't belong to the ALN.' It was his anger from the previous year. 'And then we discovered that you were highly dangerous.' The fact of the matter is that I left the place with bruises, which became a part of my official medical record. I returned to the prison, which generated an official report. The doctor is the one who takes note of the bruises. These were rare proof that there was torture committed against a prisoner who had been in custody for more than a year."[22]

The military refused to reverse the transfer of prisoners. They also force-fed other prisoners, including Elbrick kidnapper Manoel, by tying them to beds in the infirmary of the nearby state penitentiary and connecting them to IVs. After thirty-three days, the strike ended when the apostolic nuncio, the Catholic Church's diplomatic representative in Brazil, appealed to the prisoners to stop, allowing them to save face.[23]

A few months later, well before his own arrest, Alexandre visited his cousin Paulo at another penitentiary, the Casa de Detenção Carandiru. Discreet, Alexandre did not touch on the subject of the ALN. However, several months later, in a conversation with his uncle, Paulo's father, he

Figure 10. Paulo de Tarso Vannuchi's mug shot, 1976. Paulo de Tarso Vannuchi collection.

Figure 11. Paulo with father, Ivo, sister Maria Lúcia, and Neci (in swimsuit), sister of another political prisoner, at the Barro Branco political prison, late 1975/early 1976. Paulo de Tarso Vannuchi collection.

enthusiastically supported the armed resistance. Paulo recalled: "My father summed up the conversation for me and laughed: 'There came a point when I wanted to end the conversation, because, if not, he would have convinced me to join him.'"[24]

Alexandre confided to his mother, Egle Maria Vannucchi Leme, that in his fight for social justice and liberty he "was willing to pay the ultimate price."[25]

On MARCH 16, 1973, the DOI-CODI men took Alexandre to the torture chamber. "I heard Alexandre's screams," recalled Concepción Martín Pérez, an ALN sympathizer and fellow student arrested on the street and tortured at the DOI-CODI that same day after a *ponto* with Queiroz. "They themselves told me: 'That's your little buddy. That's Alexandre.'"[26] Eighteen PC do B militants in the women's collective cell could hear the screams throughout the night and into the morning hours. Turning up the volume on their radio, the DOI-CODI tried but failed to drown out Alexandre's cries.[27] As the torture continued, his screams became weaker.[28] When they finished, they brought him to the solitary confinement cell. The cell measured no more than sixteen square feet. It was so narrow that a prisoner could not lie down. It had no window or light. The guards opened the door only to provide food or take a prisoner off to the torture chamber.[29] It also had a peephole for the guards to look in on the prisoner.[30]

The solitary cell stood across from the women's cell. Neide Richopo, one of the PC do B militants, recalled that at one moment she and the other women saw Alexandre's face and waved their hands when he passed by with the officers. He did not respond in any way. Neide had previously spent a day in the solitary cell after first arriving at the DOI-CODI; she, too, was brutally tortured and, because of the trauma, had stopped eating solids, lost weight, and stopped walking. She became emaciated. Later that night the DOI-CODI men took Alexandre away for another torture session.[31] He refused to give any information to the police. According to other witnesses, when the DOI-CODI men carried him back to the cell after one of the torture sessions, he shouted: "My name is Alexandre Vannucchi Leme. I am a geology student. They are accusing me of belonging to the ALN. I only told them my name." One DOI-CODI officer said that he was "crazy."[32]

At 5 p.m. on March 17, when the jailer went to get Alexandre for another torture session, he was surprised to find the twenty-two-year-old student dead.[33]

The torturers had committed what they referred to as a "work accident"—excessive abuse and the resultant death of a prisoner who should have been kept alive to obtain additional information. Ultimately, only the torturers knew exactly what they did to Alexandre and why. No DOI-CODI person directly involved in the incident has ever granted an interview. Chaves, the São Paulo DOI-CODI intelligence analyst (see chapter 4), later spoke and testified about human rights abuses. In a 1999 interview, he confirmed this interpretation of Alexandre's death: "As far as I know, Alexandre was not on a death list, because of his importance in the context of the ALN. The targets selected and then put on the death list were important people, people who ran the organization. And Alexandre, in the final analysis, was the head of perhaps a nucleus within the university, within the student movement. . . . His death resulted from the exaggerated conduct of the interrogation and the torture. That's totally why. Excess."[34]

Paulo believed that Alexandre had suffered the same level of extreme torture he had experienced—and perhaps *because* José Ivo and then Paulo had already gone through the DOI-CODI. "Alexandre's death affected me personally and very strongly," recalled Paulo, who regarded his cousin almost as a brother.

> I always asked myself whether in dying Alexandre received a beating that had nothing to do with him. What I mean to say is, he was the third Vannucchi. The second had appeared there as a notorious liar—a guy who fooled everybody. So, suddenly they grab Alexandre and start to ask him questions. . . . I sometimes also think that wasn't the case. Sometimes I'm making myself more important than I really am. That Alexandre's story had nothing to do with mine. It's possible that they killed Alexandre without clearly knowing who he was. Where they go after him, give him a beating, and just kill him. And without any association with me. I have a lot of doubt about this. But when we fantasize, we imagine things. He arrives. "Who are you? What's your name?" "Alexandre Vannucchi." "Ah! Are you related to so-and-so? Aren't you part of the ALN? What do you mean you're

not?" Something like: "For these types we have to hit them hard, if not, they won't say a word." Something along those lines. But I'm just speculating.[35]

Indeed, the repressive forces had formed a negative view of the family. When Alexandre's father, José Oliveira Leme, searched for his son's body in São Paulo, he encountered Officer Fleury at a police station. "Of course, he comes from a family of subversives," Fleury told the father. "His cousin Paulo organizes all the subversion of students here in São Paulo."[36]

To cover up the cause of death, the DOI-CODI told the other prisoners and others who knew that Alexandre had died at the jail that he had committed suicide by slitting his throat with a razor blade in the infirmary. To lend credence to this story they decided that one of them should cut Alexandre's neck from ear to ear as his body still lay on the floor of the cell.[37] The women prisoners saw the officers dragging the bloody body. DOI-CODI personnel immediately cleaned the bloodstained floor. The jailer then staged a search for blades and other sharp instruments in the cells of the other political prisoners, telling them that a prisoner had committed suicide.[38] But the police could not keep the different versions straight. Fleury told Alexandre's father the death was an accident, whereas another officer called it a suicide. Had José Leme not insisted on obtaining a death certificate and the family not persisted in locating his body in the infamous Perus cemetery, used to hide dead revolutionaries' bodies, Alexandre could very well have become a desaparecido.[39]

THE MEANING OF Alexandre's life and disturbing demise emerged in interviews with his parents, extended family, and classmates. I gained particular insight into the situation at the USP and the DOI-CODI in early 1973 through my contact with two of Alexandre's close friends, Adriano and his wife, Arlete. In 1989, Adriano won election to the São Paulo City Council. A public school teacher, Arlete also worked as an informal political aide to her husband. In May 1997, I scheduled an interview with Adriano at council headquarters in downtown São Paulo. Knowing that a councilman in such a huge city would be extremely busy, I expected to meet for an hour at best. When I entered his office, Arlete was there, too. As we began to speak, I sensed immediately how distressing the episode had been—and how deeply they had admired Alexandre. Although I wanted to objectively understand the details of the incident, the interview became very emotional. It lasted more than three hours, during which Adriano took no calls. Nearly a quarter century after the incident, he and Arlete still felt sad and angry about Alexandre's death.

Both Adriano and Arlete became caught up in the security forces' sweep against the university and the ALN. Adriano had spent his days at the USP participating in intense, nonviolent political activity against the regime, often skipping classes to circulate around the campus. He also supported the armed resistance.[40] Arlete had recently received her USP degree in social studies. Early on the morning of March 17, 1973, DOI-CODI agents invaded Adriano's apartment. As they detained him, one slammed the butt of a machine gun into his right eye. Transporting Adriano to the DOI-CODI in a police vehicle, the officers forced him to hold a purported bomb, which they warned him not to drop. Around 11:30 a.m., they arrived at the DOI-CODI. The officers immediately started to rough him up. In the inner patio, the men ripped his clothing off down to his underwear. They made him run the gauntlet, hitting him with billy clubs and rubber hoses. Next, they put Adriano in the dragon's chair. As they tortured him, they demanded to know about Alexandre, Queiroz, and any other ALN militant about whom he had information.[41] "I perceived that they thought it took a lot of nerve to go after a ranking policeman," Adriano recalled. "That the Left could have infiltrated their security apparatus. How was it possible that Otavinho was killed? . . . That was the basic line of the initial questioning. Because Queiroz, one of our fellow geology majors, was being sought. He was nicknamed 'pope.' According to them, he had information on how the operation against Otavinho was carried out."[42] Adriano was tortured the entire afternoon and into the night. Between torture sessions they locked him in the same solitary cell that Alexandre had occupied.[43] "When I entered the cell at 6 p.m., there was a strong smell of blood, and the cell was all wet," Adriano said. "They had been washing it."[44] Adriano was sure that Alexandre must also be at the DOI-CODI. However, he had yet to learn the fate of his friend.[45]

Later that night, a DOI-CODI arrest team placed Arlete in the cell with Neide and the other PC do B militants. After Arlete identified herself as an ALN militant, the other women recounted the story of Alexandre's death. "They asked me if I knew him," Arlete recalled. "I said I did. They tried to tell me about it in as kind a manner as possible, but obviously I was extremely shocked, appalled, and scared." After finishing with Adriano, the torturers worked over Arlete for about two hours, demanding to know information about her husband, Alexandre, and Queiroz. "The whole time they were telling us to say that Alexandre had taken up arms, that he had carried out robberies, that he was an atheist," Arlete said. "It even states in my police statement that I said that he was a student and Catholic, . . . that he had not committed any robbery, not carried out any armed action, but they insisted a lot, of course, because they had killed him and wanted to fabricate a story with the statements of people who knew him, who belonged to the same group."[46]

At one point, the agents allowed Arlete to nurse Adriano in his cell after a violent asthma attack.[47] With typical cruelty, they also forced Arlete and Adriano to watch each other being tortured. "I saw Adriano being tortured on the parrot's perch, the dragon's chair, with the ferule [hand paddle], with electric shocks," Arlete recalled. "And Adriano saw me being tortured several times, but he was in very bad shape those days. One time he couldn't even stand up. They would lean him against the wall and he would slide down and sit. I had the sense that he really wasn't lucid."[48]

In another powerful interview almost a decade after our initial meeting, Arlete revealed an injury that she had only come to fathom after several years of psychotherapy in the 2000s: during her imprisonment at the DOI-CODI, she had suffered a hemorrhage that was probably a miscarriage. "I had some bleeding outside my period," she recalled. "It wasn't menstruation. . . . I hadn't had a period for more than a month. . . . Could it could have been a common hemorrhage? It could. But by the nature of it, it appeared not to be, because I got very sick. I went through this for many days and the worst of it was that I had no medical care. . . . Because I didn't say anything about it. I was afraid. They had applied shocks to my vagina. That could have caused the bleeding." The PC do B women cared for Arlete as best they could. "To tell the truth, I didn't ask for help [from the guards] because I was scared," Arlete said. "And whom would I ask anyway? The same person who would check my blood pressure and then tell them that they could keep beating me? Are you going to ask for help from that person? That wouldn't have made any sense." After her release, Arlete visited her gynecologist. Horrified by Arlete's narrative of torture, the doctor confirmed that the bleeding might indeed have been a miscarriage. "She had to cauterize the small lesions that remained from the torture," Arlete recounted.[49]

Figure 12. Arlete Diogo, 1973.
Arlete Diogo collection.

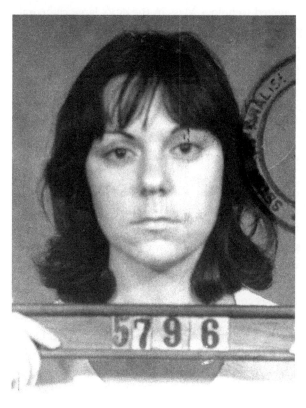

Figure 13. A police
photo of Arlete
Diogo, 1973.
Arquivo Público
do Estado de São
Paulo.

As ADRIANO AND Arlete languished in the DOI-CODI, efforts by students and Alexandre's family to locate him forced the police to create another story about his death. In false newspaper articles published on March 23, the police alleged that Alexandre had fled from his captors at a busy São Paulo intersection and was killed by an oncoming truck. As Adriano, Alexandre, and others had portrayed in the News Theater, the repressive forces commonly used stories of made-up accidents, suicides, and shoot-outs to explain the death of political prisoners.

The death of a prominent student with no proven links to the ALN and the regime's patently false version of events deeply angered the USP community and the leadership of the Catholic Church in São Paulo state. The students organized to uncover the facts surrounding Alexandre's death, while clerics issued documents of protest and said Masses in Alexandre's honor. Meeting with student leaders, Dom Paulo Evaristo Arns, the cardinal-archbishop of São Paulo, at the time the world's largest Catholic archdiocese, agreed to hold a Mass in the city's large cathedral on March 30, the day before the ninth anniversary of the military takeover. The students also garnered the support of the Brazilian Bar Association, the Brazilian Press Association, and Congressman Ulysses Guimarães, one of the leaders of the officially permitted opposition party, the MDB. The regime did not prohibit Masses per se, but Dom Paulo used this particular one as a loophole, albeit a precarious one, to criticize the regime. The decision to hold the Mass boldly confronted a government that had violently repressed public protests since 1964 and strictly prohibited them starting in late 1968.

The geology students chose classmate João Carlos Moreira Gomes to read one of the biblical passages selected for the service. João Carlos and a friend approached the cathedral, located next to the Sé Plaza. "We could see the police forces spread out all around the Sé," João Carlos recalled. To gain the courage to enter the church, he and classmate Luiz Antonio Bongiovanni each drank a shot of *cachaça* (Brazilian rum) at a bar. "When we arrived at the church, it was completely surrounded by the State Police," João Carlos stated. "Even so, we entered the church, which was already filled with people, and I went to the sacristy." There he encountered Dom Paulo and protest singer Sérgio Ricardo. Seeing his nervousness, they reassured him that he could do the reading.[50]

In the Sé Plaza, the police mounted a machine gun on a tripod, pointing it toward the entrance to the building. The scene reminded geography student Geraldo Siqueira, another organizer of the Mass, of the infamous massacre of hundreds of protesters by the Mexican police and military at the Tlatelolco Plaza in Mexico City in October 1968, less than two weeks before the country hosted the Summer Olympics. "I said: 'Are they going to repeat that here today?'" Geraldo remembered. "'My God, a government shamelessly killing students. That has already happened in Mexico.' And Mexico was not a dictatorship like the one we had. I said: 'Are they capable of doing that here?'"[51]

Three thousand people filled the cathedral, mainly USP students, friends and members of the Vannucchi family, and clergymen and others linked to the Church. With police sirens wailing outside, Dom Paulo and two dozen priests celebrated the Mass, leading the people in songs and prayers.[52] João Carlos described the moment when he read the biblical passage, which spoke of the Christian faithful's perseverance against torture, mockery, and imprisonment:

> When I rose up onto the pulpit to do the reading, the highest point in the interior of the Sé church, I could see the magnitude of the multitude that was inside the church. It really left an impression on me. At my feet I could see a very large number of photographers. Photographers and cameramen. And I noticed I was practically being investigated by the D[E]OPS [political police]. I could tell by their attitude. Not all of them, but for sure many of those photographers were there to take photos of people who could later be pursued.... A priest escorted me as I came down from the pulpit. I told him that the next day I would be traveling to the interior of the state, and in case I went missing—because I was worried about the photographs—I gave him my mother's and father's addresses. After that I watched the rest of the Mass normally.[53]

In his sermon, Dom Paulo sent a firm message to the regime: "Only God owns life. He is its origin and only He can decide its end." One of the prayers was for the release of Alexandre's cousin Paulo. Playing his guitar, Sérgio Ricardo sang "Calabouço" ("Dungeon"), a song he had just written to commemorate the emblematic death of a young student, Edson Luís,

Figure 14. The Sé Cathedral. Kenneth P. Serbin.

who had been shot by the repressive forces in Rio in March 1968, an incident that provoked protest marches across the nation and led to further deaths.[54] At the conclusion of the service, and as people left the cathedral, they sang "Caminhando" ("Walking"), also known as "So They Don't Say I Never Spoke of Flowers," a protest song by exiled composer Geraldo Vandré that the military censors had prohibited.[55] Idealistic like "Calabouço," "Caminhando" evoked the spirit of protest of the 1960s.[56]

Figure 15. Dom Paulo Evaristo Arns and other clergy at the memorial Mass for Alexandre Vannucchi Leme, São Paulo, March 30, 1973. Estadão Conteúdo.

That night, the repressive forces began a hunt for the Mass organizers, eventually arresting dozens of individuals, including many USP students and ALN sympathizers.[57] At the DOI-CODI, Major Ustra and his torturers took out their rage on the prisoners. "The day of the Mass for Alexandre everybody was beaten without knowing why, because we didn't know that the Mass was taking place," recalled Arlete.

> The day of the Mass was tumultuous. They took everybody out of their cells and beat them. . . . They were crazy, shouting, raving mad, calling Dom Paul names. They took us all out of the cells. They didn't even take us to the torture chambers. They went ahead and beat everybody right there. . . . They made all the guys parade naked in front of us women. They were crazy. They didn't say anything. How did we find out about the Mass? Four or five days later, a young woman [prisoner] arrived, a university professor and . . . PC do B contact. She told us about the Mass and its many repercussions, of the movement to organize it and how the cathedral had been surrounded.[58]

After more than four years of relative inactivity, the Mass helped to spark the rebirth of the student movement, the strengthening of the alliance between the Catholic Church and regime opponents, and a new emphasis on nonviolent resistance that contrasted sharply with the militarist approach of the ALN and other revolutionary organizations—and the dictators.[59] At a moment when peaceful resistance against the regime seemed impossible, the Mass also galvanized the USP campus as a focal point for opposition politics.[60] As a result, the balance of power between the nonviolent resistance and the repressive forces began to shift. Arlete recalled:

> The sensation I had after learning of the Mass was that they felt they had been hit hard for the first time. They had arrested the student leaders linked to the organization [ALN]. They had relaxed. When they started to see with the Mass that there was another kind of organization, organic or not, that was somewhat spontaneous but becoming a reality, they became terribly worried. . . . The dictatorship and the repression knew of this rise. They were terribly afraid of the student–Church link. They came to see that link in Alexandre and consequently in us. For example, my interrogations were very much aimed at it and how we had planned it all. They knew that we wanted the return of social activism. They wanted to know if we had discussed how that was going to be carried out. Where we were going to act. . . . They had all the power in their hands, over life, over death, over persons. They were killing us. They were torturing us. They thought they would never be punished. It's interesting how we began to perceive their fear. We were afraid. But they were also starting to feel afraid.[61]

The interrogations of Adriano focused on the same theme. "The intelligence personnel would come in and say: 'Let's quit with the chit-chat,'" he recalled. "'Let's discuss politics. We want to know in what direction this thing is going to grow. What was Alexandre Vannucchi's role in transforming the ALN into a mass organization?'" In Adriano's view, the arrest of many students not connected to the guerrilla underground thrust them into the nonviolent resistance. "You arrest a person, kill a person, and unleash a process in which you have to arrest five hundred middle-class people, some of them from the upper-middle class, the children of military officers, the children of lawyers, people who form public opinion, people from a wide variety of social backgrounds," Adriano observed. "To them at the time this all signified an enormous grassroots organization, of people who had not gone underground, all working legally in society, who had never touched a gun [or] were attached to an armed organization."[62]

The government had brutally eliminated the ALN as a military threat. However, it committed an enormous political blunder by killing Alexandre. "There are people active in their professions who, if they were run over by a car in a normal accident, thousands of people would cry for them, whereas other people can be murdered and hardly anybody will notice," Adriano observed. "The dictatorship couldn't have killed two more beloved, more significant people in their areas than Alexandre and [journalist] Vladimir Herzog. The same thing happened with the killing of Chico Mendes. The same thing happened with the death of Santo Dias da Silva."[63]

As they had in the 1960s, students led an antigovernment protest. In the view of U.S. observers in Brazil, the response to Alexandre's death represented the "strongest student political action in recent years." The Americans feared further confrontations.[64] "The ALN was in a situation where it was about to be eliminated," Adriano recalled.

> It could fight desperately in a narrow-minded way just for its survival as a political organization. Very well. I think politics can count for a lot. For that reason, Alexandre had become a revolutionary in the way defined by Ho Chi Minh: the knife in the water is the revolutionary who immerses himself in the people in such a way as not to stand out as a revolutionary. He is an everyday citizen. For example, I was noticed much more than Alexandre because of my personal characteristics, because I was extroverted, because I was more radical. Alexandre apparently was far more normal. He was a better student than I, more studious. He was liked a lot more by the professors. Taking a stand as this type of revolutionary was an amazingly wise thing to do.

With the powerful student response to the death of Alexandre, "the Médici dictatorship was reaching its saturation point."[65] In secret meetings, the Church leadership pressed the regime for justice. As the intelligence services recognized, the government now had "an Alexandre Vannucc[h]i Leme problem."[66]

The events of March and early April 1973—the start of fall and the academic year in Brazil—especially affected first-year students. In the geology program, the entire incoming class participated in the Mass. "It was quite remarkable from the standpoint of solidarity," remembered geology major Antônio Carlos Bertachini. "For me it was an act of clarification. . . . For example, we started to question the very history of the armed struggle, whether it was a coherent approach. . . . We started to debate the future stance of the movement. What to do? How to fight? What were the problems? How to face them?" The geology Centro Acadêmico had concentrated on preparing students to join the armed resistance. "But now it sought . . . a more open political stance. We understood that students needed to march alongside the rest of society. We had to start social movements."[67] The very act of organizing the Mass led USP students to hold assemblies for the first time in years. It also brought the students into contact with the clergy, opposition politicians, journalists, lawyers, and others perturbed by the repression.[68]

"From my standpoint, the Mass was an exercise in citizenship, because we were not only trying to honor the issue of a classmate's death," observed former geology major Fernando, a participant in the Mass. "It also demonstrated that people were fighting for democracy, for human rights, for liberty, and despite the fear, we were there. I believe that many people took part in the Mass in a spirit of sacrifice. People were putting themselves out there and putting their necks on the line and saying: 'I am here. I do not agree with what you are doing.'"[69] In the recollection of Luiz Antonio Bongiovanni, one of the Mass organizers and the president of the geology Centro Acadêmico, the Mass said "enough!" to the long years of repression.[70]

Bongiovanni had a *ponto* with Queiroz shortly after the Mass. Neither Queiroz nor any other person deeply involved in the ALN attended because the danger of being recognized by the police and arrested. Queiroz was not enthusiastic about the Mass as a way of defeating the regime. "The incense of the Mass is not the ascent of the masses," he told Bongiovanni.[71] Yet the Mass had congregated far more people in one protest than the guerrillas had ever achieved since taking up arms. In fact, the three thousand people in the cathedral easily outnumbered the total number of actual fighters from all forty-plus revolutionary organizations. Approximately 800 individuals participated in armed actions, and 2,112 were charged with crimes by the system of military tribunals. The Mass brought together ten times the number of ALN members involved in armed actions nationwide.[72] The guerrillas had failed to attract the people to the armed resistance, and they were unable to control any territory. The Mass was a restrained, astute, and nonviolent response to the dictators.

PRESS CENSORSHIP BLOCKED practically all news of the Mass and the attempts by the students, Alexandre's family, and others to publicize the truth of his death. To justify their actions, perpetuate the lies about Alexandre's death, and pursue the destruction of the ALN, the repressive forces continued to jail and torture USP students. On April 6, 1973, São Paulo DOI-CODI agents shot and killed Queiroz in public. By late May, the DOI-CODI men had arrested a total of forty-four USP students. On May 25, all but four of the students were released. The next day, May 26, renowned singer and composer Gilberto Gil (a future minister of culture under President Lula) performed "Cálice" ("Chalice") at the USP. Gil had just composed the ingenious song of double entendre about the regime with another giant of Brazilian music, Chico Buarque. Military censors banned "Cálice" from being played in public. One thousand students listened to Gil. This second protest once again suggested politics as an alternative to the armed resistance.[73]

Arlete spent sixty-two days at the DOI-CODI, departing in mid-May. Afterward she would have to periodically sign in at the DEOPS, where she had to listen to Officer Fleury's threatening comments. "Fleury cut off an end of my hair," Arlete remembered. "He said it was for identifying me if someday they gunned me down on the street. It was absolute intimidation." In addition to her gynecological problems, Arlete saw a doctor for a "heartburn so painful that I couldn't even stand up. I had to walk bent over because it hurt so much. I lost thirty-one pounds during those [sixty-two] days. I was already skinny before that. . . . The day my mother took me to the doctor, they followed our car. It was a climate of terror."[74]

Adriano spent ninety days at the DOI-CODI. Arlete returned regularly to visit him. "The day I left the DOI-CODI with him still there I knew what was going to continue happening to him," Arlete recalled. "It was one of the most difficult moments of my life."[75] The agents repeatedly took Adriano back to the torture chamber for interrogation. The jailers also forced Adriano to take an antidepressant. His eye became infected

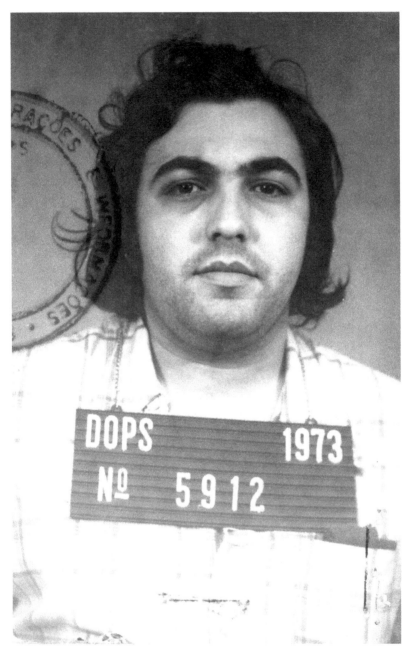

Figure 16. A police photo of Adriano. Arquivo Público do Estado de São Paulo.

from the injury on the day of his arrest.[76] He lost sixty-four pounds.[77] In mid-June, he was transferred to the Presídio do Hipódromo, a prison holding a number of political prisoners. He remained there until October.[78] Arlete frequently visited him there, too.

In October, the regime killed National Union of Students leader Honestino, whose body was never found.[79] It also sent 750 soldiers, including jungle war specialists, into the Amazon to hunt down and execute the PC do B guerrillas who had tried to establish a base of operations there. The soldiers killed some of the captured guerrillas by dropping them from planes into the Atlantic Ocean. In a few months, the PC do B was defeated.[80]

Circumstances got even tougher for the revolutionaries. In Chile, a right-wing coup against the socialist government of President Salvador Allende on September 11, 1973, eliminated a key South American safe haven for escaped or exiled members of the ALN and other organizations. In November, DOI-CODI officers tortured to death ALN guerrillas Antônio Carlos Bicalho Lana and Sônia Maria de Moraes Angel Jones.[81] On May 7, 1974, the police in Rio arrested the last active member of the ALN's military wing, Thomaz Antônio da Silva Meirelles Netto. He was never seen again.[82]

In Cuba, ALN exiles formulated a document critical of the organization's militarist tendencies. It called for ending military struggle in Brazil and a shutdown of the ALN to save the remaining fighters. However, led by Carlos Eugênio, an attempt to arrange an international congress of militants to discuss the document met with indifference among the European exiles, who had already begun to leave the ALN.[83] No political structures or any other kind of organization remained to promote the ALN's ideals. With only a few, isolated, minor armed actions thereafter, it practically ceased to exist.[84]

At the USP, the climate was grim. In December, when college graduation ceremonies were held, the class of 1973 geology majors held a moment of silence for Alexandre.[85] They simply picked up their diplomas and went home without celebrating.[86]

PRESIDENT MÉDICI TOOK pride in having directed the security forces in the cities to avoid arresting or harming people who had only superficial contact with the revolutionary organizations. He did not want the repression to affect the general populace. He ordered his agents to act "just against crime and only against criminals."[87] By the close of 1973, the regime had killed or disappeared several hundred guerrillas, with impunity.[88] However, the death of Alexandre violated Médici's strategy and brought serious consequences: Brazil's most important educational center had been politicized, along with the Catholic Church and other organizations. Also, the incident highlighted how the security forces had gotten out of hand and were building their own base of power.

On March 15, 1974, a new dictator, Gen. Ernesto Geisel, took office as Brazil's fourth military president. Opposed to the hard-liners, Geisel belonged to the so-called Sorbonne faction, which had supported the coup of 1964 but believed Brazil should have some form of Western, anti-Communist democracy. Not a democrat at heart and unopposed to the use of torture, Geisel had the most autocratic style of all of the general-presidents. Still, he understood the corrosive effect the torture centers had on military discipline and unity. He moved to eliminate them for practical, if not moral, reasons. He sought to pull the armed forces back from the brink of indiscipline and chaos caused by the battle against revolutionaries and the opposition in general. Thus, upon entering office, Geisel announced that he would initiate a political liberalization, a "slow, gradual, and secure decompression" of the dictatorship.[89] The political climate was beginning to favor the peaceful opposition.

In May 1974, Adriano, Arlete, and about a dozen other defendants accused of ties to the ALN were found innocent by a military tribunal that, like many other political trials during the dictatorship, relied on confessions extracted under torture. After the profound repercussions of the Alexandre Vannucchi Leme affair, the military personnel at the tribunal discreetly avoided reference to it.[90]

Although the dictatorship did not permit a popular vote for president and state governors, in November 1974, President Geisel, opposing the hard-liners, permitted an essentially free election for the national Congress and the state legislatures. The voters sent a sobering message to the dictators by voting overwhelmingly for the MDB in numerous contests. The progovernment National Renovating Alliance saw its majority diminish in the federal Chamber of Deputies (house of representatives) and lost sixteen of twenty-two Senate races.[91]

The years 1973 and 1974 proceeded under the gloom caused by the brutal repression of Alexandre and many others of his generation. However, the peaceful protest and 1974 election vote also discredited the violent approaches of both the regime and the guerrillas. There was new hope for a return to democracy.

The revolution had been destroyed. Brazil would not become another Cuba. However, in defeat, the revolutionaries would discover a new strategy for political change.

PART II

RESURGENCE

CHAPTER 6

Political Prisoners

After the destruction of the ALN, its surviving militants served out prison sentences, resided in exile, or lived in Brazilian society as inconspicuously as possible to avoid further persecution. They concentrated on adapting to life after their revolutionary dream. After the hope, turbulence, and violence of the ALN years, they needed to settle into a routine, and also manage their lingering physical and emotional trauma. If not in prison, they needed to earn a living. Rethinking revolutionary ideals, they also sought to resist the dictatorship nonviolently, either by organizing in prison or joining movements in the wider society.

The imprisoned guerrillas—kept in several prisons mainly in the São Paulo/Rio/Minas Gerais triangle—faced difficult conditions. At the same time, because they had inevitable daily contact with the dictatorship, they had the greatest opportunity to resist. Thus, they organized themselves as *political* prisoners: prisoners of conscience who had violated the law for political reasons. However, the government at first refused to acknowledge that designation. "The dictatorship wanted to annihilate us, not necessarily physically, but structurally, morally, politically," Manoel observed.[1]

Prison life is often a naked struggle for survival. This was especially true in Brazil, where corruption, lax enforcement of the rules, brutality, and torture characterize the correctional system. The political prisoners often witnessed and protested atrocities. Whenever the authorities held the political prisoners along with common criminals, the militants faced extreme dangers, given potential clashes with regular prisoners, sexual abuse, and chaos.

Despite censorship and strict controls in the prisons, the prisoners found ways to alert the world to their plight. Imprisoned ALN member Frei Betto, the former journalist, wrote letters to relatives and friends and kept notes about his experience. These items, including some smuggled out of prison, were published abroad. Covering the years 1969–71, the first set of letters appeared in Italy in 1971. They subsequently were published elsewhere, including in the United States, where they were issued in 1977 as *Against Principalities and Powers: Letters from a Brazilian Jail.*[2] That same year, a second set of materials appeared in Brazil, where Geisel's liberalization policies had ended censorship. The Portuguese title of the first book was *Das catacumbas*, literally, *From the Catacombs*. In these writings, Frei Betto evoked the underground struggles of the early Christian movement's resistance to Roman authority.[3] He also echoed the Brazilian Catholic Church's critical stance toward military rule. The suffering described in his and others' writings provoked international denunciation, giving the prisoners' moral ammunition against the dictatorship.

Manoel vigorously tried to organize the ALN prisoners to resist the prison authorities. After his conviction in 1970 for the Elbrick kidnapping, Manoel was imprisoned at Tiradentes in São Paulo. During the first two years, ALN members quarreled frequently. The proresistance ALN group also argued with prisoners from other revolutionary groups, who, in the eyes of the ALN, thought that passivity could win better conditions. The ALN prisoners also critically reflected on the efficacy of the armed struggle and their conduct under torture. They referred to this process as *crítica e auto-crítica* (criticism and self-criticism). The ALN group drew up a secret document in which they sought to identify the individuals and situations responsible for the many arrests and deaths at the hands of the regime. These activities unified the ALN prisoners in their ongoing resistance.[4]

To thwart these efforts, the authorities split and transferred them to different prisons. The government first moved Manoel to the Casa de Detenção Carandiru in São Paulo. After the failure of the 1972 hunger strike against the transfers, Manoel and two other ALN militants, Celso Antunes Horta and Jonas's brother Francisco Gomes da Silva, were put with common criminals in the state penitentiary, located near Carandiru. Over the next few years, the authorities kept Manoel on the move: from the penitentiary he went to Carandiru, then to Tiradentes, back to Carandiru, then the penitentiary, and finally back to Carandiru.[5]

Manoel's first stay at the penitentiary lasted nine months. He had his own cell, away from Celso and Francisco. "On the inside, each of us was isolated," Manoel recalled. "We were absolutely alone." In October 1972, in the days after his family informed him of the killing of his revolutionary uncle João, Manoel cried only when alone in his cell, fearful that a display of grief could raise suspicions and place comrades on the outside in danger.[6] He recalled:

> For me it was one of the most complicated, most difficult periods in jail ... because being absolutely alone among the common criminals is a very complicated thing. . . . I did not expose myself. So, for example, the individual cells did not have a shower head. . . . I spent nine months without showering because showering meant that I would have had to go down to the shower room with them at the shower time for my gallery and get into the bathroom with a hundred guys in order to shower. I did not do that. I knew it could cause me problems. I was a young white guy, handsome, and middle-class. They might want to rape me or do something else. . . . As best I could I cleaned myself in my cell by using the faucet. It was above the squat toilet.

Because of the strong ethic against informing, Manoel avoided contact with purported stool pigeons. He purposely cultivated relationships with the most dangerous prisoners, a respected elite who in turn respected the political prisoners because, according to the common criminals, "they [the political prisoners] didn't mess with drugs or fucking in the ass. But they weren't stupid. They were good people." Highly educated in comparison with most prisoners, Manoel worked as a bookkeeper in the prison broom factory. He won others' trust by serving as an informal counselor and by preparing documents, such as legal petitions and personal letters.[7]

In February 1973, the authorities abruptly ended their retaliatory punishment of Manoel, Celso, and Francisco. At the same time, several highly dangerous and unruly common criminals were allowed back into the general prison population after several months in solitary confinement. They wanted to retaliate for their mistreatment. "I knew that there were people there who had gone months and months in solitary confinement, without seeing the sun or receiving a visitor and living completely unprotected," Manoel said. Armed with knives, one day the angry men attacked helter-skelter. One man alone killed seven prisoners in Manoel's section of the prison, and others were killed in Celso's area. No political prisoners were hurt. However, acknowledging their precarious safety, a judge ordered their immediate transfer to Tiradentes.[8]

Manoel's experiences helped him and his comrades to organize themselves more effectively for basic survival. With the punishments over, he and a large group of prisoners were given their own wing, now at Carandiru. They won the confidence of the warden, who allowed them access to prohibited books, including Marxist literature. They bribed guards in order to obtain favors and needed items. Largely under the leadership of the ALN, the group aimed to enhance their collective well-being. They made decisions democratically, but some prisoners rejected the ALN's role. In addition to sharing chores, the men maintained group and self-discipline by exercising. "We exercised every day collectively," Manoel recalled. "Everybody got up at 6 a.m. and exercised. People who didn't belong to our group got angry as hell [laughter]. They said we didn't respect their . . . right to sleep. 'Fuck your sleep. We need to maintain our discipline. We need to keep our heads straight.'" The prisoners also did arts and crafts. Manoel learned pyrography (burning images onto leather), selling the pieces or giving them as gifts. Others drew and hung portraits of fallen comrades. The prisoners named cells after comrades, too. However, this last form of expression angered Col. Erasmo Dias, the head of public security for the state of São Paulo and a staunch anti-Communist. When he saw the drawings on a visit to Carandiru with other authorities, he exploded. He ordered all the prisoners to be sent to the penitentiary.

Manoel, Celso, and Francisco knew that the penitentiary prohibited books, which kept minds active and spread political indoctrination. The prisoners embarked on a frantic, round-the-clock mission to copy by hand as many books as possible into notebooks before the transfer out of Carandiru. "While one person copied, the others rested, slept or did something else," Manoel said. "We always had somebody copying. We were able to do that with countless books. . . . In notebooks, because I knew that the security men, during the search and seizure carried out in the penitentiary, looked for knives, drugs, and pot. They looked for things used by the common criminals. They didn't prohibit papers and written things because they were living in a different world."

Back in the penitentiary, Manoel and about thirty other political prisoners resorted to its cultural codes to creatively strengthen solidarity among themselves and with the common criminals. It was not easy. Although they all lived in the same wing, the political prisoners had individual cells. They adopted the regular prisoners' sign language. The guards understood this language, so Manoel and his comrades modified it to confuse them. To communicate with someone in a distant cell, a prisoner held out his hand in the corridor when signing, and the other prisoner held out a small mirror to read the message. The prisoners also used Morse code. They communicated with prisoners on other floors by speaking through the squat toilets, which were mere holes in the floor and interconnected by way of the sewage pipes. The common prisoners called this system the *boi*, literally, "a bull," but a word with multiple meanings in Portuguese. Hoping to help the men in solitary on the lowest floor of the prison, the revolutionaries learned their names by speaking through the *boi*. The political prisoners' lawyers then contacted students at the USP law school. The students made formal legal requests to consult with the men in solitary. In this way, the students liberated the men from the harsh treatment and in some cases obtained their release from prison. Manoel recalled:

> So along came one, two, three, and then soon thirty, forty lawyers simultaneously visiting the prisoners from solitary. The prisoner administrators didn't understand what was happening. And we told them that we were the ones arranging for the visits because the prisoners were in solitary illegally and because the disciplinary measures had no legal basis. There were no prison statutes. The whole situation was irregular and violated every human right. That's how we started our struggle, and we got all of the prisoners to join us. They came to have fantastic respect for us, because there were people leaving solitary [laughter].

The revolutionaries had forced the authorities to act responsibly.

The revolutionaries won another victory by skirting regulations regarding prison uniforms. Unlike at other prisons, here they had to wear the common uniforms. But they had arrived in the dead of winter. The prison had not yet ordered uniforms for them, including winter clothing. To keep warm the men made ponchos out of blankets. "We would go to the prison courtyard all by ourselves, without the common criminals, wearing our ponchos, and this greatly upset the prison authorities because it was the height of insubordination and they couldn't stop us," Manoel said. "Then all of a sudden, they started to prohibit it, and we insisted on the law. 'If you are prohibiting this, where is the law that says we can't cover ourselves against the cold? Where are the prison statutes? I want to see them.' Our struggle was all about the prison statutes."

As President Geisel proceeded with liberalization, the political prisoners sought other avenues of relief; no matter how skillful their resistance, being locked in individual cells hampered unity. "It was unbearable," Manoel said. "We had to get out of there." The prisoners played on the increased political sensitivity of the Geisel government during the November 1974 congressional elections. The dictatorship hoped to boost its legitimacy by allowing people to choose candidates freely. A few weeks before the election, the prisoners staged another hunger strike, demanding better conditions. With their friends and family on the outside, they carefully planned the strike for maximum political effect. Prior to the strike, for instance, a group of relatives, including Manoel's mother, took a bus to Brasília to pressure members of the Congress. Only five days into the strike, the regime made major concessions to the prisoners. It concentrated the men in a single area of Carandiru until a political prison could be built. In early 1975, all of the São Paulo political prisoners were transferred to the new facility, known as Barro Branco.

The prisoners at Barro Branco gained a certain degree of autonomy. At first the government appointed a DOI-CODI torturer as warden to intimidate the prisoners in the wake of their successful hunger strike. The prisoners opposed this man, but they could not embark on another hunger strike so soon. So, refusing to speak to the warden, they carried out a "strike of silence." After three days, he quit. The prisoners were allowed to convert three cells intended for solitary confinement into a classroom, a crafts workshop, and a library. As Manoel recalled, the remodeling broadcast a clear political message: "It was to change the character of the place, to make it impossible to use that space as a cell for punishment." On one of his visits to court, Manoel stole an official rubber stamp used by the authorities to mark books approved for prison use. "So, as we clandestinely obtained books in the prison through one of the guards and the jailkeepers, we stamped them," Manoel said.[9]

Figure 17. Political prisoners at the Barro Branco political prison, circa 1975. From left to right, standing: Ariston Lucena, Gilberto Belloque, Paulo Vannuchi, José Genoíno, and Manoel Cyrillo de Oliveira Netto; seated: Oséas Duarte, Aton Fon Filho, Reinaldo Morano Filho, Celso Horta, and Hamilton Pereira (Pedro Tierra). Paulo de Tarso Vannuchi collection.

ONE HUNDRED FIFTY miles away, separated from the Brazilian coast by a turbulent stretch of the Atlantic Ocean, convicted hijacker Colombo and scores of other political prisoners forged their own methods of resistance against the dictatorship in the prison on Ilha Grande, the largely uninhabited "big island" within Rio de Janeiro state. ALN founder Marighella and hundreds of other political prisoners had spent years on Ilha Grande in the 1930s and 1940s because of their involvement in the PCB and support for the Soviet Union.[10] Because of the long history of brutality at Ilha Grande, the political prisoners referred to it as "Ilha do Diabo," "Devil's Island."[11] Novelist, journalist, and PCB member Graciliano Ramos wrote his classic prison memoir *Memórias do cárcere* based in part on his time at Ilha Grande. "I was imprisoned on Ilha Grande with people from all of the organizations," Colombo recalled in a 2002 interview.

So I was able to have a view of things that was less about the internal workings of the ALN and more about Brazil in general, when compared to those who remained on the outside. In São Paulo the organizations were stronger, so they formed the collective of the ALN, the collective of the PCBR [Brazilian Communist Revolutionary Party]. Each organization had its own group inside the prison. At Ilha Grande we didn't. We were diluted among dozens of individuals from different organizations and different periods. When the organizations disappeared, we could lean on the comrades around us. Now, for those isolated in their own nucleus, still believing in a struggle on the outside that no longer existed, things were far more terrible.[12]

Colombo connected with Nelson Rodrigues Filho,[13] the son of Nelson Rodrigues, an ingenious playwright and journalist who staunchly supported the dictatorship and established a friendship with President Médici. Because of his fame and connections, the minister of war issued an order prohibiting physical harm to Nelson Rodrigues Filho. Code named "Prancha" (surfboard) because he was tall and skinny, Nelson Rodrigues Filho belonged to the MR-8. In 1970, before Prancha's arrest, the elder Nelson obtained from Médici permission for Prancha's safe exit from Brazil. In an act of revolutionary solidarity, Prancha refused the offer.[14] "If it's a special thing for me, I don't want it," Prancha said. Colombo recalled: "That deeply saddened his father. . . . But he would not play their game. . . . He underwent torture, interrogations."[15]

Discipline was strict at Ilha Grande, and tensions arose between the political prisoners and the prison authorities. As in São Paulo, the dictatorship mixed political prisoners with common criminals. In this case, the common prisoners had been convicted of national security violations resulting from bank robberies, a practice they adopted after learning of the revolutionaries' tactics. The latter's robberies had prompted the military to strengthen the law.[16] "As if to say, everybody who robs a bank is the same," Colombo observed. A minority at Ilha Grande, the common criminals first accepted the revolutionaries' rules. "There was no forced homosexual activity or theft among prisoners or drug use among us, and they obeyed this perfectly," Colombo remembered. "They even accepted the rules of our collective, where everything that someone got from his family was shared collectively by everybody."[17] By late 1971, there were ten common bank robbers mixed in with eighty-two revolutionaries. Over time the number of political prisoners diminished, as some finished their sentences. Fewer new prisoners entered because the repressive forces were executing more revolutionaries. Meanwhile, as the nonrevolutionary bank robberies continued, more common prisoners arrived.[18] This group included middle-class people who robbed to support drug habits. The new, nonpolitical prisoners rejected the revolutionary norms and engaged in criminal activity within the prison.[19]

In February 1972, conflict broke out between the revolutionaries and the common prisoners after one of the latter stole a political prisoner's watch. The revolutionaries punished him with a beating.[20] "The degree of incompatibility kept growing until we got to the point of physical violence, making it impossible for the two groups to continue together," Colombo recalled. "Physical violence, because they did not accept the rules of the collective. They were proliferating the use of drugs, and prisoners started robbing prisoners. These are the kinds of behaviors common in the regular prisons, and we did not accept those behaviors nor permit them. The worsening situation intensified the conflict between the two groups to the point where we started a movement demanding that we be separated from them."[21] Tensions simmered for months. In August 1972, the prison built a wall to separate the two groups. However, the militants remained vulnerable because the guards left their cells unlocked when the criminals had to walk by on their way to recreation or meals. The revolutionaries armed themselves with clubs and blades to resist a potential attack. By 1973, the common criminals outnumbered the revolutionaries. Tensions finally diminished later that year when violence between rival criminal factions left three common bank robbers dead. Focused on their own challenges, the common criminals lost interest in dominating the political prisoners.[22]

The political prisoners also complained about the primitive, precarious conditions: lack of water, horrible food, blocked sewage pipes, overcrowding, practically nonexistent medical and dental care, family visitations requiring twenty hours of travel for just three hours with the prisoners, and violence by guards against the prisoners.[23]

After several attempts to highlight their plight and obtain a transfer to a prison in the city of Rio, on May 5, 1975, the prisoners went on a hunger strike. On the outside, the prisoners' allies also pressured for their transfer.[24] President Geisel's liberalization opened up opportunities for the opposition to score political points. As a result, the strike received wide press coverage. MDB representatives read motions in Congress supporting the political prisoners. A navy boat took dignitaries to Ilha Grande to observe the conditions.[25] This was the ninth hunger strike by Brazilian political prisoners in five years. Twenty days into the strike, and in line with the liberalization, the president agreed to transfer of the political prisoners to the mainland. "Giving into a strike is hard, but I prefer to give in," Geisel said privately.[26]

Although still behind bars, the prisoners had scored an important political victory. "The fact of the matter is that we were demanding not only to leave Ilha Grande, but the creation of what was called a political prison," Colombo explained. "That put an end to the mischaracterization of us that the military had been wanting to use. With that hunger strike we got them to build an annex to the Frei Caneca just for political prisoners."[27] In August 1975, the military government moved the Ilha Grande political prisoners to the Esmeraldino Bandeira penitentiary, located in the Bangu district prison complex in Rio, where they awaited the construction of a new political prison within the city's Frei Caneca prison complex, established in the mid-1800s.[28] Located near downtown Rio on Frei Caneca Street, the Frei Caneca Penitentiary Complex ironically carried the name of an antiauthoritarian, antislavery priest executed by a firing squad in 1824 after leading a rebellion against the central government.[29] The promised facility, the Lemos de Brito Political Prison, opened in early 1976.[30]

At the Talavera Bruce women's prison, also located in Rio's Bangu complex, Colombo's hijacker girlfriend, Jessie, and her comrades also vigorously resisted the prison authorities. "We were soldiers and we acted that way," Jessie recalled. "So at first we had an extremely Stalinist organization [laughter]. It was so serious. . . . Later, we were no longer soldiers of revolutionary warfare, but a political group that put itself into the larger Brazilian political struggle." The women revolutionaries developed a strong collective. "We were very strict about that," Jessie said. "Our behavior. How we acted around the [male] jailers. How we dressed. . . . I never slept with a camisole in jail because I didn't want the guard to open the door in the morning and see me in a camisole." Instead, Jessie slept in pajamas or even jeans. "We kept our distance from the jailer on duty. . . . The fact that we were women also created many restrictions. The guys could wear shorts. There was no way we could do that. We were not in a position of strength

Figure 18. Colombo and Jessie Jane Vieira de Souza, with daughter Leta, at the Bangu prison complex, 1977. Centro de Documentação e Memória, Universidade Estadual Paulista.

around the guards." Despite staging their own hunger strike, the women did not win the right to a political prison. "We wanted to go to the same prison as the men," Jessie remembered. "We wanted them to make a wing in the prison for the women, because they had made one for the men. The fact that we were women meant that we were treated differently. For them, we were weren't that important. . . . When the liberalization advanced and anybody could visit the prisoners, everybody wanted to visit the men. Rarely did they want to visit the women [laughter]."[31]

With government permission, Jessie and Colombo married on paper in 1973. However, they still waited many months to see each other. The marriage made it possible for Colombo's family to visit Jessie at Talavera Bruce. In Rio, he too could now occasionally visit Jessie at her prison. "We went almost five years without seeing each other," Jessie recalled. "Later we got to see each other once a month. . . . And the time between visits became less and less, until at the end of our time in prison we saw each other almost every week. . . . I was the first woman in Rio to have what was called a conjugal visit. He would go to our pavilion. Our cells were individual, so we could spend almost all of our time there together. We made love and then would go over to the common area to talk to the other prisoners." In September 1976, Colombo and Jessie's daughter Leta was born in prison. "She stayed with me for three months," Jessie said. "She could have stayed with me longer. In fact, the prison had a day care center for the common prisoners. But I knew that wasn't the right thing to do. She went to live with Colombo's mother."[32]

CONVICTED OF VIOLATING national security, Manoel, Jessie, Colombo, and others faced long prison terms. However, despite the harshness of the regime, the military justice system released prisoners according to their sentences or even earlier. Many convictions were reversed on appeal.[33] Partly that was because that system, the Justiça Militar, employed many professional civilian judges. These judges were guided and frequently pressured by the military authorities, which had packed the Supreme Court with favorable appointees and removed some who disagreed with the government.[34] However, the Justiça Militar judges had leeway with political prisoners. The militants and their lawyers sought cracks in the system to secure an early release.

One perhaps unintended positive consequence of the imprisonment—
and oversight by the Justiça Militar—was to prevent the revolutionaries
dying in guerrilla actions or by execution. Paulo Vannuchi was one such
case. Resisting the prison authorities, he sought early release so that he
could resume the fight. He developed a highly contentious but ultimately
beneficial relationship with Judge Nelson da Silva Machado Guimarães.
Judge Guimarães had ordered Paulo's force-feeding during the 1972 hunger strike, but he became upset when he saw Paulo had been tortured. "At
that time I got very angry with him, because he started saying, 'Shit, that
is unacceptable,'" Paulo recalled. "I said to him: 'But your honor, you were
the one who authorized it.'"[35] Although aware of this and other atrocities,
Judge Guimarães took no action against them.[36] He also insisted on po-
lemicizing with the prisoners. "He knew theology," Paulo observed. "He
would issue sentences citing St. Thomas of Aquinas. . . . He would clash
with the prisoners. If a guy sat in front of Nelson Guimarães and said,
'I am a Communist. I don't believe in God. I'm ready to kill everybody
here,' he would treat that guy better than someone like me or the Dominicans, who said, 'No, it's Christianity that leads us to revolution.' He would
go crazy about that."[37]

In early 1975, with a third of his twelve-year sentence complete, Paulo
qualified for release from prison. However, first a hearing before Judge
Guimarães was required. The political prisoners strategized on hearings.
"Our orientation was sensible and was: 'Look, do not give a revolutionary
speech. Try to have a conversation that leads to your release, because the
important thing is to get back out there to help resume the fight.'" Paulo
stated that he no longer wanted to fight and intended to resume his
medical studies, start a family, and serve society as a doctor. At that point,
the judge asked Paulo to formally renounce his revolutionary ideals. "All
with an argument with the intention of tripping me up: 'So, sir, do you still
consider yourself a Christian?' 'Yes, I do.' 'But is Christianity compatible
with Marxism?' 'It is.' He went on a rampage. He wouldn't accept my answers. So I said, 'But your excellency, this is a philosophical question. It's
a theological question.' I wanted him to treat me objectively, under the law.
The guy would not give in." Judge Guimarães took Paulo aside to continue
their discussion in private. To support his argument, Paulo cited the case
of the Colombian guerrilla-priest Camilo Torres, killed in combat in 1966.
That example left the judge even less inclined to release Paulo. "The guy

decided that he would not let me go because if he did, I would be killed," Paulo remembered. "The guy probably helped me, because if he had released me at that time, with my attitude, I could have gotten involved again and been killed immediately."[38]

In January 1976, a São Paulo working-class PCB member, Manoel Fiel Filho, died at the DOI-CODI. As in the case of Alexandre and Vladimir Herzog, the military farcically claimed it was suicide. President Geisel, angry at the hard-liners and the security forces for attempting to obstruct his liberalization policies, acted swiftly, firing the army commander in São Paulo, Gen. Ednardo D'Ávila Mello.

The next month, Paulo had another hearing with Judge Guimarães. The judge's tone changed considerably. "The hearing really was different," Paulo recalled. "He himself didn't . . . ask any questions, just the formalities. 'If you are released, what to you intend to do?' I repeated: 'I want to return to medical school, to work, to get married and start a family.' And the guy set me free."[39]

CHAPTER 7

Moderation in Exile

Many Brazilians left their country or were forced into exile during the dictatorship (no reliable statistics exist).[1] Brazilians lived in such diverse locations as Santiago, Buenos Aires, Havana, Paris, Algiers, Stockholm, Moscow, and London. Few went to the United States, the supporter of coups in Latin America. No matter where they settled, exile had profound effects on their lives.

Living in exile in Paris, and also spending time in Moscow, ALN train robber Aloysio Nunes Ferreira Filho had an epiphany that shook his belief in Communism. As Aloysio analyzed the ALN's downfall after the deaths of Marighella and Toledo, he and exiled comrades questioned the armed struggle's efficacy. That questioning paralleled the debates among political prisoners in Brazil and within groups of still-active militants, all of whom ultimately chose nonviolent strategies. In mid-1971, ALN militants in Europe founded a dissident group called the Leninist Tendency, which demanded an end to the strictly militarist approach and a turn toward political engagement with the populace. Aloysio did not join the Leninist Tendency, but he contributed to the discussions spawning it. In August 1971, Ricardo Zarattini, one of the fifteen prisoners freed in the Elbrick operation and a leading proponent of the Leninist Tendency, penned a "self-criticism" of the ALN. It circulated widely among the exiles. Advocating the reunification of the Brazilian Left—which had fractured in

1967 after Marighella and other revolutionaries quit the PCB—the Leninist Tendency collaborated with PCB members, Brazilian revolutionary organizations, and even moderate regime opponents living in exile. "I went to Italy to speak with Zarattini," Aloysio remembered. "I wanted to help out, because I thought it was necessary to really question the road to death taken by a very large number of people, of militants, and that had no perspective of leading to victory."[2]

Aloysio's concerns eventually led him to abandon the ALN and join the French Communist Party, which followed the same political line as the PCB and the parent Soviet party: opposition to armed revolution in Brazil and peaceful coexistence with capitalism and the United States. Aloysio and other Brazilian Communist exiles helped revolutionaries fleeing from Brazil. In 1973, he reentered the PCB, which had organized a branch in Paris. "Afterwards, in my return to the Communist Party, I spent time on a regular basis with the people organizing what we could call a nonpartisan committee for solidarity with Brazil," Aloysio recalled. "There were militants from the extreme Left and Communist militants, as well as militants from the Catholic left. In that committee, we would discuss how to get into the newspapers the murders, incidents of torture, and crimes, and how to bring that information to the attention of the political and union organizations in France and Europe, and, in addition, how to support the comrades who were arriving from Brazil and needed housing, furniture, and employment. So we created the committee, the Red Aid."[3]

To support himself, his wife, Vera, and their two young children, Aloysio worked and occasionally received money from his father, a former state assemblyman and successful rancher. Vera's family also sent money. Before they bought a house in the Paris suburbs in 1976, they lived in hotel rooms and apartments lent by allies. With his Brazilian law degree and then a French bachelor's in political economy and a master's in social science, Aloysio found work as an educational administrator and college professor. From 1969 to 1973, he was one of four directors of the Institut de Recherche et de Formation en vue du Développement Harmonisé (IRFED), which trained individuals from other Third World countries to help foster economic development in their homelands. From 1974 to 1979, he taught at Besançon University. Aloysio also worked for Formation et Démocratie, an organization linked to the French Communist Party that trained labor union leaders.[4]

Although Aloysio became politically more moderate, he still followed the Soviet model. In late 1976, he traveled to Moscow to study at the Communist Party of the Soviet Union's school for the indoctrination of foreign revolutionaries and political leaders. Along with other Brazilian radicals, he engaged in a detailed study of Marx's *Capital*. However, in December he experienced a profound change of heart. Aloysio reflected on his experience:

> I spent four months there. . . . My group went there and had the privi-lege of having Armênio Guedes as the person in charge. He was the Communist intellectual who brought to the Brazilian debates about Communism the ideas of Eurocommunism that had emerged in Italy. . . . He had us read *Capital*. . . . We met Soviet leaders. Leaders from the areas of defense, economy, and culture. We could invite them to take part in debates with us. To give talks. We had autonomy to do that kind of thing. The conditions for studying were ideal because we had an enormous library at our disposal, all the necessary comforts, professors teaching small groups.

However, the Soviets did not permit their students to travel outside of Moscow.

> One thing caught my attention. I remember that at that time the president of the Chilean Communist Party, whose name was Cor-valán, was in prison in Chile. And in the Soviet Union a dissident named Bukowski was in prison. There was a prisoner exchange. Cor-valán was freed in Chile. He went to the Soviet Union. And Bukowski was set free in Moscow. He was able to go to Europe. I remember that Corvalán arrived in the Soviet Union, in Moscow, and was received as a hero with a huge party. They reported the story in the newspapers and on television. But at no time did the Soviet people learn that he had been exchanged for Bukowski. . . . I found out because by chance I had access to a newspaper of the Italian Communist Party. . . . That for me was something completely unacceptable. It was a punch to the stomach. There I was experiencing an episode of censorship of infor-mation on a very large scale. We were not allowed to photocopy docu-ments. The use of the photocopy machine was restricted and closely

guarded. We could only make a photocopy with authorization from the person in charge from the Party. As a result, all of that started to make me become very uneasy about the regime. I returned from there very despondent. But, at any rate, I thought it was possible to regenerate real socialism by democratizing it.[5]

In Aloysio's estimation, in general the "Communist Left ended up getting mixed up with dictatorship."[6]

Under Eurocommunism, the Communist parties in countries such as France and Italy charted paths independent of the authoritarian Soviet Union. For the Brazilians, building a coalition of disparate political forces became essential to fight the dictatorship. So Aloysio and many other PCB members and revolutionaries began a shift toward democracy, abandoning, as he later noted, the "ideological framework that viewed democracy as an instrument and not as a value in and of itself, . . . the idea of bourgeois freedoms as something to be overcome in the name of the dictatorship of the proletariat." "I am a man who puts liberty above everything else, and democracy as the prime value of my political action," Aloysio stated. "And the respect for human rights is for me absolutely inseparable from the idea of democracy and liberty. Respect for the individual and his or her choices. . . . The struggle against the Brazilian dictatorship was the struggle against that dictatorship and all dictatorships, of the Left and of the Right."[7] Some exiles admired the socialist systems they visited or lived in, but others echoed Aloysio's deep disappointment with the Soviet Union and Communism.[8] Shedding an authoritarian past that penetrated all of Brazilian society, many exiled Brazilian leftists came to embrace democracy. They even began to consider the positive contributions of capitalism. Meanwhile, exiled Brazilian women exposed to new currents of feminist thought began to question their subordinate position within the revolutionary Left and macho Brazilian society.[9]

Aloysio also returned from Moscow with a new love, Jussara Freire, an exiled member of the PCB whom he had met in Paris and who also joined the Moscow course. "I never cut off ties with Vera," Aloysio recalled. "We were always very close friends. . . . But we were no longer living together as man and woman. And I fell deeply in love with Jussara."[10]

Vera also had found another love and accepted the marital split. In her recollection, for revolutionaries such as she and Aloysio striving in exile to retain the level of excitement and danger of the cause, there were two options: "Get high or fall passionately in love a thousand times in order to have that level of adrenaline."[11]

DISILLUSIONED WITH THE Cuban socialist regime, Carlos Eugênio had also moved to Paris. He seemed on the verge of becoming apolitical. After so much revolutionary violence—killing and having comrades killed—he mainly avoided contact with the Brazilian activist community.[12] He met Aloysio, but they had little contact.[13] With his move from Cuba to Paris, Carlos Eugênio consciously used drugs to both relive and relieve the pain of combat in the streets of Rio and São Paulo. "These friendly drugs allow me to escape," he wrote in the opening lines of *Viagem à luta armada*.[14] Carlos Eugênio later summed up the effect of drugs as a "balm" for his open wounds,[15] ultimately stopping him from committing suicide.[16] He also used LSD and mescaline. In addition to treating his psychological wounds—he did not seek out psychotherapy in France—he took drugs out of curiosity and to obtain greater self-knowledge. Such behavior utterly contradicted ALN ethics. In all his years of armed struggle, Carlos Eugênio had no more than a drink or two, always focused on military readiness. Moreover, the revolutionaries refused to deal with Brazil's drug traffickers. Carlos Eugênio, with his notably strong psychology, avoided addiction by not establishing a routine in his usage. Remarkably, he was able to quit drugs when he wanted to and never felt the urge to restart.[17]

To the extent he engaged in politics, Carlos Eugênio followed a path similar to Aloysio's, but he still believed that armed struggle could forge social and political change. He had found the Cuban regime "absurd" because of its repressiveness and submission to the Soviet Union and its KGB agents. In one course, he listened to a Cuban military instructor, who wore good clothing and a nice wristwatch, make fun of Che Guevara. The instructor thought Che was "crazy." Carlos Eugênio still considered himself a "Guevarist" and thus a critic of how ostensibly socialist systems in the Soviet Union and Cuba reproduced rather than transformed power structures.[18] He also became deeply disappointed with Cuba's continued economic backwardness, which he attributed to its subordination to Moscow.[19]

Despite his Guevarist outlook, he, like Aloysio, saw the PCB as the most viable path to regime change. He convinced several other ALN militants in exile in Europe to join the PCB. In late 1973, during a two-week visit to Moscow, he met with PCB leader Luiz Carlos Prestes, who, after Marighella's death, had renewed ties between the PCB and the Cuban Communist Party.[20] In 1974, Carlos Eugênio requested permission to re-enter the PCB—he had quit in 1967 to join the ALN—but with the condition that the party not require him to renounce the idea of armed struggle. Armênio Guedes assented. Carlos Eugênio considered the PCB the "mother cell" for all Brazilian guerrillas.[21] Exiles from other revolutionary organizations were also sought to reunify the Brazilian radical Left.[22] The November 1974 congressional and state assembly elections ended in a surprising victory for the MDB. The most convincing showing came in the federal Senate, where its candidates received 60 percent of the votes cast.[23] The victory ratified the united front approach advocated by the PCB, many of whose members also belonged to the MDB. Leninist Tendency members were also entering the PCB.[24] Carlos Eugênio remained in the PCB until 1978. The influx of former revolutionaries into the PCB upset some ALN members who had remained in Brazil, including prisoners such as Paulo Vannuchi, who, before they recognized the inefficacy of armed resistance, sought to resume the fight.[25] This disagreement fueled deteriorating relations between the exiles and those at home.[26] However, Carlos Eugênio was convinced that a renewed guerrilla effort was doomed to failure.[27]

Carlos Eugênio sought to settle into everyday Parisian life. In his mid-twenties he had already accumulated more experiences and faced more dangers than most people over a lifetime. It was time for some normalcy, even as he recognized that his elite high school education did not qualify him for many jobs in France. He welcomed this challenge. He first worked as a bricklayer's assistant. He also worked as a carpenter and painter. With other Brazilians, he opened a moving business, and with French friends he started another business offering carpet-laying, electrical work, painting, and other household services. Carlos Eugênio also specialized in technical photography, on one occasion even entering a French nuclear power facility after allaying concerns by the police about his status as a political refugee. To avoid identification as a foreigner or refugee, Carlos Eugênio eventually learned to speak near-perfect French, earning the respect of the culturally aloof French people. "I was completely *dépaysé* [removed from one's cultural roots]," he recalled. This further distanced Carlos Eugênio from the defeats and personal losses of the revolution.[28]

Life in exile brought out other aspects of his personality, contrasting strikingly with his military toughness. In 1975, even though he lacked an undergraduate degree, Carlos Eugênio enrolled in the École Pratique des Haute Études to pursue a graduate degree in the sociology of geopolitics and defense, finishing in three years. In his thesis, he focused on the Brazilian naval servicemen's movement that, rejected by the military hierarchy, helped spark the coup of 1964. He chose the program to bolster a possible return to political activity.[29]

He also cultivated his musical interests. He had started playing piano at the age of eight and picked up guitar in his early teens. He abandoned music during the ALN period but rediscovered it with a passion in France. After studying with Brazilian guitarist Murilo Alencar, he and several other Brazilians formed a group called Ganga Zumba, honoring one of the black kings who ruled Palmares, the runaway slave colony in Carlos Eugênio's native state of Alagoas during the Portuguese colonial rule. At night clubs in Paris and on extended trips to Italy, Ganga Zumba played a wide variety of Brazilian styles, such as baião, samba, and bossa nova, as well as songs by Caetano Veloso and protest singer Geraldo Vandré. In Italy, the group also recorded some of its music. Carlos Eugênio played guitar and sang, always in Portuguese.

Carlos Eugênio eventually chose music as his permanent profession, applying to the renowned Schola Cantorum in Paris. He had to audition before one of the school's masters, the prominent musician and composer Pierre Doury. Most students used classical instruments, and many had far greater experience than Carlos Eugênio. As he watched the others perform, he feared his chances were low. Doury was wearing a suit and tie and an insignia from the French Legion of Honor. Carlos Eugênio, with jeans and a large beard, appeared with his guitar and told the professor he wanted a musical career. He proposed to play bossa nova. Bossa nova has elements of jazz, but its Brazilian roots make it unique. Like samba, bossa nova has an unusual beat originating in the rhythms brought to Brazil by the African slaves, but it is slower and softer. Samba is often danced, but bossa nova, which emerged in part from the crooner phenomenon that swept the United States and Brazil after World War II, is only sung. Spoken Portuguese can be a loud and aggressive language, but when sung it becomes alluring. Like his mentor Arnold Schönberg, Doury embraced the importance of harmony, the grammar of music. "Brazil is the land of harmony," Doury said, calling up Carlos Eugênio to perform. He played "Retrato em Preto e Branco" ("Black and White Portrait"), a striking piece about lost love composed by Antônio Carlos (Tom) Jobim (music) and Chico Buarque (lyrics). Carlos Eugênio was accepted, but on the condition that he focus on piano, a key instrument for learning music fundamentals. From 1977 to 1981, he studied under Doury, developing a great command of music history and theory. It was a salve for his history of violence and dislocation. In exile, Carlos Eugênio remembered, "music calmed me down."

CHAPTER 8

Power to the People, Brazilian-Style

Rebounding from imprisonment, in 1975 Adriano and Arlete Diogo immersed themselves in São Paulo's horrendous *cortiços*, crowded tenements where thousands of immigrants from Brazil's impoverished Northeast region settled in the twentieth century seeking work in South America's largest industrial hub. Adriano and Arlete sought to aid the cortiço-dwellers, at the invitation of the Catholic Church's Pastoral do Cortiço, a pastoral program seeking to alleviate the migrants' plight. To Arlete, they were responding to the fundamental "need to become reconnected with the people, with social movements, with the Church, to have support, so that our struggle wouldn't be limited to a half dozen who still resisted and who were being destroyed one by one." Like many militants, the Diogos were attracted to the Church and this new avenue of political action because of their Christian worldview.[1] Adriano was especially moved because Dom Paulo, the archbishop of São Paulo, had visited him and other political prisoners at the Hipódromo prison. He observed: "The wounds of prison were healed in the Church. A week after leaving jail, we already changed our tactics. We went to work right away in the cortiços. . . . You see, from 1973 until 1990, the Church was Brazil's greatest political party. Every church had political activity."[2]

Working as public school teachers, Adriano and Arlete spent their weekends in the cortiços of Mooca, a central neighborhood of São Paulo congregating Italian immigrants and their children, middle-class professionals such as the Diogos, and working-class families.[3] Most cortiços had once been mansions or other large homes of the São Paulo economic elite that emerged in the late nineteenth and early twentieth centuries with the region's coffee boom and nascent industrial expansion.[4] The cortiços generally belonged to middle-class people who had inherited them.[5] These owners subdivided each of these buildings into numerous tiny, irregular rental units, often no more than a bedroom. In the 1970s, cortiços existed in every district of São Paulo, including middle- and upper-class areas. At that time, between 10 and 20 percent of the city's population lived in cortiços, including a modern high-rise version.[6]

Along with other members of St. Raphael's parish, Adriano and Arlete studied the conditions of the cortiços and gathered statistics on the families. "There were just one or two bathrooms for about forty families," Adriano explained. "There was no green space or sunny areas, and every square inch was occupied with people. The rooms measured seventy-two square feet."[7] "The partition between the rooms was usually made not of brick, but strand board," Arlete noted. "That caused serious problems, because you could hear everything." One cortiço on Madre de Deus [Mother of God] Street housed 57 families, with some 250 people. Ninety percent of this building's inhabitants came from two cities in the Northeast state of Pernambuco, indicating how migrant networks formed in Brazil. Adriano described what he encountered:

> The Northeasterners came by the thousands looking for work and they were usually from rural areas. They considered themselves to be safe in those group dwellings, because of the architectural design closing them off from the street. It was made that way because of the very large number of rooms. And so they went out and found work. . . . But the situation was absurd. Many of the children didn't attend school, even though they lived downtown and with a school next door. They had no vaccination record cards. . . . I was born in Mooca and was a descendant of immigrants, and I never imagined that the Brazilian people . . . could live in such subhuman conditions.[8]

Arlete and Adriano witnessed even worse conditions in old movie theaters converted into cortiços. "Much worse than the favelas, much poorer," Adriano observed. "The guy ran the place like a hotel. So he wasn't subject to the rent laws, and he could raise the daily or monthly price as much as he wanted. Later violence and drugs and all kinds of terrible things arrived in the cortiços." In the early 2000s, São Paulo still had thousands of cortiços.[9]

"Our goal with all that research was to discover what were the most pressing needs of that population and how we could help them organize themselves to fight for what they needed," Arlete remembered. "We arrived at the conclusion that their biggest necessity was a day care center. So we started a campaign to obtain day care centers."[10]

Social work in the cortiços shattered the traditional concept of apolitical Catholicism held by the Diogos and especially their fellow parishioners. "We went into the cortiços to do that work with the parishioners, who were also seeing all that misery for the very first time," Arlete observed. "What struck me the most was that we neighborhood people could walk by the front door time after time and never imagine the conditions inside. . . . It caught everybody by surprise. It was for those of us who had been activists, and even more so for the middle-class people who weren't used to seeing the Church take such a position. Many people believed that the job of a priest was to say Mass and never get involved in politics."[11] Adriano noted that many middle-class people "started helping the poorest of the poor."[12]

In 1979, the Diogos' work with the mainly unskilled workers who lived in the cortiços led them to help found a local labor organization, the Associação dos Trabalhadores da Região da Mooca. It was independent of the government-approved unions that had dominated the Brazilian labor scene since the 1930s and had become weakened under the dictatorship, which appointed figureheads to run them. In the late 1970s, more than 100,000 workers toiled in approximately 1,600 factories and shops in the Mooca region, an industrial district.[13] Adriano and Arlete taught adult literacy classes to the laborers. They also visited the workers in the factories. In some instances, Adriano went to plants where better-trained, better-paid members of São Paulo's labor aristocracy worked. In contrast with these workers, the poorly treated unskilled laborers lived in "semislavery." Adriano also worked to organize the metal workers, a key group within the labor aristocracy with close links to the Church. (In addition, Adriano started working in his chosen field of geology, where he became active as a union organizer.) "We preferred doing the type of working-class organizing that was more radical, more difficult, more focused on the grassroots," Adriano recalled.[14]

Arlete also continued as a high school teacher. As a former political prisoner, she was prohibited from teaching civics but allowed to teach history, a course she used to raise political awareness among both students and teachers. Some of her former students became politically active, while others did socially oriented pastoral work in the Church. Arlete also served as the São Paulo state teachers' union representative at her school.[15]

WITH THE DEFEAT of revolutionary militarism, the *massistas* gained political strength. "Nobody talked anymore about armed resistance—it was about the grassroots movements," Adriano remembered.[16] Adriano's and Arlete's activism became part of a groundswell of nonviolent grassroots movements known in Brazil as the *movimento popular*, literally, a "popular movement," or mass social movement. *Movimento popular* is best translated as "power to the people." However, *movimento popular* had a much larger and longer-lasting social base than the Black Panthers and other small, radical movements in the United States that used "power to the people" in the late 1960s and 1970s. It reemerged from the culture of the Left that had produced nonviolent, radical initiatives in the early 1960s. They were suppressed after the coup.[17] It encompassed a wide variety of pressure groups and organizations: middle-class feminists; lower-class women's clubs combatting poverty; groups demanding better public education and transportation; Afro-Brazilians affirming black consciousness; indigenous peoples defending their lands and cultures; a labor movement independent of government-controlled unions; LGBTQ rights activists; crusaders for human rights and against torture; the proponents of amnesty for all political prisoners and exiles; lawyers, journalists, and environmentalists; and, in the wake of Alexandre's death, a renascent student movement. The *movimento popular* sprung up throughout the country. Like the Pastoral do Cortiço, many groups were tied to Brazil's Church of the Poor, the incarnation of liberation theology in the world's largest Catholic nation. Liberation theology promoted social justice. It attracted atheist revolutionaries because of roots in the Christian–Marxist dialogue begun in the 1960s. An early example of the *movimento popular* was the Catholic grassroots church communities, a network of thousands of Bible study groups that spawned social activists, encouraged by progressive Catholic leaders. Together with the Church and the MDB, the *movimento popular* drove the opposition to the military regime.[18] Adriano observed: "Why the Catholic Church? Because the Catholic Church was welcoming everybody."[19]

Paulo Vannuchi, the hardcore ALN revolutionary who defined himself as "a Christian without God," felt a powerful affinity with the Church's oppositional stance. An important step in his transformation came after his release from prison in February 1976, when he participated in meetings aimed at drawing conclusions about the ALN "self-criticism," a document produced by the political prisoners. The self-criticism had recognized the defeat of the guerrillas as the revolutionary "vanguard" and their political errors, including the overemphasis on a military solution, but still with the hope of reorganizing the ALN, Paulo observed. The conclusions discussed outside of prison were never written down, but they became an evolving guide, shared orally. As a result of this process, all of the "canons" of guerrilla warfare came into question, Paulo observed. Instead of seeking to restart the ALN, he delved into political work with the Church. He described his transition:

> The dynamic unleashed is not a one-way street—because I was a former political prisoner who would get involved in grassroots social movements. I learned things. That led to a new reflection. And it led to questioning of all the previous tactics. In my specific case, I got to learn about the realities of the working class, of a different social situation. And many of us lacked that understanding. I was from São Joaquim da Barra, that small-town atmosphere. Then came the student movement, medical school at the USP. The working class for me was hugely abstract. But later, it no longer was. I was meeting with workers on the weekends. Every Saturday. Every Sunday. Workers organizing into the alternative union movement, grassroots church communities, the working-class pastoral. . . . I became involved in working with grassroots political education, mainly with the Archdiocese of São Paulo. . . . That was really a very profound transformation.[20]

Reentering the USP in 1977, Paulo switched from medicine to journalism. He also began studying the work of Paulo Freire, a progressive educator from Recife. Freire developed the world-famous teaching philosophy known as the "pedagogy of the oppressed," as expressed in the 1968 book of that name. The Church of the Poor and its grassroots church communities mobilized through *conscientização*, or "consciousness-raising," pioneered in Freire's literacy method. In place of traditional classroom authority ("banker's education"), it proposed a democratic dialogue between teachers and students, addressing students' everyday reality.[21] Because of his ideas, in 1964 Freire was imprisoned for seventy-five days, after which he went into exile. In 1969–70, he spent a year teaching at Harvard University.

Paulo remembered how the Freire method affected him:

> You perceive the view of the relationship between a revolutionary and a worker. Or the social movement that is different from the Leninist tradition, which stated: "We revolutionaries possess revolutionary consciousness. We have what the workers do not have. We will give it to them." In other words, Paulo Freire insists on the contrary, on the idea that there is a people's wisdom that needs to be reaped and developed by the revolutionaries. Or, at the very least, the two groups have to interact. And you will explain your experience: "I was a political prisoner and lived through that. That was my experience. Are we going to organize a strike together? Well, then, it's necessary to take care of certain details. There's the political repression to worry about. It works in the following manner." And, at the same time, listen to them, as we have been doing. . . . It's like sitting in a circle where we all have things to state and to hear, to teach and to learn.[22]

As a specialist in grassroots education, Paulo in 1977 and 1978 joined Frei Betto and others to establish the Center for Grassroots Education at São Paulo's Instituto Sedes Sapientiae, an educational institute focused on social justice founded by the Catholic nun and psychologist Célia Sodré Dória. Known by her religious name, Madre Cristina, she had offered refuge to a number of political prisoners, assisted their families, and employed psychoanalysts fleeing the Argentine dictatorship.[23] The Center for Grassroots Education's pedagogy developed from liberation theology and Freire's ideas. Its students learned how to pressure for social change by organizing their neighborhoods and workplaces. Paulo observed:

> Along those lines, we became a highly sought out team because we were bringing to the table the Church's immense set of experiences, an instrument for doing political and sociological analysis that the par-

ticipants lacked. So we organized mini-courses called Mini-Course on Brazilian Reality. It began with the topic of: How does society function? Social classes, political economy, ideology. Marxist ideas from the standpoint of liberation theology. We divided the course into units. I did the History of Society. Frei Betto did Political Reading of the Gospel. He took passages that helped situate the discussion on the theme of social struggle, class struggle, ancient Palestine, new interpretations. In that context, what does a particular passage of the Gospel have to say?

As a result, participants received a basic grasp of humanity's conceptual heritage.[24]

In 1977 and 1978, as pressure against the regime grew from the *movimento popular*, the MDB, and now sectors of the business community, President Geisel accelerated the liberalization process, now known as the "political opening." In a decisive move, in October 1977 he fired the minister of the army, Gen. Sylvio Frota, a hard-liner who tried to hinder the opening. On December 31, 1978, Geisel rescinded Institutional Act No. 5, a strong signal that the dictatorship might allow a return to full civil liberties.

The *movimento popular* intensified, and a new leader emerged. In May 1978, Luiz Inácio Lula da Silva, the thirty-two-year-old president of one of the key industrial unions in the São Paulo region (the Sindicato dos Trabalhadores das Indústrias Metalúrgica e de Material Elétrico de São Bernardo do Campo e Diadema) led a rare small strike at a bus assembly plant. Silva, known by his childhood nickname Lula, had migrated from a town in the interior of Pernambuco to São Paulo state at the age of seven in 1952. He rode with his mother and siblings on the back of a large open-air truck for thirteen days, an odyssey repeated by thousands of other Brazilian families. Shortly thereafter, Lula went to work in the port city of Santos, selling peanuts, oranges, and Brazilian tapioca on the street. At age eleven, in São Paulo, he worked at a dry cleaner and as a telephone operator. On the side, he earned money shining shoes and performing other odd jobs. His family lived in conditions not much better than the cortiços. At age fifteen Lula began a career as a lathe operator. In 1963, he lost the small finger of his left hand in a factory accident.[25]

Lula joined the union in 1969, rising to the presidency in 1975. After 1964, the military had violently repressed strikes, and by 1978 Brazil had not had one for a decade. Lula's union struck because the regime had reported inaccurately low inflation statistics, leading to large drops in the value of workers' salaries. The union also wanted the right to negotiate directly with management, bypassing the traditional, government-controlled process. The sit-down action by Lula's union caught the regime by surprise. It triggered numerous other stoppages involving hundreds of thousands of workers in the greater São Paulo area through July, including white-collar employees and professionals. Because the workers sought only wage increases and did not contest the dictatorship, the government did not intervene in many of the strikes. However, the police did break up some picket lines, and the government threatened striking public employees with reprisals.[26]

Nevertheless, the 1978 strikes marked a turning point in the history of the Brazilian labor movement and in Lula's own political trajectory. "It's important to remember that 1978 was the year that I assumed a public political position for the first time," Lula later recalled. "It was that year that we organized a group of union members and went to speak with Fernando Henrique Cardoso to tell him that we wanted to support him for senator. And we campaigned for him at the entrances to factories."[27]

A world-renowned sociologist, Fernando Henrique lived in exile from 1964 to 1968, first in Chile, then in France. After his return to Brazil, he obtained a teaching position at the USP, but the dictatorship forced him to retire. In 1969, with backing from the Ford Foundation, he helped set up a research institute with ties to the MDB.[28] Fernando Henrique spent time in France again in the 1970s, where he met with Aloysio and other exiled opposition leaders. (The two had first met at the USP in the early 1960s.) Aloysio remembered favors Fernando Henrique did: "He brought me things, and he brought letters from my parents and took letters from me back to them, confidential letters that I wanted to be sure did not fall into the hands of the police, that wouldn't end up being censored."[29]

In 1976, right-wing extremists bombed the research institute—a stark warning to Fernando Henrique and other left-wing opponents of the dictatorship. However, the threats did not end their work. In the 1978 election, Fernando Henrique, running on the MDB ticket, won 1.3 million votes in the race to represent São Paulo in the Senate. It was fewer than the winning MDB candidate Franco Montoro but more than the progovernment candidate and enough to qualify him as a *suplente*, a stand-in were the seat vacated.[30] However, the progovernment National Renovating Alliance retained control of the Congress and most of the twenty-two governors' seats.[31] Geisel's choice for the presidency, Gen. João Baptista Figueiredo, the former head of Brazil's spy agency, won the guaranteed indirect 1978 election. He took office on March 15, 1979.

Just two days before, Lula led another strike, which ignited dozens more across São Paulo and fourteen other states. More than 3 million people participated. The laborers demanded more equitable treatment, an end to manipulation of wage rates, and greater independence for unions. These strikes outraged the regime and its allies in the business world. In São Paulo, the government reacted forcefully, invading churches where strikers were holding meetings. The police shot and killed Catholic union leader Santo Dias da Silva, who, just as Alexandre Vannucchi Leme, would become a symbol of resistance. Businesses fired masses of workers, and the Ministry of Labor removed Lula from the presidency of his union for two months. Businesses that wished to negotiate with the unions were warned that they would lose government credits and subsidies.[32]

In August 1979, after years of pressure from the amnesty movement, the MDB, the Church, and sectors of the *movimento popular*, the government announced the Amnesty Law. Passage of this law was fraught with political tensions and still remains controversial. The legislation allowed the return of most exiled revolutionaries and other regime opponents. It allowed the release of all political prisoners whose crimes did not involve dead victims. However, the law included language granting protection to violators of human rights.[33] As a result of the law, Manoel, Jessie Jane, and Colombo were released from prison. Aloysio, Jussara, Vera, and Aloysio and Vera's children returned from Paris. Carlos Eugênio remained absorbed in Parisian life and delayed his return.

The amnesty nudged Brazil a step closer to democracy. It affirmed a crucial historical reality: although the dictatorship executed and disappeared hundreds of individuals and tortured thousands more, it stopped far short of annihilating the radical Left. Brazil was not Chile, where dictator Augusto Pinochet's security forces killed 3,000 people, nor Argentina, where the generals' victims numbered at least 15,000. Stalin, Hitler, Mao, and other totalitarian leaders of the twentieth century brutally massacred tens of millions of people. Not just the ex-political prisoners and former exiles, but also militants such as Paulo, Adriano, and Arlete could

Figure 19. Celebrating Colombo and Jessie's release from prison: from left to right, Colombo; Jessie's mother, Leta de Souza Alves; Colombo's sister, Iná Meireles de Souza; Jessie; and Colombo's mother, Inah Meirelles de Souza, 1979. Leta had just arrived from exile in Sweden. Colombo and Jessie Jane Vieira de Souza collection.

act with less fear of reprisal after amnesty took effect—but the dictatorship continued to spy on and arrest people and tolerate right-wing terrorists.[34] Furthermore, by bringing ex-prisoners and exiles into the political process and into contact with the emboldened labor movement, the amnesty supplied the *movimento popular* and the opposition in general with new energy and ideas.

Indeed, although the dictatorship remained in place, the *movimento popular* appeared ready to progress. As Adriano recalled, workers' movements radiated throughout the São Paulo metropolitan area. He observed: "Everybody started their own movement—the health movement, the education movement, and the political movements against the dictatorship. . . . In Brazil a large mass movement was starting to emerge."[35]

CHAPTER 9

The Entrepreneurs

For Márcio Araújo de Lacerda, a student activist who somewhat ambivalently had become a guerrilla, prison provided an opportunity to rethink not just his politics but also his career. In mid-1971, disillusioned with the armed resistance and still facing most of a twelve-year sentence in his home state of Minas Gerais, Márcio built himself a work table. He began a correspondence course in industrial engineering.

Márcio believed that the resistance was doomed. He had witnessed—and admittedly contributed to—what he called the "incompetence" of the Brazilian Left. The day after the 1964 coup, he watched right-wing civilians celebrate in downtown Belo Horizonte, the capital of Minas Gerais, while his party, the PCB, did not even protest. "I stood there watching and became highly depressed and revolted with the situation, seeing the government come down without any resistance," Márcio recalled. "If there had been a serious and organized resistance, I certainly would have joined up." Márcio wanted to fight against both oppression and timidity. In 1966, he joined the army reserves—not to support or combat the repression, but to fulfill his passion for competence. He finished in first place in the infantry basic training course, displaying excellent marksmanship. "I was very enthusiastic about being a soldier," Márcio recalled. "Violence ran in my veins."[1]

However, although he enjoyed the reserves, Márcio soon sickened of the dictatorship's obsequiousness toward the United States. In 1967, after participating in student protests, he joined the Corrente Revolucionária de Minas Gerais (the Revolutionary Group of Minas Gerais), which later fused with the ALN. "I think I was much more antidictatorship than a Marxist," he recalled. The Corrente had strong ties to the local labor movement. In 1968, it helped organize a major, illegal antigovernment strike in Contagem, a suburb of Belo Horizonte, a burgeoning industrial center that symbolized the "economic miracle."[2] Given his army experience, Márcio could help train other aspiring guerrillas. He took part in three armed robberies. After one of them, to avoid police identification of their car, Márcio and his comrades blew it up with dynamite. In one failed action at a store, a comrade shot and wounded the owner, who had tried to resist.[3]

In contrast with the "camaraderie, the organization, the clarity" of the army reserves, Márcio viewed the Corrente as bungling. It had no serious security plan. Like Brazil's other urban guerrillas, Corrente members did not wear ski masks during actions. A Corrente militant spread false rumors that Márcio was an infiltrator; in Márcio's recollection, she lacked adequate training. The guerrillas had a "total lack of preparation" for interrogation by police and military investigators. Márcio observed:

> This somewhat reflected Marighella's own incompetence. . . . The way he intended to do it, it was a bit unrealistic, to go from urban guerrilla warfare to his plan of rural warfare. . . . In fact, it was all a big mistake from a political standpoint. And from a historical standpoint. He had the best of intentions, but the strategy was wrong. It really should have been a fight for democracy, not for a socialist revolution. I became resentful of the whole idea of becoming isolated, of being seen as a spy. . . . Much of my prejudice against the extreme Left also comes from that situation. And I was responsible, too, because I was also a militant. I also committed errors of judgment. I could have been tougher in my opposition, once I saw how fragile things were. I was also responsible for not putting a stop to things soon enough.[4]

Márcio observed that, for a young person, clandestine revolutionary warfare "was a very confusing thing. And we didn't have sufficient information to correctly evaluate what was happening." Márcio's judgment was further clouded by his relationship with his first girlfriend, also a Corrente member. Many of Brazil's revolutionaries entered the fight through such personal connections. "Although it may appear somewhat irresponsible, I perhaps stayed on in the organization in part because of her," Márcio admitted. "It was one of those romantic illusions, because I saw what was wrong with the organization and told myself, 'Oh, this is a mistake.' But I stayed on."[5] Márcio recalled:

> I remember the conversation I had with her. I said that I understood that the path of armed struggle, of urban guerrilla warfare and even the idea of the *foco* [Cuban-inspired, small-scale operations] was incorrect, that the surviving groups at that point were already practically destroyed. But still more people were going to die. . . . They would be exterminated. It was a technical matter. But I understood that in the long run the mass movement in Brazil could obtain access to power. The possibility that one day there could be an armed struggle, a bloody revolution, could not be eliminated. But it would be the result of a mass movement, not as the result of that crazy strategy that we had attempted.[6]

Many former guerrillas took pride in their actions, but Márcio did not. "I think it was a waste of life—not just mine, but everybody's," he said. "You can be proud to the extent that you can say, 'Look, it was something I did out of conviction, unselfishness, and the possibility of sacrifice. It was a noble cause.' That's fine. But I'm very rational about it. From a political standpoint, the cause was mistaken. The people were good and politically aware, . . . but the job was done badly. . . . This is the outlook of the manager, of the entrepreneur. . . . The entire scene was bad."[7]

Márcio's final moments as a Corrente guerrilla proved disastrous. On April 26, 1969, he tried to flee from police waiting for him when he arrived home. As they were about to capture him, he threw away his gun and surrendered. The police took him to local military interrogators. Standing now before soldiers and a colonel who expected him to spill his guts about his activism, Márcio sarcastically shouted, "Good morning!" After he denied any knowledge of guerrilla operations, the soldiers began to throw punches. Suddenly, looking up at a blackboard, Márcio saw that investigators had listed the name of every important member of the Corrente, including him, and the operations in which they were involved. Feeling completely demoralized, he lost the desire to resist. However, the authorities lacked one important piece of information: the location of a load of stolen dynamite that Márcio had hidden for later use against the regime. They demanded that he take them to it. Márcio recalled: "I told them: 'I'll take you, because, fuck, the way this badly organized revolution is going, some crazy guy could get that dynamite and kill a bunch of innocent people. I don't want that to happen.' The way I saw it, that dynamite was supposed to be used against a military objective, not for terrorism." When Márcio and the police arrived at the hiding place, they discovered that someone from the Corrente had removed the dynamite.

During the most difficult phase of his interrogations, one guard "hit both my ears with cupped hands and with tremendous force," Márcio recalled. "My ears rang for a very long time," he said. "I still have some kind of lesion in my ears."[8]

Márcio was convicted of subversion. He spent the first ten months of his sentence at a Minas Gerais penal colony also used to hold suspected militants. He was then transferred to the political prison in Juiz de Fora. At first, Márcio found prison unbearable.[9] He asked a friend to sneak in money and a gun so that he could attempt an escape. Fearing for Márcio's safety, the friend refused.[10] Over time, Márcio adapted, turning prison into a test of perseverance, solidarity, and leadership. More than the revolution, prison allowed Márcio to experience egalitarianism and cooperation because the prisoners shared material possessions and gathered frequently to discuss their problems. As with the ALN prisoners in São Paulo, Márcio had spent long hours evaluating the guerrillas' ideals and strategies and contemplating his future.[11] He reconnected with Corrente members and other revolutionaries. The prisoners protested for better conditions. However, without relinquishing his opposition to the dictatorship, Márcio also struck up a convivial relationship with prison officials. Noting Márcio's leadership qualities, the officials transferred him and another prisoner to cells closer to the commandant's headquarters. Márcio debated politics with the authorities, and they allowed him to watch the 1970 World Cup—Brazil's victory was used as regime propaganda—on the television in the officers' canteen. (The soccer broadcasts were among the first live TV events in Brazil, thanks to the military's inclusion of Brazil in the international satellite transmission system.) To conform with revolutionary norms, the Corrente prisoners wanted Márcio to formally lead their group. Because of his skepticism about the revolution, he refused, but he participated in a two-week hunger strike in early 1971.[12]

Figure 20. Márcio Araújo de Lacerda in the uniform of the army reserves. Márcio Araújo de Lacerda collection.

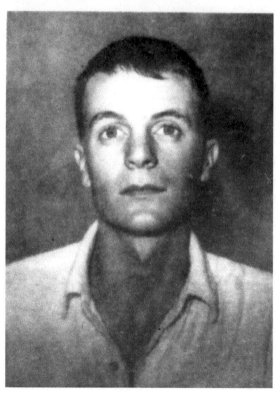

Figure 21. A police photo of Márcio. Arquivo Público do Estado de São Paulo.

Discreetly, Márcio made a half-hearted attempt to argue for the end the guerrilla struggle. "I regret not having been more incisive, more aggressive, on that matter," Márcio said. "I was afraid of being accused of dropping out to pursue personal interests. . . . Anybody who tried to [be more incisive] could even be killed the same way that Márcio [Leite] was. They shot him dead in the street." Risking his reputation and physical wellbeing, Márcio officially resigned from the Corrente. "One morning I had a flash of clarity about what I wanted for my life: to get out of [prison] as soon as possible," Márcio recalled. "I concluded that I was incompetent as a politician. I had no vocation for that. . . . In other words, I was incompetent in both the external and the internal struggle. . . . I didn't play games very well. I concluded that I was an entrepreneur. I liked to organize things and engage in teamwork. To do that I needed to get out of prison, return to life, finish my degree, and start to work. I imagined that I could perhaps help to change the country some other way in the future. I sought out the rest of the group and requested a meeting. I told them, 'Look, I'm formally resigning from the organization.'" Márcio's departure remained a secret, known only by his fellow inmates. They respected his decision. Despite their political disagreements, he maintained solidarity with them. When the most radical prisoners wanted to riot over the quality of the food, Márcio convinced them not to.[13]

In late 1971, as Márcio worked on the correspondence course, a solicitous judge arranged for his transfer to a rural prison at the town of Neves, Minas Gerais. The judge had perhaps learned of Márcio's moderation and likely had the support of the military's own moderates in effecting the transfer. "We believe that you are above all an entrepreneur," one major confided, in Márcio's recollection. Neves was less harsh. It had a soccer field and even a cinema. Márcio worked as a librarian, then in the pharmacy. He spent many hours in the radio repair shop, fixing things for free for the prisoners. He could use the skills he had learned in technical school as a teenager and honed as an employee of the Minas Gerais telephone company, Telemig, before his revolutionary activities. After Márcio's successful adaptation at Neves, the judge again intervened favorably. After agreeing not to participate in politics and to report to the police three times a week, Márcio won what he termed a "somewhat crooked" conditional release from prison in January 1973.[14]

I FIRST LEARNED ABOUT Márcio in an astonishing interview in 2001 with Ricardo Apgaua, a fellow local PCB member who had helped Márcio enter the Corrente. By 2001, Ricardo was a real estate agent in one of Belo Horizonte's upper-middle-class districts. Ricardo had developed an appreciative yet highly critical view of socialism, especially regarding its approach to economics. Eagerly flouting what he saw as some Brazilian leftists' dogmatic nationalism and socialism, Ricardo pointed to the economic inefficiencies of Allende's socialism in Chile. Ricardo unabashedly backed probusiness policies, saying that they did not have to diminish social justice and human rights. His former revolutionary comrades tagged him as a "neoliberal," a pejorative term for many on the Latin American Left. In Ricardo's view, they failed to comprehend that social conflict and class struggle were not the only paths to sociopolitical progress. He urged me to interview his longtime friend Márcio.[15]

Márcio displayed the typical personality of the *mineiro,* a person from Minas Gerais, a hilly region once rich in gold and diamonds still resplendent in iron ore and other key natural resources. Discreet and laconic like many mineiros, Márcio was an extremely private person. He refused to tell the story of his guerrilla past to the Brazilian press, and at first he seemed unwilling to speak with me. Extremely busy, he traveled frequently. I politely pressed for an informal, get-acquainted meeting. Finally, in mid-2002 we arranged to meet in Brasília, the ultramodern, rationally planned capital adorned with the masterpieces of Communist architect Oscar Niemeyer, one of the designers of the UN headquarters in New York.

Márcio came from humble origins in the interior, but he looked like one of the strikingly handsome actors in Brazil's world-class, prime-time soap operas. Tall with a good physique, he was white and had slightly wavy blonde hair, quite unusual in a country where most people had dark or tan skin (except for the south, which was populated with many people of Italian, German, and Polish extraction). The Lacerda family came from the north of Portugal, he explained, which had people of Germanic extraction.[16]

To our pricey lunch in Brasília, Márcio brought two cell phones. Phone-tapping had become a common part of Brazilian political intrigue, and, with his mineiro cautiousness and experience in telecommunications, Márcio played it safe by obtaining a second, secure phone for sensitive

matters. He was now in the national spotlight. He brought two newspaper articles and a magazine piece that identified him as the fundraiser
for presidential candidate Ciro Gomes, a young, outspoken defender of
Brazil's national interests and business community, representing the Partido Popular Socialista (Popular Socialist Party), the renamed but dwin-
dling PCB.

I interviewed Márcio during a weekend in 2003 and another in 2005,
both in Minas. We held additional, shorter meetings in 2004 in Brasília
and 2006 in São Paulo. Our final interview took place in Belo Horizonte
in 2015. For the first two interviews, in line with mineiro hospitality, I
stayed in the guest room of the family mansion on the outskirts of Belo
Horizonte, where Márcio lived with his wife, Regina, with space for the
extended family. A recent acquisition, the 10,000-square-foot home included an indoor swimming pool, a home theater, two offices, a banquet
area, and an exercise room where personal trainers met with family members. The home had a computerized system for security and climate control. From the living room, I could gaze at verdant mountains and valleys.
Like many well-off Brazilian families, they had a staff that included a cook,
drivers, and maids. The mansion was beyond the wildest dreams of most
Brazilians and even most Americans, but it wasn't ostentatious. Márcio
and Regina could easily have afforded something even bigger and more
luxurious. For years, they had lived austerely, plowing profits from their
two companies into business investments.[17] I joined Márcio, Regina, and
their three adult children for lunch and dinner, and Márcio and I relaxed
in the private sauna.

One evening, dispensing with his driver, Márcio drove me to the spots
in Belo Horizonte where he had carried out guerrilla actions and had ultimately been arrested. Whereas Márcio was the assailant in 1969, now as
a member of Brazil's socioeconomic elite he was a potential target. Brazil's
stark inequality hit home. To defend against armed robbery and kidnapping, Márcio's imported Audi had bulletproof windows, an accessory purchased in Brazil more than in any other nation.[18]

Another evening, at a wedding party for a young couple from the
mineiro elite, Márcio and I mingled with the upper crust, some of whom
were guiding Brazil into prosperity. We circulated among the other guests
on the grounds of the exclusive Belo Horizonte club and maneuvered our
way in the balmy night around elaborate decorations. Márcio introduced
me to Vice President José Alencar Gomes da Silva, a wealthy industrialist

from Minas and a member of the Liberal Party. I also greeted Frei Betto, at the time a special assistant to President Lula and whom I had first met in the early 1990s. Márcio seemed well-connected on both the Left and the Right. Diversity within the ALN once again influenced the path of its ex-combatants.

IN THE 1970S, Márcio attempted to reenter the telephone business as policymakers during the "economic miracle" embraced state-led crony capitalism and emphasized infrastructure projects and the expansion of middle-class housing. His entrée into telecommunications began long before the advent of cell phones, in a low-technology country with large numbers of households without access to residential landline telephones. Such was the situation throughout the developing world, which depended on American and European companies for telephone technology. Before the start of the dictatorship, only a small minority of Brazilians, mainly in large urban areas, had telephones. American and Canadian companies primarily controlled Brazil's telephone system, doing little to expand it. If a town had service, residents had to walk to a public telephone station to make calls.[19] Long-distance calls could take several hours to arrange. In Rio, almost all of the phone cables had deteriorated so much that lines went dead during rains.[20]

In 1980, Brazil still had just one home telephone for every 16 citizens, and only one public pay phone for every 2,291 inhabitants. (Brazil's 1960 and 1970 censuses did not include data on telephone ownership. By comparison, in 1980, 93 percent of U.S. households had a telephone.) Still, that represented progress. After 1964, the generals stimulated, coordinated, and standardized the dissemination of telephones and landline wiring, built a microwave transmission system to enable interstate communications, and, between 1975 and 1985, integrated a confounding patchwork of 862 small telephone companies into a national system with just 133 firms. Minas Gerais in particular underwent much centralization. Starting in 1974, Brazil's telephone system linked to INTELSAT, the International Tele-communications Satellite Organization, used to facilitate domestic long-distance calling.[21] Prior to 1964, some state governments had expropriated the holdings of the U.S.-based International Telephone and Telegraph (ITT) corporation, actions that created friction between the United States and Brazil. Despite the military regime's initial pro-American stance, in telecommunications it continued on a nationalistic path, acquiring ITT's holdings in Brazil and blocking proposals from ITT and a Japanese firm for other domestic projects. Under the military's expansion policy, despite the low number of household phones, by 1982 every Brazilian municipality had telephones. So did more than four thousand villages and rural areas.[22]

The generals wanted to maximize residential telephone coverage and make it affordable.[23] The military's involvement in telecommunications dated back to the late nineteenth century, when it played a critical role in extending the nation's telegraph system into Brazil's vast interior.[24] To regulate the expansion and establish firm political control, the dictators created several new governmental bodies. In 1965, they set up Embratel (the Brazilian Telecommunications Company). The opening of the Ministry of Communications in 1967 made telecommunications a cabinet-level matter. The key body for centralizing the phone system was Telebrás (Brazilian Telecommunications), a federal holding company set up in 1972 to oversee public and private initiatives. To encourage further technological progress in telecommunications-related areas, the government opened agencies to research computers (Cobra) and digital technology (Digibrás).[25] The government initially funded Telebrás with the staggering sum of $820 million. By 1974 it recorded an income of $585 million. By 1985 the figure had climbed to $2.44 billion. A World Bank report stated in 1984: "It is, by far, the largest telecommunications system in the developing world and the world's tenth largest."[26] In 1976 Telebrás created its own research arm, the Center for Research and Development, which sought to stimulate innovations in phone technology.[27] Nationalistic military officers played a big role in Telebrás and the other agencies. They sought to increase Brazil's industrial capacity to avoid importing telecommunications equipment, further reducing foreign firms' participation in the industry. Some of the military administrators worked for the same powerful intelligence services involved in the repression of the Left.[28] With an eye to both national security and business opportunities, Brazil also pursued an armaments industry, aircraft manufacturing, and nuclear energy capacity.[29]

Márcio, recognizing the country's deficits and both personally idealistic and professionally ambitious, faced an extremely complex challenge. After 1973, political liberalization and the rise of the nonviolent opposition provided entrepreneurial capitalists a greater chance of success. However, Márcio needed to maneuver through a nontransparent system steered by cronyism. Ultimately, he needed to find allies within that system who shared his goal of economic and technological development, turn that system to his advantage, and avoid abandoning his ideals. In effect, by seeking to competently expand phone service, he aimed to create an entrepreneurial version of the *movimento popular*, all while carrying the stigma of ex-political prisoner. In 1973, Márcio twice sought to return to his old job at Telemig, but intelligence officers entrenched in the federal bureaucracy blocked him. He found work at a financially shaky telephone installation and construction company.[30]

Márcio noticed a simple but significant gap in the burgeoning phone industry: a number of firms installed underground lines, aboveground lines, and street poles, but nobody specialized in installation of lines and telephones inside individual homes and businesses. With Regina as his partner, Márcio started a business to fill this niche. In 1967, Belo Horizonte, a city of about 1 million people, had only 20,000 telephones, mainly equipment from the 1930s and 1940s. In the early 1970s, Telemig aimed to install 100,000 telephones just in that one city. Márcio and Regina named their company Construtel, a name derived from the phrase "construção em telecomunicações" (telecommunications construction).[31]

"I didn't want to own a business," Márcio recalled. "I started my own business because they closed the doors." He commented: "I was married. I earned a good salary. But I was frustrated, because the company where I worked wasn't modern. I was studying business administration. I knew telecommunications. . . . I felt an enormous need to have a space where I could exercise my creativity, my own specific way of doing things."[32]

Márcio believed strongly that installers needed special training to serve residential and business consumers. He explained this to the Telemig executives. "Because of their lack of experience, they imagined that the same workers who installed the above- and belowground lines would also perform this other, more delicate service," Márcio explained. "I said, 'Look, that's not a good solution, because they are two different kinds of service. They're people with different qualifications. There is a different kind of training.'" A psychologist, Regina played a leading role in choosing Construtel employees. The company sought people "reliable from the standpoint of customer relations, capable of entering into people's residences without causing any difficulties and with ease of communication, skills, and willing to do manual work," Márcio said. "Because in Brazil . . . the prejudice against manual work still persists. Certainly thirty years ago . . .

it was very strong. In fact, when I left the interior saying that I was going to take a technical course at a time when people left only to become lawyers, doctors, and engineers, it kind of shocked people. They would say: 'Wow, you're going to get your hands dirty with grease?'"[33]

In mid-1975, Márcio and Regina sold two pieces of land to raise initial capital, and they hired sixty people. Construtel immediately won a contract with Telemig. It gained further stimulus from the fact that Telebrás's consolidation of the industry led to bigger firms. For them, Márcio's plans for large-scale installation made even more sense.[34]

However, with Geisel's liberalization still in its early phase and the hard-liners threatening to scuttle it, military intelligence took careful note of Construtel's presence in the market. To avoid political problems, Márcio and Regina registered Construtel in her and her brother's name. But Márcio's former boss at Telemig tried to get the company's contract canceled. "There's a Communist starting a business in a sensitive area," he was said to have told the authorities, as Márcio learned at the time. However, shielding Construtel against the military hard-liners, the air force general presiding over Telemig maintained the contract, with the recommendation that Márcio keep a low profile. Then a military prosecutor alleged that Márcio's release from prison was illegal. This was no small thing; another Corrente member had to return to prison after the Supreme Military Tribunal, the military's highest court, ruled against his special release. The Tribunal considered returning Márcio to prison, too. He went to Brasília to meet the judges, including the liberal-minded Gen. Rodrigo Otávio Jordão, whose son worked in telecommunications. Jordão supported Márcio, but he was just one vote. To avoid arrest in the event of a negative decision, Marcio went to Argentina to await the full Tribunal's judgment.[35] "I went to the worst place in the world to await the decision," Márcio reflected. "It was on the eve of the coup against Isabelita [Perón, the president of Argentina]. . . . I wouldn't be able to return to Brazil. I was going to have to seek asylum in an embassy. And it would have caused chaos here, because the company would have to continue operating, but Regina wasn't going to want to stay here without me."[36]

Regina visited the Tribunal judges to persuade them to vote in Márcio's favor. She obtained the assistance from a leading MDB congressman, Lysâneas Maciel, who lent his official car for making the rounds in Brasília. Before entering one notoriously lecherous judge's home, Regina grabbed a revolver from the trunk. "She entered the guy's house armed,"

Márcio remembered. "And at one point the guy, despite the fact that she was almost six months pregnant, gets up close to her and says, 'Ah! From what I hear, terrorists' girlfriends like sex a lot.' And she threatened him. She said, 'Don't get any closer or I will kill you.'"[37]

In February 1976, by a vote of 4–3, the Tribunal confirmed Márcio's freedom. However, his political problems continued. In Rio, a large group of military hard-liners in the local bureaucracy blocked Márcio from even registering to bid for telephone contracts. "Until the amnesty was approved [in 1979], I lived in a constant state of fright," Márcio recalled. Even into the early 1990s, Márcio continued to encounter resistance from military operatives.[38]

But Construtel thrived. Márcio found allies among the military engineers and telecommunications specialists who shared his patriotic vision of Brazil's technological future. They impressed him with their competence. Márcio explained:

> The regime had various facets. So you had to know the differences. The military wasn't a monolithic structure. I was dealing with military personnel from communications engineering in the air force, the army, and even the navy. These people were highly educated, and politically they did not identify with radicals of the cavalry. In other words, they had vision. . . . Not just professional vision. They included the best that the armed forces had to offer. . . . People of high intellectual level, technical training, national vision, patriotism, honesty. I didn't have to give a single penny to anybody in order to win my space. . . .
>
> What took place in the telecommunications field was an alliance among highly professional military personnel, technicians and nationalists, young engineers, good-natured executives, all with a goal of developing the country. So these people spent their time innovating and investing with the idea of development in mind. And despite my history of opposition to the regime and my imprisonment for violent actions, at bottom they sympathized with who I was. Why? They weren't the so-called mastodons or gorillas. The other day I was conversing with an admiral in Brasília, a highly educated man, who had just come back to Brazil after commanding an aircraft carrier that Brazil recently brought from France. . . . And he told me: "The irony of that period is that there were good people on both sides, and all of

them were interested in their country." I said: "You're right. We were victims of the Cold War."[39]

Márcio received vital support from a father of modern Brazilian telecommunications, Gen. José Antônio de Alencastro e Silva. A nationalist but coup opponent, Alencastro was labeled a Communist by radical right-wing elements of the regime. But he survived those accusations. A military engineer, Alencastro presided over Telemig from 1972 to 1974 and then Telebrás from 1974 to 1985. "He was very much inspired by Bell Labs," Márcio recalled. "He advocated for Brazil to set up the same thing. So he created the Center for Research and Development, based on the American experience." Years later, when President Figueiredo visited a telecommunications fair in Brasília, Alencastro steered him to Márcio's booth and enthusiastically endorsed his work.[40] "I wanted to help Márcio," Alencastro recalled. "I knew him as a very human person who, because of his independent political development, did not get a very good reception in his field of work. I made no distinction between a Márcio, a Pedro, a Paulo, a João, or anybody else as long as he showed himself capable of performing the work that we needed done. . . . Why block the way of a young man who had fought for his political ideals? It doesn't matter whether he was right or wrong. They were his ideals."[41]

Márcio and Regina worked to spread the word about Construtel's capabilities. In August 1976 they drove throughout Brazil, introducing themselves to local telephone company executives. "We drove more than five thousand miles in two weeks," Márcio remembered. Construtel received no contracts, but Márcio had made valuable contacts for future business. Shortly before the Tribunal's decision in early 1976, he had received a letter of inquiry from Telebrasília, the state telephone company in the capital. By year's end, Construtel had its second major contract. The demands for phones quickly reached fever pitch. "It was happening everywhere," Márcio remembered. "The country had gone many years without installing new lines." Márcio next conquered São Paulo state, the most powerful region of the South American economy. He used a letter of recommendation from Telebrasília. Márcio recollected: "I went to São Paulo in 1977, 1978, with the name of a contact. I called him from the airport. He said, 'Come on over and meet with me.' I got there and said, 'Look, you must be having some problems in installing new lines.' He said, 'I certainly am!' So I showed him the letter from Telebrasília, and I immediately got a con-

Figure 22. A Construtel worker in the early 1980s in the city of Ouro Preto, Minas Gerais. Márcio Araújo de Lacerda collection.

tract."[42] São Paulo was a mother lode for Construtel. In the 1980s, the company employed as many as three thousand people there. Construtel also entered the market in Rio de Janeiro, Pernambuco, and Mato Grosso.

Construtel was leaving its mark on Brazil: in the 1980s it became the country's largest installer of telecommunications networks.[43] Márcio gained prominence by helping Brazilians, dispersed over half a continent, come together as a modern nation. In 1989, Construtel expanded to Chile, later entering Argentina and Bolívia. In the late 1990s, Construtel and other businesses started by Márcio had annual revenues of more than $100 million.[44]

Márcio lived a paradox. He loved business, but he still adhered to many revolutionary ideals. And, although working with the military, he wanted a return to democracy. "For a long time, I lived enormous conflicts of conscience," he recalled, adding that he discussed his situation with a psychotherapist. "Sometimes I even had difficulty in getting close to the people who worked with me, because of those conflicts. With them I had a relationship of capitalist and worker. But once I resolved the conflict and was able to understand the difficulties I was having, I felt better."[45]

For Márcio, being an "entrepreneur" meant departing from traditional capitalism. One key influence was the American management specialist Peter Drucker. He read Drucker's *The Effective Executive* and *Managing for Results*, practical guides for businessmen that were translated into Portuguese and published in Brazil in the late 1960s. Drucker's writings helped Márcio understand the importance of a participatory business model. His experience as a political prisoner reinforced the focus on the business as a whole. "You can also be an entrepreneur by organizing an action that is more collective in nature," he said. "An entrepreneur in the sense of planning, organizing, executing, and controlling. Not necessarily in the sense of augmenting your capital. Because you can be an internal entrepreneur. While being an entrepreneur, you can be an executive, but not necessarily a stockholder. I always was able to separate my position as a stockholder from that as an executive. . . . I never felt as if I owned the bench where I worked, because for me a business is a social entity with a certain autonomy." According to Márcio, he accumulated profits not for personal benefit, but to keep Construtel on a constant curve of upward growth.[46]

Discouraging authoritarian attitudes at Construtel, Márcio built a new model for Brazilian business, one in which loyal workers meant higher productivity. In comparison with developed countries, urban workers in mid-twentieth-century Brazil labored in precarious conditions and earned miserably low wages. In the countryside, unskilled workers faced even harsher conditions, little better than what slaves had experienced. Both ignorant of better possibilities and demoralized by their struggle, most everyday Brazilians faced their station in life without active complaint. The hope of improving this situation had led young, idealistic people into the Corrente.[47] Once, after inspecting a Construtel installation job in the small city of Ipatinga, Márcio ate dinner with the team of thirty employees. "It got late," Márcio recounted. "I hadn't checked into any hotel. I said, 'Ah! I'll just sleep here.' So I got my bag. I got into one of the bunk beds in the workers' quarters and slept there with them. This was so extraordinary for them. They had never heard of a business owner sleeping in a bunk bed among the workers. And it wasn't at all demagoguery on my part, because I had been to prison and lived in student dorms and students' quarters at technical school. For me, it was something normal that a person would do." Márcio encouraged employees to join in decision-making and engage in constructive criticism. He also promoted corporate financial transparency, and he established a substantial profit-sharing program that favored the lowest-earning employees. The employee "doesn't want to be a number, a cog on the wheel," Márcio said. He rewarded employees based on merit, even when this meant bending or disobeying Brazil's paternalistic labor laws. "What used to exist was a paternalistic relationship, one where the kind father helped out his employees in moments of difficulty by giving a little bit here, a little bit there," Márcio explained. "Brazilians have always liked that kind of leader. Then, all of a sudden somebody comes along who, in addition to helping out in difficult moments and treating them well, tried to reward them based on merit. That was innovative." It also contradicted revolutionary notions of equality, which dictated that all workers receive the same pay.[48]

In 1977 AND 1978, while Márcio kept a low profile as an ex-political prisoner and focused on building Construtel, a small but prominent group of Brazilian business leaders joined the *movimento popular*. Like Márcio, business people in general had good personal connections with the military government, but they had little say in setting policy. Many business leaders still supported military rule, but the sense of exclusion helped push others into the opposition. As had Lula and the trade unions, businesses were also forming independent organizations to express their views more strongly. These efforts strengthened the prodemocracy movement.[49]

In 1979, Márcio founded another company, Batik. It developed a new technology "made in Brazil," a high-technology telephone exchange system using unique, low-cost, compact digital switching equipment. Batik helped challenge the foreign dominance of telephone equipment sales in Brazil.[50] In the 1970s and 1980s, digital switching equipment became the most attractive segment of the global telephone market. These systems worked faster and better and were easier to maintain than the much older electromechanical devices.[51] Batik was one of six Brazilian companies that produced the new digital systems. Four of them used technology developed by Telebrás's Center for Research and Development. Political concerns and budgetary limitations caused the launching of the Center's technology to fall behind by years. Foreign companies also continued to pressure, with success, for a substantial share of the Brazilian market. As a result, Telebrás fell far short of its goal of using only Center technology in Brazil's switching equipment, but the agency stimulated the creation of dozens of Brazilian companies and brought Brazil international recognition.[52]

Batik helped fill the technological gap left by the government. Independent of Telebrás's Center, it developed its own technology, entering the market with government approval.[53] To expand the telephone system into the many small towns of Minas Gerais, Telemig, strapped for funds, had pulled out of storage old German-made mechanical telephone switching systems from the 1930s. These would not do for modern telecommunications, so Telemig requested bids to convert them into the standard electromechanical telephone exchanges. This helped stimulate the idea for Batik. Renato Vale, a former political prisoner, had some expertise in telecommunications. He suggested to Márcio that they take on the business of building the electromechanical trunk lines for Telemig. Márcio, Renato, and a third partner, Francis Lopes, started Batik in a garage at the back of the Construtel property. Márcio underwrote Batik with a large amount of Construtel capital. Rushing to register the company, Márcio chose the name "Batik" on the spur of the moment as he walked through a famous street fair in Belo Horizonte where artisans displayed their batik-like creations. The word echoed the first two syllables of the Portuguese word *batimento*, or "beat," which was also a technical word Márcio had learned in studying electronics. "Francis was very good in electronics, and Renato knew telecommunications signaling," Márcio remembered. "I had the money, the infrastructure, and the will to build an industrial enterprise." They won a contract with Telemig and soon began supplying phone companies in other Brazilian states facing the same technological deficit.[54]

Significantly, Batik moved beyond electromechanical technology. Born at the dawn of the microprocessor era, it pioneered using that technology in telephone exchanges in Brazil's small towns. The microprocessors allowed the equipment to perform a vastly greater number of operations, and more complex ones. Except for the processors, Batik produced everything locally. Batik employed Brazilian university computer scientists as consultants. It also set up a research laboratory and master's degree program in telecommunications software at the local federal university. "Because we were already making all the electronic parts for the electromechanical exchange, I thought, 'Why not make a completely electronic exchange?'" Márcio said. "The small-size exchanges of that era, the ones with 50, 100, or 200 lines, were all still electro-mechanical. . . . And no manufacturer, not even the multinationals, had a completely electronic [small-size] exchange in Brazil. Only the large-size ones." Without receiving any direct subsidies, Batik beat to the punch a Brazilian government project seeking to develop a similar technology with millions of dollars of public assistance. "You've got an exchange with 256 lines," Márcio explained regarding Batik's new technology. "So, with the model we made, you can put one next to it, then another, and then another, each one complete with all of the elements and with one processor communicating with another, in a network. This was not a model with the giant, central processor controlling all of the functions of an exchange. It was a model with a *network* of processors. This was its originality." To make the expansion financially viable, Batik signed agreements with municipalities and received payments directly from customers.[55] In Minas Gerais, Batik designed an initiative called Project Bandstand, which installed the local telephone exchange underneath the traditional bandstand located in the town square, the center of civic attention. The bandstands protected the equipment from the elements.[56] "It was a marketing success," Márcio said of the new technology. "And we took the market for small exchanges away from the multinationals."[57]

Batik established exchanges in thousands of towns and cities. It helped usher Brazil into a new era, transforming the telephone from a big-city luxury into an item of middle-class necessity. Before Batik's telephone exchanges, people in a small town might wait hours to make a call. Now they could do it immediately, explained Marcello Guilherme Abi-Saber, a former Corrente member who had regularly visited Márcio in prison (but denied him the gun and money he wanted for an escape), and who wound up working for both Construtel and Batik.[58] Márcio reminisced:

I had a very good feeling about developing something. A telephone exchange is something that's almost alive. It has to function twenty-four hours a day, seven days a week, for twenty years. It's a piece of equipment that never stops. When it does stop, it's chaos. So it's got to be of high quality. . . .

[At Batik] you took on a project, developed it, manufactured it, and took it to get installed and up and running in a city. You got to see the local populace take part in it through the community project. The telephone system is something that very intensely affects the lives of people. So, in addition to the technological aspect and the money earned, it was satisfying to be providing a service in the public interest.[59]

Figure 23. Márcio (center) explains Batik technology to Vice President Aureliano Chaves, with, at far left, Congressman Paulino Cícero and business leader Stefan Salej looking on at a technology fair, circa 1982–83. At the far right is Paulo Slander, a Telemig executive. The man at Márcio's immediate right is unidentified. Márcio Araújo de Lacerda collection.

Figure 24. The Batik factory floor in the late 1980s. Márcio Araújo de Lacerda collection.

Márcio, Ricardo, Renato, and Marcello were not the only ex-revolutionaries to go into business. Percival Maricato, who gave up a comfortable middle-class existence as a drug company salesman in São Paulo to join the ALN because of its call for national liberation, was brutally tortured and spent two years in prison. After his release in 1973, he entered the restaurant business. He later established a successful legal practice, representing a variety of clients, including unions and environmentalists. Politically, Percival aligned himself with the MDB. He joined other progressive-minded entrepreneurs seeking to humanize capitalism and emphasize human solidarity. He saw no contradiction in being a capitalist with a social conscience. "I consider myself a social democrat more than anything else," he observed. "I believe socialism is the ideal system, but I don't think humans are prepared for it. In fact, back in those days I very much thought this way already. Because humans are egotistical, they're impatient, and they're hardly unselfish. Only a minority is unselfish. So it's no use wanting a system that people won't accept."[60]

Whereas Márcio and Percival embraced business, other ex-ALN members entered the private sector out of necessity. Maurice Politi, an Egyptian-born Jew and political prisoner in São Paulo, went into exile in Israel in 1975. After marrying and starting a family, he was anxious to return to his adopted country and live close to his wife's homeland, Argentina. He worked as an executive for Société Générale de Surveillance (SGS), the Swiss-based multinational product and business accreditation service, landing a position in São Paulo. When they arrived in Brazil, his wife was pregnant with their second child. "I had to start there and earn money to support my family," Maurice remembered. "I lived in a one-bedroom apartment that my father had, but with no furniture. . . . I entered the world of business in order to survive."[61] After his retirement in 2007, Maurice dedicated himself to raising awareness about the dictatorship's atrocities, including a year working in the national Secretariat for Human Rights.[62]

Manoel, the man who wounded the U.S. ambassador, resumed his truncated career in public relations. Because a condition of his release from prison required a commitment of employment, Manoel got a cousin in the business to promise a job. The cousin was José Carlos Cavalcante Mendonça, known as Duda Mendonça, one of Brazil's most successful public relations men at the time and later its best-known political image-maker.

Moved by Manoel's struggle, Duda supported the 1979 amnesty campaign by signing a petition and fashioning an international-award-winning ad for the campaign.[63] The position had the added advantage of being in Manoel's home state of Bahia, far from the main guerrilla circuit of Rio and São Paulo. Manoel's success reflected the continuing importance of family ties in Brazil and Manoel's (and most other guerrillas') middle-class status. Even though the revolutionaries claimed to speak for the lower classes, they used class connections to rebuild their lives after defeat. Brazil remained a society of inequality and privilege. A ten-year prison term would have severely restricted most people's professional and social prospects. However, Manoel had a high profile as a political prisoner. For the Brazilian Left, there was no shame in his actions. The job with Duda eased his transition to life in society.

I found from my survey of twenty-six other former ALN militants that five worked as small business operators. Others entered a variety of fields: four engineers, two doctors, two economists, and teachers and university professors.

THE FORMER ALN militants who entered private business exemplified once again the diversity of ideas about revolution within the ALN and in the paths chosen after the defeat of violent resistance.

Márcio achieved a unique feat in the history of Brazil's revolutionaries: without firing a shot, he produced better lives for many by creating jobs. In an ironic twist of the dictatorial era, Márcio collaborated with the military's nationalistic, technologically oriented sectors to massively expand key infrastructure. His work facilitated a common goal of the Brazilian Left and Right: consolidating Brazil as a nation-state. Rapidly conquering new markets, Márcio became wealthy pioneering a new era of Brazilian capitalism. The rise of telecommunications helped make Brazil a modern consumer society, but residential home phones remained a privilege of the middle and upper classes.[64] (As General Alencastro observed in 1990, Brazil had failed to achieve the goal of universal landline telephone service—an important indicator of modern development.[65])

In his entrepreneurial evolution, Márcio tried to preserve many egalitarian ideals of the revolution. Frequently, authoritarianism and corporatism—a model of society as a body in which all parts work together under the direction of the head—have marked the political culture of Latin America. This combination made Latin American political and business relations highly paternalistic.[66] Many Latin Americans struggled to shed this ethos. Márcio represented a new generation of Brazilian business people, workers, and public administrators who rejected authoritarianism and deemphasized corporatism. Though Márcio helped bring modern business culture to Brazil, Construtel and Batik were born within the old system and benefited from it. The companies did not receive direct financial assistance from the state, but one of Batik's early investors was the government's national development bank. Telebrás nurtured the environment in which Márcio's and numerous other private telecommunications companies could flourish, shielded at least partially from foreign competition. As in so many instances in history—including the case of the United States—in Brazil a *state-led* capitalist system used government support for vital infrastructure to spur economic growth and produce private capitalist success. The state-led system meant mixed results for the overall economy. On the one hand, it stimulated the creation of much industry and infrastructure. On the other hand, the apex of this model in the 1970s coincided with the initial shrinkage of Brazil's industrial sector (deindustrialization), because it seemed to harm long-term private investment.[67] Nevertheless, Márcio and his business collaborators contributed to the erosion, albeit ever so slightly, of crony capitalism by helping to introduce technological innovation and entrepreneurial thinking.

PART III

RULE

CHAPTER 10

From Bullets to Ballots

President Figueiredo took office in 1979 committed to President Geisel's political opening but with only a vague promise to "make Brazil a democracy."[1] Geisel had added a year to his successor's term, extending Figueiredo's potential time in office to 1985 and dictatorial rule to a total of twenty-one years. The PCB and the MDB advocated for a unified opposition to push for a peaceful end to the dictatorship. The *movimento popular*, the independent union movement, and other factions were positioned to join the united front. To preempt such unity, the generals adopted a divide-and-conquer strategy. By declaring the 1979 Amnesty Law and allowing the return of exiles and the release of political prisoners, the government increased the number of its opponents. This heightened the possibility of infighting on the left.

In November 1979, the government reinforced this strategy by reforming the party system. It abolished the National Renovating Alliance and the MDB and allowed new parties to form. Most of the National Renovating Alliance members and other prodictatorship politicians entered the Partido Democrático Social (PDS, Social Democratic Party), which, despite its name, maintained a conservative outlook.

This all fostered a party system that became a confusing alphabet soup that continues to this day. As expected, the Left splintered into a series of smaller parties. The MDB became the Party of the Brazilian Democratic Movement (PMDB). The PMDB attracted many followers, but so did the newly formed Partido Popular (PP, Popular Party), the Partido Trabalhista Brasileiro (PTB, Brazilian Labor Party), and the Partido Democrático Trabalhista (PDT, Democratic Labor Party). The PCB, the PC do B, and other, smaller communist parties remained illegal but worked within the legal parties. The PCB and the former members of the revolutionary MR-8, in particular, worked within the PMDB. Another significant leftist party, the Partido dos Trabalhadores (PT, Workers' Party), emerged under Lula's leadership. It attracted people from the unions, the grassroots church communities, the intelligentsia, and the former revolutionary Left. However, many ex-revolutionaries joined the PDT and other parties. (My survey of twenty-six former ALN members demonstrated that fifteen affiliated with the PT at one time or another. Five had belonged to the PCB at some point. Three had affiliations with the PMDB, two the Partido Verde [Green Party], one the PDT, and one the PSDB. Six professed no party affiliation. Some switched parties.) The government and its right-wing political allies in the PDS, who formed the largest single political force as guaranteed by the regime, easily outmaneuvered the opposition parties to build a commanding majority in the Congress. In yet another political manipulation, the government postponed the municipal elections of 1980 for two years.

In April 1980, Lula led yet another wave of strikes. The strikes involved fewer people than the 1979 walkouts but were better organized. In São Paulo, the grassroots church communities and the Church leadership lent their full support. The military government harshly repressed the strikes, using armored vehicles and helicopters and arresting workers and even lawyers who supported the strikers. Lula was arrested, held at the DEOPS for a month, and removed from the union leadership. The 1980 strikes, embodying working-class resistance to the dictatorship, became a key reference point in the nonviolent struggle for democracy.[2]

A slowing economy combined with rising inflation increased the pressure for strikes in the late 1970s and early 1980s. Under Figueiredo, the economy performed poorly. After the global spike in oil prices and interest rates in 1979, Brazil's foreign debt ballooned to $100 billion, among the world's highest. In late 1982, the government declared that Brazil was close to insolvency. Seeking relief, it renegotiated the debt with the politically unpopular International Monetary Fund, the virtual representative of the U.S. and European powers, which could prescribe onerous financial solutions. In 1983, inflation reached 211 percent and unemployment rose, plunging the country into recession.[3] Brazil restricted imports and boosted exports. To cover trade deficits and alleviate the foreign debt, it devalued the *cruzeiro* by 30 percent. The government also controlled wages and credit and increased taxes.[4] In 1983, a general strike involving an estimated 2 million to 3 million employees became a virtual national day of protest.[5] The economic crisis led the Figueiredo government to slow infrastructure expansion, the pride of Médici and Geisel and entrepreneurs, such as Márcio. By 1984, insufficient telecommunications investment slowed telephone expansion, causing a shortfall of 1 million lines in Brazil's urban areas. Whenever subscriptions for new lines were announced, prospective buyers formed long lines at telephone company offices. A vigorous black market sprang up, with sellers charging several thousand dollars per number.[6]

The outlook for democracy appeared grim. Resisting the political opening, the military hard-liners hoped to extend dictatorial rule beyond Figueiredo. Right-wing terrorists attacked newsstands that sold left-wing newspapers. A secretary at the Brazilian Bar Association was killed by a letter-bomb sent by such terrorists. However, on April 30, 1981, an army captain and sergeant linked to the intelligence services botched a terrorist attack at Rio's Riocentro convention center, where 20,000 people had gathered for a party to celebrate May 1, Labor Day. The soldiers' bomb accidentally exploded in their car, killing the sergeant and seriously wounding the captain. The Riocentro incident turned the political tide against the hard-liners. Right-wing terrorist attacks halted. The push for a return to civilian rule gained momentum.[7]

In the highly anticipated 1982 election, the opposition parties collectively garnered more votes than the PDS, which nevertheless still remained the largest party and, forming an alliance with the moderate PTB, maintained its majority in the Congress. The PDS also continued to dominate the electoral college (as defined and manipulated by the dictatorship), scheduled to meet in January 1985 to choose the next president— again with no popular vote. However, in 1983 and early 1984, the *movimento popular* mushroomed into urban street protests involving millions of people who demanded *diretas já* (direct presidential elections *now*). These were the largest protests in Brazilian history up to that moment. The *diretas já* campaign suggested that the masses might triumph over militarism. Utterly nonviolent, it captured the people's imagination in a way that the guerrillas had failed to achieve in 1969. Expectations for a return to full democracy ran high. However, in April 1984 the constitutional

amendment for a direct election failed to achieve the two-thirds vote necessary for passage in the Chamber of Deputies. The PDS had prevailed,
dashing the people's hopes. The Brazilian populace acquiesced in the decision, conducting no further protests.

Instead of an election, the stage was set for a transition to civilian rule
via negotiations among the military and political elite.

As BRAZIL LURCHED toward a potential democracy, the former ALN revolutionaries sought to reaffirm themselves professionally and politically.
They still shared the common goal of removing the dictatorship. However,
with the return of parties and civil liberties, peaceful political action became the norm. Elections became the new arena of struggle, and control
of governmental institutions the new goal. Some former revolutionaries
aspired to positions of leadership, including public office. Instead of bullets, they now focused on ballots.

The former ALN members differed in their views of democracy,
capitalism, and vision for Brazil's future. In the new electoral system, this
meant that they sometimes competed with one another.

Building on its electoral victories as the old MDB, the PMDB
emerged as the largest, initially most influential of the new antidictatorship parties. Its rising stars included Franco Montoro, elected governor of
São Paulo by an overwhelming margin in the 1982 election, and Fernando
Henrique Cardoso, who, having qualified as a senatorial substitute in the
1978 election, assumed Montoro's seat in the Senate in March 1983.

Via the PMDB, former exile Aloysio quickly emerged as one of Brazil's new political leaders. Through old contacts he joined a research project
on Brazilian federalism. He also worked as a lawyer, his chosen career before the ALN. He obtained a master's degree in law at the USP, working
nights as a teaching assistant. In 1981, he became a state's attorney for the
state of São Paulo, primarily serving as a public defender. Aloysio also focused on rebuilding the PCB. Despite attacks on the leftist press by right-
wing militants, he helped run a new, nationally distributed party newspaper
called *A Voz da Unidade* (*The Voice of Unity*), an echo of the united front
strategy. "I reentered the PCB and the MDB, as all of us Communist militants were doing," Aloysio observed. "There was no contradiction. And
within the MDB, we showed the greatest openness. We Communists were
the ones who thought that we should accept [into the MDB] anybody

who was against the regime, for whatever reason." Aloysio also helped nurture the newly formed PMDB. On Friday afternoons, he left work in São Paulo to drive almost three hundred miles to his hometown of São José do Rio Preto (hereafter referred to as Rio Preto), in the northwestern part of the state. There he spent the weekends setting up a local section of the party, aiming to "redemocratize" the country. "There I was known and had a circle of my friends and my father's friends," Aloysio recalled.[8]

In 1982, Aloysio won a seat in the Assembléia Legislativa de São Paulo (São Paulo State Assembly) on the PMDB ticket. In Brazilian legislatures, representatives are not chosen from a specific district, but from a general pool of candidates from the entire city or state, but many politicians do indeed have a geographical base of support. Aloysio's father contributed substantially to the campaign and arranged for critical support from allies around Rio Preto.[9] (Aloysio also continued in the still illegal PCB.) His centrist stance contrasted with what he viewed as the PT's more sectarian approach. The PT attracted more radical former ALN members and was less interested in alliances with centrists. Aloysio observed:

> The Montoro government had to live with [President] João Baptista Figueiredo. It was a very tense and delicate situation. From our perspective it was important to maintain the unity of everybody who wanted to redemocratize the country, a *wide-ranging* redemocratization. Unity within the party, that was the principal instrument of redemocratization, the PMDB. . . . At that time the PCB was also taking on—at least in the very strong faction of the PCB with which I was affiliated in São Paulo—democracy as a permanent value, and an appreciation for the institutional aspects of the democratic system, something not so appreciated by the PT, because of its extreme leftist elements.[10]

In what would become a hallmark of his career, Aloysio had begun to advocate for strong political and governmental institutions.

Building a statewide political following, Aloysio rose into the PMDB leadership. As a legislator, he focused on remedying the ecological devastation caused by the industrial and population boom in the greater São Paulo area. He created and led the Permanent Committee for the Defense of the Environment, addressing sanitation and land use.[11] Governor Montoro selected Aloysio as leader of the PMDB bloc in the state assembly.

Figure 25. A state assemblyman and rising star in the PMDB in the 1980s, Aloysio (left) had contact with top party leaders, such as Fernando Henrique Cardoso (right). Aloysio Nunes Ferreira Filho collection.

With thirty-eight of seventy-seven seats, it was the largest bloc.[12] "The leader commands all of actions of the bloc in the state assembly," Aloysio explained. "He discusses the bills that are going to be voted on and seeks to define the bloc's position on the votes. In a large bloc this is not an easy task, because it has lots of wings."[13] As the PMDB leader, Aloysio became a member of the party's state-level executive commission. He rose to the position of secretary-general, renewing contact with Fernando Henrique and meeting other key PMDB leaders.[14] He traveled around the state and did media interviews. He participated in the governor's weekly staff meetings covering finances, social issues, infrastructure, and economic development. Aloysio also aided Montoro in pushing the *diretas já* campaign and was "was intensely involved in mobilizing people and building alliances."[15]

LULA AND THE founders of the PT were skeptical of the transition to civilian rule and the type of representative democracy envisioned. According to its Charter of Principles, through the electoral process the party aimed to establish a socialist system with "a government of the workers."[16] Events elsewhere could be seen as empowering workers. In 1979, supported by Cuba, the leaders of the Nicaraguan Revolution installed a socialist government in that country. In a very different setting, the following year the Solidarity movement in Poland demonstrated the power of worker protest against the Communist state under the leadership of Lech Walesa, an electrician. In Brazil, the workers' power increased under the leadership of a uniquely Brazilian creation, the PT, an unusual alliance of independent union leaders, former Marxist-Leninist revolutionaries, Trotskyist groups, and radical Catholic activists.[17]

Lula became a national figure. In some ways, he fit the ideal profile sought by many ex-revolutionaries: a person of humble origins rising up to challenge the dictatorship and Brazil's oppressive socioeconomic system. Furthermore, one of Lula's brothers belonged to the PCB and had been tortured. However, contrary to his image at the time, Lula himself was emphatically not a revolutionary—perhaps not even a leftist.[18] "Lula's the type who, when he talks about us, the picture he had of us when he saw the 'wanted' signs for the terrorists was: 'No. They really are terrorists [laughter]. The sooner they are captured, the better for Brazil, because Brazil will be on the right path,'" Paulo Vannuchi observed. "It's the hard realization of how disconnected the vanguard, which fought heroically and fulfilled important roles, was from the masses and their understanding of things."[19] In his youth, Lula viewed the 1964 coup favorably. Whereas other Brazilians protested and took up arms to oppose the dictatorship in the late 1960s, he initially showed no interest in politics.

Lula's formative experience came from his work in factories and his role as a union leader negotiating with capitalists, not fighting to eliminate them. Despite the military repression, the São Paulo labor aristocracy that he led benefited from economic growth. Lula emerged *after* the worst repression ended and President Geisel's decision to start restoring civil liberties. Because of Lula's stance, the PT presented far less a threat to the capitalist system than its rhetoric indicated. Unconcerned with ideology, Lula projected the PT as a new development in Brazilian society that sought to bypass traditional ideologies and political practices. Indeed, although Lula led massive strikes, his "new unionism" movement rejected the government-controlled labor system and fought to negotiate freely with employers, a central characteristic of modern capitalism. On this point, Lula coincided with key business leaders, who belonged to the country's most prominent chamber of commerce and industry, the Federação das Indústrias do Estado de São Paulo. Moreover, the PT emerged within the framework of a party reform designed by the military—not outside the system, as the revolutionaries had attempted. Lula and ex-revolutionaries formed an alliance to defeat the dictatorship and build a new party. Whereas the ex-revolutionaries offered the party their professional and organizational skills, Lula as party leader mediated among the various factions, always avoiding doctrinaire positions.[20] His leadership neutralized the more radical plans for Brazil's socioeconomic transformation. He and the unionists accepted revolutionary rhetoric and socialist goals, but the party put forth no concrete plans for the kind of socialism it desired or the means to achieve it, and it had no answers for key questions, such as the fate of the legal system. More than ideology, it was the action of the unions, the social movements, and the grassroots church communities that guided the party.[21] The emphasis on action in some ways resembled the strategy of the ALN. Brazilian political and institutional pragmatism had come into play.

Although not revolutionary, the PT was crucial to Brazil's democratization in the early 1980s. It innovated politically with its emphasis on workers' interests, internal democracy, and accountability to members. The party sought to change society from the bottom up and to instill notions of effective citizenship and democratic participation. It roundly rejected elite political negotiation to solve Brazil's problems. Because of these multiple goals, the early PT existed as both movement and party. More than any other party, the PT tapped into the enthusiasm and innovation of the *movimento popular*. It attracted tens of thousands of young, idealistic militants dedicated to ending the dictatorship and building social justice. Whereas the Elbrick kidnappers and their comrades in arms had failed to galvanize the nation in the late 1960s and early 1970s, the PT members worked tirelessly to win over the populace. Nevertheless, intraparty tensions developed between the emphases on mass mobilization and institutional, representative politics.[22] Moreover, political reality would have a moderating influence on the PT as it learned how to administer Brazil's governmental institutions.

For Adriano and Arlete, the São Paulo activists, political moderation began with their decision to join the party. They were steeped in the radical currents of the *movimento popular*, and they distrusted the PMDB. Initially, they also thought that the PT might indeed be too moderate. "We were very suspicious," Adriano recalled, "that the PT, at the time it was being founded, could become another bourgeois party like the MDB, although the PT had its origins in the workers' struggles." Their suspicions also flowed from "the influence the ALN had on us and because of the tougher opposition of the [local] metalworkers, who at first were against the creation of the PT. . . . We had been influenced by that group, which we did political work with in the factories in Mooca." However, when the Diogos learned that former ALN members, other ex-revolutionaries, and former student radicals were helping to organize the PT, they decided to join.[23]

The founding members of the PT included Marighella's widow, Clara Charf, and José Dirceu de Oliveira e Silva (hereafter referred to as Dirceu). One of the most prominent of the 1960s student leaders, Dirceu had been among the fifteen political prisoners released in exchange for Ambassador Elbrick's freedom. Dirceu went to Cuba, where he joined the ALN. He left for the dissident MOLIPO (Movement for Popular Liberation), a small group that emphasized renewing the fight in Brazil. Dirceu underwent plastic surgery to make his face less recognizable. In 1971, he returned to Brazil clandestinely in MOLIPO's ill-fated attempt to reinforce the armed struggle. One of the few to survive the onslaught against MO-LIPO, he assumed a new identity, working as a clothing salesman in a small town in the southern state of Paraná, where he married and had a son. With the declaration of the 1979 amnesty, Dirceu went to Cuba to reverse his surgery. In Brazil, he reassumed his original identity and immediately reentered politics. In January 1980, he met Lula, who invited him to join the PT. Dirceu quickly established himself as a key advisor to Lula. Seeking to steer the PT toward electoral success, in the 1990s and 2000s Dirceu strove to remove its extreme-Left elements.[24]

The party developed thanks to its members' efforts to attract new members and become involved in campaigns and local government. To that end, Adriano and Arlete helped set up a party branch in the Mooca region, first focusing on recruitment.[25] In 1982, Adriano worked on the successful campaign of Luiza Erundina de Sousa, one of the PT's most radical activists, for São Paulo's city council. To escape military repression, Erundina had migrated from the Northeast to São Paulo in 1971. With strong ties to the progressive Church, she threw herself into São Paulo's *movimento popular*. "I worked for her like crazy," Adriano remembered. Erundina made Adriano an aide. Erundina practiced a proactive form of civil disobedience. "She was the councilwoman of the favela people and of the land invasions," Adriano continued. "That was her motto." Adriano worked side by side with Erundina as she helped poor families resist eviction from favelas and squatter settlements. Whenever they failed to get eviction orders suspended, they joined affected families in confronting the police carrying out the orders. Once, Erundina, Adriano, and local residents blocked police from entering a favela for forty-eight hours.[26] Their actions paralleled a growing rural squatters' movement and efforts to protect native peoples and settlers in the Amazon and other regions.

Erundina and Adriano also collaborated with families aiming to set up new squatter settlements. Adriano recalled one episode in the distant Itaquera district, where middle-class residents threatened to torch the squatters and the moving trucks delivering their belongings. For two weeks, the squatters had to take refuge in a day care center. "Every weekend she took part in an invasion," Adriano recalled. "We would get arrested every weekend and then released. Every weekend she would get in trouble, always with the help of priests, with nuns."[27] Adriano ran the risk of reprisal from the same repressive system that had imprisoned him and continued to closely monitor the opposition. After one particularly brutal skirmish, Adriano and Erundina suffered heavy bruises from the blows of billy clubs.[28]

Despite the tumultuous tactics, Adriano and Arlete gained valuable lessons in institutional politics. Adriano recollected: "We started to learn how to . . . elect city councilors, representatives, senators, governors. How a party is formed, a legal party with a strong influence of the Catholic Church." His four years on Erundina's staff were insightful: "I learned that stuff, first about legality, the new rules, what it meant to be a representative. And, second, the legality of being linked to a movement. How to be a representative connected to the *movimento popular*. It was a beautiful time because it was when the campaign for direct elections was being organized."[29] Adriano also produced reports for key council investigations spearheaded by Erundina. The inquiries aimed at improving housing conditions for the poor and preventing floods in their neighborhoods.[30]

The PT dominated Adriano's and Arlete's lives. With their young daughter, Janaína, tagging along, every Saturday they attended daylong meetings. "I'll never forget one Mother's Day when I was elected in my region as the delegate to the Unified Workers Central congress," Arlete remembered. "I went to the congress instead of spending the day with Janaína. . . . Our lives as militants involved extreme sacrifices. . . . I had to do it all myself—mother, wife, and militant. Experience had made me tough as steel. How was I going to retreat now?"[31]

As THE PT grew, militant Paulo Vannuchi, a founding member of the party, took part in a simple yet brilliant clandestine project to demoralize the dictatorship. More ingenious than the Elbrick kidnapping, the project did not involve guns, but documents. Some of its few plotters took advantage of the bureaucratic routine of the Brazilian army. Though the risks were huge, participants were so vigilant that the ruthless intelligence and security services suspected nothing. The project aimed to expose the dictators' modus operandi—torture—to the Brazilian people with irrefutable evidence. Paulo—a foiled revolutionary and victim of torture—gained a second chance to create a revolution. This time it would be a revolution in human rights echoing indignantly throughout Brazil with the words "torture never again."

The project was known as "Brasil: Nunca Mais" (BNM, Brazil: Never Again). It was conceived by Archbishop Dom Paulo and Presbyterian pastor Jaime Wright, the Brazilian-born son of American missionaries. Pastor Wright's brother, Paulo Stuart Wright, a politician-turned-revolutionary, disappeared in 1973. Beginning in late 1979, BNM lawyers, who also represented political prisoners, obtained legal, routine twenty-four-hour access to the military tribunal court documents kept on file with the Supreme Military Tribunal, in Brasília. (The same body had approved Márcio Lacerda's release from prison.) Nearby, BNM set up an office with several photocopy machines. Over the next several years, with the machines running constantly, the project managed to copy 707 court cases involving cases of subversion and torture—nearly a million pages. In numerous trips by plane and bus, BNM couriers transported the documents to São Paulo. Microfilms of the documents were sent to Europe as a backup.[32] The cases included detailed testimony given by political prisoners about torture, the perpetrators, and the interrogation centers, including the São Paulo unit where Elbrick kidnapper Jonas and Alexandre Vannucchi Leme were killed. The ultimate goal was to publish evidence, produce a "reckoning with torture" and torturers as an act of "justice," and "to create a new humanity."[33]

The BNM team included journalists and others who organized, summarized, and analyzed the information about torture and torturers. Frei

Betto was an important writer. A key attorney was Luiz Eduardo Green-halgh, a defender of political prisoners and a leader of the amnesty movement. Both had ties to the PT.

In the words of Pastor Wright, Paulo was the "central figure" and "the man who conceived and directed the entire project." Paulo analyzed and summarized each of the 707 cases.[34] He also did the final rewrite and edit of the material to be published.[35] In a 2001 interview, Paulo offered his memories of BNM and the need for absolute secrecy:

> For many years the project worked with a very small team, fewer than ten people. And in the final phase, when there was an enormous quantity of material accumulated, we needed to hire about thirty, perhaps forty people. At that moment, we were more vulnerable. It's one thing to have half a dozen people, all of them knowing one another well and trusting one another. Later, when we had a group of forty, we had to recruit without knowing them very well. In that phase, we had to switch to three different locations quickly because there were suspicions. We had to exclude some people because they behaved strangely: "Could the police have infiltrated the team?" . . .
>
> I was working in two places: at Brazil: Never Again and at Sedes Sapientiae, in the same building. It was on two different floors, the Center for Popular Education was on the lower floor, and Brasil: Nunca Mais was on the upper floor. And when I told the team at the Center for Popular Education that I had to go out for a while, my colleagues got upset. They said that I shouldn't be absent, because our work was going well and I was an important part of the team. I had to say that I was going to work here [at BNM], but I couldn't tell them about the work. So I would say: "It's human rights research for the Archdiocese of São Paulo and involved the military regime, something very secret." And at that time people were sufficiently politically aware for them to just accept what I said, without asking questions. One or another were dying to know: "What is it? What is it really?" There was a program in that same period called Clamor [a project involving political exiles from other Latin American countries], and I lied to people to let them think that my work involved problems outside of Brazil. . . . Nobody found out. We didn't even tell our families. We also spoke to them about it in general terms. . . .

Then the PT was born, and it started to get organized. So I also had my political activity. And as an activist I was called upon to offer professional advice. So there came a moment when I also split my time. We also understood early on that Brazil: Never Again was something you couldn't work on all day long. It was something you gave just six hours to, because nobody could withstand more than that.

Participation in the BNM came at a great personal cost. Paulo recalled the effect of the intense work:

I have some side effects from Brazil: Never Again. I almost don't notice anything from torture, very little. I have a dislocation, and some back problems. Very slight. But at Brazil: Never Again I developed an allergy to photocopies and had to work for years wearing a mask, because otherwise I couldn't do it. My hand broke out in sores all over. It makes sense, because of the photocopy chemicals.... And all allergic reactions are psychosomatic. So it was evidently something that I, in doing that work, was reliving from all of those experiences I had lived. And that became an allergy. It gets into your skin. I had to use gloves, my skin all irritated from the inside out. And there was no way to avoid it. I needed to do the work. We had established goals. A certain number per week in order for the project to advance. So we said: "No, it's got to be no more than six hours per day."[36]

To use his grassroots political education in building the PT, Paulo took on an additional job as an aide to Devanir Ribeiro, a PT councilor on the São Paulo City Council. Paulo also began to specialize as a political analyst. In the early 1980s, he became an assistant at the PT's National General Secretariat. There, Paulo had his first contacts with Lula, the PT president.[37]

REFLECTING THE PLURALISM of the ALN and the diverse adaptations in the postrevolutionary period, other former militants looked beyond the PMDB and the PT.

After their release from prison in 1979, Jessie and Colombo reunited with their daughter Leta. Without jobs or college degrees, they took refuge in the working-class city of Volta Redonda, with the help of the local Catholic bishop, Dom Waldyr Calheiros de Novaes. Volta Redonda was the site of the government-owned Companhia Siderúrgica Nacional (CSN, or National Steel Factory). Located sixty-five miles from Rio, the city and its plant were hotbeds of union organizing and political activity. The dictators declared this strategic region an area of maximum interest for national security. A progressive and staunch defender of human rights, Dom Waldyr had clashed frequently with the military. As part of his pastoral outreach, he had visited Jessie and Colombo in prison every two weeks. In Volta Redonda, he offered them housing in a neighborhood with strong grassroots church communities, and he hired them to edit the local Catholic newspaper. However, local anti-Communist priests and nuns treated Jessie and Colombo with hostility because of the couple's support for the amnesty and the Nicaraguan Revolution. "They thought that the amnesty was a middle-class thing that workers had nothing to do with: those people of the armed resistance, the terrorists," Jessie remembered. "They thought: 'they're going to harm the standing of our bishop.'" Unable to fit in, Jessie and Colombo returned to Niterói, across the bay from Rio. To survive, Colombo worked various jobs, including construction (poorly paid in Brazil) and selling homemade jewelry at a street-side stand. Jessie worked for a left-wing magazine and studied for a bachelor's degree in history.[38]

In Niterói, a canvasser seeking signatures required to create the PT knocked on their door. Jessie recalled: "I said to Colombo: 'Let's sign up. At least we'll be helping to bring into existence one more party.'" Disorganized and weak, the Niterói section founders cast about for leadership and convinced Colombo to be their first president. However, they thought that the party in Rio de Janeiro state lacked a sufficiently progressive agenda.[39] As a result, Jessie and Colombo started gravitating toward the PDT (Democratic Labor Party), albeit more with an eye to its impressive politicians rather than to the party organization. In a reflection of how personal connections and regional diversity affected political paths, most former ALN revolutionaries in Rio also opted for the PDT. They included Carlos Eduardo Fayal de Lyra, who took a leading role in establishing the PDT locally.[40] Rio formed part of the political power base of the charismatic Leonel Brizola, the brother-in-law of deposed President Goulart and one of Brazil's leading nationalist politicians. As the governor of the state of Rio Grande do Sul in the early 1960s, Brizola took control of some

Figure 26. In 1971, President Médici visited the National Steel Factory in Volta Redonda, an area of national security and hotbed of political activism. Iconographia.

public utilities owned by U.S.-based multinational corporations, including ITT. In 1982, he won election as governor of Rio de Janeiro state. He used the position to rebuild his national political following, interrupted by the coup and fifteen years in exile (1964–79), spent mainly in Uruguay but also with travel in Europe and the United States. Under Brizola, the PDT adopted a European democratic-socialist stance combined with an emphasis on new Brazilian themes, such as fighting racism, child poverty and abandonment, and for women's rights and improvement of the educational system for the masses. The PDT advocated *socialismo moreno* (literally, dark-skinned socialism), a Brazilian brand of socialism.[41]

Colombo and Jessie supported José Juarez Antunes, the most prominent labor leader of the 1980s in Volta Redonda and a politician with independent, antidogmatic views. A veteran employee of the CSN, Juarez participated in the MDB starting in the mid-1970s. Colombo and Jessie met him in the broad-based amnesty movement of 1979.[42] "We were born on the left," Jessie remembered. "Suddenly we meet this person from a world very different from ours. . . . He also had never met anybody like us.

Because of that we developed a great friendship."[43] In 1980, Juarez ran unsuccessfully for the presidency of the Volta Redonda Metalworkers' Union, which included CSN's workers. Representing the PT, in 1982 Juarez lost a bid for the Rio de Janeiro State Assembly but used the campaign to expand his base among the workers. Because of his growing influence, the CSN fired Juarez. To continue the legal qualification as a metalworker required of union members, he took a job in a small backyard lathe shop.[44]

The next year, Juarez won the union presidency. Colombo assisted by putting Juarez in touch with left-wing politicians, who donated to the campaign. In June 1984, Colombo helped Juarez organize the first strike in the CSN since its launch in 1941. Twenty-two thousand workers walked off the job in a mainly symbolic sit-down action that broke the taboo against strikes in the highly sensitive area.[45] "The CSN lots its virginity," the workers quipped.[46] While the workers occupied the factory and kept its essential operations going, family members congregated outside. Thousands of local residents marched in the streets to support the strikers. When a group of union members influenced by radical Trotskyists wanted to shut down the blast furnaces—a highly risky procedure that could make the factory inoperative—Juarez convinced the majority of the workers to reject the plan. The government put the army on alert but did not send in troops. When local police arrived, the strikers prevented them from taking violent actions by offering them food and refreshments—which their superiors had neglected to provide—and engaging them in conversation. Colombo remembered:

> This was all happening in the heat of the *diretas já* campaign. Lots of enthusiasm.... From time to time Juarez came out to negotiate something, to make some contact, but most of the time he kept on inside. I was nearby coordinating the contact with the press, with our supporters, with all of those from many places who were in solidarity with us, and with what was being discussed outside the factory. The discussions were taking place both inside and outside the factory, and that influenced the leaders. Our role was to have their back and to discuss every move. It was a very explosive situation.... A strike controlled by the workers had never occurred. If anything went wrong, it would be disastrous for the entire country. Volta Redonda had a huge responsibility.

Five days into the strike, with the CSN's administrators mainly refusing to negotiate, Juarez called an end to the stoppage, with no material gains but proof that the workers could strike. He had emerged as a rival to Lula. "Lula is a guy who discovers politics by way of the union, while Juarez discovers the union by way of politics," Colombo observed. "Two inverse movements that arrived at the same point at the same moment."[47]

In Jessie's recollection, Colombo helped Juarez develop consistent positions and counteract the simplistic outlook of the younger, more radical union activists, such as the Trotskyists. "Because of that, he became the key political advisor to Juarez," Jessie recalled.[48] Complementing each other, the two men divided responsibilities. "The activists gravitated towards me and the masses around Juarez," Colombo remembered.[49] After the strike, Colombo formally joined Juarez's staff, commuting between Niterói and Volta Redonda. "I put out the bulletins," Colombo continued. "I did the newspaper. I coordinated the distribution of leaflets. I became the political point man in the union. The point man for contact with other movements, not just in the cities but around the country, in an integrated manner. There were few metalworker unions affiliated with the Unified Workers Central outside of São Paulo. Only a few went into the Workers Central without the support of us in the Volta Redonda union. Financial support, personnel, cars, support in any way possible." In 1985, Juarez quit the PT after it expelled delegates who voted against the party line in the indirect presidential election. "On that day, he no longer felt himself represented, nor representative, and soon he came into the PDT," Colombo recalled. "And Juarez was the second to become affiliated with the Unified Workers Central in Rio de Janeiro, but people looked askance at him, because he had quit the PT. . . . He didn't fit in anywhere. He transgressed equally on the right and on the left."[50]

That year, Jessie and Colombo also formally joined the PDT. In the 1985 Volta Redonda elections, PDT candidate Marino Clinger won the race for mayor. "We understood that we needed to take power in the city because the CSN had always dominated the mayor's office," Jessie observed. "It was necessary to have a mayoralty not linked to the company in order for you to have a very clear distinction of powers. The CSN is one thing, the union another, and the city yet another."[51]

Other ex-ALN members completely avoided party politics in the early 1980s. Márcio concentrated on business and his family. So did the one-time kidnapper Manoel Cyrillo. "I had been struggling for democracy," he recalled.[52] After the stresses of guerrilla warfare, torture, and prison, he believed that he had contributed enough of his life to politics. In Salvador, Bahia, he worked for his publicist cousin Duda Mendonça. He married Lúcia Cabral Jahnel, who had visited him regularly at the Barro Branco political prison. Lúcia later became a physicist. They had two daughters, born in 1981 and 1983. Manoel adopted his wife's daughter from her previous marriage to another man, who was an ALN member and a childhood friend of Manoel. His daughters occupied much of Manoel's free time, with weekly visits to the beach and the zoo. "When I left prison, I wanted to have children," Manoel remembered. "I wanted to have the opportunity to raise my children and create people with ideas in their heads that I thought were good. What I had wanted for my country I now wanted for my family. I wanted to be a model father."[53]

Carlos Eugênio, the gunman-turned-musician, left the PCB in 1978 while still in Paris studying under Doury. Whereas most exiled Brazilians hurried home after the 1979 amnesty, Carlos Eugênio went to Brazil only in 1981: his father was dying. Carlos Eugênio had not officially received amnesty. Moreover, the army convicted him in absentia of desertion for his 1969 abandonment of the Copacabana Fort to fight for the ALN. With a warrant issued for his arrest, Carlos Eugênio went underground again. In early 1982, he gained asylum in the French ambassador's residence in Brasília. With publicity in French and Brazilian newspapers, Carlos Eugênio's case reached the Brazilian Supreme Court. The judges ruled in his favor, granting him amnesty.[54] He settled in Rio, where he started a new career giving private music lessons. He also played acoustic, electric, and bass guitar in nightclubs with the group Conjunto Mais Café.[55] Carlos Eugênio received invitations to join the PT but rejected it as nonleftist, that is, too supportive of the status quo.[56] Instead of institutional politics, he gave talks and participated in political study groups. "It was my way of doing politics," he recalled.[57]

DESPITE THE FAILURE of the *diretas já* amendment, the political momentum had shifted decisively against the dictatorship. Lacking legitimacy and leadership, the fatigued military government fulfilled its plan to relinquish power to a civilian. Although the promilitary PDS might have decided the election with its majority in the electoral college, the party imploded after a liberal faction exited to form the Democratic Alliance with the PMDB and other parties. As its candidate, the Alliance chose the Minas Gerais governor, Tancredo Neves, a seventy-four-year-old political veteran who had joined the MDB in 1966, switched to the Popular Party (PP) in 1979, and entered the PMDB after it merged with the PP in 1982. After intense negotiations guaranteeing the armed forces a strong role in the future civilian government, on January 15, 1985, Tancredo carried the vote in the electoral college, defeating PDS candidate Paulo Maluf. (Protesting the indirect election, the PT abstained from the voting in the electoral college. It expelled three dissident delegates who voted for Tancredo.) It would be a transfer of power, albeit a negotiated one.

However, on the eve of his March 14 inauguration, Tancredo fell gravely ill. Military and political leaders held urgent discussions with colossal constitutional implications. They decided that Vice-President-Elect José Sarney—a leading pro-military politician added to the ticket in a political compromise—would be sworn in on March 15. Tancredo died on April 21, Tiradentes Day, a national patriotic holiday honoring the martyred forerunner of Brazilian independence. The following morning, Sarney was officially confirmed as president. With a staunch ally in the presidency, the military fared far better.

Months later, on July 15, 1985, democracy and human rights received a powerful boost. Without announcement—and to the complete surprise of the still-existent, formidable military intelligence services—four thousand copies of the secretly published book *Brasil: Nunca mais* appeared on the shelves of bookstores throughout the country. "We did not announce the publication . . . beforehand because we didn't want to run the risk of it being confiscated," the head of the Catholic publishing house Vozes explained.[58] *Brasil: Nunca mais* revealed for the first time the severity and extent of the repression. It quickly became one of the most popular nonfiction books in Brazilian history, shooting to number one on the bestseller list, staying there for twenty-five weeks, and selling 200,000 copies in two years.

Perhaps more than a civilian president, the publication of this anonymous memoir of terror symbolized the end of military rule. It became especially popular among the young adults who had come of age during the dictatorship. Around Brazil, human rights organizations began to sprout up, adopting the name Torture Never Again. Thanks in part to the book's revelations, President Sarney on September 23 felt obliged to sign the UN Convention against Torture. On November 21, the Archdiocese of São Paulo released a list of 444 torturers identified by BNM. Newspapers across the country published the list, putting the spotlight on abusive security agents now in prominent positions, including Colonel Ustra, the former head of the São Paulo DOI-CODI, now military attaché at the Brazilian embassy in Uruguay.[59] Prefaced by Dom Paulo, *Brasil: Nunca mais* did not divulge the names of Paulo Vannuchi, Frei Betto, or any of the project's other participants. "It's not the intention of this Project to collect evidence to be used in a Brazilian Nuremberg," the anonymous introduction stated. "The Project is not moved by any desire for revenge. In the search for justice, the Brazilian people have never been motivated by feelings of revenge. The intention of the work is to have an impact, by revealing to the national conscience, under the light of denunciations, a dark reality kept secret in the dungeons of the prolonged political repression after 1964."[60]

Yet Brazil's return to democracy was complicated. Some of the dictators in neighboring Argentina had gone to prison. Brazil's 1979 Amnesty Law and the precarious transition of 1984–85 echoed *Brasil: Nunca mais*'s recommendation against prosecution of torturers. A civilian, allied over the previous two decades with the armed forces, sat in the presidential chair, but Brazilians continued to yearn to choose their leader in an election. Brazilian democracy would require strengthening not only in the areas of civil and human rights but in public administration, the combat of corruption, and economic recovery.

CHAPTER 11

A Proletarian versus a
Free-Marketer for President

With the civilian government in place, Brazilians started to repair the political, social, and economic damage of the dictatorship. The armed forces, despite having relinquished formal control of the government, still held considerable power. High-level officers held six of two dozen cabinet-level positions in President Sarney's government, each concerned with military and intelligence matters.[1] The military cast a shadow over Brazilian society during the entire Sarney presidency. Despite this, the government finally permitted the Communist parties—the PCB and PC do B—to legally register, and it instituted less-demanding rules for creating new parties. A total of twenty-two formed. These included the Partido Socialista Brasileira (PSB, Brazilian Socialist Party), which had been active from 1947 to 1965, but it was banned by the dictatorship and restarted with new members.[2] The PMDB, PT, and other parties continued to flourish. Politics was far more open than during the military era.

On the economic front, Sarney and his advisers waged a seemingly unending battle against inflation. In March 1986, the president announced a freeze on prices and the introduction of a new currency, the *cruzado*. For the first time in more than a decade, Brazilians' salaries did not erode, and the purchase of consumer goods rose, as did consumption of meat, a luxury for poor Brazilians. A TV news report showed one citizen, one of many so-called Sarney's inspectors, ordering the closing of a supermarket in the name of the president because it had violated the price freeze. The sudden economic recovery created unprecedented public euphoria. It also paved the way for the crucial election of November 15, 1986, the first fully free national election since 1960. The election included the participation of illiterates, who numbered almost a quarter of the adult population. They earned the right to vote for the first time in Brazilian history via a constitutional amendment passed by the Congress in 1985.[3]

Brazilian voters selected a new Congress, which would also function as a National Constituent Assembly charged with replacing the constitution imposed by the generals in 1967 and amended substantially in 1969. President Sarney and many other politicians switched to the PMDB, which voters associated with the successful cruzado. A centrist alliance of the PMDB and the Liberal Front Party (which absorbed the PDS dissidents who supported the Tancredo Neves candidacy) won a smashing victory: all governorships, three-quarters of the Chamber of Deputies, and 80 percent of the Senate.[4] The PMDB was the dominant partner of the alliance and scored the biggest victory by any party in contemporary Brazilian history.[5] Politicians now joined the PMDB not for its center-left ideology or history of opposing the dictatorship, but because of its popularity. It had metamorphosed from an opposition party to an electoral machine. The election confirmed the reality of many democracies: economic issues deeply influence voters.

However, the cruzado program proved to be little more than a temporary, artificial strategy. The government faced an enormously difficult challenge. It had to break the economic, social, and psychological cycle of inflation, deeply reinforced by more than a decade of military-imposed indexation—the automatic adjustment of wages, contracts, and other prices. Rather than apply a gradual policy reached by political consensus, the Sarney government tried to wean Brazilians from inflation by way of an economic shock ostensibly without financial or social cost. It propagated the illusion that popular enthusiasm could override economic reality. By early 1987, the cruzado program collapsed and inflation returned. The prize freeze and 1986 economic boomlet had produced serious shortages of key goods, including meat. Supplemental beef imports, however, arrived late and were of poor quality. To do business, both companies and consumers looked for ways to skirt the price controls. Inflation roared again, becoming hyperinflation and reaching a monthly rate of 26 percent in May and June 1987. President Sarney and his frequently changing advisors sought to repair the economy, introducing yet another currency, the *cruzado novo* (new cruzado). It failed. People and businesses quickly learned to anticipate the government's moves, undermining the intentions of its policies. Meanwhile, the PT, the Unified Workers Central, and other labor organizations promoted nationwide strikes to protest economic policy and demand better wages, with limited success. Brazil once again had to suspend payments on its foreign debt, becoming an outcast in the international financial community. By the end of Sarney's term in early 1990, the monthly inflation rate had reached 80 percent, throwing the economy into disarray, discrediting him as a leader, and eroding the popularity of the PMDB and the Liberal Front Party. Struggling financially, Brazilians spent their paychecks as quickly as possible to keep ahead of daily price hikes. The poor economic performance cast doubt on the overall effectiveness of Brazil's new democracy.[6]

The economic uncertainty was paralleled by the uneven, sometimes tumultuous efforts of the Constituent Assembly to produce a new constitution. Many of the left and center-left representatives wanted Brazil to adopt a parliamentary system, seemingly the most appropriate for the country's many parties. But they lost to the larger, generally more conservative bloc, which favored a presidential system, in large part to maintain Sarney's power. Indeed, Sarney and the majority pushed through a provision extending his mandate another year, to March 1990. Despite the disputes over the form of government, the final draft of the constitution firmly established Brazil as a capitalist democracy. The conservative majority had blocked radical measures, such as redistribution of land, which would have impinged on private property. Nevertheless, the document aimed to address numerous social concerns, such as the right to strike, maternity leave, health, education, and environmental protection. It also reduced some of the concentration of power in the federal government created under the military, devolving greater political and administrative responsibilities to the states and municipalities.[7] However, Brazil remained a highly centralized nation, with issues such as taxation remaining in the hands of the federal government. The Constituent Assembly ratified the new constitution on October 5, 1988. Brazil had a solid plan to move beyond the military phase. However, major tasks remained: first, implementing the new constitution and, second, dealing with the myriad of political, social, and economic challenges to make Brazil a prosperous, stable, and just nation.

WITH FREEDOM OF EXPRESSION and civil liberties restored, Brazilian citizens openly debated their nation's future. The Constituent Assembly revealed the different tendencies. The PMDB split when voting on the system of government and the length of Sarney's term. The minority left wing exited the organization to form the Partido da Social Democracia Brasileria (PSDB, Brazilian Social Democratic Party). Prominent PSDB leaders included former governor Montoro and senators Mário Covas and Fernando Henrique Cardoso. Former student leader José Serra, a member of the Chamber of Deputies, also entered the PSDB. Nevertheless, the party supported the new constitution. The PT did not, declaring that it was "essentially conservative, anti-democratic and anti-popular," but the party did accept its legitimacy.[8] Running in São Paulo state, Lula had garnered 650,000 votes in the 1986 election for the Constituent Assembly—the most in the nation—but he made little attempt to influence the proceedings. At this point, for Lula and the PT, the impetus for political and social change had to come from outside traditional institutions.[9]

During this period, Aloysio established himself as a centrist concerned with efficient government. Despite his affinity with Fernando Henrique, Serra, and other PSDB luminaries, Aloysio remained within the PMDB because of its important role in ending the dictatorship and the continued influence of its PCB militants. In his second term in the São Paulo State Assembly, continuing as the leader of the PMDB bloc (1986–90), Aloysio participated in preparing a new state constitution, which was mandated by the federal constitution. He led the campaign for a state constitutional amendment raising the allocation of tax revenues to double support for research in higher education and other institutions. Another Aloysio amendment assigned 30 percent of the state budget for education.[10] Aloysio used his power to block the adoption of many "popular amendments," introduced via petition, which often promoted the special interests of public employees. "Therefore, my job was a defensive measure for avoiding the linkage of salaries, automatic promotions, the accumulation of bonuses, fundamentally a series of pressures from those special interests, which, if given in to, would have disastrous consequences for the functioning of the state," he recalled. "It was a political battle against special interests."[11]

Figure 27. Continuing as a leader of the PMDB bloc in the state assembly, Aloysio played an important role in the drafting of the São Paulo state constitution in the late 1980s. Aloysio Nunes Ferreira Filho collection.

COLOMBO CONTINUED HIS WORK with labor leader José Juarez Antunes in Volta Redonda. In 1986, Juarez won a second term as the Volta Redonda Metalworkers' Union president. Running on the PDT ticket and with the support of Colombo and the union, Juarez was also elected to the Constituent Assembly with fifty thousand votes, the third-highest tally in Rio de Janeiro state.[12] Colombo became Juarez's official congressional political advisor. "We would go to Brasília and back together," Colombo recalled. "We would stay in the same apartment. I also started spending time with the other workers, the other union leaders at the Constituent Assembly. . . . I was often the point man with the PDT, because Juarez was an unknown quantity."[13] Jessie commented: "Juarez in the PT was on the right; in the PDT he was on the extreme left [laughter]."[14] Outsiders attributed Juarez's leftist positions to Colombo, the ex-revolutionary. In reality, Juarez arrived at his own conclusions after detailed discussions with Colombo. Colombo also built ties with Lula and other prounion members of the Constituent Assembly.[15]

In the Constituent Assembly, Juarez attempted to modernize worker–business relations. As Lula did, he saw Brazil's labor laws as archaic and harmful to the working class.[16] Established in the 1930s, the laws were systematized in 1943. Though ostensibly intended to protect Brazilian workers and professionals, the system violated union autonomy and freedom without delivering on its most basic promises of rights and benefits. Brazilians felt as if they were drowning in a sea of labor regulations. Lula called the system—in a reference to the military repression—the Institutional Act No. 5 of the working class.[17] However, the workers in Volta Redonda feared that attempts at reform could backfire. "And in a certain way, we aligned ourselves with the idea of allowing those rights, which are sacred: the Bible of the workers, period," Colombo commented.[18] The Constituent Assembly kept the system in place—an impediment to the idea of open and free negotiations between workers and employers. This system has survived into the present.

In 1987, Jessie, after completing her history degree the previous year at the Universidade Federal Fluminense in Niterói, moved with Leta to Volta Redonda to be with Colombo. She helped open a community cultural center. She also focused on the history of the local working class, starting a school for union members. There Jessie set up an archive for the documentation produced by the metalworkers' union. The school published a magazine focusing on the history of Volta Redonda. She still commuted to her job at the left-wing magazine in Rio. She entered the prestigious master's program in history at the Universidade Estadual de Campinas (UNICAMP, State University of Campinas), located 200 miles from Volta Redonda in São Paulo state, further complicating her travel schedule.[19]

In 1988, Jessie and Colombo joined Juarez in his bid for greater power: the mayoralty of Volta Redonda. He still had two years in his congressional term. Brazilian politicians regularly seek executive positions because of their prestige, the access to budgetary resources, and the platform to reach yet higher office. In Juarez's case, the mayoralty would let him continue the work of the outgoing PDT mayor, Marino Clinger. He wished to implement his own vision for a local government independent of the power of the massive state-owned CSN steel factory and dedicated to improving the lot of the workers. After a tense PDT convention in which Juarez's forces battled the conservative wing of the party, he emerged as the party's candidate. "It was truly an epic campaign," Jessie remembered.[20]

The campaign coincided with continued unrest at the CSN. The workers demanded a wage increase and improved working conditions, including six-hour shifts to allow for proper rest, as required by the new constitution. They staged a three-day strike in May, leading to intervention by the army and no concessions by the CSN. On November 7—eight days before the Brazil-wide vote for mayors and city councils—the workers struck again. They took control of the factory, quieting the blast furnaces but not turning them off. Fifteen thousand workers were inside. The government sent two thousand soldiers to try to force them out. The army stationed small tanks and other heavy armaments just outside the CSN. The soldiers had colored their faces for combat. To foil the military, the strikers entered into the steelworks, a highly dangerous area of the factory difficult to access, especially for outsiders. When soldiers tried to enter, the workers beat them back by throwing stones. The army cut off the electricity and water supply and sent in only milk and orange juice, hoping to exhaust the workers and give them diarrhea.[21] The government sent Roberto Cardoso Alves, minister of industry and commerce, as lead negotiator. Alves attempted to delegitimize the strike and, echoing the discussions begun by Brazilian economists about a dramatic shift in policy away from government involvement in the economy, publicly suggested that the CSN be privatized. The local populace protested privatization, proclaiming that the factory was a public good.[22]

The army blocked Juarez from entering the factory. On November 9, after company officials denied most of the union's requests, the workers voted in two assemblies—inside and outside the factory—to continue the strike. They converted a forklift and other work implements into weapons. That night, Volta Redonda became a battleground, with soldiers attacking people on the streets with billy clubs and bayonets and smashing storefronts. Soldiers entered the factory firing teargas canisters, hitting workers with clubs, and shooting guns. Three young workers died inside the CSN, and dozens were wounded. The soldiers nearly destroyed two of the three blast furnaces—the very property the government claimed to protect with military action. On November 10, the workers withdrew from the factory. However, the strike continued. They also sent in teams to save the blast furnaces.[23]

Learning about the incident through television and press reports, many Brazilians became aghast at the violence against fellow citizens. The indignation benefited the Left. On November 15, Juarez won the election for mayor. In São Paulo, Adriano Diogo's mentor, Luiza Erundina, an underdog candidate running on the PT ticket, shocked the national political establishment by winning the mayor's race.[24] Also on the PT ticket, and with Arlete serving as his campaign manager, Adriano won election to the São Paulo City Council with the fifth-highest number of votes.[25] The next day, Dom Waldyr, the local bishop who had welcomed Jessie and Colombo to Volta Redonda after their release from prison, held an outdoor Mass with four other bishops to mourn the deaths of the three workers. The bishops criticized the government. As a steady rain poured on the thousands gathered in the Brazil Plaza, the bloody clothes of the three dead workers hung from a large cross, symbolizing their sacrifice.[26]

On November 21, sixty thousand workers, family members, and Volta Redonda residents circled the CSN in a massive hug in a sign of respect for the factory as the heart of the local economy, for solidarity, and in support for the strike. Two days later, after the workers secured key demands, such as a six-hour shift and a wage increase, Juarez called the strike to an end. Taking office as mayor on January 1, 1989, he appointed Colombo as his chief of staff for political affairs and Jessie as his secretary for cultural affairs. Juarez immediately began to practice a form of grassroots democracy, convoking workers' assemblies at the entrance to the CSN to pressure the city council on proworker measures. Juarez also personally took measures to the council offices with a message, urging members to vote immediately. "Because if not, the message would end up in the bureaucracy and never be voted on," Colombo recalled. "A way of administering the city was emerging that was going to become an example for the rest of the country—to govern together with the people." Their comrades throughout Brazil were impressed.[27]

It would not be so simple. "It was a lot of romanticism on our part to think that we would be able to confront all of those powerful interests with impunity," Jessie recalled.[28] After the Mass for the dead workers, Dom Waldyr received a visit from two policemen from an investigative team set up by Governor Brizola to investigate the infamous death squad that operated in Rio and nearby. According to the officers' intelligence, the squad aimed to kill both the bishop and Juarez by running their cars off the road. Dom Waldyr passed on the information to Colombo and started riding buses.[29] On February 21, 1989—just fifty-one days into his administration—Juarez died in a suspicious car accident on the way to Brasília. "They murdered Juarez," Colombo said as he hugged a union leader.[30] Dom Waldyr also concluded that Juarez had been assassinated. Accident investigators concluded that Juarez's car had been hit hard from behind, projecting his car and body into a tree. But the authorities never investigated the purported killing.[31] A massive crowd—120,000 people—attended the burial ceremony for Juarez, including Brizola, Lula, and PCB leader Luiz Carlos Prestes.

At Jessie's suggestion, the city planned to erect a monument to the three dead CSN workers designed by Oscar Niemeyer, the world-renowned architect responsible for so much in Brasília. "At the time Juarez died, we were preparing a super-radical May Day," Jessie remembered.[32] On the morning of the monument's inauguration, May 1, Labor Day, army men blew up the monument. Union members wanted to have the monument reconstructed, but, on Niemeyer's advice, the broken pieces were preserved on the site to recall the military's violence.[33]

"The army was run out of town, chased out with the people booing them," Colombo recalled. "And the general who commanded the invasion told the press that there would be consequences, that there would be payback."[34] He and Jessie believed that corrupt elements within the Volta Redonda government, including politicians who allied with Juarez to get elected, contributed to a conspiracy to murder Juarez. They later recognized that they failed to grasp local politics, which contributed to the animosity toward Juarez. "The fact of the matter is that we didn't really know the city," Jessie observed. "We lived in the city's working-class area, but the city was complex. . . . So you have the problem of the complexity of power, of the state. You don't know the multiple interests in play. You'll only find out when you disturb those interests. It took us a long time to understand."[35] After Juarez's death, Colombo and Jessie quit their jobs. With Leta they left Volta Redonda for the state of Espírito Santo to seek new work.

THE TRAUMA OF Volta Redonda revealed how badly Brazilian society needed a change not just in the national leadership but also in political practice. Because of the precarious economy and weak public finances throughout the "lost decade" of the 1980s, Brazilian economists and policymakers had begun soul-searching about the state's future role in the economy. Some leaders began discussing the need to reform the state-led model of Brazilian development, including protection of the domestic market from foreign competition and the subsidizing of private and public businesses.[36] Crony capitalism was coming under attack.

The new constitution stipulated that voters would directly select a new president. The election's first round was scheduled for November 15, 1989, the centenary of the Brazilian republic. If no candidate received more than 50 percent of the votes, a runoff between the top two vote-getters would take place on December 17. The election potentially provided a clean break with a major legacy of the dictatorship: Sarney's indirect election. For the first time since 1960, Brazilians could vote for president. Because of mandatory voting for everybody over eighteen and under seventy, turnout was 88 percent, with 72.3 million people casting first-round ballots. Seventy percent of voters were selecting a president for the first time.[37] Brazilians participated in the election hoping for economic restoration and the creation of a more just and democratic society.

Of twenty-one candidates in 1989, a relatively unknown politician, Fernando Collor de Mello (hereafter referred to as Collor)—brash, young, right-wing—took the early lead. The field included well-known leaders, such as Lula, Brizola, Covas, and Fernando Gabeira of the Green Party, one of the Elbrick kidnappers. The PT considered but quickly rejected Gabeira as Lula's vice presidential running mate in a PT/Green Party coalition because of his supposed incompatibility and free-spirit views: after returning from exile in Europe, he had worn a crocheted lilac thong to the beach in Rio and given interviews in which he supported environmentalism, feminism, and LBGTQ rights. Later, Gabeira supported the legalization of marijuana. In 1989, he ran under the banner of the Green Party.[38]

Collor came from a traditional oligarchical family in Alagoas, Brazil's second-smallest and second-poorest state, where Carlos Eugênio had grown up. Collor had backed the dictatorship, serving as a mayor of Maceió, the capital, while a member of the promilitary National Renovating Alliance, and also in the Chamber of Deputies as a PDS representative. In 1989, with the other parties running their own candidates, he ran on the ticket of a party created specifically for his candidacy, the Party of National Reconstruction. Presenting himself as an outsider, Collor fulminated against the Sarney administration and traditional politicians who represented the elite.[39] Still, Collor was the grandson of Lindolfo Collor, who served as minister of labor in the 1930s. His father was Arnon de Mello, a senator from Alagoas, who had shot dead another senator on the floor of the federal Senate but received no jail time—a typical outcome for the wealthy and powerful. Riding the wave of public indignation about the kind of privileged public employees targeted by Aloysio and others, Collor played heavily on his reputation as the "caçador de marajás," the "privilege buster." ("Marajá" is Portuguese for "maharajah," a way of describing public employees with very high salaries obtained through connections and dubious means.)[40] Attacking state intervention, Collor's message resonated with the emerging doubts about the government's economic role, calls for the loosening of import restrictions, and the proposal to privatize state-run enterprises.[41]

Backed by conservative politicians, business leaders, Neo-Pentecostal and evangelical religious denominations, and especially the powerful, universally watched Globo television network of the oligarchical Marinho family, Collor consolidated his lead in the polls. On June 4, the Communist government in China sent tanks into Peking's Tiananmen Square against protesters demanding freedom. Hundreds of people died. On November 9, six days before the election, the world witnessed the fall of the Berlin Wall, the greatest symbol of the Cold War and of Communism's restrictions. The anti-Communism of U.S. president Ronald Reagan, British prime minister Margaret Thatcher, and Pope John Paul II had triumphed. Astonished, the radical Left everywhere began soul-searching about its ideals. Collor handily won the first round of the election on November 15 with 30.5 percent of the votes. Lula edged out Brizola for second place with 17.2 percent. (Gabeira had one of the lowest tallies, with less than 0.2 percent of the total.) In the second round, Brazilians faced a choice between two diametrically opposed candidates: Collor, the movie-star-like proponent of the free market, and Lula, the bearded former union leader and founder of a party preaching socialism but maintaining flexibility.[42]

The titanic struggle between a proletarian and a son of the elite captured the imagination of an electorate polarized between the backers of the social status quo (including the supporters of the military dictatorship) and activists from the *movimento popular*. Collor appealed to Brazilians by striking a macho pose and railing against corruption, while Lula stressed his working-class origins. Each day Lula moved closer to Collor in the polls. He won the first of two televised debates on December 3. Lula clearly had the momentum.[43]

Both campaign staffs dug up dirt on their opponent. In Collor television ads, a former girlfriend of Lula, Miriam Cordeiro, with whom he had two children, claimed that he had once suggested she have an abortion.

Abortion is illegal in Brazil and, at that time, permitted only in instances of rape, incest, and danger to the life of the mother. Lurian, Lula's adolescent daughter from this relationship, was the supposed object of the potential abortion. Paulo Vannuchi, a member of Lula's campaign team, was traveling with the candidate to Campinas and Belo Horizonte as these events unfolded. "In the last week, when we returned in the early morning hours, at the airport there was a group of PT people waiting to tell Lula that Miriam Cordeiro had appeared on television and talked about it," Paulo remembered. The team debated tactics. "They wanted him to have him get his daughter, Lurian, to speak badly of her mother. He would not allow it."[44] Without saying a word, Lurian briefly appeared alongside her father in his own spot as he declared, "Lurian is the result of an act of love."

Lula had selected Paulo to handle counterintelligence against Collor. The accomplished central figure behind the best-selling *Brasil: Nunca mais* remained unknown to the public. After Lula entered the second round, he gave Paulo a stack of news clippings about eighteen inches high regarding Collor. Paulo spent a week studying the clippings. He also did his own research.[45] He recalled: "At the time I was certainly the most knowledgeable person about Collor de Mello in Brazil. . . . I made a report. . . . I systematized everything." For example, Paulo described the case of Ana Lídia, a young girl from Brasília who died in a notorious incident. "[Collor] did not take part in the murder," Paulo reported to Lula. "What happened was that he was in the country home where she was because he was part of the group of friends and went there." Paulo also obtained "very clear testimony" of Collor's usage of cocaine. In addition, the document focused on political themes, including Collor's extravagant spending on personal items, such as a private jet, while serving as governor of Alagoas. "There were insinuations of homosexuality, which his brother later mentioned," Paulo recalled. The documentation also included reports of Collor's deals with the sugarcane growers of Alagoas. In exchange for campaign donations, Collor arranged for extremely generous tax exemptions that put Alagoas into a long-term debt crisis. Because of his knowledge of Collor, Paulo participated in the meetings held to prepare Lula for the debates.[46]

However, Lula refused to use any of the personal material against Collor. Paulo continued: "After I presented the information to Lula, he said: 'No. I don't want to go down that path. Cocaine, or whatever. I'm not going to do it. . . . We are going to have a political debate.'"[47] Just two days after the Lurian revelation and three days before the election, Lula entered the final, crucial debate virtually tied with Collor in the polls. However, Lula now appeared timid. Without mentioning Lurian, Collor won the debate. Globo TV's infamous, tendentious report on the highlights of debate footage, broadcast the next day, magnified Collor's apparent superiority.[48] "Lula, taking the ethical path, got screwed because the attack against him was personal, with the Miriam Cordeiro incident," Paulo observed, acknowledging that Lula could have performed better in the final debate.[49] On December 17, Collor won the election with 53 percent of the vote (35.1 million) to Lula's 47 percent (31.1 million).

Paulo believed that Lula made the right choice regarding negative campaigning. "In fact, I believe that the logic can be reversed," Paulo said in a 2001 interview. "Can a Collor win an election with a maneuver like that? Yes, he can. . . . He wants to preserve the system of domination, of corruption. Now, you can win an election by a trick, by making a shocking revelation at the last minute. . . . In a PT government with Lula as leader, you need to win when there are the basic fundamentals of hegemony to support that government. If you win by chance or by trick, the government won't last long, just three months, just six months and it's over. And then the Left will have to wait fifty years to rise up again. So, I have the impression that Lula's decision was a wise one."[50]

WITH COLLOR'S ELECTION, Brazil completed its transition to democracy, but the military still loomed large, as Brazilians witnessed at Volta Redonda. It remained for Collor to attempt to constrain its power.

The new, postauthoritarian Left had made a spirited entrée into presidential politics. Lula emerged as its undisputed leader. Paulo formed part of an increasingly confident group of PT officials and professionals who made the party an organized, serious electoral competitor. With the fall of the Berlin Wall, the PT's support for socialism remained vague. However, it now recognized that it needed to support democracy as a value in and of itself, not merely as a tool to achieve power. The PT had become the country's main opposition party, and its acceptance of the electoral process strengthened democracy for Brazil as a whole.[51] As demonstrated by Lula's reaction to the Lurian episode, the PT also stood out as prizing ethical behavior.

At the time, some Brazilians speculated about the scenario of a Lula victory. Would the armed forces have allowed Lula to actually take office? This question is unanswerable.[52] However, the difficult experience of Juarez in Volta Redonda suggests that a Lula government in the early 1990s would have faced fierce opposition. Brazil had a finely written constitution, but the rule of law remained weak. Furthermore, violence could trump peaceful political solutions. Without stronger democracy, neither a socialist nor capitalist system could achieve sustained benefits for society as a whole. Jessie and Colombo had learned that ideological and political fervor weren't sufficient for acting as public administrators, that achieving power did not mean keeping it. Transforming society was far more difficult than the revolutionaries had imagined. Confronting entrenched power, they recognized the need for far greater persistence—and flexibility—than they had initially imagined.

As policymakers had begun soul-searching about the economy, the Brazilian Left expressed deep concern about both old and new social challenges, including drug trafficking and urban violence, land conflicts in the countryside, abandoned children, and the devastation of the Amazon.

In 1990, it was President Collor's turn to attempt his own, capitalistic revolution.

CHAPTER 12

Revolutionaries in Suits and Ties

When President Collor took office on March 15, 1990, he froze every Brazilian's bank account in an attempt to halt hyperinflation. He hoped to drastically reduce the circulation of money. Even those paying for urgent medical operations and other emergencies could not make immediate withdrawals. People started suing the government to gain access to their money, while powerful special interests skirted the rules. Collor also controlled prices and wages, and he restored the name *cruzeiro* to the currency. His economic program became known as the Collor Plan. However, within months inflation returned. A second plan also failed. By mid-1991, monthly inflation climbed to 20 percent. Politically inept and lacking congressional support, Collor came under intense attack as revelations emerged of massive financial corruption in his campaign and administration—including accusations leveled by his brother Pedro. Collor personally benefited. In 1992, the PT and other opposition parties called for Collor's impeachment. Thousands of youthful protesters filled the streets demanding the president's ouster and an end to unethical political practices. In September, the Chamber of Deputies voted articles of impeachment against Collor. The Senate tried and convicted him on December 29, 1992, even though he had resigned that day. He was thus banned from political activity for eight years. Though Brazilian democracy appeared dysfunctional—Collor was ousted by a weak, fragmented multiparty system, and this first postdictatorial elected administration was

Figure 28. President Fernando Collor de Mello. Fotos Públicas.

a disaster—it had withstood a major test: its institutions had functioned constitutionally, and the military had not intervened. Vice President Itamar Franco took office, forming a clean coalition government that brought political stability and eventually tamed inflation. Brazil's elected leaders had listened to the voice of the people.[1]

Despite Collor's failures, he had successfully initiated a two-track program to modernize the economy and attack crony capitalism: privatization of state-run companies and elimination of the decades-old policy—shared by both democratic and military administrations—of protecting the domestic market from foreign imports. Shortly after Collor's exit, the government privatized the giant CSN, a leading symbol of Brazil's state-led capitalism.[2] Many state-owned firms had suffered huge financial losses because of mismanagement, political manipulation, and the expectation that they underwrite governmental social and cultural initiatives. Privatization ratcheted back—but did not eliminate—state-led capitalism.[3] Collor instituted other reforms, aiming to reduce the bloated federal bureaucracy, make the economy more competitive, and improve the quality of Brazilian-made goods.[4] Collor also shut down the military's nuclear weapons program. Many former leftists resisted the socioeconomic reforms, blocking, for example, the privatization of Petrobras, but they did not provide new alternatives. The tensions between proponents of the so-called neoliberal reforms and their vigorous opponents in the PT, the unions, and the nationalistic Left colored Brazilian politics deep into the twenty-first century.

However, certain reforms did appeal to others on the left, including former PCB members and revolutionaries who rejected the anti-neoliberal outlook. They recognized that the world was changing. In December 1991, the Soviet Union had collapsed, while in Communist China reformers strove to stimulate capitalist development. In October 1992, as Brazil anticipated Collor's ouster, a group of forty-four intellectuals, professionals, politicians, union leaders, and others issued a provocative manifesto titled "For the Future of São Paulo," addressing the city but also sending a message to the nation. The signers included opponents of the military regime, such as José Ibrahim, a former union leader, member of the VPR (People's Revolutionary Vanguard), and political prisoner freed in the Elbrick action. "As a response to the people's demand for morality, the democratic solution regarding President Collor must not serve as a pretext for interrupting but instead facilitating ... the continuation of structural reforms aimed at the economic, social, and political modernization of the country," the brief document began. Observing the need to repair the "broken-down infrastructure" of the country's leading economic hub and create a "broadening of social policy," the manifesto stated that "it is necessary to attract private capital for those services that must and can be privatized." With the reforms "it will become possible to modernize the city's structures, stimulating the creation of jobs, and make municipal services more rational and efficient, thereby improving the quality of life for the populace."[5]

The manifesto took a stand regarding the November 1992 runoff in the mayoral election to replace outgoing incumbent Erundina. (Running for the PMDB, Aloysio had finished third in the first round, which had nine candidates.) The second-round conservative candidate was Paulo Maluf, the prodictatorship politician who had served as the regime-appointed mayor of the city and became the military's preferred candidate in the indirect presidential election of 1985. He was the outgoing state governor. His opponent was Eduardo Suplicy, a member of the MDB in the 1970s and the first senator ever elected by the PT, in 1990. (Governing Brazil's largest city brought more clout than serving in the Senate.) Citing the need for "administrative experience" but without naming Maluf, the document clearly favored him.[6] So Maluf used the manifesto in campaign publicity. It created friction between Suplicy and the signers, who had been his allies against the dictatorship.[7]

Suplicy especially criticized manifesto signer Rodolfo Konder, a journalist, former PCB member, political prisoner, and the director of Amnesty International in Brazil from 1980 to 1990. Having supported Konder during his imprisonment at the São Paulo DOI-CODI, Suplicy unsuccessfully demanded political loyalty.[8] When Maluf won easily, Konder was appointed to head the city's Secretariat of Culture. "The old Brazilian Left hasn't realized that the world has changed," Konder said in a newspaper interview. "It's still hidden behind the Berlin Wall. It doesn't see that the Cold War is over. . . . The way the PT has acted, we need to react against its political correctness, its sectarianism, which boos anybody who disagrees, which likes to antagonize. . . . I am a nonpartisan neoliberal. Socialism is dead."[9]

As a top assistant, Konder chose Itoby Alves Corrêa Jr., an attorney, promoter of Brazilian–Cuban relations, and unsuccessful PSDB city council candidate in 1988. Itoby was one of Marighella's most reliable deputies.[10] He also signed the manifesto, angering some former revolutionaries.[11] In Itoby's view, former revolutionaries needed to learn the art of politics. "In Cuba people gained recognition with the number of their attacks, not the raising of political awareness," he reflected in 2001, noting his own transition from revolutionary authoritarianism to social democracy and admiration for centrists such as British prime minister Tony Blair and French prime minister Lionel Jospin. "If the revolutionaries had won, I wouldn't be here today. I'd have gone before a firing squad."[12]

For Manoel, as the capitalist West was taking its victory lap, the time had arrived to savor his achievements in public relations. He had done well, handling major accounts at his cousin Duda Mendonça's firm in Bahia. After his wife's work as a physics professor took them to the city of Campinas, near São Paulo, in 1985, Manoel first struggled to open his own business. However, he eventually established himself as a leader in the Campinas/São Paulo market. In 1992, Manoel won an international public relations award for a 1991 Christmas greeting that he had designed for the Sanyo Corporation in Brazil. Instead of a greeting card, however, Manoel produced a four-minute video on the Amazon region, the headquarters of Sanyo's Brazilian operations. Manoel titled it *Çuikiri*, which means "green" in a Brazilian native language. As Manoel recalled, the video was a natural for a manufacturer of video cassette recorders and televisions. The company distributed the cassette to its business associates. In January 1993, Manoel, his wife, and the president of Sanyo in Brazil traveled to New York City for the awards ceremony.[13]

Manoel had no difficulty entering the United States, despite his record as one of Ambassador Elbrick's abductors. That contrasted sharply with at least five visa denials for journalist Gabeira, the most famous, but tactically one of the least important, of the people involved in the kidnapping.[14] "I went to the consulate with all of the necessary documents," Manoel recalled. "The first document was a telegram from the festival organizers stating that I had won the gold medal. Also, the telegram from the American branch of Sanyo saying that I could visit their offices. I filled in everything correctly. I was completely honest. So, there was that classic question: whether you have ever had any kind of link with a party or institution or anything like it connected to international Communism. I put down that yes, I did." Manoel believed that the U.S. authorities knew his identity. However, when he retrieved his passport, the consular

Figure 29. Manoel, in 2015, holding his 1992 New York Festivals public relations award. Kenneth P. Serbin.

official asked him no questions. He received a visa valid for ten years, the maximum. "The visa was granted because of the political situation," he concluded. "The day I landed in New York, I was in the hotel lobby. I was watching President Clinton's inauguration on TV. It was a different time for the United States, one that had little to do with the period of the elder [President] Bush or his son."[15]

The moment produced a supreme irony: the anti-imperialist guerrilla, the man who had wounded the U.S. ambassador, received a capitalist award in the heart of the empire. "In my heart I laughed a lot," Manoel remembered. "I walked up onto the stage with everybody clapping. Then the gold medal, the prize, the photos. I felt redeemed in the heart of New York City [laughter]. There's meaning in that, isn't there? It was very interesting. The only thing missing was Sinatra singing 'New York, New York' [laughter]."[16]

STARTING IN MID-1994, the Itamar Franco administration (1993–95) successfully halted inflation with a new economic plan implemented by Fernando Henrique Cardoso, the prominent opponent of the dictatorship whose think tank had been bombed by right-wing terrorists. Fernando Henrique had first served as Itamar's foreign minister (1992–93), then as minister of finance (1993–94). Some saw the capable and experienced former academic and senator as a de facto prime minister.[17] Brazilians had suffered through eight changes in the currency in ten years—and rampant inflation.[18] As Fernando Henrique later noted in his memoir, "All of us had nightmares about people running around with suitcases full of worthless cash. This would cause unimaginable riots and social unrest." Inflation facilitated corruption at all levels of society: account balance sheets became unreliable, and the declining value of money encouraged embezzlers to steal even more. It discouraged foreign investment and dissolved trust in public institutions.[19] Conceived with greater expertise than previous programs, the successful *Plano Real* (*Real* Plan) relied on fiscal restraint by the government at all levels, a large reserve of U.S. dollars in Brazil's accounts, and a downward pressure on local prices with the increase of imports. The plan lent its name to a new currency, the *real*. Inflation, 40 to 50 percent per month in early 1994, by December had dropped to just 1 percent.[20] The *Real* Plan became the most successful economic stabilization program in Brazilian history.[21] It allowed businesses, middle-class consumers, and especially the poor the ability to rationally plan their budgets for the first time in decades. Then Fernando Henrique rode this success to victory in the 1994 presidential election on the ticket of the PSDB, which had drawn leftists when it split from the PMDB in 1988. He handily defeated Lula, his main opponent, and the other candidates in the first round. During his two terms in office (1995–2003)—defeating Lula again in 1998— Fernando Henrique kept inflation low, but at the cost of extremely high interest rates and slow economic growth. As Fernando Henrique himself publicly observed, the *Real* Plan raised living standards by making high-protein foods such as yogurt and chicken affordable to the poor.[22] Millions of poor people benefited, with 6 percent of the population rising above the poverty level just in the first two years of the *Real* Plan.[23] Despite often being painted as an elitist by opponents, Fernando Henrique became the favorite politician of the poor, but his popularity fell as he neared the end of his second term. A left-wing intellectual had delivered with a centrist agenda.

Figure 30. President Fernando Henrique Cardoso. Fotos Públicas.

Defeating inflation allowed Fernando Henrique to focus on his primary goal of stabilizing Brazilian democracy after the transition from military rule and the inauspicious Sarney and Collor governments. Fernando Henrique eliminated military control over the armed forces by abolishing the cabinet-level positions for the heads of the armed forces and creating a civilian-led Ministry of Defense. In 1995, he sanctioned a law establishing a commission to officially recognize the government's responsibility in the death and disappearance of opponents of the dictatorship and to compensate their families, without overturning the 1979 Amnesty Law, which shielded torturers from prosecution. That initiative reflected a broader concern with human rights and social justice. With pressure from landless rural workers, Fernando Henrique redistributed land to poor families in the countryside. However, he faced harsh criticism from many for seeking a constitutional change permitting a second presidential term. His cabinet ministers and supporters in the Congress successfully pushed for the constitutional amendment, which also allowed a second consecutive term for governors and mayors. Although seen as self-serving and resulting from dubious deal-making, reelection fostered stability by allowing greater continuity in government. In contrast with the free-for-all nature of the 1989 presidential election, politics under Fernando Henrique tended to center on two main parties, the PSDB and the PT. Though unlike the United States' two-party system, this situation nevertheless contributed to stability. Politically the Fernando Henrique era was one of the calmest in modern Brazilian history.[24]

Fernando Henrique also sought to modernize Brazil's economy. Although he had nationalist leanings, he sought to adapt his country to the post–Cold War order dominated by the United States. In his view, Brazil should not resist intensifying globalization but take advantage of it.[25] Fernando Henrique adopted some of the same strategies as Collor. Via constitutional amendments, his administration privatized state-owned businesses in mining, electricity supply, and telecommunications. The government partially privatized Petrobras; it maintained control of the firm but ended its monopoly on oil exploration and refining. It allowed private investors to buy stock in Petrobras and Brazilian and foreign partners to participate in exploration. In 2000, Petrobras was listed on the New York Stock Exchange.[26] It introduced greater transparency in accounting and corporate governance, laying the groundwork for increased foreign investment. Upgrading its facilities and diversifying its activities, Petrobras became an international company.[27] However, Fernando Henrique did not fully embrace neoliberalism. In some instances, he *reversed* Collor's policies: he reestablished moderate protectionism in international trade and used national industrial policy to protect key sectors, such as the automobile industry.[28]

Fernando Henrique reformed the banking system, which had come to rely on easy profits from high inflation. He augmented the power of the central bank. A new Fiscal Responsibility Law increased transparency and accountability in the use of public funds. He sought to make government more responsive, especially to the poor, whom public employees commonly viewed as supplicants rather than citizens with a right to quality services. Thus, he professionalized the civil service, greatly increasing the number of college graduates in its ranks. He universalized access to public education and public health services. He created public assistance programs, such as Bolsa Escola, a scholarship program aimed at encouraging needy families to send their children to school regularly instead of having them work to support the household.[29] During his administration, significantly more people attended high school and college.[30] Historically, most government social spending went to the middle class in the form of public pensions and subsidies to higher education. Bolsa Escola marked the first time that major government spending went to the poor. Fernando Henrique was also the first president to acknowledge and combat racism in a country that professed racial harmony but reflected racial hierarchy.[31] Under the leadership of José Serra, minister of planning and budget (1995–96) and of health (1998–2002), the government and civil society implemented an AIDS prevention and treatment program widely considered the best in the developing world and even a model for developed countries. The initiative included domestic production of many of the drugs in the so-called anti-AIDS cocktail and heavy pressure on multinational pharmaceutical firms to lower the prices of patented AIDS medicines by more than half. Brazil thus halved the AIDS death rate between 1996 and 2002.[32]

In all, Fernando Henrique's efforts represented the most ambitious attempt at reforming Brazil in decades.[33] Though imperfect, these reforms moved Brazil significantly away from crony capitalism.

However, other economic challenges limited Fernando Henrique's success. Economic crises in Asia (1997) and Russia (1998) and state governments' inability to reduce spending led to a draining of the dollar reserves needed to keep the *real* stable, resulting in currency speculation.

This predicament forced the administration to seek a massive loan package from the IMF and other sources totaling $45 billion, secured in large part because of Fernando Henrique's good relationship with President Clinton. As a result of the crisis, in January 1999, the start of Fernando Henrique's second term, the government had to devalue the *real* by almost 100 percent, from one to two *reals* per dollar. Despite these economic shocks, inflation remained low. In 2000, the country performed well. In 2001, however, government mismanagement of the power grid led to severe rationing, forcing people to take shorter showers, for example. With further devaluation of the *real* and the negative effect of the 9/11 terrorist attacks on the world economy, Brazil had to borrow another $15 billion from the IMF.[34] By the end of Fernando Henrique's second term, the economy became sluggish, causing unemployment and debt to rise and wages to stagnate.[35]

IN FERNANDO HENRIQUE, Brazil had a president who had vigorously (and peacefully) opposed the dictatorship. His election had great symbolic importance. Continuing a trend begun with the 1979 Amnesty Law, during his administration former revolutionaries and other regime opponents participated freely in politics. Some rose to leadership positions. Both collaborating and competing, they strove to strengthen and manage the democratic and capitalist system that they had previously attacked. The strong political affinity and mutual trust between Fernando Henrique and Aloysio exemplified this process. They maintained close ties even after Fernando Henrique left the PMDB in 1988 to cofound the PSDB.

Aloysio, after two terms in the São Paulo State Assembly, ran for vice governor of São Paulo in 1990 with successful PMDB gubernatorial candidate Luiz Antônio Fleury Filho (no relation to the infamous Officer Fleury), a law professor and prosecutor who had become state secretary for public safety. To get involved in electoral politics, the ex-revolutionaries sometimes had to work with people who were somewhat tainted, at least by association: Fleury was the political godson of his predecessor, Orestes Quércia, a PMDB boss notorious for his alleged corruption.[36] Fleury defeated Maluf in the second round. The vice governorship was a ceremonial position, but during Fleury's administration (1991–95), Aloysio twice served as secretary for metropolitan transport, overseeing public transportation in the São Paulo megalopolis. He negotiated hundreds of millions

Figure 31. A moment from the 1990 PMDB campaign for São Paulo governor by Luiz Antônio Fleury Filho: in the front row (from left to right), Fleury's wife, Ika; Fleury; Aloysio; Aloysio's wife, Jussara; the couple's two daughters; and Congressman Michel Temer, future president of Brazil. Aloysio Nunes Ferreira Filho collection.

of dollars in loans from the World Bank and the Inter-American Development Bank for long-term projects to expand and improve train and subway lines. One subway line was the first in the world to receive World Bank financing.[37]

The Fleury–Aloysio administration became embroiled in one of modern Brazil's most infamous human rights scandals. In the first round of the abovementioned 1992 São Paulo mayoral race, the PMDB called on Aloysio to run in the first round against Maluf (the eventual victor), Suplicy, and six other candidates. The first round took place on October 2. The day before, police under the command of the state's secretary for public safety, a Fleury appointee, massacred 111 men at the Carandiru prison. The officers served in the Polícia Militar, not actual military police but a branch of the regular police primarily in charge of street and traffic patrol. Previously controlled by the military regime, the Polícia Militar failed to shed their repressive tendencies after the return to civilian rule.

With Aloysio already running behind in the polls, the incident sealed defeat for him and the PMDB.[38]

Aloysio later described the massacre as "disgraceful" and a "huge tragedy" that cost him votes. The evening before the election, without knowing of the massacre, Aloysio had to take a detour around a police blockade as he headed to a campaign event. He could see helicopters flying near Carandiru. "I only heard about what happened at Carandiru on the day of the election, at 6 a.m., when I went to a television studio," he recalled. "On election day, everybody talked about it. My first interview that day was about Carandiru, about which I was totally uninformed." The massacre made international headlines, reinforcing the image of the Brazilian government as a violator of human rights. However, Aloysio did not blame Fleury. "It would have been demagoguery and disloyalty on my part if I had said: 'I'm resigning, because the governor was responsible,'" Aloysio recalled, noting that Fleury, as secretary for public security, had instituted the first human rights course at the Polícia Militar's academy. "That was an operation by the Polícia Militar, obviously without an order from the governor. . . . In my opinion, what happened was the fault of the [successor] secretary for public safety. The secretary must have gone to the prison certainly already knowing what was going on." The secretary for public safety resigned, and Fleury removed all of the police commanders involved in the massacre. "It was an act of savagery by the Polícia Militar," Aloysio asserted. Of 120 officers initially accused, the only person convicted in the killings was police colonel Ubiratan Guimarães. Free on appeal, he was ultimately absolved, because the courts accepted his argument that he was acting on orders. Unconcerned with human rights, many Brazilians approved of the massacre. "Afterwards this criminal was elected to the state assembly," Aloysio recalled. "And the number that he chose as his candidate number was 111. He was elected with a huge number of votes."[39]

Despite their best intentions, the civilians now running Brazil seemed powerless to stop human rights abuses worse than any single act committed by the dictatorship. Political and economic reforms were insufficient. Brazil also required deep social reforms.

In 1994, Aloysio ran for a seat in the federal Chamber of Deputies. Though Brazilian congressional candidates vie for votes across an entire state, Aloysio focused on the region around his hometown of Rio Preto. In Brazil, as in so many places, all politics is ultimately local. He drew voters who identified with him politically and others who recognized that he would work to resolve local problems.[40]

I FIRST MET ALOYSIO during a short, get-acquainted meeting in 2001 in his general secretary's office at the Palácio do Planalto, the presidential palace in Brasília. The Planalto's elegant exterior, designed by Niemeyer, belied its drab interior. The contradiction embodied both Brazil's grandeur and its reality as a developing country. Dressed in a suit and tie as required by the Planalto dress code, I sat across from Aloysio at his work desk. We spoke about the history of the ALN. Later, for three days in August 2002, I immersed myself in Aloysio's campaign—now under the PSDB banner—for a third term in the Chamber of Deputies.

From São Paulo, I flew two hours to Rio Preto. Aloysio and his press aide, Gisele Sayeg (who would become his third wife), awaited me at the airport. As Aloysio drove me to his ranch house, the three of us discussed the diplomatic acumen of the Catholic Church, the 2002 presidential campaign, and his Italian ancestry. The region also had attracted many Lebanese immigrants, Gisele's forebears. One of Aloysio's grandfathers had used savings from city jobs to buy a coffee plantation. Aloysio owned part of that land, on which he grew coffee, cassava, and coconut and rubber trees. Aloysio now considered himself "rich," a member of the country's "economic, intellectual, and political" elite, but he had always worked for a living. He was an energetic guide to his region.[41]

Rio Preto lies about a hundred miles west of the city of Ribeirão Preto, the hub of a wealthy agricultural area known as "the California of Brazil." Ribeirão Preto highlighted São Paulo state's central role in the national economy, exemplifying Brazilian progress, despite deep social inequality in the region. According to Aloysio, the Rio Preto area had become Brazil's largest producer of latex (the product of rubber trees), surpassing the output of the vast Amazon region. Cattle farming formed another base of the local economy. The region also had a number of small industries and a strong service sector, including sixty college-level programs and a medical cluster. We toured one of the local hospitals and its associated medical school. Several physicians had connections to the American medical community. Aloysio was greeted enthusiastically at the two institutions and, in his congressional role, listened to requests for assistance with their various institutional needs.[42]

Aloysio campaigned intensively, walking through urban neighbor-hoods and traveling by car around the region to meet with voters and po-litical contacts. During a lunchtime gathering at a *churrascaria* (Brazilian barbecue restaurant), he conversed with grassroots health workers and advocates for the disabled, alcoholics, and children with Down syndrome. He also visited day care centers for needy children, many suffering from medical conditions. Our stops included Aloysio's campaign headquarters and congressional office, where I met several relatives and three veteran PCB militants who had supported Aloysio since the 1960s. Aloysio was completely transparent, allowing me access to meetings and private con-versations.

Although an atheist, Aloysio respected voters' diverse religious beliefs. In a poor neighborhood, he talked at length with an Afro-Brazilian woman from Bahia who practiced *candomblé*, an African religion of the slaves and still adhered to by millions. In that same neighborhood, I counted seven different Protestant evangelical churches along a one-mile commercial strip. That evening, we visited the Assemblies of God con-gregation in the city of Catanduva. Eyeing potential votes, Aloysio gave a speech to about 80 pastors and 2,500 of the faithful. Aloysio had the sup-port of one key pastor, Daniel Palmeira, a highly popular city councilman and candidate for the state assembly. Aloysio's whip in Catanduva, a Catholic councilman, had sealed the alliance with Palmeira. Many in the church wore campaign T-shirts displaying Aloysio's and Palmeira's names.

In his speech, Aloysio extolled the faith of the audience. He urged them to vote for Palmeira, a politician with "clean hands." "I, like you, be-lieve in liberty," he said, referring to Palmeira. "Those who follow the word of God in the evangelical churches aren't after anything for themselves. They just want the liberty to practice their religion." Aloysio stated that he wanted a just country without prejudice and with dignified work for the common people. He referred to the work of pastors and believers who had rescued young people from addiction, edified families, and preached in difficult places, such as prisons. Later in the evening, we visited a Catholic fair in Catanduva. Aloysio shook the hands of dozens of people, including a sugar plantation owner and a priest. Noting Aloysio's presence, a bingo-caller repeated his name frequently over a loudspeaker. The gam-bling, beer drinking, and smoking of the fair attendees contrasted sharply with the ecstatic singing and prayers at the Assemblies of God church. Aloysio was comfortable in both settings.[43]

Eᴀʀʟɪᴇʀ, ᴅᴜʀɪɴɢ ʜɪꜱ ꜰɪʀꜱᴛ ᴛᴇʀᴍ in the federal Chamber of Deputies (1995–99), Aloysio had actively supported a reform of the Polícia Militar, proposed by Fernando Henrique, which essentially ended the practice of allowing criminally accused officers to be judged by their fellow policemen. He recalled it as "one of the most important and most difficult legislative battles" in his ten years as a congressman. Opposed to this reform, the Polícia Militar's lobby was "very strong," he added. An effort by Fernando Henrique to transfer all allegations to the civilian justice system, rather than just "malicious crimes against life," was defeated.[44]

Aloysio served as the vice leader of the PMDB bloc. Aloysio initially opposed the PMDB's participation in Fernando Henrique's government; he thought that the party should back the president's reforms but maintain a critical political distance. However, Aloysio soon became one of the president's staunchest supporters. In fact, Fernando Henrique considered nominating Aloysio as minister of transportation, but internal PMDB politics prevented it. "The party didn't want someone in that cabinet position who was very close to the president," Aloysio recalled. He supported the reforms to further deregulate the economy and reduce the role of the state. So did the majority of the PMDB bloc. They also advocated for the constitutional amendment to permit a second presidential term. Aloysio and allies helped: "We negotiated the highly necessary political deals needed."[45] Writing in his diary, in December 1995 Fernando Henrique expressed his admiration for Aloysio's abilities and how badly he wanted him inside the executive branch: "As political coordinator, the only one I see right now that I like is Aloysio Nunes Ferreira. I don't know if it will be possible to nominate him. . . . That's the reality of politics. I'd like to have somebody to be able to clarify things for me a little, to receive the party leaders."[46] In Aloysio's estimation, Fernando Henrique's election represented "the surmounting of a deep crisis of hegemony in the country that had existed since the end of the military regime." Only Fernando Henrique had the capacity to unite sufficiently large sectors of the Left and the Right to open the economy and improve the social safety net: on the left, the PT opposed reform; on the right, the Liberal Front Party (which absorbed the more liberal elements of the promilitary PDS) benefited too much from the use of political patronage to want to change the system. Because key, nationalistic PMDB leaders in the state of São Paulo disapproved of the reforms, in 1998 Aloysio switched to the PSDB.[47]

As with most of Fernando Henrique's reforms, the privatization of the telecommunications sector involved controversy. Aloysio sat on the congressional committee in charge of the pertinent legislation. In a 2004 interview, he rejected the criticism—leveled by Márcio and others—that privatization occurred too rapidly, thus preventing Brazilian firms from surviving foreign competition. Aloysio explained:

> Privatization took place as the result of a constitutional amendment that went through a long process in the Congress, almost a whole year. Afterwards, it was followed by a general telecommunications law that was widely discussed and debated in the Congress, in business circles, and by the public. It is one of the best-conceived laws that we have in Brazil, which guarantees universal service and the oversight of a regulating agency to verify quality of service. The results are there for people to see. Brazilian firms could participate, but they didn't have enough capital to do so.

Despite the many improvements in telecommunications fostered under the military, Brazil still experienced serious bottlenecks. Aloysio continued:

> I want there to be enough telephones in Brazil for everybody to be able to talk. Before the privatization, telephone lines were so valuable that they became an object of trade. When you filled out your income taxes, you declared the number of telephone lines you owned. It could take two to four years just to get a telephone line installed. Now it takes two weeks. And it's accessible to anybody, whether a landline or a cell phone.
>
> The Brazilian telephone system has neither the capital nor the technology to be able to buy a telephone company? Then let them find another business. The fact is that the state-owned system, besides having exhausted its investment capacity, had enormous featherbedding for political purposes and became one of the most important factors in the exchange of political favors. Twenty-seven public companies at the state level, with five boards of directors at each one to be staffed by political favorites. And there weren't enough telephones in Brazil. The technology was backward. If the way to end that predicament was to privatize and allow in foreign companies, then so be it. That's the price you have to pay.[48]

During Fernando Henrique's two terms, the number of telephones per 100 people increased from 8.4 to 30. The total number of landlines nearly quadrupled, and the number of cell phone lines went from 800,000 to 81 million.[49] A decade after Fernando Henrique's departure, Brazil's cell phone operators claimed that their customers talked more on the phone than any other people on the planet.[50]

Similarly, Aloysio rejected the label "neoliberal" for Fernando Henrique's government. "I think that 'neoliberalism' was a way for our adversaries to attack our government," he insisted. "What President Fernando Henrique did was to recover the possibility for the state to intervene in the economy, in the implementation of social policy. The Brazilian state was in a meltdown. Financial crisis. Fiscal crisis. Total lack of credibility. . . . So, what Fernando Henrique did was to reorganize the Brazilian state." As with many other countries, under Fernando Henrique, Brazil followed the pro-free-market, pro-balanced-budget "Washington Consensus" not because of some conspiratorial pressure from the United States and the international financial community, but in response to Brazil's unique circumstances, Aloysio maintained. "I can say so because I took part in many . . . budget meetings," he recalled. He continued: "Globalization requires all nations to carefully manage their budgets. Privatization is the result of something else, the end of the model created by Getúlio Vargas, when the state drove business activity."[51]

Still considering himself a leftist, Aloysio nevertheless diverged sharply from others' doctrinaire positions. He believed that Brazil's leaders needed to govern with flexibility. He elaborated: "I'm a leftist, in the sense that I want the world in which I live to be free of prejudice, in which human relations are based on reason, on fraternity. I consider myself to be a child of the Enlightenment, as all socialists are." Brazil needed to address its "scandalously unequal" society. "However, I don't believe in a utopia as I once did—the utopia of socialism," Aloysio said.[52]

In 1998, Aloysio easily won election to the Chamber of Deputies for a second term (1999–2003). In 1999, Fernando Henrique tapped him as general secretary, a cabinet-level position as the administration's primary liaison with the Congress and the state governors, who in Brazil hold substantial sway over federal congressional delegations. Aloysio served in this post until November 2001. With the economic crisis at the start of Fernando Henrique's second term, political turbulence in the Congress increased substantially. With an eye to the 2002 presidential election, the

PSDB's two main allies, the centrist PMDB and the right-wing Liberal Front Party, became rivals and started jockeying for influence. Meanwhile, led by the union-driven PT, the far-left opposition amplified its attacks on the government with public protests and allegations of corruption, even calling for the ouster of Fernando Henrique and for new elections. In Aloysio's eyes, the opposition sought to "undermine the government." However, Fernando Henrique remained in firm control. With Aloysio's assistance, all of Fernando Henrique's proposed measures passed in the Congress.[53]

As the general secretary, Aloysio strengthened his dialogue with Dirceu, the former ALN and MOLIPO member, now the president of the PT, and seen by many as Lula's éminence grise. "The president thought it important that his government have such a dialogue with the principal opposition party," Aloysio recalled. "We did nothing without me informing the president or Dirceu informing the leadership of the PT. . . . Based on our old friendship, we had a relationship of mutual trust in handling questions that involved the relationship between the PT and the administration."

This former revolutionary and participant in the ALN's spectacular 1968 train robbery next lived a historical irony as remarkable as Manoel Cyrillo's triumph in New York: rising to the top of Brazil's justice system. To replace a retiring justice, Fernando Henrique asked Aloysio to join Brazil's Supreme Court. "But I thought that my vocation was really in politics and not on the bench," remembered Aloysio, who declined. However, shortly thereafter, in November 2001, he did accept the similarly prestigious job of minister of justice. Aloysio took over the position from José Gregori, a human rights lawyer who had helped institute Fernando Henrique's human rights policies.

Because of the volatility of Brazilian politics, a cabinet post can be brief. Aloysio spent only twenty weeks as minister of justice; in mid-2002, he had to resign in order to run for reelection in Congress. Nevertheless, he accomplished a number of goals and handled political hot potatoes. "The problems at the Ministry of Justice are all huge ones, with huge repercussions," Aloysio explained. "And they are crises that appear without any warning. . . . I had serious crises to deal with: the murder of the [PT] mayor of Santo André, the murder of the [PT] mayor Campinas, both preceded by a series of threatening e-mail messages directed at the leaders of the PT that led one to believe that there might have been a wave of political assassinations. Later it was discovered that the e-mails were sent by a mentally ill person."[54] The man received court-ordered psychological treatment. However, the actual crimes were never solved. The January 2002 killing of Celso Augusto Daniel, the mayor of Santo André, a working-class suburb of São Paulo and a PT stronghold, had serious political implications. His death involved torture. Police detectives, the Polícia Civil, blamed common criminal kidnappers. However, prosecutors asserted that the killers acted to prevent Celso Daniel from revealing financial corruption within the PT.[55] The two crimes' potential political effect on the government was enormous. However, Aloysio maintained official distance. "I established a standard, during my time at the Ministry of Justice, of never interfering, of never digging too much into police investigations," he recalled "The investigations of the Polícia Federal are forwarded to the Ministério Público [prosecutors] and not to the minister of justice."[56]

Aloysio also dealt with the invasion of the president's family's ranch by squatters from the Landless Rural Workers' Movement, a key component of the *movimento popular*. He directed the court-ordered withdrawal of the workers. Aloysio won a political battle to keep within the ministry an agency to fight monopolistic and anticonsumer practices by banks. The Central Bank wanted to take over the agency. "The president decided that dispute in my favor," Aloysio recalled. Aloysio increased the demarcation of native peoples' traditional lands as guaranteed by the courts. He sent bills to Congress aimed at overhauling Brazil's national criminal code, the Código Penal, established in 1941. That process is ongoing. Under Aloysio, the ministry established a series of international agreements to fight money laundering. Aloysio also successfully promoted alternative sentences—such as community service—for illegal drug use.[57]

As both general secretary and minister of justice, Aloysio respected the conventional interpretation of the 1979 Amnesty Law as shielding the dictatorship's human rights violators from prosecution. Nevertheless, with the president's consent, he did hinder the careers of some of those agents, many of whom continued in law enforcement or the military. "For example, I blocked promotions," he remembered with pride. For Aloysio the amnesty did not represent a draw between the military and the opposition, but a victory for the latter. "Because today I can say that I was a member of the Communist Party, that I was a member of the ALN," he continued. "I experienced the ideological evolution of my generation and I came to be a part of the government of the Republic, just as Dirceu has done. We can say that without any reproach.... Our past did not become an obstacle to our political rise."[58]

FERNANDO HENRIQUE'S REFORMS profoundly affected Brazilian business, including Márcio's telecommunications firms. The public firms that provided Márcio with opportunities passed into private hands. The privatization of Telebrás was one of the largest in Latin American history. Embratel was also sold.[59]

By the late 1980s, Márcio had expanded into the international market. Construtel won an important contract in Chile in 1989. In the 1990s it entered Argentina and Bolivia. In 1996, he established profit sharing on a reverse sliding scale: the lower the employee's salary, the greater the proportion of profits received. That year one-third of Batik's profits went to the employees. In Marcello Abi-Saber's recollection, this magnitude of profit sharing was unique in Brazil. It encouraged workers to take greater responsibility for company performance, pointing out, for example, wasteful use of resources. When he later sold his firms, Márcio distributed profits again. The eventual sale of Batik to Lucent in 1999 resulted in distributing $1.5 million among 280 employees.[60]

The quest for equitable business practices produced another great paradox for Márcio. He had abandoned the revolution to become a capitalist, but he ultimately performed the revolutionary act of transferring capital to his employees. Márcio's business practices indicated both the profound moderation of the Brazilian Left *and* the preservation of some of its core ideals. The social justice Márcio had failed to achieve through violence finally came to fruition in a nonviolent democratic capitalist system. As a radically democratic entrepreneur, Márcio embraced a demanding work ethic but also the value of compassion, a belief in others' potential, and respect for other points of view. He wanted to diminish socioeconomic oppression and close the gap between rich and poor. He also donated as much as 500,000 *reals* ($500,000) per year to charity.[61]

The economic reforms came at the height of Construtel's and Batik's technological, managerial, and financial success. Márcio astutely saw the proverbial handwriting on the wall and knew that his companies, despite their agility and innovativeness, could not compete with the multinational behemoths poised to expand into Latin America.[62] Meanwhile, Brazil's telephone companies began to demand financing of their equipment purchases at very low interest rates—something Márcio's firms could not provide.[63] To brace Construtel for the impending foreign competition, in 1993 he sold a 51 percent share to the Italian firm Sirti. The contract stipulated that the Brazilians and Italians would jointly manage the company. Sirti also bought 35 percent of Batik. Márcio explained: "At the beginning of the nineties, I watched the Spaniards advance in Chile. I was very worried about the privatizations, and my thesis was the following: there's not going to be any more room for Brazilian companies. Whoever doesn't have an alliance with a foreign group will be gone. . . . A while later, in Chile, as a result of our alliance with the Italians, we signed an enormous, a gigantic contract. In other words, my strategy was right. But here in Brazil their help wasn't as important. They became more like spectators. They just wanted their dividends, and they didn't get involved in management."[64]

As mentioned above, in 1999, Márcio sold Batik to Lucent. He also sold another large share of Construtel to Sirti. In 2001, Márcio bought back all of Construtel's shares at a much lower price. Construtel's traditional telecommunications business was diminishing, in large part because of falling prices and profits in the face of the foreign competition. The foreigners were playing market hardball: a supplier to Telefónica, Construtel had to sue the Spanish company for failing to pay. "The suppliers got strangled," Márcio recalled. By 2003, in a "strategic retreat" from the foreign-dominated market, he would shut down the telecommunications wing of the company. Construtel laid off two thousand employees, paying the full severance as required under Brazilian law. The shrunken Construtel, run by Márcio's two sons, shifted into geoprocessing, a technology for managing electrical, gas, water, sewer, and telephone networks. A holding company invested part of Márcio's capital in a mutual fund targeting Brazilian high technology start-up companies.[65]

Márcio viewed the sale of his companies as a defeat.[66] He had donated 200,000 *reals* ($200,000) to Fernando Henrique's 1994 campaign.[67] Although Márcio aligned with no political party, his nationalistic outlook led him to criticize the way in which Collor and then Fernando Henrique carried out economic reform. He especially disapproved of the latter's propping up of the *real* by increasing the national debt. "This tied the government's hands when it came time to do things," Márcio opined. "It made it difficult for the government to plan, and it destroyed what little was left of industrial policy." He criticized the two presidents' approach to privatization and foreign competition:

> Collor blew open the economy, reduced import duties, and favored the denationalization of industry without getting anything in return. No country reduces barriers and taxes for the whole world without negotiation, without something in return. . . . Privatizing industries without an industrial policy was a crime. I called that initiative the "creation of import corridors," "the creation of a reverse protectionism." Everybody spoke badly of the protectionism that Brazil had created. The way they carried out the privatizations, they created protected markets for imported products. It was technological colonialism. . . . They could have carried out privatization with the obligation to buy products made in Brazil, with preference for technology developed locally. They could even have used foreign companies. Lucent sold many Batik exchanges in Brazil after the privatizations. In fact, practically everything that Lucent sold was from Batik. Lucent wasn't able to sell its large system here. And the government could have kept golden shares in those companies.[68]

The crisis in Márcio's companies symbolized Brazil's shift away from emphasis on homegrown businesses and government-led economic development.

Still, the sale of Márcio's firms made him wealthy. No longer driven to succeed, he worked less. In 1998, the family moved into the mansion outside Belo Horizonte. Later they bought a catamaran anchored in the Caribbean. Regina became a renowned psychotherapist and expert in alternative therapies, and Márcio planned future projects to educate needy children.[69]

THE PT HAD COMBATTED Collor, establishing a shadow cabinet as a platform for criticizing his policies. Paulo Vannuchi, the former political prisoner and human rights activist, served as its executive secretary. As the Collor government ended, the PT established a think tank, the Citizenship Institute, to furnish Lula, the party, and a potential PT presidential administration with a policy agenda for such issues as housing for the poor, hunger relief, and public safety. Paulo became one of the Citizenship Institute's key administrators and thinkers. It became increasingly active as Lula and the PT vociferously opposed practically all of Fernando Henrique's policies. Paulo also provided regular analyses of politics and current events for the Sindicato dos Metalúrgicos do ABC (a leading union in metropolitan São Paulo's industrial region), the Unified Workers Central, and other labor organizations. Such labor work kept him "grounded in reality." At the Citizenship Institute, where Lula kept an office, Paulo resolved problems for him and tackled special assignments. In 1994, he served as the coordinating executive secretary for Lula's unsuccessful presidential run.[70]

To sharpen his analytical skills, in 1996 Paulo entered the USP master's program in political science. His studies provided fresh ideas for his political work.[71] They also helped him rethink socialism. Over the ensuing five years, he prepared a 300-page thesis titled "Democracy, Liberalism, Socialism and the Contribution of Norberto Bobbio." Dedicated to his murdered cousin Alexandre, the thesis echoed the post-Soviet angst of Brazil's socialists, who criticized Fernando Henrique's reforms yet searched in vain for a new model. Paulo probed the thought of Bobbio (1909–2004), a prolific, vastly cultured Italian legal and political philosopher, to understand the shortcomings of socialism. Bobbio provided an invaluable perspective because, emphasizing political dialogue over attack, he both sympathized with and critiqued Marxism. As a result, he gained respect on both the right and the left. "The big problem of inequality among individuals and peoples in this world has persisted and is severe and unbearable," Bobbio stated in 1994. "Historic communism failed. But the challenges it posed continue." This fact particularly concerned Brazil, "one of the world champions of inequality," Paulo wrote.[72]

However, in Bobbio's estimation Marxism had erred profoundly by not recognizing key achievements of classical liberalism—the balance of powers, the rule of law, respect for the individual, political pluralism, and the defense of human rights—as gains for all people and not just the so-called bourgeoisie. Bobbio concluded that, above all else, nations needed to embrace democracy. He did not speculate on socialism's future. Nor did Paulo, though his exploration of Bobbio's support for liberal democracy reinforced his own democratic commitment. Paulo wrote: "Hostile to the focus on the idea of revolution in Marxist thought, Bobbio's reformist approach invites revolutionaries of all stripes to modernize the very idea of

Figure 32. Luiz Inácio Lula da Silva during a break in a candidates' debate in the 1994 presidential campaign. Kenneth P. Serbin.

revolution without appealing to dogmatism, testing to see how far revolution can combine with the dispute for power via democratic means, which presupposes full acceptance of the rules of the game."[73]

In the mid-1990s, Lula used the Citizenship Institute as a base for his Citizenship Caravans, during which he traveled throughout Brazil to strengthen his ties to the poor and widen the PT's base. Unlike most Brazilian politicians, except for his one term in Congress, Lula built his base out of office. No longer a metalworker, he also had left the leadership of the union movement. Linking himself to the grassroots, he became a perennial, professional candidate for president. Indeed, the Citizenship Institute helped him become autonomous from the PT—but the party's dependence on him as its most visible figure grew.[74]

The PT bureaucratized in a way that reinforced Lula's charismatic leadership but distanced the organization from the grassroots: elected PT officials took control of the party from the idealistic activists who had electrified it in the 1980s. As a result, activism in the streets diminished. "All the revolutionaries, all those political groups put on suits and ties, ran for city council, ran for mayor, took jobs in the ministries," observed Adriano, a staunch PT member especially concerned about the role of the grassroots. "In Brazil the Left became institutionalized. . . . We could even say that this represented the destruction of the *movimento popular* from the Trotskyist point of view." Dirceu, himself a member of the Chamber of Deputies, led this process as PT president. The PT had never formally adopted or renounced Marxism, and now it struggled to redefine its vision of socialism. In 1990, Dirceu commented privately that the party needed to abandon so-called real socialism, that "unburied cadaver." In reality, socialism became irrelevant—because Brazil was making social progress under Fernando Henrique and the PT itself was adopting a much more moderate, pragmatic stance. Even before the federal telecommunications reform, PT mayors Antonio Palocci of Ribeirão Preto and Luiz Eduardo Cheida of Londrina, Paraná, privatized their cities' public phone companies. The PT also began to become involved in corruption: Paulo de Tarso Venceslau, one of the Elbrick kidnappers and an aide in the PT-administered mayoralty of São José dos Campos, São Paulo, accused individuals close to Lula of transferring public funds into the PT's coffers. For his whistle-blowing, Venceslau was fired and expelled from the party— reportedly at Lula's insistence. The scandal suggested that the PT differed ethically less from other political parties than it had claimed. Thus, the

PT grappled with the tension between the thirst for social justice and the quest for power.[75] The incident served as a portent of future scandals.

The PT penetrated the political system especially at the local level. In 1994, for instance, it had 53 mayors, 77 state representatives, and 1,400 city council members.[76] As a first-term PT São Paulo City Council member during the mayoral administration of Erundina (1989–92), Adriano shed his role as agitator to become an institution-builder. He defended the interests of the Erundina administration in the city council and elsewhere. In fact, he displayed greater moderation than the mayor, who had been elected with much support from the poor. He disagreed with her efforts to govern independently of the PT (and its alliances with other parties) by relying solely on the *movimento popular*. By 2001, he had settled in the party's centrist faction, dominated by Dirceu.[77] Nevertheless, Adriano still mingled with the poor in his base in São Paulo's extensive, impoverished East Zone, a focal point of progressive Catholicism. Adriano worked to get the city to pave roads, introduce new bus routes, prevent floods, and clean up contaminated land and water. He collaborated with activists such as Valdênia Aparecida Paulino, a human rights lawyer of humble origins. Working with protest rappers and other youths, Valdênia sought to protect children and teens from violence and to promote their rights as citizens. Lyrics from a popular song echoed in the neighborhood: "It's time to come together / To make the favela a place of pride / Now let's unite and start to protest." In a gesture of political moderation, Adriano also worked closely with the business-backed group Commerce for Social Service, which supported the social, cultural, and athletic development of the local populace.[78]

With Maluf's victory in the 1992 mayoral contest, Adriano's second stint on the city council (1993–97) became a "term of resistance."[79] "I specialized in causing trouble for Maluf," Adriano recalled, laughing. "It was very difficult. I have to recognize that he is a very powerful enemy, very intelligent, very well-connected. . . . Someday, if I ever become mayor of São Paulo, I want to get to know the city as well as Maluf. He knows all the ins and outs of the bureaucracy."[80]

Adriano had a long history with Maluf. He first clashed with Maluf during his undergraduate years at the USP, when Maluf served as the dictatorially appointed (and notoriously corrupt) mayor; Maluf had refused a demand for discounted bus fare for students. Working as a São Paulo state geologist during Maluf's governorship (1979–82), Adriano helped to organize opposition to Maluf's controversial state-owned oil exploration firm Paulipetro, which was accused of wasteful spending, corruption, and being harmful to Petrobras's interests.[81] Now, after Maluf's election as mayor, Adriano helped organize grassroots protests against the administration prompted by Maluf's cavalier attitude toward the poor. In late 1993, Adriano and angry favela dwellers clashed with Maluf over his decision to transport household trash to a nearby dump designated for just scrap and rubble, thus endangering residents' health, the local environment, and the city's water supply. The city ignored a court order, using police officers to escort garbage trucks through a barricade set up by the residents. After Maluf won an appeal, the local residents destroyed the facility. "They set the entire dump on fire," Adriano recalled. "The repercussions were so serious that I was afraid of getting arrested. Of course, I never incited anyone to commit violence, but the violence there was spontaneous, explosive."[82] In another political battle, Maluf canceled the city's garbage recycling program—the first in Brazil, and begun under Erundina as a result of Adriano's legislative initiative. During the era of Maluf's successor and protégé Celso Pitta (1997–2001), Adriano skirted the cancellation by connecting small-scale recycling cooperatives with private firms that purchased the materials.[83] These disputes highlighted the harsh environmental reality of a municipality with 10 million inhabitants where much garbage was still incinerated because of the lack of dumps.

In his third and fourth terms on the council (1997–2001, 2001–2005), Adriano denounced inadequacies and corruption in the semiprivatized municipal health system started by Maluf and continued by Pitta. Adriano decried Maluf's cancellation of vaccination programs and AIDS-prevention initiatives.[84] He presided over a city council investigation of allegations of fraud, embezzlement, official misconduct, and other accusations against the Pitta administration and his city council allies. The final report, issued in 2001, concluded that Pitta had tacitly agreed with the illegal practices. It recommended criminal prosecution of the perpetrators.[85] "Six billion *reals* were spent," Adriano remembered. "It was to launder money, to pass on money to others. . . . That money disappeared. People did not get the services they needed. This destroyed the health system in the city of São Paulo. . . . It was white-collar crime, organized crime."[86] No one was ever convicted—an example of a drawback of Brazilian democracy. A 2008 news article reported that a number of the wrongdoers were suspects in other health system fraud cases.[87]

Throughout his time on the city council, Adriano worked in tandem with Arlete. In addition to managing his campaigns, she served as a political advisor to Adriano and the group of activists, local leaders, and PT members around him. Retired from teaching and related union activity, Arlete also helped coordinate Adriano's staff, drafted legislation, and, with the many demands on him, managed his official schedule. She also helped spearhead an initiative to educate grassroots activists about policy and politics.[88]

AFTER THE CALAMITIES OF Volta Redonda, Jessie and Colombo found no relief from political strife as they pursued activism in the state of Espírito Santo, located to the northeast of Rio de Janeiro state. In 1990, Perly Cipriano, a former ALN member whom Colombo had met in the Frei Caneca prison, and Jessie's brother, Juca Alves, a local political activist, helped the couple find positions. Colombo also reconnected with two leading local politicians, Vitor Buaiz of the PT and Vasco Alves de Oliveira Junior of the PSDB (no relation to Jessie and her brother), allies of deceased Volta Redonda mayor José Juarez Antunes in the Constituent Assembly. Working on her master's degree in history, Jessie joined an effort to set up a municipal archive in the state capital, Vitória, governed by Buaiz. When the project failed, she went to work for the Federation of Social Service and Educational Organizations, helping unionize workers in miserable conditions in the cellulose industry.[89]

Colombo became the secretary of transportation for the city of Cariacica, a bedroom community—which he called an "immense favela"—furnishing labor to the industries around Vitória. As part of a potential national democratic leftist front to counteract the influence of the powerful, Mayor Vasco Alves appointed staff from various left-wing parties. For instance, Colombo was in the PDT, but Juca, named secretary of planning, belonged to the PT. In Jessie's and Colombo's recollection, Cariacica was extremely violent. Just after their arrival in December 1989, a local priest engaged in the *movimento popular* was murdered.[90]

Upsetting the local elite with his plans for social improvements, Vasco Alves was removed from office by the city council, only to be reinstated after a campaign by his allies and a federal court order. Now Colombo could help set up public transportation in Cariacica. "People would walk kilometers in the dirt, in mud," he recalled. The city bought new buses, and passengers rode for free. Colombo also assisted the mayor with administrative, political, and grassroots-city initiatives. "We had to put sewers in so many neighborhoods and on so many streets that we set up our own terra cotta pipe factory," Colombo remembered. The project employed both public employees and local residents. "Entire neighborhoods that benefited took part," he noted. "During the week and even on the weekend all the city's machinery, which was scarce, would be sent to one neighborhood to dig the holes, with the residents working alongside. And they would serve a huge amount of food, with the neighborhood women cooking for all those people who were working." After Braspérola, a Swiss-Brazilian company that produced world-class wool, refused a city order to remove a long security wall on public property that impeded pedestrians, Vasco Alves led Colombo, city employees, and angry residents there and destroyed it with city-supplied dynamite. "That's how bad the confrontations there got with the powerful," Colombo recalled.[91]

In early 1993, Colombo and Jessie's daughter, Leta, now sixteen, wanted to return to Rio, so the family moved. Jessie worked again for the left-wing magazine. She also entered the doctoral program in history at the Universidade Federal do Rio de Janeiro. Colombo became a special assistant to Governor Brizola (PDT), elected to a second term in 1990. Colombo served as a liaison to PDT subgroups in the state of Rio de Janeiro. In 1994, the head of the PDT's union groups convinced Colombo to run for the Rio de Janeiro State Assembly. However, without sufficient financial backing from the party and business donors, he failed to win a seat.[92]

Colombo and Jessie's allies' electoral fortunes in Espírito Santo drew them back to the state: the PT's Buaiz became governor with the support of the PDT, and Juca entered the state assembly. Continuing work on her doctorate, Jessie obtained an adjunct professorship in history at the Universidade Federal do Espírito Santo. Buaiz tapped Colombo to run the state's Central de Abastecimento (CEASA, or Food Distribution Center), a public network of distribution centers and markets set up during the dictatorship to centralize and assure supply of cities and towns with foods produced by private farmers. Seeking to improve Espírito Santo's CEASA, Buaiz and Colombo clashed with the deeply entrenched interests: farmers unwilling to return loaned government equipment and a staff of unreliable political appointees hostile toward innovations like computerization.[93]

"There was a constant conflict between private interests of the public employees and the public interest," Colombo explained. "They very easily and deliberately opposed any attempt at reform. . . . I couldn't fire anybody. Their political patrons came around all the time." Laughing, Colombo underscored his frustration, referring to Jessie's previous observation when working for the city of Volta Redonda: "'Colombo, I discovered that there is no such thing as a public servant. There are only public enemies.' Because government bureaucracy is always against the people."[94] Just as Márcio did, Jessie blamed corporatism as the underlying cause. She considered public administration in Brazil a "syndicate that exists to reproduce itself." She saw no easy solutions, but improved education could help. "It's basically a problem of cultural heritage," she observed. "How do you change the culture of a country? . . . How do you establish the division between public and private, which in Brazil is very problematic, and private not just in the personal sense? Something can be private in order to benefit a group. Defining what's public and private in a patrimonial country like ours is very complicated. That would require a revolution in a cultural sense. . . . This is not only a problem for the Right. It's also a problem for the Left."[95]

Buaiz boldly implemented a creative solution for the food distribution predicament. "It was very difficult, so Vitor Buaiz decided to close down [CEASA] and start a new one," Colombo explained. "And he took advantage of the incentive that Fernando Henrique provided allowing the firing of all employees when a business was closed." Created in 1998, the new enterprise took the name Agricultural Development Company. It could hire based on people's abilities, not political connections. He could now confront the farmers. "All of this was done on the eve of an election, and we had to practically set up a military operation to recover machinery that was on ranches being used by the ranchers," he recalled. "We had to hire a trustworthy individual to go to the countryside, with a driver and truck, to get the machines, and with backup from the Polícia Militar."[96]

In 1998, Jessie returned to Rio to complete her doctorate, awarded that year. Colombo remained in Vitória into 1999 to finish his work for Governor Buaiz. Jessie soon put her historical expertise and political experience to work. In January, after winning election on a leftist coalition ticket with Brizola's enthusiastic support, Anthony William Garotinho Matheus de Oliveira took office as the governor of Rio de Janeiro state (1999–2002). Garotinho appointed Jessie as director of the Public Archives of the State of Rio de Janeiro. First, she reorganized and cleaned up the facility, left in deplorable condition by the previous governor's administration. The archives included the highly significant and highly sensitive files of Rio's political police during the dictatorship. Jessie could now help shape the way future generations of Brazilians would remember the struggle between the military government and guerrillas, such as herself. She waged a fierce political battle with the Polícia Civil (the investigative branch of the police force) to control the building where the political police had operated during the dictatorship. Jessie wanted to transfer the public archives to that building, which would represent a moral victory for the opponents of the dictatorship and defenders of human rights. It would transform the building from a symbol of repression into one of transparency and the search for historical truth. Garotinho approved the plan. However, the police refused to relinquish the building, claiming to need it for a museum and police officers' club. Garotinho's successor, Governor Benedita da Silva of the PT, maintained police control, but the building still formally belonged to the public archives.[97] The dispute exemplified the conflict over the historical memory of the dictatorship in other areas of Brazil.

After his return to Rio, Colombo joined an extraordinarily large group of former revolutionaries hired to work in Garotinho's Secretariat of Labor (SETRAB). The secretary of labor was Jaime Cardoso, a political prisoner sent into exile in 1971 along with sixty-nine other prisoners freed in exchange for the release of the Swiss ambassador. A former militant for Vanguarda Armada Revolucionária Palmares (VAR-Palmares, or Palmares Armed Revolutionary Vanguard), Jaime was also secretary general of the PSB, the Brazilian Socialist Party. Patronage of different sorts took place at SETRAB: eight other ex-revolutionaries got positions. Colombo coordinated a team that conducted oversight of the secretariat's contracts with nongovernmental organizations (NGOs) providing worker training. "The uniqueness of the Secretariat for Labor is not just that the secretary took part in the armed Left, but also that he hired comrades that developed an extremely close relationship while in exile," Colombo recalled. "We developed an affinity based on our historical affinity, and we used that in our task of managing well something that already existed."[98]

SETRAB provided an avenue for ex-guerrilla and musician Carlos Eugênio to enter formal politics for the first time. In the early 1990s, he had continued to focus on music. Along with a friend, in 1992 he became an entrepreneur by opening a music school in Ipanema called In Concert. It reached a regular enrollment of more than eight hundred students. Carlos Eugênio left the school in 1995 to write his controversial memoir,

Viagem à luta armada (discussed in chapter 4), followed by a second book on the same theme.[99] In April 2000, during a dinner at the legendary Café Lamas, host to Rio's radical intelligentsia in the 1960s and reunions of former revolutionaries in more recent years, Carlos Eugênio told Secretary of Labor Jaime: "We weren't defeated. Our platform was better than the Right's." Jaime agreed. Carlos Eugênio was about to turn fifty. People deserved a second chance in life, he believed. A few days later Jaime offered Carlos Eugênio a newly created position, one that enabled him to promote at least some revolutionary ideals: ombudsman for the working class of the state of Rio de Janeiro.[100]

The former executioner of traitors and enemies of the revolution now worked in the executive branch. As his main responsibility, he represented workers before the SETRAB and other state agencies, often when they did not comply with labor regulations. He mediated strikes and other labor disputes. Responding immediately to workplace complaints, he encouraged employer–employee negotiation, thus avoiding the more formal and potentially more bureaucratic, time-consuming recourse of the labor courts. Carlos Eugênio helped set up thirty-nine centers and two mobile units dedicated to registering workers for benefits, such as unemployment pay and training programs. As a tribute to two fallen ALN guerrillas, the centers were named after the brothers Iuri and Alex Xavier Pereira. In tandem with other sectors of the secretariat, the ombudsman's office helped people find jobs, join cooperatives, open small businesses, and secure small loans. The office helped meet the demand for specific types of labor sought by employers; it identified government agencies, unions, and NGOs to provide the necessary training. Carlos Eugênio and the secretariat focused primarily on the unemployed, favela residents, people in areas controlled by drug traffickers, and the minimally educated. In all, under Garotinho, SETRAB trained or retrained tens of thousands of workers. It also established initiatives for the disabled and mentally ill.[101]

In a 2002 interview, Carlos Eugênio described a typical person assisted by SETRAB: a fifty-two-year-old unemployed black woman living in the Complexo da Maré, a large, low-lying favela located on the proverbial other side of the tracks, Rio's North Zone. Carlos Eugênio emphasized the importance of SETRAB's First Job program, which helped youths enter the job market. SETRAB provided incentives to employers, who had to pledge not to lay off anybody upon hiring a youth. Carlos Eugênio believed strongly that First Job provided an alternative to the drug trade, which attracted many teens and even children. First Job was better than putting more police on the street, Carlos Eugênio affirmed. "A little populism never hurt anyone," he observed.[102]

Ultimately, Carlos Eugênio and the ex-revolutionaries at SETRAB resolved to "clean up institutions" and "punish" corruption.[103] His office helped recover 3 million *reals* spent improperly on training programs.[104] "Nobody is here to engage in corruption or get rich," he observed. They had once proven themselves as guerrillas. Now they wanted to demonstrate that they could run a government agency honestly and competently while lifting up Brazil's downtrodden and emboldening them to exercise their rights as citizens. That was the true meaning of being a "public servant." He concluded: "We knew how to destroy the state, but also how to build it."[105]

CHAPTER 13

The "American Dream" in Power

By early 2002, Lula was poised to join the global establishment.

That year he made his fourth attempt at Brazil's presidency. The PT had moderated substantially as it became ever more integrated into the government and the political system. Dirceu had transformed the PT into a decidedly non-Marxist, reformist social-democratic party.[1] Chairing Lula's campaign, Dirceu tapped Paulo Vannuchi to coordinate his staff. With the economic difficulties at the end of Fernando Henrique's term, Lula was the early favorite. However, Lula had never received more than 32 percent of the vote. To achieve victory, Lula, Dirceu, and the party leadership resolved to boost the PT candidate's popularity and make him more palatable to middle- and upper-class people fearful of his supposed socialist bent. They pragmatically planned the campaign. To reinvent Lula's image, the PT hired Manoel's cousin Duda Mendonça, who had become one of Brazil's leading political consultants. He had particularly gained fame—and opprobrium on the left—for helping Maluf's 1992 mayoral campaign. Lula trimmed his beard, donned business suits, and, instead of fiery rhetoric, described himself as the nonthreatening "little Lula of peace and love."[2] "It's the notion of moderation," Paulo later observed. "In other words, let's confirm an image of maturity."[3] Duda's polished media spots reinforced this image. To fund its efforts, the PT started taking in large corporate donations.[4]

Despite the PT's criticism of Fernando Henrique's conservative ties, Lula chose as his running mate José Alencar, a wealthy businessman and senator from Minas Gerais. Formerly of the PMDB, in 2002 Alencar joined a small conservative party, the Liberal Party, linked to evangelical Christians who had vociferously opposed Lula in past elections. Alencar helped calm fears that Lula would attack business and capitalism. Reflected throughout 2002 by speculation against the *real* in anticipation of a Lula victory—it fell to almost four per dollar—those fears threatened to destabilize the economy.[5]

Lula received praise from an unexpected quarter. At a press conference in Brasília in early June, U.S. ambassador Donna Hrinak, a George W. Bush appointee, was asked whether the Bush administration feared a Lula presidency. Hrinak said that she understood Lula well, because her father had been a steelworker. She admired Lula's rise from poverty to the apex of Brazilian politics. Because of press speculation about Lula, Hrinak wanted to say something upbeat. She told the reporters that "Lula is the personification of the American dream." For the Brazilian business community, Hrinak's words amounted to an endorsement of Lula as someone who could support their interests.[6] For the first time, a representative of the U.S. government had spoken of the Brazilian Left in such terms. For many Brazilians, it proved that the PT had indeed changed.[7]

The most critical moment in the remaking of Lula took place on June 22, 2002, when he read a "Letter to the Brazilian People" during a PT meeting. Later referred to sarcastically by some Brazilians as a "Letter to the Bankers," the document reassured the world that a PT government would continue the capitalist program of Fernando Henrique, including the former president's emphases on macroeconomic stability, control of inflation, and fiscal equilibrium.[8] Lula had willingly been co-opted by the international financial and economic elite.[9] To rescue Brazil from impending financial turmoil and the potential global economy repercussions, the Fernando Henrique government negotiated a $30 billion loan from the IMF, the largest it ever made to any country. Lula and the other opposition candidates all publicly pledged to honor the conditions of the loan, the funds from which would arrive mostly during the next administration.[10]

Working with Dirceu, Aloysio helped set up an official meeting between Lula and Fernando Henrique to discuss the loan. Aloysio also arranged secret meetings between Dirceu and the president to discuss the IMF agreement and other issues. Fernando Henrique not only had to share his logic but also get a read on Lula's reaction, recalled Aloysio: "Imagine if Lula had reacted and said: 'That agreement will only last until the end of the Fernando Henrique government. When I take office, it will not longer be in effect.' He needed to talk with Lula to agree on the political language that would be used by the government and the opposition. . . . During critical moments of the campaign, we had those contacts and avoided dramatizing the situation and feeding into the idea that the PT in power could mean chaos for the economy."[11]

THE GOVERNMENT ANNOUNCED the IMF agreement on August 7, 2002. On the morning of August 10, I went to the Citizenship Institute, the PT think tank, where Lula and two other key PT leaders were preparing to campaign in the city of São Paulo. The PT candidate for governor of São Paulo was José Genoíno, a rare survivor of the PC do B's Amazonian guerrilla effort and now an influential PT congressman. The PT mayor of São Paulo was Marta Suplicy, the ex-wife of PT senator Eduardo Suplicy and a famous psychologist and TV personality. She had defeated Maluf in a 2000 campaign intensely focused on the corruption of the Maluf and Pitta administrations.

Paulo Vannuchi had arranged for me to ride in the Lula motorcade. It was one among a myriad of tasks he handled during the taxing campaign, and not always the intellectual work that he enjoyed at the Citizenship Institute. "My job was to be a pivot, somebody who remained at campaign headquarters all the time and who had access to the main campaign coordinators," Paulo recalled. He resolved disputes among party rivals, kept Lula connected to the *movimento popular*, and handled logistics for key meetings. He helped prepare the visit to Brazil by the American civil rights activist Jesse Jackson. At a First Baptist Church event in São Paulo, Jackson called Lula a symbol of hope in the same vein as South African leader Nelson Mandela and Martin Luther King Jr. Paulo coordinated intelligence and counterintelligence regarding other candidates—the "nitroglycerine of the campaign"—and contributed material for potential use in TV spots and debates. He helped formulate parts of Lula's platform, and he joined meetings of prominent pro-PT intellectuals to critically analyze the campaign.[12]

Paulo also provided ideas for the plank on ethics and anticorruption measures. Along with others in the party, Paulo was concerned about the "troubling indications" of corruption in the Santo André mayoral administration of Celso Daniel, who was murdered in January 2002. Paulo said to Lula: "Look, any wrongdoing in the party, the PT is going to pay triple the political price of anybody else."[13]

I first observed Lula in person in October 1989 during a campaign speech in the impoverished outer Rio neighborhood known as Vila Kennedy, a large public housing project built in a 1960s urban renewal program aimed at removing favela-dwellers from the city's prosperous districts. Using the gesture that reflected his humble origins, Lula raised his left hand to reveal his missing pinky, lost while operating a lathe as a young man. Although Lula lost to Collor, the campaign generated great enthusiasm and hopes for future PT successes.

By 2002, Lula's party had become a Brazilian political institution. The cover story of the business-oriented newsmagazine *IstoÉ* declared: "Lula isn't scary anymore," the headline stamped over a picture of a smiling Lula in a white shirt and dark tie. The article discussed his plans to "humanize Brazilian capitalism."[14]

Lula's motorcade had an official escort of motorcycle police, adding an air of legitimacy. As we passed through one lower-middle-class neighborhood, small groups of people gathered on street corners to wait for him. However, no multitudes appeared at any stop that day, even in lower-class neighborhoods. Several Brazilian observers of the race commented to me that year that it lacked excitement, but Paulo later observed that in Recife and other cities in the Northeast, Lula's birthplace, record crowds turned out. Still, in São Paulo, the nation's largest city and where Lula grew up, no major rally took place.[15] The spontaneity and radicalism of 1989 had given way to the political sobriety and media-focused efforts of Lula and Dirceu in 2002.[16]

I rode in the second car with Gilberto Carvalho, the campaign chief of staff and a member of Lula's inner circle. He provided honest insight into Lula's outlook. An ex-seminarian from the neighboring state of Paraná, Gilberto had plunged into the radical Catholic movements of the late 1960s and early 1970s. He and others abandoned the seminary to live in a favela in Curitiba, the state capital. Inspired by French and Brazilian worker-priests, he also took a job in a factory. In 1979, he helped organize a major industrial strike in Curitiba. Gilberto became a key link between the *movimento popular* and the PT, running the party's grassroots political literacy initiatives. Rising within the party, he joined the Lula campaign in May 2002.[17]

Figure 33. Lula greeting a girl during a campaign stop in a lower-class São Paulo neighbor-hood, August 2002. Kenneth P. Serbin.

Gilberto emphasized that Lula had not abandoned the basic prin-ciples of social justice, refined under the tutelage of Catholic progressives such as Frei Betto and famed liberation theologian Leonardo Boff. How-ever, in Gilberto's view Lula had through experience also developed great political flexibility. Lula rejected dogmatism. He had declared himself a "socialist" in a general sense, without adhering to any model. After the fall of the Berlin Wall, Lula did not change his values but his tactical approach to power. Gilberto, not without qualms, extended this analysis to the 2002 election:

Sometimes I myself worry about the certain pragmatism that has taken over Lula. He actually was the person in the party who most battled for, who most fought for the alliance with the Liberal Party, which in theory is a party that doesn't have much to do with the PT or would have practically nothing to do with the PT. However, Lula became convinced—this is my opinion—that whenever an alliance could be made with a party and we maintained control of the alliance and, naturally, as long as they are not parties linked to corruption or the dictatorship, but even if they are center-right parties, as in the case of the Liberal Party, as long as we control the process, there is no risk in making the alliance. As he had very strong personal and political connections to José Alencar, who is a senator who had belonged to the PMDB and later joined the Liberal Party, he was determined to carry out the idea of an alliance with that party. He was able to convince the party, at least the majority of the party, to go ahead with the alliance. That reveals a pragmatism different from the past. It occurs to me that Lula, I would say, got tired of being only in the opposition.

Similarly, Gilberto believed that a President Lula would develop a pragmatic, results-oriented relationship with the United States, as long as it did not try to dominate Brazil. "I never saw on Lula's part, as a position of principle, antagonism towards the United States," Gilberto observed. "He got on extraordinarily well with the American ambassador. He told us that it was a very pleasant conversation. He was also very happy when she said that he, in some ways, represented the history of the American dream, that is, the person who rises from below."[18]

TWO EMBLEMATIC MOMENTS in the campaign signaled how Lula intended to govern. In the first, during an interview on August 29 on a popular morning TV program, Lula praised Médici, the most repressive of the dictators, as a way to criticize what he saw as a lack of strategic economic planning by Fernando Henrique. "In 1970, at the height of the military dictatorship, when President Médici was persecuting my comrades in the PT, we were experiencing the greatest creation in jobs in the country's history, with economic growth at 10 percent per year," Lula said. "The military leaders, with all their defects, thought about Brazil strategically, because they built Proalcool [the alcohol-run car program], they built the petrochemical complex, they built a reasonably good telecommunications system."[19] Lula wanted to increase the capacity of the internal Brazilian market to produce and consume.

The second moment came the night of October 3, just after the final nationally televised debate of the first round of the election. Confident of their chances in the October 6 vote, Lula, Duda, and other advisors and friends celebrated at an exclusive restaurant in Ipanema. With great fanfare, Duda bought Lula a present: a bottle of Romanée-Conti, a fine French wine drunk only by the wealthy, for more than 6,000 *reals* (about

$1,700). It provoked criticism. "It doesn't make sense that a presidential candidate says the things Lula says (the story of the woman beggar with a child in her lap, for example) and later washes down the truffles of his ravioli with a bottle of Romanée-Conti at the table," wrote veteran political columnist Elio Gaspari. "The scene is pathetic. Assuming that Lula believes in what he says, he found himself in a situation where it will be difficult for him to recognize himself."[20]

Oblivious to or unconcerned about the Médici era and that wine bottle—or perhaps because of them, because they, too, wanted a stronger country and to enjoy some luxury—Brazilians embraced the Lula candidacy. Lula faced three major opponents in the first round: José Serra of the PSDB, Garotinho of the PSB, and Ciro Gomes of the Popular Socialist Party, the former PCB. Lula won 46.4 percent of the vote, more than double the 23.2 percent of second-place Serra. Garotinho received 17.9 percent and Ciro 12 percent. The lack of a majority necessitated a runoff on October 27; Lula won a smashing victory over Serra: 61.3 to 38.7 percent. For the first time in the history of Brazil, a left-wing party took power at the federal level.[21] He became the first president of working-class origin in Latin American history. After the election of the socialist Salvador Allende in Chile in 1970, Lula's rise represented the most significant institutional success in the history of the Latin American Left.[22]

The night of October 27, PT supporters rejoiced in the streets. In São Paulo, Lula and his campaign occupied the five-star Hotel Gran Meliá. Paulo had handled logistics. There he celebrated with Globo TV news anchor and friend Chico Pinheiro and Pinheiro's broadcaster wife, Carla Vilhena. Later Lula, the campaign staff, and guests joined the crowd on the Avenida Paulista. "We not only won, but we won without any alarm, with no risk of 'Well, the military is not going to allow Lula to take office or Bush won't allow it,'" Paulo remembered of that night. "Nothing at all like that. Something very normal." Paulo understood the enormous challenge of transforming Brazil. He knew that the PT could not start humanity "from scratch." Nevertheless, after frequenting the Palácio do Planalto in the early days of the Lula government, he felt the "tremendous satisfaction of seeing the possibility of carrying out a transition like this one, which could put Brazil on the road to justice, to solidarity, without having to resort to widespread violence—a civil war—in the way I saw it when I became a militant at age seventeen, eighteen, something my children won't have to do. That gave me a sense of victory."[23]

Figure 34. President Lula. Wikimedia Commons.

In 2006, Lula won reelection in another landslide, defeating former São Paulo governor Geraldo Alckmin of the PSDB by 61 to 39 percent. On balance, over his two terms Lula delivered on his promises. The economy grew, living standards rose substantially for the poor, and the political system remained stable. He achieved such successes with a mix of economic conservatism, redistributive social policies, and effective, extensive pork barrel public works. He bolstered Brazil as a democratic and capitalist nation. However, the Lula administration also left a paradoxical legacy, since it both fought and contributed to corruption.

On the economic front, Lula proceeded cautiously—even more so than some conservative adversaries thought necessary.[24] In an era of vast U.S. public deficits, the IMF agreement required federal budget surpluses amounting to 3.75 percent of the GNP. In the first few years, the Lula government exceeded those requirements. Lula named Henrique Meirelles, a PSDB politician and bank executive, to head the Central Bank, and the opportunistic, proprivatization ex-mayor Palocci as the minister of finance. Meirelles kept interest rates high, and the value of the *real* recovered substantially. It continued to appreciate throughout the Lula era. Thus, Lula kept the currency stable and inflation low.[25]

Lula increased government intervention in the economy, largely through traditional mechanisms such as tax incentives and subsidized credit. He also increased the number of ministries and public employees. These developments reaffirmed state-led capitalism as Brazil's economic model, albeit within the framework established by Fernando Henrique.[26] Indeed, the PT reinvented state-led capitalism, with the state no longer acting as the main driver of development but as a coinvestor with the private sector. The government continued the Collor–Fernando Henrique approach of improving the performance and governance of the remaining state-owned firms, getting the largest of them listed on the Brazilian stock exchanges. The government's development bank also loaned large sums to private and state-owned companies, thus picking winners and partly reviving crony capitalism.[27] Lula pushed through a controversial reduction in Brazil's comparatively generous social security system in order to reduce its enormous deficits,[28] but the reform's long-term effectiveness was unclear.[29] Overall, Brazil was so financially stable that in 2009 it became a net creditor to the United States—and the fourth largest U.S. creditor overall. That stability helped Brazil to withstand the Great Recession of 2008–2009 better than most countries, including the United States.[30]

During the Lula years, Brazil solidified its position in global capitalism. After Brazil paid off its IMF loans early, in 2007, 2008, and 2009, the international credit rating agencies raised Brazil's credit rating to the highly desired investment-grade. Foreign investment flowed into Brazil; in the developing world, only China received greater direct investment. By the end of Lula's administration, the main Brazilian stock exchange, the Bolsa de Valores de São Paulo (BOVESPA, starting in 2008, BM&FBovespa), had grown to the world's fourth-largest stock market in terms of market value. Brazil had developed one of the world's most diversified economies, with a GDP of nearly $2 trillion. Brazilian conglomerates in food and steel expanded into international markets and—in a reverse of the imperialism once attacked by the ALN and Lula—acquired American companies such as Anheuser-Busch. Embraer ranked as the world's third-largest aircraft maker, furnishing the U.S. market and others with commuter and executive jets. In 2007 alone, at least fourteen Brazilians became billionaires, and in 2008 the country had 220,000 millionaires—more than India, which had six times the population. To end Brazil's dependence on the United States as its major trading partner, the Lula administration vastly expanded commercial ties with other countries. In 2009, China became Brazil's new leading trade partner—leading to fears that Chinese exports might supplant key local products, such as shoes. Despite poor basic infrastructure, such as roads, by the end of the Lula era, Brazil had more computers than the rest of Latin America combined, producing significant gains in business productivity. The boom also led to more spending on luxuries. In many respects, Brazilian capitalism was both agile and dynamic.[31] Along with rising prices paid by China for Brazilian foodstuffs and raw materials, Lula's policies led to a doubling of the economic growth rate compared to the Fernando Henrique years.[32]

However, Brazilian capitalism still had many flaws. Whereas twentieth-century industrialization had reduced Brazil's vulnerability by reducing its dependence on exports of commodities such as food and raw materials, under Lula these categories dominated once again, albeit some of the new commodities, such as ethanol and soy, involved technological aspects that produced positive spillovers into the economy.[33] Because of Lula's caution, Brazil's growth rates actually lagged behind most of the rest of Latin America, which also benefited greatly from the boom in China and India. Brazil's per capita economic growth also remained one of the region's lowest.[34] Under Lula, the economy created more jobs than the administrations of Sarney, Collor, Itamar, and Fernando Henrique combined: 10.5 million, a half million more than Lula had promised in 2002. Even so, continuing a long-term trend, about half of the economically active population still worked in the so-called informal sector, where people paid no taxes but also received no government benefits or legal protections.[35] The informal sector only started to decline significantly several years after Lula left office.[36] In addition, many of the jobs created were short-term. Reflecting a trend in the United States, Brazil relied increasingly on outsourcing, which accounted for 25.5 percent of the formal labor market in 2011. Self-employment also rose. Overall, labor unions lost ground, a grand irony for a former union leader.[37]

In November 2007, national euphoria set in when Petrobras announced the discovery of between 5 billion and 8 billion barrels of oil in a field known as Tupi, 160 miles off the coast of Rio de Janeiro. It practically doubled Brazil's proven reserves.[38] Petrobras executives said that Tupi could have as much as 80 billion barrels.[39] The oil is located in the so-called subsalt, a deposit below a thick layer of salt underneath the sea floor. For Latin America, estimates placed Brazil second only behind oil giant Venezuela in total reserves. Petrobras soon found additional subsalt reserves. Brazilian officials began boasting of the possibility of oil self-sufficiency. The discoveries set off debates regarding Brazil's concessions policy (a Petrobras monopoly versus the inclusion of private companies), the massive human and material infrastructure needed, and environmental effects.[40] Regarding potential royalties, the government suspended auctions involving private companies interested in Tupi. The Congress passed a law giving full control to Petrobras; potential profits would go into a sovereign fund dedicated to public investment in research, culture, education, and environmental preservation.[41] Despite the many complexities, the subsalt discoveries further burnished Brazil's reputation and Lula's political image. In September 2010, Petrobras finalized a stock offering to underwrite a $225 billion investment to develop the subsalt. Lula declared it the "greatest capital-raising in the history of world capitalism."[42]

MANOEL, A LULA SUPPORTER, found his public relations career revived thanks to Petrobras. After his many successes, in 2001 Manoel had plunged into deep psychological depression, the long-term result of violence and imprisonment. "I blew up my entire business," Manoel recalled. "I stopped caring for my appearance, my clothing, my teeth, my hair. And my agency. I unconsciously embarked on a process of self-destruction, because of the illness, because of my past problems. There's no mystery in it. It was the consequence of torture." With antidepressants and the help of a therapist recommended by another former ALN member, Manoel overcame the crisis—but without recovering his clients. In 2003, through another ALN connection, Manoel landed a public relations job at Petrobras's world headquarters in downtown Rio.[43]

At first, Manoel helped select and critique the materials of outside public relations firms. In 2004, another former revolutionary at Petrobras, Maria Augusta Carneiro Ribeiro, learned that Manoel was working there. A former MR-8 guerrilla and one of the fifteen prisoners (and the only woman) released in exchange for Ambassador Elbrick, Maria Augusta served as ombudsman, a new post set up by the PT to impartially receive complaints from and resolve disputes among employees. Under the privatization of Petrobras, the government retained considerable control. Maria Augusta had Manoel transferred to her department in an act of political and personal solidarity. The ombudsman's office sponsored employee volunteer projects. During one party to celebrate the projects, Manoel gave a short speech about the significance of his presence at Petrobras. He recalled the moment in 1969 when he saw the words written on the prison wall sixteen years earlier by another political prisoner, the beloved author Monteiro Lobato: "The oil is ours." After Fernando Henrique's privatizations, nationalistic sentiment had returned to Petrobras. Maria Augusta defended human rights within Petrobras and through many of its undertakings around Brazil. Manoel publicized the office's purpose and activities within the firm. Manoel also developed a successful media campaign for the exclusive, high-powered mix of Petrobras gasoline used in victorious Williams Formula 1 race cars. The campaign aimed to boost consumption of Petrobras's domestic gasoline.[44] Many Brazilians passionately follow Formula 1 racing, and the country's drivers rank frequently among the world's best.

Because of its abundant capital, Petrobras had become one of Brazil's biggest underwriters of films, cultural activities, and community social projects. After switching to the communications department in 2006, Manoel helped produce photo exhibits and publicity films highlighting the projects that brought the greatest political dividends for the firm. The production teams traveled around the country. "I went to the most fantastic places in Brazil working for Petrobras," Manoel observed. In the Amazon, where most travel is by river and access to services difficult, Manoel and the team documented the work of a floating medical clinic. According to Manoel, under the PT, Petrobras made selection of the projects more transparent to avoid political favoritism. "The PT democratized Petrobras's budget," he observed.[45]

ALTHOUGH BRAZIL REMAINED starkly unequal, the lives of the poor improved considerably under Lula. Extending Fernando Henrique's policies, he added programs of his own. A low-income consumer credit program injected billions of *reals* into the economy. He cut taxes on basic food and household items.[46] The government provided benefits to people with special needs and the impoverished elderly. It launched new services, such as dental clinics.[47] It supported small businesses and agro-industrial cooperatives. It also started the Electricity for Everybody program to bring power to poor areas, and it built public housing in an initiative baptized My House, My Life. The administration expanded Fernando Henrique's Bolsa Escola (scholarships for needy children) into a massive welfare program, Bolsa Família (family assistance), which sent monthly payments to registered low-income families with children in school.[48] Bolsa Família became the largest public cash transfer program in the world, with more than 13 million families enrolled by 2012.[49] Certified recipients withdrew funds electronically from a federal bank, thus bypassing the traditional distribution of government assistance by local politicians and eliminating potential manipulation of the program.[50] To ensure effective use of the funds, the government selected women as the vast majority of Bolsa Família recipients.

Like Fernando Henrique, Lula devoted an increasing percentage of the GNP to social spending. The lower classes especially benefited from an impressive 52 percent increase in the minimum wage over eight years. As Lula had hoped, the redistribution of income expanded Brazil's domestic market—something economists and historians had long identified as a severe weak point—and helped create a "new middle class." The term "middle class" was relative: the new middle class had a standard of living closer to the working and lower-middle classes of the developed world. Nevertheless, by 2009 Lula's policies had lifted 28 million people—14 percent of the population—out of poverty.[51] For first time in modern Brazilian history, inequality had dropped. During the "inclusionary decade" that began in 2001, inequality fell to a record low, with the incomes of the poor growing at triple the rate of those of the rich. For the first time in its history, Brazil became a middle-class-majority society in terms of consumption. Under Fernando Henrique, the poverty rate dropped from 43 to 35 or 36 percent of the population. Under Lula, the number fell to 20 percent.[52]

Earnings improved for people traditionally marginalized in Brazil: women, blacks, rural workers, participants in the informal sector, and those residing outside the relatively developed triangle of São Paulo, Rio de Janeiro, and Minas Gerais.[53] Paradoxically, especially for the Left, many benefiting from Lula's policies had no link to the *movimento popular*, the PT, or any other left-wing party. Many of these people had nevertheless seen Lula in person in the citizenship caravans of the 1990s.[54] A shift of lower-class loyalty to Lula—combined with the exit of middle- and upper-class supporters disturbed by the high levels of corruption starting in 2005—became especially clear in his 2006 reelection and second term.[55] Also, Lula's policies negatively affected the traditional middle class, which now paid more for the labor-intensive services it relied on (maids and nannies, for example). Overall, this class's standard of living declined in relation to the upper class. Its support for the PT began to erode.[56]

Despite the nascent political tensions, Lula brought poor Brazilians a step closer to the American dream of a secure, middle-class lifestyle. He strove for a capitalist model that resembled the mid-twentieth-century New Deal of President Franklin Delano Roosevelt. But access to consumer goods did not alone mean a middle-class life. To achieve Rooseveltian standards, Brazilians on the rise needed to improve the quality of their lives by gaining access to better jobs and housing and better public services, such as the health system, education, and transportation. In reducing inequality, Lula had reversed the negative trend started under the dictatorship. Some likened the creation of Bolsa Família with the Social Security Act of 1935. More ominously to some, Lula and the PT wanted to match another FDR achievement: to win four consecutive presidential terms, perhaps more. It wasn't implausible. Quickly, the PSDB and other parties had voiced support for Bolsa Família. Lula made poverty reduction a permanent part of the Brazilian political equation.[57]

IN THE QUEST to help Lula construct a Brazilian New Deal, Paulo acted counterintuitively: he turned down the chance to become a ruler. Instead of accepting Lula's offer in 2002 to work as a prestigious special assistant in the Palácio do Planalto—or perhaps even as Lula's personal secretary— he opted to develop a new initiative, the Youth Initiative, at the Citizenship Institute. Seldom had Paulo felt so torn as he did about his decision to remain outside the government.[58] In the end, he believed he made the correct choice.[59]

Paulo introduced some revolutionary thinking into Lula's view of power. The stress of the campaign, which Paulo expected to continue in the Planalto, convinced him to remain in São Paulo. An intense work schedule including many nonintellectual tasks, he thought, would rob him of the time he needed to "create, to formulate." "And it wasn't just a matter of refusing a mission," Paulo affirmed. "I had the conviction that it wouldn't be the most efficient way of contributing." Lula had told him, "I want you with me as one of my gurus" and the "people we'll have beers with at night," but Paulo considered that a "very idyllic outlook on Lula's part," given the stresses of governing. And although Paulo said he would join the government if there were "extreme circumstances," he said personal considerations—a two-year-old toddler and a wife (his third) with a psychoanalytic practice in São Paulo—that hindered a move. "But, above all, I think the government needs to have trustworthy supporters outside the government," for instance, continuing in São Paulo working in the Citizenship Institute and with the grassroots. "Lula agreed with me completely."[60]

Informally, Paulo did assist Lula with some matters. He confidentially helped select cabinet members, vetting powerful, high-profile politicians.[61] In December 2003, he accompanied the president on his historic, controversial trip to five Arab nations, the first-ever visit by a Brazilian president to the Middle East, in an effort to project a more proactive role for the country in the world and generate business for Brazilian firms.[62] Mainly, though, the unobtrusive Paulo dedicated himself to the Citizenship Institute, which had no official link to the government, and to his work as a union advisor. Paulo became the Citizenship Institute's executive coordinator. He could exercise power without being in power. "I believed the Youth Initiative had a beautiful program that I could be focusing on," he stated. "And if there hadn't been somebody like me willing to get it started and do the networking and building, it might never have gotten off the ground."[63]

In 1990, the Congress had passed the Statute for Children and Adolescents in an attempt to secure the constitutional rights of individuals ages eighteen and under. Paulo spearheaded the Youth Initiative, helping to bring the issues of youth (defined as ages fifteen to twenty-four) onto the governmental agenda. In contrast with traditional, bureaucracy-driven programs, Paulo used the PT's participatory model to consult with youth leaders, specialists in youth issues, NGOs, and others in a series of meetings

Figure 35. Paulo outside the headquarters of the Sindicato dos Metalúrgicos do ABC, São Paulo's industrial region, 2006. Kenneth P. Serbin.

around Brazil in 2003 and 2004. Three thousand people took part in the process.[64] At an initial brainstorming session at the Citizenship Institute in June 2003, twenty-five participants identified the main problem: a "huge gap in language between the people who make policy, or try to make policy, and youth," according to the meeting minutes. The participants noted the absence of working-class youth voices and the lack of a youth policy from the PT and other parties. Other topics included work, education, culture, sports, health, mental health, sexuality, drugs, violence, and legal rights.[65] Significantly, the initiative rejected Brazil's traditional, narrow emphasis on "juvenile delinquency"—exacerbated in the country's violent detention centers—in favor of viewing youths as citizens and protagonists of their own lives. After receiving the initiative's broad-ranging conclusions, in February 2005 Lula established a National Youth Policy. It created a National Secretariat for Youth, National Youth Council, and ProYouth, the National Program for the Inclusion of Youths.[66] "It was really a theme the country had not paid attention to," Paulo said.[67]

The national secretariat was significant but only a first step. It also administered ProYouth, the flagship of the Youth Initiative. Indeed, Pro-Youth produced the most concrete results,[68] joining a larger endeavor by the government to transition workers into the formal job market.[69] Brazil's youths were unemployed at twice the national rate.[70] Because ProYouth addressed diverse needs and ideological outlooks, including those of business, it garnered the most political support of all the initiative's proposals. It focused on unemployed working- and lower-class youths, especially those who had not completed junior high. Participants took a twelve-month course to complete junior high, receive job training, and work on a community project.[71] Significantly, ProYouth aimed to prepare youths for new types of work as traditional industrial, agricultural, and service jobs disappeared because of mechanization and computerization. Brazil's youths could now learn to care for children and the elderly, participate in combating dengue fever, educate people about AIDS, or work to protect the environment. Classes started in July 2005. Hoping to enroll 1 million students per year, the Lula government budgeted 300 million *reals* for ProYouth, subject to annual congressional approval. The course provided a 100-*real* stipend—more than what families received from Bolsa Família (a maximum of 95 *reals* for a family with three children). Because of budgetary limitations, the government established a minimum age of eighteen for enrollees.[72]

In 2007, the government included rural youths and younger adolescents in ProYouth.[73] By Lula's last year in office, the government estimated that 2 million youths had participated.[74] A study of urban participants found that those completing the program performed well academically, even though more than 40 percent dropped out, a rate similar to that of the public schools.[75] The government trained many in ProYouth, but it put forth no statistics on how many obtained jobs in the private sector or started small businesses.

Paulo then took on the Project for a National Policy to Support Local Development, which offered federal assistance to catalyze sustainable projects. Lula also implemented massive projects, such as the Program to Accelerate Growth (PAG), which invested in more than three hundred public and private infrastructure projects, including roads, railways, power plants, ports, airports, and refineries. The government obtained funds for PAG from Petrobras, private investors, and other sources. Some projects went to large, politically connected construction companies: a consortium led by Construtora Norberto Odebrecht, the country's biggest construction company and owned by Emílio Odebrecht, won the bid for one of the largest projects, a hydroelectric dam in the Amazon. (The firm later became implicated in a massive bribery investigation known as Operation Car Wash; see chapter 14.) The PAG also supported community infrastructure in poor areas. By 2010, the PAG had injected $200 billion into the Brazilian economy. That year the government announced PAG 2, with a goal of investing more than $500 billion. The PAG helped enhance both Lula's legacy and the PT's chances in the 2010 presidential election.[76]

In the political arena, Lula practiced "peace and love." He skillfully balanced the many competing interests of a large and diverse society with a political spectrum much broader than that of the United States. Of all the presidents, Lula picked the greatest number of cabinet ministers who had resisted the dictatorship.[77] The most prominent was Dirceu, the chief of staff and second most powerful person in the government. Lula also brought on board Dilma Rousseff, who had belonged to VAR-Palmares (Palmares Armed Revolutionary Vanguard). She served as minister of mines and energy and then chief of staff. She led the way in defining the rules for the subsalt oil. She was also known as the "mother of the PAG."

The Lula administration most decidedly avoided radical actions. It sought to bring political and social conflicts under the purview of the bureaucracy—as opposed to clashes in the streets.[78] Lula and the PT thus avoided the radicalism of left-wing governments in other South American countries.[79] The PT also abandoned any pretense of governing with the transparency and high level of citizen participation it had promoted at the local level in the 1990s. Lula represented the triumph of pragmatism.[80] Depending on his audience and political needs, Lula could play the role of fiery speaker or conciliator. In one observer's words, his government "simultaneously antagonized and reconciled, denounced and built consensus, inflamed and cooled down."[81]

Significantly, the PT reneged on its historic promise to carry out a massive redistribution of land to the rural poor. This would have alienated the large landowners of the powerful agribusiness sector (soybean producers and cattle ranchers, for example) and property owners in general. Fernando Henrique's government actually had redistributed far more land. The Lula government extended handsome subsidies and other privileges to agribusiness. Although bringing Brazil international recognition, the rise of agribusiness jeopardized the environment because of deforestation and harmful agricultural practices. The rural *movimento popular* felt betrayed by Lula and the PT.[82] Brazil had abolished slavery in 1889, but it had yet to address the equally important, centuries-old problem of control of the land by a few.[83] Under Lula, agricultural exports made up 4 percent of GDP and 97 percent of trade surpluses.[84] Thus, agribusiness consolidated its position as a key economic driver, further drawing Brazil into the global capitalist system. While China became the workshop of the world, Brazil became its farm.[85]

The far Left understood Lula's approach all too well. Some prosocialist groups and leaders of the *movimento popular* quit the PT. Despite Gilberto Carvalho's role as Lula's link to the grass roots, many progressive Catholics distanced themselves from the government. Frei Betto, a special presidential assistant, resigned in late 2004 in frustration over the watering down of a program to eradicate hunger. He denounced Bolsa Família for creating dependence on the government and failing to provide job training, and he criticized the administration for abandoning the *movimento popular*.[86]

Many PT members and other citizens became disillusioned after the stark revelation that the party had lost perhaps its most precious political capital: clean government. In February 2004, Dirceu assistant Waldomiro Diniz was revealed in a video soliciting a bribe, destined for the PT, from a leader of Rio's infamous numbers racket. Other denunciations of corruption followed. Feuding internally, in February 2005 the PT lost the speakership of the Chamber of Deputies to Severino Cavalcanti, a member of the Progressive Party. Unaligned with the government, the Progressive Party counted Maluf among its key members. Without the speakership, Lula lost critical support for his legislative goals.

On June 6, 2005, Congressman Roberto Jefferson revealed a bombshell. A member of the PTB, one of the small, conservative parties in the PT coalition, Jefferson disclosed that the PT had engineered an illegal party-switching and vote-buying scheme to preserve the coalition and the congressional majority. The arrangement was known as the "mensalão," the "big monthly allowance" paid to individual representatives, using illicitly obtained funds. Jefferson implicated Dirceu and other PT leaders. Most people did not recall the regional PT scandals of the 1990s, but it became clear that graft and illegal payments had been fueling the party's campaigns and offshore accounts.[87] Maintaining the coalition also fueled the large growth in the number of ministries and public employees.[88]

The day after Jefferson's revelation, Paulo described the situation as "the most difficult moment of the Lula government." In his analysis, the Waldomiro scandal "struck at a fundamental aspect of the party, which was its moral force and transparency." The situation was worsened by Dirceu's involvement, "a former militant of the underground movement" key to coordinating the government and mediating the PT's internal factions. Cavalcanti's election and Jefferson's revelation shook Paulo's confidence in the PT. "Personally, I have told people that it was the first time that I felt shame," Paulo admitted. "Our defeat in the election for the Speaker of the House had begun within the PT. The PT did not demonstrate unity, seriousness, a commitment to the country required of a party in power." The Jefferson episode "wears down the government," Paulo added. Lula was too generous, even naïve, in forming alliances with "false" allies such as Jefferson. Paulo believed that the broad, democratic, left-wing front nurtured by the PT over decades now ran the risk of failure.[89]

"A government like Lula's must not hesitate," Paulo emphasized. The president needed to root out and punish corruption. From 2001 to 2003, Paulo had co-organized a series of Citizenship Institute seminars focused on a campaign promise: the reform of Brazil's political system. On July 1, 2003, Lula officially presented the resultant book to the leaders of both the Senate and Chamber of Deputies.[90] In the preface, Lula underlined the need to "combat corruption and the promiscuity between public and private actors."[91] The book reflected on ways to eliminate slush funds, money laundering, and other illicit practices. The problem was "profoundly rooted in the political and business culture of Brazil," American political scientist David Samuels wrote in a chapter on campaign finance. Samuels suggested that Brazil consider public financing of campaigns, a limit on contributions, and the reform of tax and banking laws to encourage transparency.[92] In 2005, the problem seemed worse than ever. "Candidates' financial statements are totally fictitious," Paulo affirmed. "Everybody knows that. Fernando Henrique does. Lula does.... The country has not yet made up its mind to say: 'Let's have an open debate about this among ourselves. Let's change this thing.'" As they did in the United States, Brazilian courts needed to confiscate wealth gained via corruption, Paulo added. If not, corruption—even with jail time—would remain attractive.[93] The problem went far beyond Lula and the PT. However, Lula did not seem to take to heart his think tank's analysis and recommendations.

Days after Jefferson's denunciations, Dirceu resigned, as did former guerrilla Genoíno, who had become the party president after his unsuccessful bid for governor of São Paulo. The secretary general quit, and the party later expelled its treasurer. During an interview in Paris on July 15, 2005, Lula publicly acknowledged that the PT was no different from any other Brazilian political party: "What the PT did from an electoral standpoint is done systematically in Brazil."[94] On August 12, in a speech on national TV, Lula asked the Brazilian people for forgiveness and stated that he felt betrayed, but he did not say who was responsible. The scandal damaged the party's reputation more than Lula's. Small, ultraleftist parties wanted to impeach Lula, but the PSDB and other major opposition parties did not agree. With Lula gaining popularity thanks to the growing economy, both sides wanted to avoid an open confrontation.[95]

Paradoxically, although few noted this at the time, the PT became caught up in its own campaign against corruption. The mensalão and Lula's reaction to it contradicted his administration's significant advances in the prosecution of white-collar crime, made possible by the improved investigative power of the Polícia Federal (Federal Police, the equivalent of the FBI). The Polícia Federal had obtained autonomy under Lula and increased collaboration with other federal investigative bodies. The Lula government also expanded the Comptroller General's Office, created in 2002 by Fernando Henrique.[96] Overall, an improvement in these and other institutions made the country a victim of its own success: increased exposure of corruption raised people's opinion of those institutions but also led to greater dissatisfaction with the status quo.[97]

SEEKING TO OVERCOME THE mensalão crisis, in July 2005 Lula introduced budget cuts that resulted in eliminating or downsizing some cabinet posts. One agency that lost cabinet status was the Secretaria Especial de Direitos Humanos da Presidência da República (SEDH, or Special Secretariat for Human Rights of the President of the Republic), created by Fernando Henrique in 1997 and raised to a cabinet-level position by Lula in 2003. Nilmário Miranda, a former revolutionary and political prisoner, prominent PT politician, and leading human rights advocate, stepped down as the head of the SEDH. However, under pressure from human rights groups and recognizing the symbolic downgrade, Lula reestablished the SEDH at the ministerial level.[98]

Lula made Paulo the new head. On December 6, 2005, Paulo met with the president to discuss the nomination. "Human rights are the center of my life," Paulo told Lula. Paulo recalled: "He trusted my ability to dialogue, especially with the social movements. He would personally help me in any way I needed."[99] Paulo officially took office on December 21, 2005. As a former political prisoner and victim of brutal torture, how did he react to becoming the minister of the SEDH? "My activism was already focusing on the recovery of the historical memory and the settling of accounts, and these were part of a much wider range of interests that were just as central as those others or even more so," he said in a 2006 interview.

> For example, the idea of building a country without poverty, without misery, without unemployment. I even have a hard time establishing relations with some of the groups of the families of the dead and disappeared. There are a few of these small groups that spend all of their time just on that issue. And even when I say, "Why don't we start a movement against the torture that exists today?," it's as if that matter was unimportant. Torture with dignity was only the kind that was in the past. That's completely unacceptable. I mean, the torture that affected me, that affected my relative, my cousin, that killed my comrades is still present today.[100]

Even with his broad interpretation of human rights, Paulo focused on the military-era atrocities daily. He confronted serious political obstacles, including Lula's hesitancy to antagonize the armed forces.[101] Paulo had recognized this political conundrum in 2003, discussing the infamous officer who had tortured him. "If I'm going to want mess with Ustra, I'll need to decide whether starting a fight with the army, by getting Ustra and putting him in jail, is worth it in terms of a pragmatic cost-benefit relationship," Paulo affirmed. "We want to govern."[102] In December 2005, Lula assured Paulo that he wanted the armed forces to finally open up their archives from the dictatorial era.[103] Lula also wanted clarification of the circumstances of, and responsibility for, the deaths and disappearances, including location of graves.[104] That month the government opened relevant files of Brazil's CIA, the Agência Brasileira de Inteligência (ABIN), transferring them to the National Archives in Brasília. The predecessor to the ABIN had aided the repressive forces and spied on regime opponents. However, with the military archives still closed, Paulo sought the preservation of existing records (including digitization) and warned officials about the legal consequences of hiding or destroying documentation. "You always need to dialogue very judiciously with the military," Paulo observed. "The Brazilian armed forces still need to attain a greater awareness of the rule of law, and of the fact that the military regime really represented a break with the democratic system."[105] Paulo recognized that, unlike in Argentina, Chile, and Uruguay, where former dictators and their agents faced punishment and mass public protests, "in Brazil, unfortunately, we no longer have any large movements with society discussing the military regime. Here the movement involves more of an awareness-building about human rights by researchers, journalists, and the activists."[106] In this atmosphere, Paulo had to exercise extraordinary patience and self-control.

Because of the Lula administration's decision to appeal a 2003 court ruling requiring the military to turn over all information about the missing Araguaia guerrillas, at SEDH Paulo revitalized the government commission set up in 1995 to recognize the government's responsibility for atrocities and compensate families. In a difficult dialogue with the angry Araguaia families, Paulo defended Lula's government but also sought to facilitate the search for the hidden graves. The government commission set up a DNA bank to help identify the remains. "I personally don't think it's advisable that the government raise the question of punishment," Paulo observed. "That subject is one for the human rights movements and the relatives to raise, according to their particular positions. Because what we're doing here involves the idea of revealing what happened. It's about the right to memory and truth."[107] In 2007, the SEDH published a 500-page report of the government commission, *Direito à Memória e à Verdade: Comissão Especial sobre Mortos e Desaparecidos Políticos* (*The Right to Memory and the Truth: The Special Commission on Dead and Disappeared Political Militants*), with descriptions of the abuses of each of the 475 recognized victims of the dictatorship. Twenty-two years after the end of the dictatorship and the publication of *Brasil: Nunca mais*, the government had finally issued an official report on the atrocities.[108] Shortly thereafter, the government dropped its appeal of the Araguaia decision.[109] However, the military's archives remain closed.

Though Lula officially received the Madres de la Plaza de Mayo, the mothers of the Argentine desaparecidos, he did not have a ceremony for the Brazilian families.[110] The president did share a few moments with some of the families at the launching for *Direito à Memória e à Verdade*. Lula promised to find the bodies of the disappeared.[111] However, in eight years his government located not a single desaparecido. Paulo remained deeply loyal to Lula, but he believed that the government needed to act faster and do more. He noted that Lula had arrived in power aiming to do the opposite of what opponents feared: "to beckon for a grand national accord without revenge. So, he did not attack the military in the way some might have expected. . . . He did not want to dwell on the past."[112]

In December 2009, Paulo proposed the creation of a National Truth Commission to investigate—but not punish—human rights violations during the dictatorship. The proposal was part of the third National Plan for Human Rights, launched by the SEDH. The Truth Commission would have the power to request documents, reconstruct incidents, explain the practice of torture to the public, and locate the remains of the desaparecidos.[113] Defense Minister Nelson Jobim and the heads of the army, navy, and air force threatened to resign, offended because a potential commission would investigate human rights violations committed specifically "in the context of political repression."[114] In Paulo's estimation, they sought to provoke an incident in order to block the potential candidacy of Dilma Rousseff in the 2010 election. In what Paulo later described as a "lynching" and the "strongest ideological attack suffered by the Lula government," conservative media outlets attacked other aspects of the National

Plan for Human Rights, such as women's reproductive rights.[115] Paulo argued that a Truth Commission actually favored the military, because it would demonstrate that only a fraction of Brazil's many military men had committed abuses.[116] He also threatened to resign. Lula, Paulo, and Jobim negotiated a compromise; Lula removed the offending phrase about political repression. He set up a commission to study the commission, a maneuver that put the process well into 2010, a presidential election year.[117] Some interpreted Lula's ambiguous actions as a way to "wash his hands" of the matter,[118] leaving it for the next administration.[119] The controversy also raised concerns that a truth commission could upset the conciliation resulting from the 1979 Amnesty Law, which protected torturers from prosecution.[120]

In a historic decision in April 2010, the Supreme Court rejected a formal request from the Brazilian Bar Association to revoke torturers' protection under the amnesty. Paulo condemned the ruling.[121] On November 24, 2010, the Inter-American Court of Human Rights unanimously found the Brazilian government guilty of causing the disappearance of sixty-two Araguaia guerrillas. The sentence required Brazil to identify and punish the perpetrators and prohibited the use of the Amnesty Law to impede the process.[122] Though Brazil had ratified the American Convention on Human Rights, it resisted implementing the ruling.

Because they represented an unresolved, highly charged history, issues regarding the dictatorship made up nearly all of the media coverage of the SEDH. However, the ministry dedicated nearly all its resources to other human rights matters, involving tens of millions of citizens.[123] "Human rights is a huge area," Paulo observed. SEDH focused on the rights of children, adolescents, youths accused of crimes, the LGBTQ community, the elderly, and the disabled. The ministry combatted child labor, the sexual exploitation of children and adolescents, and international trafficking of children. It also denounced violence against the natives, attacks on small rural landholders, and slavery, which persisted in some areas of Brazil. It contributed to joint operations against death squads and inhumane treatment in prisons. SEDH produced unprecedented human rights education campaigns, including the participation of top soccer teams, who wore uniforms with a symbol promoting the rights of the disabled. SEDH also worked to educate police forces about the need to respect human rights.[124] SEDH helped organize Brazil's periodic national human rights conferences. Under Paulo, the most critical took place in 2008. It marked the sixtieth anniversary of the UN Declaration of Human Rights, a historic moment because of the UN's call to nations to formulate their own human rights strategies. Twelve cabinet members joined Lula at the opening. Two thousand people participated, helping lay the basis for the idea of a Truth Commission.[125] SEDH also fought the practice of torture in police stations with awareness campaigns.[126] SEDH grew significantly. In the mid-2000s, the SEDH had a staff of just 200 people and no official budget. When Paul left office in 2010, he had doubled the staff and obtained from Lula a 650 percent increase in the now-official budget.[127]

Despite its peripheral status within the Brazilian government, the SEDH had a significant international profile. Though Brazil became known for violations of human rights, its dictatorial legacy made it one of the few nations with a cabinet-level human rights post. Although they competed fiercely in other areas, the PT and the PSDB developed a consensus on human rights. In the words of Paulo Sérgio Pinheiro, a SEDH head under Fernando Henrique, Brazil had thus acquired an international reputation as an "honest broker" in human rights. Paulo Vannuchi had a "line of ambassadors" wanting to visit him, but not the U.S. envoy. Paulo also opened discreet discussions with China, seen as a serious violator of human rights.[128] Paulo chafed when in 2006 a U.S. State Department analysis lowered the grade of Brazil's human rights record. The report detailed numerous abuses. Paulo pointed out that the report ignored abuses at U.S.-controlled prisons in Cuba and Iraq. It also ignored "important changes that we introduced." Moreover, Paulo pointed out, Brazil had signed key international human rights treaties, and, unlike the United States and Canada, was represented at the Inter-American Commission on Human Rights.[129] As in the 2010 ruling against the Brazilian government, that commission sent its decisions to the Inter-American Court of Human Rights for judgment.

On balance, the progress on human rights of the Fernando Henrique/ Lula era was mixed. In a 2010 report by one of the most important human rights think tanks, former SEDH head Paulo Sérgio described "the contradictory situation of human rights in our country," with significant institutional and policy improvements and the growing mobilization of civil society, but still many abuses. In Paulo Sérgio's analysis, Brazilians could no longer blame just the legacies of the dictatorship; despite socioeconomic progress, the democratic system had failed to reduce violations substantially. For example, homicide rates remained alarmingly high—in

2006, 26.3 per 100,000 inhabitants, compared to 5.2 in the United States and 1.46 in France. In 2016, the rate had grown to 29.9, producing 61,619 murders. In 2017, it reached 30.8, with 63,880 murders. The state had no control over many favelas and remote areas of the country, where lawlessness and corruption reigned. The Brazilian state had done nothing to reform the repressive police system and ineffective judiciary, which vast numbers of Brazilians could not access. Most Brazilian politicians ignored human rights, and officials who were conscientious about the matter were stymied in finding practical ways to implement them.[130] Like administrations before it, the Lula government failed to reduce criminal violence, and violence by both drug traffickers and the police against the poor. This became starkly evident in May 2006, when a prison-based criminal group, the First Command of the Capital, unleashed an attack on São Paulo, killing officers, burning buses, and shutting down the city completely. More than five hundred people died.[131]

Paulo frequently wrestled with a widespread bias: the impression that "human rights are for defending outlaws." In Paulo's view, the human rights community needed to combat this false notion through cultural programs and other means.[132] Another, deeply imbedded problem was the sense of impunity that dominated the country. Like the unprosecuted dictatorship's torturers, many human rights violators walked free.[133] A small ministry could not possibly address all of the many violations in a population of almost 190 million. Brazil still had much work to do.

DURING THE LULA ERA, other members of the ALN cohort rose to key leadership positions. Having retired from business, Márcio had entered politics for the first time in the 2002 election. Distrustful of the PT's radical elements, in the first round he became the de facto campaign manager for Ciro Gomes of the Popular Socialist Party, the former PCB. He donated 900,000 *reals* to the effort. Márcio was drawn to Ciro's nationalistic economic stance, support for industrial policy, and acerbic critique of Fernando Henrique's opening of the economy.[134] Rewarding Ciro's support in the second round, Lula made him head of the Ministry of National Integration. Largely concerned with the impoverished Northeast, National Integration was seen as one of the most corrupt, least financially accountable ministries. Márcio became Ciro's executive secretary, the second-in-command. Ciro and Márcio found the ministry in a state of chaos.[135]

Márcio called it a "pork barrel operation" used for political interests rather than the national good. Since the military era, he estimated, corruption had resulted in billions of *reals* in losses to the ministry.[136]

Consistent with his ideals of business competence and entrepreneurship, Márcio applied a "cultural shock" to improve the ministry. "We need clarity on the cost-benefit of things," Márcio explained in a 2003 interview. "We need to define priorities, create performance indicators, and include in the cost of our actions the salaries of our employees. The government doesn't do this." Tracking losses resulting from corruption, Márcio attempted to recover the funds. He encountered far more administrative procedures in government than in the private sector, yet in his view they did not improve performance or eliminate corruption. In one sector of the ministry, he found employees working in an authoritarian culture, with no staff meetings. "The simple fact that I sent an e-mail to the employees was a cultural shock [laughter]," Márcio said.[137] After heavy floods in early 2004 left 300,000 Northeasterners homeless, Márcio and Ciro advised Lula to avoid sending relief funds via politicians, susceptible to being skimmed, and channel assistance through a new kind of interagency effort. The ministry provided tons of food and medications, thus avoiding outbreaks of epidemic disease.[138]

Ciro and Márcio fought to make the ministry generate ideas and incentives for Brazil's regional development, especially in the Northeast. Key proposals included a regional Northeast railroad.[139] The most ambitious—and controversial—project aimed to bring the waters of the São Francisco River to thousands of families and farmers vulnerable to the deadly drought cycles of the Northeast region. A major campaign plank of Lula, the irrigation project would include numerous dams and thousands of miles of pipelines and canals. Opponents argued that it would threaten the ecosystem and benefit large landowners, harming the poor. The government used eminent domain to remove people from land needed for the project. Despite the controversies, the Lula administration forged ahead. The potential for the Brazilian economy was enormous—but so was the risk. Some irrigation projects flourished, while others failed because of inadequate technological investment and marketing. Though aimed at helping Brazil achieve water security,[140] the São Francisco project suffered several delays.[141] As of mid-2018, the government had not completed it.

Márcio's government service came with a high personal cost and risk to his reputation. With mass layoffs at Construtel as he shut down his

Figure 36. Márcio in Rio in 2007. Kenneth P. Serbin.

business and began his work at the ministry, Márcio apparently contradicted the assumption of many Brazilians that all politicians are corrupt.
"Everybody thought that I had gone into government to increase my business, but I'm cutting back," Márcio commented.[142] On August 2, 2005,
Márcio became erroneously implicated in the mensalão scandal when the
press published articles citing a Polícia Federal investigation alleging that
he had received 457,000 *reals* from a mensalão bagman.[143] Márcio denied
any wrongdoing, but resigned immediately. To clear his name, he spent
350,000 *reals* of his personal funds on lawyers and a public relations specialist. The bagman admitted that he had incorrectly implicated Márcio.
After eight months of work, including a deposition to the Polícia Federal
and visits to congressional representatives, Márcio obtained an official ex-
oneration. He was the only individual declared innocent in the mensalão.
Tired of the matter, which had deeply embarrassed his family, Márcio
declined to return to the Ministry of National Integration. He learned
a valuable lesson about Brazil's politics and media. "I was the one who
had to prove I was innocent," he later observed. "Things are completely
distorted."[144]

Márcio's experience in Brasília increased his political stock. Starting in June 2006, he coordinated the regional development initiative of the Federation of Industries of the State of Minas Gerais. Letting his hair and beard grow, he also spent time sailing his boat in the Caribbean in order to recover from the stress and ponder his future. In 2007, he became the secretary of state for economic development in the cabinet of Minas Gerais governor Aécio Neves da Cunha of the PSDB.[145] Aécio was the grandson of Tancredo Neves, the president-elect who had died in 1985.

Aécio paved the way for Márcio to run in 2008 for mayor of Belo Horizonte, Brazil's fourth largest city, with 2.5 million people as of 2000. The outgoing mayor, Fernando Pimentel of the PT, had participated in a failed attempt by the VPR in 1970 to kidnap the U.S. consul in Porto Alegre.[146] He and Márcio met in the political prison in Juiz de Fora; the two later worked together at a telecommunications company before the start of Construtel. In 2002, Márcio donated to Pimentel's successful vice mayoral campaign (Pimentel became mayor after the winner quit for health reasons).[147] From opposing parties, Pimentel and Aécio backed Márcio's candidacy as a trial balloon for a possible national alliance of the PSDB, the PT, and other parties. Ciro played a role, too. They hoped that a center-left bloc could attract voters by eliminating the need to form coalitions with the PMDB and the other, smaller parties interested only in pork. "Lula himself took part in the negotiations, and they reached the conclusion that Belo Horizonte could be a laboratory for the establishment of that third way," Márcio recalled. "To that end, I could be the consensus candidate." As a result, Márcio ran on the ticket of the PSB with the support of both the PT and the PSDB, defeating the PMDB candidate in the second round. It was as if the Democrats and Republicans had jointly backed a third-party candidate for mayor of Chicago. The Belo Horizonte election became the focus of national attention, further boosting Márcio's political profile and Aécio's presidential possibilities.[148]

Márcio approached the mayoralty with the same practical, collaborative emphasis he had at Construtel and the ministry. He and his advisors drew up a strategic, twenty-year plan for governing and improving the quality of life in Belo Horizonte by improving public transportation, education, health, and the environment.[149] Márcio made political appointments of eleven former Construtel and Batik executives and employees, including longtime friend and ex-Corrente member Marcello Abi-Saber.[150] Overseeing an annual budget of 10 billion *reals* (about $5.9 billion) and nearly 50,000 public employees, Márcio introduced meritocratic criteria for political appointments by having a human resources firm administer vocational tests. "People were scandalized at first," Márcio said. He noted that government procedures often changed slowly, requiring new laws and regulations and surmounting bureaucratic inertia; pork-oriented parties opposed Márcio's rejection of their job candidates. "On the tests the applicants answered hundreds of questions over a three-hour period," he commented. "You end up with people who are qualified, motivated, and dedicated to a shared objective." To review progress on city priorities, Márcio's administration held staff meetings that included top managers and also technical personnel from all city departments. "It's a space for criticisms, suggestions, and accountability," Márcio observed. "There's no party clique here, no ivory tower, no black box. That's how it is in a business, right? So people criticize me for not being a politician, and I say that it's because I don't allow the formation of fiefdoms.... With the passage of time, good people, leftists, those with a humanistic view of the world came to see that I had a . . . strategy that incorporated elements borrowed from private business but that also aimed for inclusion, justice, and progress."[151]

Overall, Márcio got high marks from the Belo Horizonte population. In December 2010, at the midpoint of his administration, an opinion poll canvassing Brazil's eight leading cities asked citizens to rate their mayor's performance. Márcio had the highest approval rating.[152]

In SÃO PAULO, PT veteran Adriano's career took an unexpected turn that led him to become even more politically moderate—and more accepting of capitalism. In the 2002 election, Adriano stepped up from the São Paulo City Council to the São Paulo State Assembly. In January 2003, with two years still left in her term, São Paulo mayor Marta Suplicy replaced the head of the city's Secretariat for Green Matters and the Environment with Adriano. He now called on his experience as a geologist and specialist in public sanitation. On leave from the assembly, for the first time Adriano worked in the executive branch. In a July 2003 interview, Adriano marveled at Lula's moderation as he himself sought to adapt to new circumstances. "I was very afraid that the Lula government would become an ultraleftist government and isolated like all of the leftist governments of Latin America," he stated. However, Adriano was "utterly surprised" by the fact that the Lula government was "level-headed," even "on the conservative side." Lula had "more of a centrist ethos." "On the other hand, I'm in a quandary as to whether that centrism, that conservatism, might result in a lack of creativity and independence on the part of the president," he observed. "But I think I prefer that conservative model that lasts longer as opposed to a more leftist, more popular government that lasts less. . . . I believe Lula has become a statesman."[153]

Adriano took charge of environmental affairs in a city of 11 million people surrounded by industrial suburbs with another 9 million inhabitants—the globe's third-largest urban area. Over the preceding 140 years, São Paulo had experienced the fastest big-city growth in human history.[154] During Adriano's two years in office, the secretariat advanced on several fronts, including a system to test cars for pollution violations; the establishment of large, environmentally protected areas; cleaning of dumps; a renewed emphasis on recycling; and an initiative to involve the populace in ecological matters. Adriano and his staff administered the city's thirty-two parks, an immensely valuable resource in a highly polluted megalopolis with very little green space.[155]

The secretariat had an extremely small budget, about $25 million, mainly for operating expenses. It set aside only a few hundred thousand dollars for investments and projects. Adriano met this challenge by reaching out to the corporate world, securing sponsorships worth millions of dollars. Funds for various projects came from Petrobras, the Pão de Açucar supermarket chain, Nestlé, the Spain-based Telefónica, the Fundação Roberto Marinho (named after the powerful founder of the Globo network), the bicycle-maker Caloi, and other sources. The secretariat also obtained assistance from the Inter-American Development Bank. Private investment in public areas was very new in Brazil. "I see no problem in having the private sector, especially the multinational corporations, which make so much money here, donate some of their money to the people," Adriano commented. "That's part of their marketing. Now, if you want to say that the model has changed, I agree: it has changed. In the past worse things were done without the relationship becoming apparent."[156]

Adriano's most important accomplishments involved the reorganization of the city's central park, the Parque do Ibirapuera, whose designers included famed architect Niemeyer. Opened in 1954 during the commemorations of the city's 400th anniversary, Ibirapuera became internationally renowned as a place for concerts and other cultural events. For residents of São Paulo, it was a place to exercise and relax, but only partially escape air pollution, because of high levels of contamination. According to Adriano, the mismanaged park had lost too much green space. "Obviously the Parque do Ibirapuera is the postcard image of the city of São Paulo," Adriano noted. "Every day I met with business people who wanted to do a project with the secretariat involving an investment in the Parque do Ibirapuera, either concerning sports, equipment, music, or culture." The secretariat invested 100 million *reals* of private money in the park for its fiftieth anniversary in 2004. Adriano recovered green space by removing parking lots and other paved areas, and he cleaned up the park's three artificial lakes. Cars were banned. The secretariat removed a city building with its hundreds of employees, regulated pet use, repaired the park's planetarium, introduced bike paths, and added a colored water fountain display set to music. It converted an abandoned building into a museum presenting the history of slavery and Afro-Brazilian cultures. In the crowning achievement, Adriano arranged for a $7 million donation from the Italian multinational TIM, a major provider of cell phone service in Brazil, to construct a Niemeyer-projected indoor/outdoor auditorium for musical performances. It included facilities for poor children to receive free music lessons. "A park does not exist without culture, in part because environmental issues are much more a cultural one than a biological one," Adriano stated.[157]

Adriano's executive experience and collaboration with the private sector transformed his political ideology. Before the secretariat, he admittedly had "zero" contact with the private sector. "I used to think it was like entering criminal territory, a quagmire, that I could compromise my image, my biography," Adriano said. Now he believed that cooperation with business was "necessary." Business had "good people" and an "intelligent" side, which included a willingness to create a vision of "social responsibility." Adriano believed that he had not compromised his underlying values, but that he had become a better, more nuanced politician. "I did not become corrupt," he said. "And I grew. I became a much more mature person. . . . We need to break away from the prejudice of purely and simply saying 'no.' 'No. I won't speak to business people,' for example. That's absurd. Now, what you can't give up is to say 'no' to corruption, 'no' to things involving favoritism. Now, just because a guy is a business person doesn't necessarily mean that he's corrupt or seeking to corrupt someone. The world is not divided between the good and the evil." Adriano still considered himself a "social democrat tending towards a socialist." "A socialist is someone who

Figure 37. Adriano in 2007. Kenneth P. Serbin.

knows how to get along with business people without giving up the need to redistribute wealth," he concluded. "A socialist is a team player."[158]

Completed under Adriano, the Ibirapuera auditorium actually opened in late 2005 under the administration of PSDB mayor José Serra, who defeated Marta Suplicy in 2004. Aloysio served as Serra's secretary for governance. After Serra's election as São Paulo state governor in 2006—a platform for a presidential run in 2010—Aloysio became his chief of staff for political matters. Despite the PSDB's refusal to seek Lula's impeachment, Aloysio criticized the president's "sentimental, somewhat pro–Third World rhetoric, with a certain anti-American flare." Lula also had a "chimerical idea to form a strategic axis with China, which obviously wants nothing to do with such an idea." He believed that overall the PT had achieved little.[159]

However, Aloysio did believe that Lula's election was historic. He explained in a 2004 interview:

Lula is an important figure in Brazilian politics. He represented a sector of Brazilian politics that needed to acquire governmental experience. It was natural that it got a chance to enter the federal government. It had already been in state governments, municipalities. It resonated with the public, with social movements. . . . I thought the PT's arrival in power was important—of course, I wanted Serra to win—because it meant the end of ideological litmus tests in Brazilian politics. People can no longer say: "So-and-so cannot enter the government, because he's a leftist." . . . The way they are running the government is another matter. For me it's been a major disappointment.[160]

Aloysio believed that Lula had full knowledge of the PT's corrupt practices.[161]

After Adriano and Arlete separated in 2002, Arlete no longer worked in politics. She declined a call by activists to run for city council in 2004. She no longer believed that political parties were necessary for social activism. "There are many other paths," she affirmed. "Party life sometimes forces you into a more restricted outlook, because there you have the principles of the party, the organization, the leadership." She wanted to focus on her family (two grandchildren) and explore other facets of life. She underwent psychoanalysis, enrolled in adult continuing education classes, and wrote a graduate thesis on the history of the dictatorship's official pedagogical materials. She gave public talks about her participation in the resistance—including her torture and the miscarriage it provoked. She wanted to help Brazil avoid repeating its dictatorial horrors. Arlete sang in a university chorus that partnered with a chorus at a detention center for teenage girls. There she befriended a seventeen-year-old Evangelical woman who had been raped by her stepfather when she was thirteen and was now the single mother of three children. The woman took part in an occupational training program sponsored by the state government and with underwriting from Avon and Votorantim, a Brazilian industrial conglomerate. "She has a marvelous voice, the joy of living," Arlete observed. "She did the program at a hair-cutting school, so she'll have a profession. . . . I think that we need a new way of viewing that type of work and not to judge it as just pure charity. Today, to get something done, you need partnerships, you need less prejudice and more solidarity. Because this way things get done."[162]

In Rio, Jessie, Colombo, and Carlos Eugênio remained outside the orbit of the PT and PSDB. They criticized Lula's government for its refusal to push for greater social reform. Colombo belonged to the PSB.

Figure 38. Arlete in 2006. Kenneth P. Serbin.

Jessie had no party affiliation. They saw little difference between the PT and PSDB: neither party challenged the status quo.[163] In their eyes, Lula had long ago lost his working-class ties. "I wanted to believe . . . that the PT would do things that were part of the tradition of the Left," Jessie commented. "They could have summoned the people to participate in things that I think are fundamental, for example, educational issues, mobilizing young students, a little like the literacy campaign the Cuban Revolution did."[164] As dean of the college of arts and sciences at the Universidade Federal do Rio de Janeiro, Jessie battled the same type of gross bureaucratic inefficiency and lack of accountability that she and Colombo had encountered in Volta Redonda and Espírito Santo. At least under Lula the federal universities significantly increased competitiveness in faculty hiring.[165]

Carlos Eugênio's experience at the Secretariat for Labor under Rio governor Garotinho led to his reentry into politics. In April 2002, he campaigned for Garotinho's wife, Rosinha, who succeeded her husband as governor. She ran on the PSB ticket. Carlos Eugênio recruited members

Figure 39. Carlos Eugênio doing political work in São Paulo, 2006. Kenneth P. Serbin.

for PSB at the grass roots, including in Rio's violent favelas. Now armed only with the shield of democratic politics, the former guerrilla had never been so vulnerable as he was now in drug traffickers' territory. Carlos Eugênio became one of the PSB's top political advisors. Although PSB members took part in the Lula government, Carlos Eugênio viewed the PSB as an authentic alternative to the PT. In 2004, he assisted Erundina's campaign to retake the São Paulo mayor's office, this time on the PSB slate. Unlike most of his ex-revolutionary peers, Carlos Eugênio believed that Lula should have confronted the international capitalist system in the way Hugo Chávez had done in Venezuela. Lula's embrace of the system, he thought, saved him from impeachment in the mensalão scandal. Lula was a political genius, but he lacked a coherent plan for the nation. Bolsa Família rescued families from poverty, but the banks had record profits, Carlos Eugênio affirmed. The PT had helped "domesticate" Brazilian democracy and the Left. Lula drank Romanée-Conti while many favela residents lacked clean drinking water. (In 2007, 13 percent of Brazilians had no access to tap water.) "I was deeply troubled by that," Carlos Eugênio commented. The once "glamorous" PT was now losing its appeal. He considered the Lula government's overall conduct a defeat for the Brazilian Left worse than the defeat of the armed struggle. On the international level, the Left had practically disappeared. In his estimation, Brazilian society remained so deeply unequal that it still might require a violent "institutional rupture" to bring about social justice. Carlos Eugênio saw preparation of a new generation of militants as the only hope for the Brazilian Left. He maintained contact with young grassroots anarchists anxious for social change but rejecting party politics.[166]

LULA'S OPINION POLL approval rating in late 2010 hit 87 percent, the highest in Brazilian history for the end of an administration.[167] Lula demonstrated not only that he was a political survivor, but also that he had connected with Brazil's underprivileged. "What was done over five hundred years you can't rebuild in two," Paulo heard union leaders say of the historic injustices that they believed Lula was working to eliminate.[168] Lula's approach was gradual.[169] He had the good fortune of leading Brazil on the upswing of an internal economic cycle strong enough to help the country weather the Great Recession of 2008–2009. He celebrated Brazil's securing of the right to host two events of international prestige: the 2014 World Cup in soccer and the 2016 Summer Olympics. Lula had successfully prepared the terrain for his successor. A four-term PT hold on the presidency appeared very much possible. Two years after Lula left office, Brazil passed the United Kingdom to become the world's sixth largest economy.

The Brazil that the ALN had once wanted to revolutionize had changed profoundly under Fernando Henrique and Lula. A nation of have-nots was rapidly tilting toward a nation of haves. Poor Brazilians had little interest in political ideology. They wanted their leaders, however imperfect, to help them thrive.

However, the seeds of future difficulties were also planted during the Lula years. Corruption remained deeply ingrained in many sectors of Brazilian society. Under Lula, it had reached unexpected levels, perhaps damaging the country's political institutions.[170] Despite improvements in the civil service, federal public servants remained focused on admissions exams, salary scales, and political concerns to the detriment of performance and a more nimble response to citizens' needs.[171] Keeping the *real* overvalued brought short-term gains but also caused long-term problems, such as high interest rates, a huge rise in the country's internal debt, dein-dustrialization, and a shift to exporting primary goods rather than more complex industrial goods. This situation kept Brazil in a subordinate position in the global economy, with less opportunity for technological advance. The government failed to use the proceeds from the subsalt oil to correct these imbalances.[172] A key historical question emerged: Had Brazil once again wagered too much on a primary export, as it previously had done with sugar, gold, diamonds, and coffee?

Lula reduced inequality through welfare payments, but his government failed to invest in critical infrastructure and long-term social investments—factors that acted as a drag on the economic competitiveness and dynamism necessary for stability.[173] Indeed, Brazil's annual productivity gains trailed the developed world and East Asia, and its level of investments remained low. The state-led capitalist model had stimulated little innovation in business.[174] Violent criminal organizations such as the First Command of the Capital continued to flourish. Support for the human rights of common citizens remained low. Regarding the government response to trafficker violence in Rio, where police laid siege to some favelas in 2007, Lula stated: "You don't deal with crooks by giving them roses or treating them delicately."[175] Thus, the government's policy of "pacifying" the favelas relied on what one scholar called the "coexistence of *welfare* and *warfare*."[176] The universal public health and educational systems remained precarious.[177] Poor education produced a shortage of skilled workers, further hampering social and economic progress.[178] In 2010, 56 percent of Brazilian homes still lacked basic sanitation.[179] Brazil had gone from being the third-most unequal country in the world to about the fifteenth. It still had a long way to go to improve living standards.[180]

For now, at least, the American Dream remained just that—a dream.

CHAPTER 14

An Ex-Revolutionary at the Helm
Encounters Turbulence and Hostility

The undisputed leader of the PT, Lula by 2010 oversaw an economy grow-ing at a rate of 7.5 percent. Rewarding a competent and loyal minister, he handpicked Dilma Rousseff as the party's presidential candidate in that year's election.

Dilma had a more radical background than Lula, but she had never before run for public office. Her father had emigrated to Brazil from Bul-garia, marrying a woman from Uberaba, Minas Gerais. The couple settled in Belo Horizonte, where Dilma was born in 1947. Like many radicals, she moved from student politics into revolutionary organizations as the dic-tatorship deepened. In 1969, she entered the newly formed VAR-Palmares, a fusion of two groups that, like others, sought to overthrow the regime. The organization was inspired by seventeenth-century resistance against Portuguese colonial rulers at the runaway slave colony Palmares. In July 1969 in Rio, the group stole a safe containing $2.5 million (approximately $18 million today)—the largest take by any terrorist or revolutionary group in the world at the time. Dilma, who did not take part in the theft, sided with a faction that favored grassroots political organization, but she did support the armed resistance. On January 16, 1970, she was arrested in São Paulo by DOI-CODI agents who had been on her trail. Seeking informa-tion about her revolutionary activities, over the next twenty-two days in-

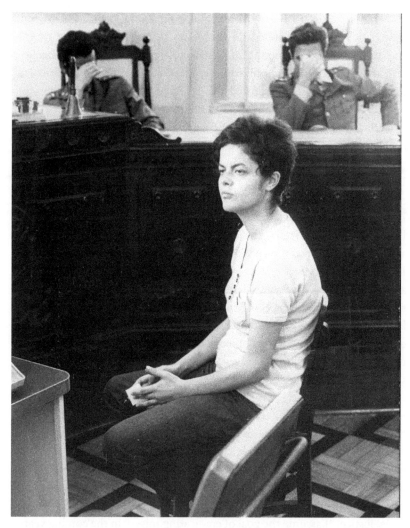

Figure 40. Political prisoner Dilma Rousseff at a military tribunal in Rio, November 1970. Photo by Adi Mera, Fundo Última Hora, Arquivo Público do Estado São Paulo.

terrogators at the DOI-CODI tortured Dilma numerous times, shocking much of her body, including her nipples and head. She was eventually transferred to the Tiradentes prison, from which she was released in November 1972 after the Supremo Tribunal Militar reduced her forty-eight-month sentence to twenty-five.[1]

Dilma settled in Porto Alegre, the capital of Rio Grande do Sul, Brazil's southernmost state and the political base of President Vargas and President Goulart and also Brizola. After completing her bachelor's and master's in economics in the late 1970s, Dilma joined Brizola's social-democratic PDT. From 1986 to 1988, she served as the secretary of finance—the first woman in Brazil to hold such a position—under Alceu Collares, the PDT mayor of Porto Alegre. After Collares became governor, Dilma held the post of secretary of mines, energy, and communications from 1993 to 1994, and again under PT governor Olívio Dutra from 1999 to 2002.

Disappointed with the PDT's failure to seal an alliance with the PT, Dilma switched to the latter in 2001. Her performance and expertise led Lula to name her first as minister of mines and energy then later chief of staff. Untouched by the mensalão, Dilma became Lula's political protégé. In 2009, she survived a bout with lymphoma. Despite a social taboo against discussing cancer, her defeat of the disease strengthened her emotionally and politically. Seeking the presidency and riding on Lula's popularity, Dilma handily defeated José Serra of the PSDB in the second round of the 2010 contest. "Serra is someone of the same origins, the people who resisted the dictatorship," observed Adriano Diogo, who knew Serra from school days. "It was a battle of the giants."[2]

"The fact of my election, beyond what it represents for me personally, is a demonstration of the democratic advance of our country: for the first time a woman will preside over Brazil," Dilma declared in her victory speech. "I therefore want to register here my first commitment after the election: to honor all Brazilian women so that this event, unprecedented until today, becomes a natural occurrence." Dilma was also Brazil's first president who had been a revolutionary. She emphasized the quest for social justice: "I assume the goal of eradicating misery in the coming years, but for this I humbly request the support of all that can help our country to overcome the abyss that still separates us from being a developed nation."[3]

With Lula placing the presidential sash on her, Dilma took office on January 1, 2011. All but one of the nine main former ALN interviewees voted for Dilma in the second round. All viewed Dilma as a continuation of Lula. Her supporters agreed on the dually historic significance of her election. "I thought it was very important to have two things joined

Figure 41. President Dilma. Fotos Públicas.

in a single person," Arlete commented, noting Dilma's female and ex-revolutionary status. "It was very powerful," Jessie said, adding that Dilma's past participation in Jessie's preferred party, the PDT, added to her appeal. "For you to have an idea, in Niterói there were never more than four women at the same time on the city council, in this city of 200,000 inhabitants," Colombo observed. He, Carlos Eugênio, and other activists had decided to put up Carlos Eugênio as a congressional candidate as symbolic support for Dilma's candidacy. He received only 576 votes, but gave numerous talks aiming to draw alienated youth into the electoral process. Márcio campaigned for Dilma in Belo Horizonte. "Women who took up arms had to break many different kinds of taboos," he asserted. "Most of them were very special women, including Dilma." "It was a tremendous utopia, a tremendous hope," Adriano remarked. "She invited all of her cellmates to her inauguration," Manoel Cyrillo stated. "That was beautiful."[4]

Paulo witnessed Lula's elation at the first cabinet meeting after Dilma's victory. Elbrick kidnapper Franklin Martins, Lula's press secretary, was also present. Paulo recalled:

He [Lula] talked during the cabinet meeting not just about the joy of having the first woman president, but also continuing the symbolism of his own election as the first metalworker, union leader, and migrant, without a college degree. And he [Lula] interrupted the part about her being the first woman to say: "I want to tell you, Franklin and Paulo"—two ministers who had participated in the underground resistance—"that your generation has come to govern." So I was very excited, because Lula has a different view about the period of the armed resistance. It was his sign of respect for us despite the disagreement over the methods of the armed resistance. It was also meaningful for my personal history because I was right on the other side of the wall at the Tiradentes prison.

For Paulo, Dilma's rise to power represented a historic turnaround in which individuals once considered the internal enemies of their countries—José "Pepe" Mujica in Uruguay, Michelle Bachelet in Chile, and Salvador Sánchez in El Salvador—had become rulers.[5]

Dilma had ample support in the Congress. The PT's record number of congressional seats (88 of 513) gave it the largest bloc of representatives, whereas the PSDB bloc declined substantially from sixty-six to fifty-three seats. Nevertheless, the PSDB won eight of Brazil's twenty-seven governorships, more than the PT (five) or any other party, including São Paulo and Minas Gerais.[6] Somewhat like Democratic/Republican politics in the United States, PT/PSDB polarization was increasing. The support of tens of millions of voters made the PSDB a formidable opponent for the new Dilma administration.

PSDB stalwart Aloysio, however, voted for Serra. With electoral support from Serra and Fernando Henrique, Aloysio emerged as a key Dilma opponent after an astounding come-from-behind victory running for a national Senate seat from São Paulo in the 2010 elections. He garnered 11.1 million votes, more than any other senator in Brazilian history.[7] Aécio Neves entered the Senate for Minas Gerais with 7.5 million votes, the third largest in the election. Thinking he had lost, Aloysio shared dinner and a bottle of wine with Gisele before going to bed. "My children woke me up, banging on the bedroom door," Aloysio remembered. "'Dad, you won the election. You are in first place.' Then it was party time. I became very excited. I had hypertension, something that had never happened to me before. . . . My candidacy and election to the Senate were the high point of my long political career. . . . Despite all the defects of our political system, it is an important institution. It is Brazil's strongest representative body."[8]

Aloysio was unimpressed by the emphasis on Dilma's revolutionary past. "It's been a long time," he observed. "There's no reason for me to say, 'Wow, great, an ex-militant!' Especially because I believe the [resistance] was a disaster." Aloysio believed that Dilma had demonstrated "personal courage, strong values." But he saw little importance in her sex. "She's a woman. . . . That's not an attribute that leads me to imagine that she can perform differently than a man. I'm a man who's a feminist, for example." He held the standard view that her election revealed the people's desire to retain the economic gains of the Lula years. "I don't believe it was a turning point in Brazilian history," he stated. "Lula's election was. Fernando Henrique's election was. But Dilma's was not." Aloysio quickly became "disappointed" by her rule: "I thought that she could have set up . . . an administration with a wider political base, an administration of effective reforms, an administration capable of attracting people, of breaking that 'Taliban' phase of the PT, someone capable of governing magnificently."[9]

At first, however, things looked good: in Dilma's first hundred days, the economy created 798,000 jobs.[10] Inequality continued to diminish under Dilma, with the poverty rate dropping from 20 percent under Lula to just 15.1 percent in 2013.[11] But Lula had put Dilma in one of the worst possible situations for an incoming president in a developing country. The overappreciation of the *real* had produced long-term dangers for the economy. With a strong currency, more Brazilians could afford to visit Disney World and shop in New York, but the country's industries contracted because they could not compete with imports made cheap by the deceivingly favorable exchange rate—not to mention China's continued ascent as a manufacturing superpower. Under Lula and especially Dilma, a long trend of deindustrialization accelerated. In effect, although some saw Dilma and Brazil as protectionist, the overvalued currency had done the opposite, weakening domestic industry. In addition, Dilma continued raising the minimum wage, even without an attendant increase in Brazilian workers' productivity.[12] The crisis of the euro and European debt, with the threat of national bankruptcy in Greece and elsewhere, further complicated matters. To maintain the support of the international financial community courted so judiciously by Lula, Dilma maintained budget surpluses and low inflation. However, during her first year in office, the growth rate dropped to 2.7 percent. She attempted a mix of stimuli, including a partial devaluation of the *real*, but in 2012 the growth rate fell to just 0.9 percent. Brazilian businesses lost overall competitiveness, and they became pessimistic about the economy.[13] This was a rapid and dramatic turnaround from Lula's boom.

Despite the worrisome scenario, Dilma had become more popular in her first two years than Fernando Henrique and Lula had been at the same point.[14] People had not yet felt the effect of the slowing economy. Dilma further boosted her ratings in the polls by taking a hard line against malfeasance. During her first ten months, seven ministers (including five holdovers from Lula's cabinet) resigned because of allegations of corruption. She also began to cultivate her own image, emphasizing her managerial proficiency in contrast with Lula's hands-off, avuncular style.[15]

However, Dilma faced serious social challenges unresolved under Lula. Because people now saw Bolsa Família as a right, maintaining the program brought her no additional political benefit.[16] Many working-class people still felt left out of the progress of the Lula era. The rule of the PT had not eliminated the brutal and disdainful treatment of workers by big construction companies awarded government contracts. (In contrast with the United States, construction workers in Brazil receive low wages.) As a result, 2011 brought strikes and protests from state-level public-sector employees and workers in large construction projects tied to the PAG (the massive public works program), the 2014 World Cup, and the 2016 Olympics.[17] Many families lost their homes to make room for the new facilities; the government reneged on its promise to relocate them.[18] When federal workers went on strike in 2012, Dilma sternly reminded them that they had received wage hikes above the inflation rate during the Lula years.[19]

As they had with Lula, significant sectors of the *movimento popular* became disillusioned with Dilma, especially because of her support for the massive Belo Monte hydroelectric dam in the Amazon, the abandonment of agrarian reform, and a failure to protect tribal lands. She did little better than pay lip service to the settling of accounts with the dictatorship. In November 2012—twenty-seven years after the end of military rule—she promulgated the creation of the National Truth Commission to investigate the deaths and disappearances carried out by the armed forces. However, the Truth Commission lacked punitive powers, and it could not compel the armed forces to hand over documentation regarding the desaparecidos. Furthermore, Dilma impeded the search for justice by opposing review of the 1979 Amnesty Law.[20]

By 2013, the economic slowdown started to produce political difficulties for Dilma. Undoing some of the 1990s reforms, she increased political interference in state-owned enterprises.[21] Supporters in civil society, the business community, and the international financial sector that had backed Lula started to abandon Dilma. Her rigid, managerial style prevented an effective political response. Although determined and public-spirited, Dilma was an ineffective politician.[22] The PT had lost momentum.

To FORESTALL GROWING INFLATION, in late 2012 Dilma asked all governors and mayors to postpone a scheduled increase in municipal bus fares until June 2013. After the increase took effect, on June 6 members of the Free Fare Movement—which, among other demands, wanted free or lower fares—led a protest against the measure involving about one thousand people in downtown São Paulo. The local police repressed the demonstration with tear gas and rubber bullets. That day Brazilians learned that the global economic ratings agency Standard & Poors had classified Brazil as an investment risk because of low growth and rising government spending. The next day, five thousand pro–Free Fare demonstrators blocked a main avenue, prompting a similar police response and the arrest of fifteen young adults, including USP student leaders and members of ultraradical groups.[23]

What came next stupefied the Brazilian political, academic, and media establishment. These elements had failed to perceive signs of discontent, which had also appeared, albeit in different contexts, in the Arab Spring of 2010, the Occupy Wall Street movement of 2011, and the Turkish protests of May and June 2013. In an explosion of frustration, indignation, and postmodern self-expression, throughout the rest of June 2013, more than 1 million Brazilians took to the streets, holding more than 700 protests in 360 cities. (Some sources put the numbers at more than 500 cities and between 10 and 15 million protestors.) Calling for everything from improved public services to greater respect for the marginalized, protestors attempted to occupy city council chambers, state assemblies, and gubernatorial offices. Others blocked traffic on highways. With police trying to protect property and keep the demonstrations peaceful, 6 people were killed, and 150 were arrested.[24] In some cases, the police harassed or brutally beat demonstrators and journalists.[25] On June 19, the authorities in the states of Rio de Janeiro and São Paulo rescinded all fare increases.[26]

Seeing their government spend billions of dollars on the World Cup and Olympics, the demonstrators demanded improved public transportation, education, crime control, and medical facilities. Leaderless and autonomous, individuals and groups of protestors voiced a polyphony of demands. On June 20, the day of the largest protests, with more than 1 million participants across the nation, placards wielded in Rio stated "Free bus fares," "Homophobia is a crime," "The Polícia Militar must be abolished," "Join the march for marijuana," "It's my body," "Zero intolerance," "Stop the violence: Afro-Brazilian religions deserve respect," "Rio is ours, not the construction companies'," and "I want a health system up to FIFA standards." (FIFA, the Fedération Internationale de Football Association, sponsors the World Cup and requires host nations to upgrade or build stadiums to very high standards.) Many protestors wore Anonymous masks, a global symbol of antigovernment, antiestablishment sentiment.[27] Groups of youths known as "Black Blocs" used violence and vandalism in their protests, but most Brazilians rejected that attitude.[28] Concerned primarily about the declining economy and protecting their establishments from the Black Blocs, business owners refrained from commenting on the protests.[29] One scholar observed that the Black Blocs aimed not to instigate violence but defend protestors against police repression.[30] A July 2013 poll revealed that 89 percent of Brazilians supported the protests.[31] For a few weeks, the protestors commanded the attention of their government and society.[32] Displaying the flag and singing the national anthem, they engaged in a massive display of civic nationalism.[33] With rising expectations in the wake of the Lula boom, they wanted their country to achieve First World status.[34]

Pundits, politicians, and former revolutionaries struggled to interpret the protests. The events of what came to be known as "June 2013" transformed the Dilma administration and former revolutionaries into the guarantors of public order and thus the foes of protests. Boxed in, their responses could recall the dictatorial repression. "We want to suppress vandalism," declared former Rio de Janeiro governor Benedita da Silva, now a PT congresswoman. Aldo Rebelo, a PC do B member serving as sports minister, proclaimed that the government would not tolerate protests against the Confederations Cup, a soccer tournament held in Brazil that year as a prelude to the World Cup. Minister of Justice José Eduardo Cardozo of the PT offered states' Polícia Militar units funds to fight destruction of property. He announced that the government would monitor the demonstrations. Whereas PT discourse defined incidents of police beatings as a "confrontation," it classified attacks on private property, a symbol of capitalism, as terrorism. Indeed, in the wake of the protests, PT senator Jorge Viana advocated the passage of an antiterror law. Only far-left sectors of the party condemned such criminalization of the protests. Adriano was one of the few PT politicians to defend jailed demonstrators.[35]

Dilma defended the right to protest. However, the events of June 2013 cast her in a role similar to that of these other PT leaders. On June 20, the police blocked protestors trying to invade the Palácio do Itamaraty, the headquarters of the Ministry of Foreign Relations, located yards from the Congress and the Palácio do Planalto. Fully mobilized, the presidential guard called on army troops to protect the president, who was taken from the Planalto to her official residence, the Palácio da Alvorada (Dawn Palace). Few in Brazil would have predicted that one day a PT president would rely on the armed forces to shield her from a potential clash with demonstrators.[36] In a nationally televised address on June 21, fifteen days after the protests began, Dilma stated that she would meet with the (purported) leaders of the protests but that her government would "not compromise on violence." She promised to improve public services, including the creation of the More Doctors Initiative. After meeting with Free Fare movement leaders three days later, Dilma proposed the convocation of a Constituent Assembly to address political reform.[37] The populace and the Congress dismissed that idea as irrelevant, as they did the call for a national plebiscite on political reform. This major defeat weakened the president's political standing.[38] Unable to comprehend and assimilate new ways of protest, and constrained by its status as the ruling party, the PT had lost the street.[39]

"The country . . . was shaken by a political phenomenon still difficult to decipher," Paulo affirmed. "It's good that the country has had this type of protest. In few countries can the president tell the public that she was proud of such protests, when the tendency is to do what the president of Turkey did or what was done to the leaders of the Arab Spring, to say: 'No, the people want too much.'"[40]

In Belo Horizonte, about 100,000 demonstrators clashed with police outside the stadium hosting a match in the Confederations Cup.[41] In Brazil, governors oversee public safety and local police, not mayors. So Márcio, as mayor, did not become the target of protests, despite a brush with alleged nepotism regarding his son Tiago. In 2009, he had named Tiago to a high-profile, unpaid post involving the World Cup. In 2011, faced with a suit by state prosecutors, Márcio removed Tiago. He later defended Tiago's designation. The incident did not affect his political standing; in 2012, he easily won reelection on the PSB ticket.[42] Despite his revolutionary past, Márcio skeptically viewed the 2013 protests as the result of several factors, including young radicals "against this, that, and everything else." He recognized the frustration over public services but did not fully agree that it had caused the protests. "Public services in Brazil aren't as bad as people say," he maintained.[43]

Some observers in Brazil initially dismissed the protests. However, in the aftermath of June 2013, a key causal pattern emerged. With basic survival now secure, members of Brazil's "new middle class" started to focus on the quality of life—the better jobs, housing, and public services that the middle classes in developed countries enjoyed. Relative prosperity had also led members of this class to become more critical of governmental institutions.[44] Márcio's comments seemed off the mark. Brazilians had become deeply dissatisfied with poor public services while paying the highest taxes in Latin America, even as corruption continued. At the same time, the partial success in combating corruption raised people's expectations and increased frustration with the status quo.[45]

Many Brazilians, especially young adults, detested what they perceived as their leaders' sly, cynical, and arrogant way of governing. From their perspective, the political class—including the PT—swept the nation's problems under the rug while spending billions of dollars on public relations. Official publicity spots especially irritated the populace because they inaccurately portrayed the country as running smoothly. After the initial Free Fare movement actions to block fare increases, the protestors were decidedly nonpartisan. They were also mainly middle-class, but other social groups participated. They did not protest against the Dilma government per se, but they also did not identify with her, Lula, or the PT. They were angry at the party leadership's embrace of the notoriously corrupt Maluf. Allied with the PT, the *movimento popular* was mainly absent from the protests. The demonstrators believed corruption was out of control, and, indeed, the government appeared incompetent. A widely seen TV report about the abandonment of the expensive São Francisco irrigation project—a Lula promise partially implemented under Ciro and Márcio—reinforced that image. Brazilians with any means sought to secure private health insurance, which freed them from the serious difficulties of the public system. In some cities, scheduling an appointment with a doctor in the public system could take ten months, and the patient might not actually see the doctor until years later. Seven hundred cities lacked doctors. Above all, protestors complained about public transportation. Many citizens spent several hours getting to and from work in crowded buses and trains. Poor service also reigned throughout the private sector, frequently becoming the target of the country's comedians. Congress reinforced the image of incompetence: instead of responding genuinely to June 2013, it started debating the infamous "gay cure" (transformation of homosexuals into heterosexuals) promulgated by some of Brazil's conservative churches. Even worse, it considered a constitutional amendment to restrict the powers of the Ministério Público, the federal prosecutor's office in charge of investigating political corruption. Under pressure from protestors, the Congress ultimately voted down the measure.[46]

The virtual home for protests was the social media site Facebook. Most demonstrators had learned about the protests via Facebook, where people posted news about the events and their reactions to them. In some countries, Facebook activism substitutes for political activism, but in this case people left their comfort zone for the streets.[47] The protests were completely unorganized, without planned routes, start or end times, megaphones, loudspeakers, or stages. The lack of leaders, or in some cases multiple leaders, made it difficult for police and government authorities to negotiate with protestors.[48] People at the June 20 Rio protest used smartphones to watch live transmission of the demonstration from other locations or live social media channels. Independent journalists and demonstrators captured video of police brutality.[49] From just 3 percent in 2000, the number of Brazilians with Internet access had jumped to 45 percent in 2012.[50] That year, Brazil registered the world's largest increase in new Facebook members.[51] In June 2013, almost 100 million people—half of the population—had access. Seventy-one percent of youths described the Internet as their best political tool. Few politicians fathomed the profound shift from traditional demonstrations to a new, digital activism in which the grassroots interconnectedness of social media trumped TV. June 2013 laid bare traditional politicians' distance from the streets—real or virtual. Most did not even use e-mail. Although Dilma had used her laptop in Lula's cabinet meetings, an unusual practice, after her 2010 victory she turned off her Twitter account. She reactivated it after June 2013. Leadership and communication were becoming more horizontal, with YouTube videos of June 2013 activists drawing millions of views. In effect, the protestors pursued their own political reform by bypassing traditional leaders and organizations.[52]

As PRESIDENT, DILMA had no role in the mensalão trial of 2012, held in the Supreme Court. It resulted in the historic convictions of Dirceu, Genoíno, and other public figures. Because the convictions represented a victory against corruption, they temporarily boosted Dilma's popularity—until the aftermath of June 2013.[53] The televised sentencing of the mensalão defendants in November 2013 fed Brazilians' moral indignation. This increased opposition to Dilma.[54] The Supreme Court sent all twelve defendants to prison. After that, the political situation deteriorated further. In 2014, the economy registered almost zero growth, and unemployment started to rise.[55] So did inflation. The political system became evermore unwieldy, with nearly three dozen political parties.

Investigations began to reveal that the mensalão paled in comparison to what actually occurred under Lula and Dilma. Much of the wrongdoing involved Petrobras, a favorite target of corrupt officials because it was awash in cash and involved in numerous construction projects.[56] During the Lula administration, when Dilma sat on the board of Petrobras, the company purchased the Pasadena Refining System Inc. refinery near Houston, Texas. In a series of transactions starting in 2006, Petrobras paid $1.18 billion for the nearly century-old facility, almost thirty times the value a Belgian company had paid for it in 2005. The government accounting office found eleven former high-level Petrobras managers responsible for the bad deal and froze the assets of the company's former president, José Sérgio Gabrielli.[57]

Known as Operation Car Wash, another investigation by the Polícia Federal and federal magistrates into money laundering and government corruption led again to Petrobras. Under the terms of a plea bargain, former Petrobras manager Paulo Roberto Costa, who had stood in as president when Gabrielli traveled abroad, revealed improprieties in the Pasadena purchase and other business deals.[58] Though it's impossible to know whether any of the dictators or other civilian presidents were more corrupt than the PT,[59] Operation Car Wash was the largest corruption probe in Brazilian history. It revealed billions of dollars in kickbacks from Petrobras projects to Petrobras officials, directors of Petrobras contractors, politicians, and the PT and PMDB.[60] It was modeled in part on the "mani puliti" (clean hands) investigation that rocked Italian politics in the 1990s. The Italian case, which also involved the state oil company, virtually destroyed the Italian Socialist and Christian Democratic parties.[61] In 2016, the U.S. Department of Justice revealed that Operation Car Wash's investigation of the Odebrecht conglomerate had become the world's largest bribery case.[62] Tainting Petrobras's reputation for competence and professionalism, the Brazilian scandal undermined the company's entrepreneurial viability. The company had become a tool of nationalist interests, with some of its questionable activities resembling those at the less successful and less reputable national oil firms of Mexico and Venezuela. The investigation revealed how the Lula and Dilma administrations had used the oil giant to attempt to perpetuate the PT in power by using stolen funds for political purposes. At the same time, the oil exploration euphoria of Lula's second term faded as the company faced unforeseen technical and financial challenges in developing the subsalt fields.[63]

The World Cup in June and July 2014 ran smoothly and without protests. However, the Brazilian national team's embarrassing 7–1 semifinal loss to Germany dashed the hopes of a championship at home. The defeat eliminated the chance of an upward soccer bounce for Dilma in the opinion polls in that year's reelection campaign.

The 2014 race, the closest in modern Brazilian history, was also the most rancorous, with the PT in particular relying on negative campaigning.[64] Dilma and Vice President Michel Temer of the PMDB—a coalition of political convenience—again headed the PT ticket. The PSDB, choosing Sen. Aécio Neves for its presidential slot, then announced Aloysio as its vice presidential candidate. As in the United States, vice presidents in Brazil have little practical function. However, because of the volatility of Brazilian politics, they have four times taken office because of the death or resignation of the president. The PSDB ticket joined two successful vote-getters from the country's two largest states, Minas Gerais and São Paulo. At sixty-nine, Aloysio was one of the party's most experienced leaders. As he later explained, he provided valuable advice to Aécio, who was fifty-four, helping Aécio attempt to "defeat the PT by mobilizing São Paulo." He helped Aécio prepare for the debates, provided suggestions for commercials, and aided in analyzing PSDB polls. Aécio and Aloysio felt the brunt of the PT's attacks. "They claimed that I was a drug trafficker, can you believe it?" Aloysio recalled. "And they told lies about every part of my life. They were saying that I was against the Truth Commission—I reported the bill to the Senate. That I was antigay—no, on the contrary."[65] In early and mid-October, opinion polls indicated that Aécio had slightly overtaken Dilma.[66] However, on election day, October 26, the president won by a slim margin, with 51.64 percent of the vote. Nevertheless, in contrast with the PT's overwhelming victories in the previous three elections, the extremely close vote signaled a potential political shift. "In the immediate aftermath, it seemed as if we had created an enormous amount of energy," Aloysio observed. "That awoke, I think, enormous civic excitement that had lain dormant. And, at the same time, it would put in check the PT's domination, which had appeared to have installed itself permanently."[67]

In São Paulo, in another indication of the PT's diminished appeal, Adriano lost his first election ever, a bid to become a member of Congress. As his eight-year tenure in the São Paulo State Assembly came to an end, Adriano completed a mission that he had embraced passionately during his second term: the establishment and leadership of Brazil's very first state-level truth commission. It was inaugurated in May 2012, just a few days before the National Truth Commission. In Adriano's estimation, the work of the São Paulo commission provided political support for the national commission. He believed that his commission raised awareness among Brazilian youths about the atrocities of the dictatorship and the need for strong human rights policies.[68]

Supported by Paulo Vannuchi, the National Truth Commission issued its final report in December 2014. Seen by many critics as weak, the Truth Commission did not resolve a single disappearance or death. It moved Brazil ahead only modestly in terms of government and military accountability, a key component of democracy.[69] Outside the cabinet after Lula's presidential administration ended, Paulo continued to advise the former chief executive. He did so at the former Citizenship Institute, renamed as the Lula Institute. It was no longer part of the PT but directly linked to Lula. In June 2013, Paulo was elected to the Inter-American Commission on Human Rights of the Organization of American States for the term 2014–17.

Both Adriano and Paulo voted for Dilma in 2014. In São Paulo, Arlete continued her search for personal and familial fulfillment, but she was ever attentive to politics and supportive of Dilma. Manoel had retired from Petrobras, and Jessie and Colombo also readied for retirement. They, too, had all voted for Dilma. Carlos Eugênio left the PSB, disillusioned with what he saw as a rightward shift. He voted for Dilma in the second round, but he had cast no ballot in the first round. The 2014 polarization between the two main parties had an early portent in Márcio's 2012 reelection as mayor of Belo Horizonte; he scored a substantial victory, but this time without the joint PT-PSDB backing he had received in 2008. Indeed, after enthusiastically supporting Dilma in 2010, Márcio vowed not to publicly support a candidate in 2014. He did not reveal his vote. "My only involvement in the campaign was this: during Aécio's last public appearance, when he went to the Serra da Piedade [a shrine] to pray, I was at his side," Márcio commented.[70]

The anti-Dilma forces intensified. Just two days after the vote, on October 26, 2014, a group of individuals, presumably Brazilian, demanded in a petition on the U.S. White House website—open to the public—that the administration of President Obama intervene in Brazil to prevent "Communist expansion" by the Dilma government. The U.S. embassy issued a statement affirming that the petition did not reflect any official position of the U.S. government and that the White House had publicly congratulated Dilma on her reelection. Without demanding a recount, on October 30, the Aécio–Aloysio campaign demanded an audit of the vote and the voting system, casting doubt on the election. Electoral officials denied the request. On November 1, 2014, a small group of protestors on the Avenida Paulista called for Dilma's impeachment. A few called for the return of military rule. Eduardo Bolsonaro, a congressman-elect and the son of prodictatorship congressman Jair Bolsonaro, declared that, had his father entered the presidential race, he would have "shot" Dilma. The authorities did not detain the younger Bolsonaro.[71] Jair Bolsonaro was elected president of Brazil in October 2018 (see chapter 15).

Starting her second term, in early 2015 Dilma embarked upon what some analysts described as a "honeymoon in hell." Dilma had not won approval of a single executive-initiated bill in 2014—a historic first in the postdictatorship era. The balance of power in the Chamber of Deputies shifted to anti-Dilma forces, led by a newly chosen Chamber speaker, Eduardo Cunha. A conservative evangelical and former radio personality, Cunha pushed through numerous measures to curtail Dilma's executive and political power. An atmosphere of political chaos set in. The situation worsened with revelations by Operation Car Wash investigators, including news of the continued theft of tens of millions of *reals* from Petrobras.[72] Cooler heads in the opposition, including Fernando Henrique, publicly opposed Dilma's removal from office.[73] Nevertheless, on March 15 more than 2 million people across the nation protested against corruption and the government, demanding Dilma's resignation or impeachment. It was the largest protest in Brazilian history after the 1984 *diretas já* demonstrations. The people in the streets were accompanied by a *panelaço*, people banging pots and pans in their apartment windows to show their disapproval of Dilma.[74] In May 2015, Dilma's opinion poll approval rating fell to a meager 7 percent—the worst in Brazilian presidential history to that point.[75] (Later, President Temer's rating would reach as low as 3 percent.) Sixty-three percent believed that she should be impeached. Brazil seemed headed for an unprecedented stress test of its democracy.[76]

CHAPTER 15

Brazil Five Decades after the Kidnapping

On July 14, 2015, I met Manoel in São Paulo's financial center, near the Avenida Paulista. We stood not far from where he had run into the police dragnet in September 1969 following the kidnapping—and Manoel's wounding—of Ambassador Elbrick in Rio. We got into Manoel's four-wheel-drive vehicle and headed out of the city. I remembered Manoel's story of perilously negotiating the city's streets to avoid capture. This time, another American at his side, the intent was not to kidnap. Manoel had invited me to spend an evening at his recently finished second home in the small, rustic mountain town of Gonçalves, Minas Gerais, about eighty miles away. On the phone, he had described the place as a calm, enjoyable setting for the final interview for this book. In addition to Manoel, during my July 2015 trip to Brazil I would be able to interview all the other former militants, except for Carlos Eugênio, who had suffered a second, serious heart attack a few months before and had moved outside Rio to recover. (In 2017 and 2018, he battled cancer of the larynx.) I aimed to obtain their views of the Lula and Dilma administrations. I also wanted to hear how Brazil's mixed progress fit—or did not fit—with their vision for the nation nearly five decades after the ALN abducted Elbrick. Former radicals had joined Brazil's leaders. What did the nation have to show for it?

After several hours on the road, during which we discussed Brazilian politics, we arrived in Gonçalves. Night had fallen, and Manoel put the vehicle into high gear to ascend a steep, unpaved road through a densely wooded area leading to his house, where his wife, Lúcia, awaited us. Manoel, who would turn sixty-nine later that month, had left Petrobras in 2010. Lúcia had retired as a physics professor. Their home stood at the crest of a hill in the Serra da Mantiqueira, a large mountain range in São Paulo, Rio de Janeiro, and Minas Gerais. Nestled in a small valley, Gonçalves had only a few thousand residents. People of means were building impressive homes in the surrounding hills. It remained an inconspicuous alternative to other towns in the area that had become busy resorts for middle- and upper-class families seeking respite from congested Rio and São Paulo. Manoel and Lúcia's large but unostentatious home had a spectacular vista of the hills. "In my universe, 'serra' was only going to be Sierra Maestra," Manoel, laughing, told me as the two of us sat in his living room after dinner. He was referring to the mountains where Fidel Castro had hidden at the start of the Cuban Revolution. "It never had anything to do with the Mantiqueira."[1]

Manoel had come out a winner in the Brazilian state-capitalist system. "I'm privileged to have this here and for having been able to retire," he observed. "I recognize that." In addition to his Petrobras pension, he received a monthly compensation, granted to many victims of the dictatorship.

Figure 42. Manoel in July 2015 at his retirement home in Gonçalves, Minas Gerais. Kenneth P. Serbin.

Manoel saw capitalism as "a step ahead in world social progress" that helped Brazil overcome its "feudal" and "archaic" aspects. He agreed with the PSDB's emphasis on capitalism, but he thought that the party failed to transform Brazil into a social democracy. The PT had come closer to that goal. "There was nothing revolutionary about it," he commented. "It did not threaten for one instant any economic sector. Never had bankers won and profited as under the PT administration. Never was property so respected as under the PT administration. Never was freedom of the press elevated as under the PT administration. But, on the other hand, never had so many people at the grassroots benefited so much."

In Manoel's assessment, in 2015 President Dilma created a political crisis because she abandoned the progrowth strategy that had brought the PT success for twelve years. Accepting the recession, she handed the crisis to the opposition "on a silver platter."[2] The PT had de-emphasized political education, thus failing to demonstrate that a progressive public policy needed to be consolidated and preserved over the long run. With the "catastrophic" corruption scandals and proposal to impeach Dilma, the PT was "annihilated" as a "mass political party of major importance." In power, the PT mistakenly adopted the posture of the traditional elite. "They thought they had become a part of the dominant classes and, therefore, had the right to steal, to commit all of that social promiscuity, to carry out those swindles, which the dominant classes have done here for centuries," Manoel commented. Preserving their own interests, the traditional elite abandoned the PT, allowing it to be exposed.

For Manoel, Brazil's underlying problem was lack of democratic consolidation—the final step in the transition from military rule, which included strengthening democratic institutions, values, and practices. One key cause, despite Brazil's economic significance, stemmed from its subordinate role in the global system. Manoel was still an economic nationalist. He thought that Brazil's capitalist class remained subservient to foreign interests. Domestically it allied itself with powerful, ultraconservative rural landowners to the detriment of small farmers and landless laborers. Manoel believed that Petrobras was the victim of the Car Wash investigation. He fully supported the campaign against corruption and for greater transparency. However, he strongly criticized frequent press leaks by corruption investigators because they compromised the inquiries and were susceptible to political manipulation, which Dilma pointed to as the cause of her declining popularity.

Another facet of democratic consolidation concerned transitional justice: the redress for the human rights abuses of the dictatorship. Manoel considered the National Truth Commission important, but believed that Brazil needed to do more. "Such transitional justice needs to take place in Brazil and definitely needs to punish whoever committed crimes, even if those criminals are subsequently amnestied," he stated. Endemic police violence continued because of the impunity associated with the dictatorship, he added. Blaming PSDB authorities, Manoel disapproved of how the Memorial of the Resistance—the former cells of the São Paulo political police converted into a museum—downplayed both his experience there and the severity of the repression. In his spacious Gonçalves front yard, Manoel planned to build a memorial for two persecuted relatives: Maria Guimarães Sampaio, a cousin who had visited Manoel in prison and supplied basic necessities (she died of cancer in 2010), and João Carlos Cavalcanti Reis, the uncle who had politicized Manoel and fought for the ALN and MOLIPO before his assassination in 1972. Manoel intended to publicly inaugurate the memorial, with ex-revolutionaries present. He wanted to "pay tribute . . . to all of the victims of the dictatorship. Everybody, even those who are unaware even today that they were victims of the dictatorship. Because we all suffered, not just those who died or were in prison. . . . Brazil lost its project as a country, as a nation. It was abandoned. A colossal legion of reactionaries was created." As if caught in a time warp, Brazil still had anti-Communists when most of the world had moved beyond the Cold War.

A third facet of democratic consolidation reflected the lack of a clear break with the military era. This resulted from the gradual, highly controlled political opening, which permitted the prodictatorship political forces to continue ruling the nation and block social, cultural, and political progress.[3] In contrast with Paulo's and Aloysio's claim about the ultimate victory of the revolutionaries, Manoel asserted that the promilitary forces had maintained power. According to him, the fact that nobody in Brazil could pinpoint the moment full democracy returned proved that it had not occurred. Thus, he referred to Brazil as a "semidemocracy,"[4] but he recognized Lula's rescue of millions from poverty as significant. In the long run, he was also optimistic about Brazilian politics. Just as many had observed about the June 2013 protests, Manoel pointed to social media and new technologies as new "arms" for disseminating alternative political ideas.

Manoel believed that he had maintained a revolutionary vision. "Life is dynamic," he commented. "Everything is in motion: the universe, nature. I think that essentially my political ideas did not change—acknowledging progress, respecting nations. . . . Whenever I speak about the United States, I try to speak about the American state, the American administration, and I defend the American people. One has nothing to do with the other. I'm not the one who changed. I think it's the world that changed." Manoel asserted that if Ambassador Elbrick were alive, he would continue to "understand our reasons" for the kidnapping.

THE OTHER FORMER ALN members also maintained that they had not compromised their basic political values but had adapted to changing circumstances. In July 2015, the workaholic, abstemious Adriano—out of public office for the first time since 1989 but not ready to retire at age sixty-six—bemoaned the difficult transition to informal political activity. He was anxious to outline the conclusions of an investigation he had led in his final months in the São Paulo State Assembly regarding atrocities linked to hazing in the state's public and private universities, including the USP medical school: dangerous drinking competitions, illegal drug usage, trafficking in women, and rape. "Hazing is a form of torture," Adriano had said when the report became public in March 2015.[5] The problem was deeply rooted in Brazil's university culture. "Because it's not just about hazing," he observed in our interview. "It's about the whole structure of power that is developed within the universities." Adriano sought other ways to advocate for human rights, pushing for the São Paulo municipal truth commission. Profoundly disappointed by Dilma's refusal to publicize and build on the work of the National Truth Commission, Adriano sought to spotlight human rights by collaborating on the matter with the Brazilian Bar Association and promoting human rights research.[6]

Adriano blamed Dilma's deteriorating political situation on a "bloodless coup" by enemies who isolated her from the Congress. He cited a swing toward conservativism in initiatives such as a bill to try sixteen-year-old criminal suspects as adults. Dilma herself contributed to that trend by including a symbol of Brazilian conservatism, Kátia Abreu, in her new cabinet. In Adriano's eyes, Dilma was politically inept. Her administration prioritized institutional and technical relationships over politics.

"So I think Lula's big mistake was having supported Dilma's reelection," Adriano observed. "I think her model is completely different from his." Having prioritized the central government, the PT had lost a large number of seats at the state and local levels. "So we didn't run a campaign for president. We ran a campaign for queen." For Adriano, the postdictatorship model of multiparty congressional coalitions supporting the president no longer worked. Dilma's presidency marked the end of an era.[7]

Moreover, despite the reduction in poverty and increase in employment under Lula, Brazil's return to its historic role as supplier of raw materials condemned workers to manual tasks or low-technology service jobs. "The laborers never qualify to do anything else," Adriano asserted. "You've got a wonder of a country where people work at what? At telemarketing. . . . We no longer have what we used to talk about, a strategic plan, a way of forming a new society with a new youth." This created political bottlenecks. "Because we've got 40 million people who've been benefited from inclusion, their level of hope and of consumption is completely different from when they didn't have a credit card or a bank account. A young man is going to go to college and then live in a favela? . . . I just think that nobody can deal with redistribution of wealth exclusive of political consciousness."[8]

Arlete, at sixty-nine, was enjoying retirement, focusing primarily on her continuing education classes and her grandchildren. She considered Adriano's exit from government "a lamentable loss," especially because he had championed human rights. Arlete mainly blamed the PT for the corruption scandals and Dilma's political crisis. However, sharing a widely held view, she believed that the courts and the media used a double standard in singling out the PT compared with other scandals. She agreed that a new wave of conservatism and prejudice helped cause Dilma and the PT's difficulties. As seen in the March 2015 protests, for the first time since 1964, conservatives marched in the streets. After the dictatorship, it seemed that conservatism "had become somewhat diluted," Arlete commented. "But that's not what I've seen lately," she continued. "I don't mean just in a political sense. I'm talking about how they view minorities, sexuality, religion."[9]

In June 2015, an anti-Dilma car sticker became available at an online store. Designed to fit over the opening of a gas tank, it showed a fake image of a smiling Dilma with her legs spread and her vagina at the opening where the gas nozzle is inserted. Arlete attributed the sticker to Brazilian machismo. "For a while it had been, let's say, sort of weakened or camouflaged, making it appear that we had evolved further but in reality hadn't," Arlete remarked. "But it's present in politics! It's striking, unfortunately. Just look at the number of men in public positions. I believe that the populace itself has gotten better, but it still votes according to machismo." After the federal Secretariat for Women prompted an investigation, the vendor stopped selling the sticker. Arlete noted even deeper hatred of Dilma in public protests and the calls by some for a return to military rule. "I get very worried, because we gave so much of our youth for this country to redemocratize, to liberalize," Arlete said. "And I see my grandchildren and get worried about them. I thought that I'd be handing them a Brazil that had progressed further."[10]

OUTSIDE RIO, in a bucolic area of Niterói, I had lunch with Jessie and Colombo at their simple but charming home set among tall trees. Good-naturedly, Colombo joked that no American had previously come to their

Figure 43. Jessie and Colombo at their Niterói home, July 2015. Kenneth P. Serbin.

"safe house." At sixty-five, he had not worked for some years because of health issues, but he collaborated with Carlos Eugênio and others on a blog disseminating political news and analysis from leftist standpoints. Jessie, now sixty-six, was ready to retire from her professorial post at the Universidade Federal do Rio de Janeiro.

Jessie saw the National Truth Commission as an important but limited achievement. She and Colombo received no invitations to testify before a Rio de Janeiro state truth commission or participate in related initiatives. "We're airplane hijackers," Jessie commented. "That's not very noble," Colombo added wryly. Conservative politicians still viewed them as "terrorists," she said.[11]

Jessie still supported Dilma, but believed her second term had become "complicated" by her embrace of a more cautious, probanker economic policy. Brazil had improved greatly under Lula and Dilma, but many young people, especially blacks, still lived miserably and suffered from "absurd" police violence. "Rio de Janeiro is a big favela where the police kill boys every day," Jessie remarked. "And they kill with indifference. The thing about [trying minors as] adults is a scandal. It's yet another manifestation of the slave era." Like the rest of the country, Rio still had too many teen mothers, Jessie added. Bolsa Família helped, she said, but families needed much more, such as daylong schools that kept students off the streets and away from violent drug traffickers and police. Brazil's mammoth social contrasts persisted like "Seattle on one side and the slave quarters on the other." Many in the traditional middle class resisted the rise of the poor, opposing such advances as the More Doctors Initiative and a 2015 law creating new protections and benefits for the country's millions of domestic workers. "It's a society so absurdly slavocratic that it doesn't even have a plan for capitalist development," Jessie concluded.

She and Colombo expressed indignation at how some conservatives publicly referred to Dilma as a "cow"—including on the floor of Congress. "That's immoral," Jessie observed. "And the idea that Dilma is authoritarian: if it were a man, they wouldn't say that." Conservative politicians were embracing ignorance, she believed. "We don't even have the classic right-wing guy who's erudite."

Forlorn about Brazil's political future, Jessie and Colombo no longer belonged to any political organization. Ultimately, although they recognized progress under the PT, they did not see capitalism as a long-term solution to Brazil's ills and inequality. "I also don't believe in structural change via the legislature," Jessie concluded. "What a utopian society would be like and whether it will take the name of socialism, I don't know. What's certain is that we won't see it."

IN BELO HORIZONTE, in the third year of his second term as mayor, the sixty-nine-year-old Márcio continued to refine the model of government that couples business efficiency and social inclusion. Brazil's governmental bodies were so ossified that creating even minor business-style professionalism was significant. In his speeches, Márcio stressed the role of elected officials and public employees as servants of the people, who should expect quality government. "If you begin promising things that you're not going to do, it's a total disaster," Márcio told the PSB party congress in 2014. "People want transparency, honesty, credibility. They want us to work. Nobody is obliged to become a public administrator.... So if you're going to do it, do it right!"[12] Márcio's staff streamlined the municipal bureaucracy, updated its computer systems, and improved responses to citizen requests. Employees assisted millions of people annually personally, via telephone, and via the Internet. Residents' requests were georeferenced to measure the demand for services in particular areas.[13] Known as BH Resolves, Márcio believed that this system improved the climate for entrepreneurs and investors. To prevent corruption in city contracts, Márcio tripled the number of auditors and set up an anticorruption secretariat.[14] Márcio's administration especially took pride in expanding schools and preschools in working-class areas. The preschools were built with municipal and federal funds. Private companies often participated in the construction as part of the PT's federal push to encourage public–private partnerships, stimulate the economy, and speed completion of projects. Under Márcio, Belo Horizonte constructed preschools using local labor and environmentally sustainable designs.[15] In 2015, Belo Horizonte had more public–private partnerships than any other state capital.[16]

Márcio reveled in his contact with the public during the festive inaugurations of schools and other events. In contrast with his awkward diction in our early interviews, Márcio had become a polished public speaker and good conversationalist.[17]

His political profile grew. In 2012, Belo Horizonte hosted the five-day international meeting of the organization Local Governments for Sustainability in preparation for Rio+20, the follow-up to the historic UN

Figure 44. Márcio with a constituent at the Belo Horizonte municipal soup kitchen, July 2015. Breno Pataro, Prefeitura de Belo Horizonte.

Earth Summit on the environment and development, held in Rio in 1992. "The world is aware today that mayors and cities must be protagonists of the changes that humanity requires," Márcio stated in our 2015 interview at Belo Horizonte city hall. "Because it's in the cities that people live and where things really happen." Representatives of four hundred cities from more than seventy countries participated. In April 2015, fellow mayors in Brazil chose Márcio as president of the National Mayors' Conference, which represented nearly two hundred cities and advocated on municipal matters.[18] In July 2015, Márcio and five other mayors joined their counterparts from fifty-nine other cites in meetings at the Vatican in Rome to discuss the implications of Pope Francis's controversial, progressive encyclical on climate change, *Laudato Si'* (May 2015), subtitled *On Care for Our Common Home*. Márcio handed Francis a letter, titled "Declaration of Brazil's Mayors," outlining the country's goals for combatting climate change. It called on wealthy nations to provide resources and technology to developing nations.[19]

In our 2015 interview, Márcio elaborated on how local actions protected the environment. He pointed to the three-year, billion-*real* implantation of MOVE, a bus rapid transit (BRT) system, developed first in Curitiba and adopted in numerous countries, to make mass transportation more efficient and attractive. MOVE—its name based on the common verb "move" in English, Portuguese, and Spanish—shortened commutes and diminished the use of cars. With modern, air-conditioned buses running in dedicated lanes in the middle of city streets, MOVE transported 500,000 passengers daily. "The system permitted the removal of hundreds and hundreds of buses from the streets, especially here in the downtown area," Márcio explained. "So traffic got better. The problem is that, in the last ten years, the number of cars has doubled and the streets are the same ones. This is a problem for the entire country, and for other countries, too. It's the automobile culture."[20] Transportation was just one factor in sustainability. Cities still awaited quality urban planning, including laws to regulate Brazil's disordered growth, building height, and neighborhood population density—goals Márcio had started to implement.

Márcio recognized that Brazil faced even larger challenges. Whereas cities in the developed world had hundreds of kilometers of subway lines, São Paulo had only seventy and Belo Horizonte only twenty-eight. "But it's very expensive!" Márcio said. He described the federal government as virtually bankrupt, leaving no funds to invest in critical, sustainable infrastructure. Márcio blamed this on Brazil's underlying economic problems, corruption, and lack of political foresight. "This country has never had austere administrations!" Márcio asserted. "So Lula arrives and says: 'Let's have the World Cup in twelve cities.'" FIFA had recommended eight. "The interest we pay on the debt annually in Brazil would be enough to resolve all of our immediate problems of mass public transportation in all of the metropolitan regions," Márcio continued.

In Márcio's assessment, the scandals of the Lula/Dilma era demoralized the Brazilian Left and fed a newly powerful conservative movement. Márcio stated:

> That means the growth and flowering of a Right in Brazil, a Right that is even a little more modern, but capable, also, of recruiting followers. Brazil has never had a Right that has called itself the Right. As the opposition, the PT defended the values of the Left, and, in power, it has become demoralized. In contrast, the Right says: "Wait a minute, we are better than those people. We can say we're rightwing, because we advocate the opposite of what they do." So, the PT

succeeded in gestating a Right, with the actual appearance of the Right, which never existed before in Brazil. There are people who even defend the superiority of the strongest, of the most intelligent, and say that poor people are lazy. At least we've got a Right. Now it's up for a new Left to emerge, other than the PT.

Dilma's record left Márcio with a mixed appraisal of Brazil. In his view, despite the PT's expansion of technical and university education, the economy lagged in productivity and competitiveness. Brazil lacked innovation in technology, human resources, and education. Though Brazil was a country of entrepreneurs, the educational system, dominated by obsolete "Marxist cliques," inculcated Brazil's youth "with a perverted view of reality, a view of justice that is anticapital, antientrepreneurial, antiproductivity, that even advocates that there be no comparison of people, of results." He added: "The schools don't teach the least bit about the values of the democratic rule of law, of respect, and of the obligations people must have." High taxes, bureaucracy, contradictory environmental legislation, and the burdensome labor laws all hampered entrepreneurs, Márcio added. Meanwhile, some Brazilian businesses still depended on the state. "It's a sick society," Márcio concluded.

> We've got a majority that only thinks about the short term, about consumption. It's a society that likes to copy any novelty that arises in Europe or the United States, which is valuable because it came from there. It's very difficult to construct a positive identity, because people don't respect their racial origins, the image of their own parents. They don't value their birthplace. Those who don't have a strong identity and respect themselves aren't capable of constructing anything of quality. Who are we? A multifaceted society, including in terms of regions, with very fragile political institutions disrespected by the populace. So the question is: Who will lead us? Who will show us the way?

AT THE LULA INSTITUTE in São Paulo, the former president and his allies tried to defend Dilma and regain the PT's political momentum. After I met Paulo Vannuchi at the Lula Institute for our interview, he drove me to the bank employees' union building for an institute-sponsored talk by liberation theologian and longtime PT supporter Leonardo Boff. Paulo intro-

Figure 45. Paulo (left) listens to presentation by liberation theologian and PT supporter Leonardo Boff, July 2015. Kenneth P. Serbin.

duced Boff to the audience of PT followers, union members, and Catholic activists. Echoing *Laudato Si'*, Boff criticized the world's unequal accumulation of wealth and warned of environmental disaster. The world needed a new paradigm of production and consumption. In Brazil, the PT needed to abandon the "vice of power" and rediscover grassroots activism.[21]

After the presentation, Paulo drove Boff's partner Márcia Miranda, Boff, and me to the Lula Institute. Lula gregariously greeted us. Lula, his two guests, and Paulo met privately for two hours while I awaited Paulo in a lounge, where I discussed the political crisis with PT Congressman Carlos Zarattini, the son of Ricardo Zarattini, one of the political prisoners released in the Elbrick operation.

I began recording my interview with Paulo as he drove us later to his office at the regional metalworkers' union headquarters in São Bernardo do Campo, the same city where Lula lived. At sixty-five, Paulo continued to passionately defend human rights. At the Inter-American Commission on Human Rights he reviewed petitions from victims of human rights violations in Argentina, Bolivia, Paraguay, and Uruguay. The right for a victim to have his or her own country investigated was unique to the

Americas. In Brazil, this bolstered the rights of abused women and combatted slavery, but, unlike in other countries, it had not yet meant the
punishment of military-era torturers. Paulo believed that Brazilian democracy had advanced to the point where the Amnesty Law, which protected the torturers, could be revoked. He envisioned that standardized
postdictatorship truth commissions could be stimulated by the Inter-
American Commission. He also focused on building its capacity to
monitor and denounce violations of economic, social, and cultural rights
in the countries under its jurisdiction.[22]

Paulo blamed both sides of the political fence for Dilma's crises. He
criticized the refusal of the PSDB and the Democratas (the former Liberal Front Party) to accept the results of the 2014 election as a key undermining factor of Dilma's second term. In Paulo's opinion, they should not
have targeted Dilma, because she personally was not corrupt. The political
situation had become increasingly characterized by "paranoia" and "profound irrationality." But he also faulted Dilma for failing to communicate
and remaining politically inactive between the election and the inauguration. She lacked "Lula's democratic creativity." The revelations of corruption represented a "trauma" that degraded a party that had succeeded in
revolutionizing Brazilian politics, Paulo said. Paulo thought that Dilma's
impeachment, though it might benefit the Left by freeing it from responsibility for the bad economy, would be a "coup," an "antidemocratic folly."
He observed: "Paradoxically, the coup could also benefit us in this way:
good, you see how they are acting? Elitism once again." Even so, the PT
had been remiss. "The PT up to this point has not demonstrated an understanding of what happened—which I consider absolutely imperative,"
he stated. "In other words, we must carry out an unsparing analysis of our
organization."

Paulo reflected on how his study of Bobbio had ultimately made him
more "eclectic" in his political outlook and analysis of Brazil. He now had
both a more realistic and more humanistic attitude toward politics and
life. He, too, saw Brazil as subordinate to foreign powers and unable to
escape the legacy of slavery. "Brazil's capitalist strength is not capable of
creating a business class with the ability to say: 'No, I will believe in my
country, I will invest, I will build,'" Paulo commented. Brazil still needed
some form of socialism. However, "socialism" for Paulo now signified gen-
erosity, solidarity, sustainable development, respect for diversity of opinion,

and profound respect for democracy as a value, not as a political instrument to be manipulated. "Our project is about a democratic revolution," Paulo affirmed. "So we want to keep the idea of revolution. I won't condemn the revolutionary that I once was, but I will affirm: today I am a revolutionary and, like all of us, I seek to be more revolutionary today than I was back then, because back then I was not able to analyze the context in the way I can today." Socialist experiments had erred gravely in abolishing private property. "The socialism that we want to construct is not the socialism of the 'new man,' of the 'new woman'—nobody knows whether he or she will ever arise—but a socialism with the real human beings that we have today, with all their virtues and defects," Paulo continued. "And, of course, the socialist agenda is one that accounts for the challenges of daily survival: 99 percent of union leaders will take better care of their private own cars than of the union's fleet [laughter]. So the challenge is to create a society in which public goods are treated with the same affection that you treat your own things." Just as Arlete, he had come to reject politics as the totality of life. "The night of lovemaking with your wife, with your girlfriend, is difficult if it's also political," he concluded. "That foolishness has to stop. There is a private life, too."

IN BRASÍLIA, former vice presidential candidate Aloysio became a leader in the effort to impeach Dilma. Aloysio had recently turned seventy, the first of the nine interviewees to reach that milestone. When not observing him at work in the Senate, I lodged in a guest room at his official Senate residence. The morning of the July 6, we took a long, vigorous walk, discussing Brazilian culture and politics. In his Senate office, I watched Aloysio take a phone call from Fernando Henrique, discuss with the Tunisian ambassador Brazil's need for an antiterrorism law, and listen to the Paraguayan ambassador report on the vast support in his country's senate for Aloysio, Aécio, and other Brazilian senators who had been rebuffed in their attempt to meet with opposition leaders and support democracy in troubled Venezuela. Aloysio invited me to join him in a staff discussion of a bill to better protect citizens' private information in a world of cyber insecurity. In another meeting Aloysio, two staffers, an accounting professor, and representatives of the government accounting office analyzed possible illegal fiscal maneuvers by the Dilma administration.

Aloysio explained his suspicions. "The illegal fiscal maneuver is a practice that the government has engaged in for some time, which consists of the attempt to hide government spending in order to maintain public accounting within the limits of a law that is very important, the Fiscal Responsibility Law," he affirmed. The law, dating from the Fernando Henrique era, was crucial to enabling credibility with investors and rating agencies. "The illegal fiscal maneuvers consist of hiding public expenditures as credit operations," he explained. The government paid for Bolsa Família, My House, My Life, and other popular programs via the federal treasury and government banks. However, because of the declining economy and lower tax receipts, the banks had to make the payments using their own credit. "The federal government is allegedly carrying out credit operations with the very banks that it controls, which is prohibited by the Fiscal Responsibility Law," he said, calling it a crime. Aloysio and other opponents of Dilma suspected that she had committed these irregularities in 2014 and 2015. "It's fiscal belt-tightening," Aloysio observed. "The gov-

Figure 46. Aloysio at work in his Senate office, July 2015. Kenneth P. Serbin.

ernment spent more than it could, especially last year, an election year. And to justify and cover up those expenditures, which were not authorized in the budget, it carried out that type of credit operation." Aloysio believed that, if proven, the maneuvers would represent an impeachable offense.[23]

Later, on the Senate floor, Aloysio countered the accusation by PT senator Gleisi Hoffman, Dilma's former chief of staff, that the PSDB was trying to "destabilize" the Dilma government and attempt a "coup." "It's a form of escapism on the part of progovernment forces to avoid confronting the real problems that President Dilma is facing," he declared. "The cause was the actions of fiscal irresponsibility, the frenzy of spending to win the elections by pumping up social spending." Aloysio reminded Hoffmann that the government accounting office could judge whether illegal fiscal maneuvers had occurred. The PSDB, he noted, had also officially requested an audit of the results of the 2014 election because of Dilma's "abuse" of power. Dilma's popularity was plummeting, and all of Brazil knew it, he added. "Obviously, I do not desire a traumatic ending to this process," he stated. "I lived through the effects of institutional rupture. That will not occur in Brazil. Whatever the result of the legal proceedings, it will be respected."[24]

Aloysio blamed the crisis on corruption and Dilma's political ineptitude. The PT's corruption was a "stain" on the entire Brazilian Left, harming the reputations of PT leaders, he remarked in our interview. "Lula is shameless," he said. "Today he is a person obsessed with money. He became a millionaire. He used power to enrich his family." Aloysio pointed to the case of Lula's son Lulinha, a São Paulo zoo employee who used his connections to start a business that he later sold for 5 million *reals*. According to government investigators, Lula illicitly acquired a triplex apartment in the seaside town of Guarujá built by the OAS conglomerate, a main target of Operation Car Wash. "He's gone around the world as a lobbyist for construction companies," Aloysio asserted. "So I've lost respect for him. And he was the mentor of the political system that produced the mensalão and the oil corruption."

Aloysio recognized but did not identify with the resurgence of conservatism. Those advocating a return to military rule were "inconsequential." Whereas the youth offenders bill proposed that sixteen- and seventeen-year-old suspects be automatically treated as adults, Aloysio's version recommended such status only for violent crimes and only after determination by a juvenile court judge. Eighty-seven percent of Brazilians supported the more punitive version. Aloysio viewed his bill as a way to "hold back a little the wave" of support for the tougher measure.[25] The proposal was not taken up by the Senate, leaving the legislative status quo in place. Aloysio supported the decriminalization of abortion, legal only in cases of rape, incest, danger to life of the mother, and anencephaly (absence of the brain). Conservatives staunchly opposed a change in the law. Dilma, although initially indicating in 2009 that she favored decriminalization, changed her mind in the 2010 campaign against the vociferously pro-life Serra.[26] As president, she avoided the issue, a sign of the PT's unwillingness to push on controversial social issues. "That's not a matter for the penal code," Aloysio commented. "I've already said that. There is no reason to punish a woman who has already been punished by the fact of ending a pregnancy."

Despite its progress, Brazil to Aloysio remained an unequal society with a mediocre capitalist system. He admired capitalism's promotion of individual creativity and the free market as "a mechanism for distributing opportunities." However, Brazil's capitalism was "uncompetitive, a capitalism burdened with rules" that benefited politicians and bureaucrats but not consumers. "Our capital markets are very weak," Aloysio observed, citing Brazil's subordinate position in the international sphere. He called the socialist option "an illusion." "So it's better to improve capitalism, civilize it, tame it, temper it with humanism, with social policies," he said. Despite its vast inequalities, Brazil was a "society on the move. With major challenges, including in the political arena." The return of mass demonstrations was "an enormous challenge to the politicians. How do we tie into that? How do we relate to a movement without it running us or us running it?" Innovative in multiple ways, Brazilians had "high aspirations." Democratic culture had expanded greatly, in Brazil and around the world, he thought. "Brazil today is an open society, a society with numerous career possibilities," he said. "There is no political-ideological organization that is banned, that is delegitimized. I'm enjoying this, this new situation in comparison with the one I lived during the dictatorship and even before the dictatorship, a society then with few choices for those interested in politics." According to Aloysio, prejudice was also diminishing. "The campaign against discrimination, against homophobia, against violence— these are themes that I wasn't very aware of in my youth," he concluded. "Today they are central for me."

IN LATE 2015, the economic recession deepened. Members of the new middle class began to drop again below the poverty line.[27] On December 2, speaker Cunha of the PMDB unleashed the impeachment process by officially accepting an accusation of illegal fiscal maneuvers filed by two attorneys, one a former PT member, the other a former minister of justice under Fernando Henrique. Cunha acted in revenge for the investigation into his own purported illicit fortune, with millions of dollars deposited in Swiss bank accounts. Operation Car Wash revealed more details of the world's biggest corruption scheme. For the first time, leading government officials and corporate executives were convicted on corruption charges *and* were going to jail, thanks to vigorous investigation by the Polícia Federal and a new generation of democratically minded prosecutors and judges. The Dilma administration's attempts to steer the media and weaken federal accountability institutions did not gain traction in the governing coalition or in society.[28]

As anger against corruption and Dilma increased, the push for her impeachment grew. At 6 a.m. on March 4, 2016, the Polícia Federal raided Lula's apartment in São Bernardo do Campo, took him into custody, and questioned him for three hours as part of the probe into his connections to the crimes investigated by the Car Wash: influence trafficking, the beachfront apartment in Guarujá, and a country estate in Atibaia, São Paulo. Nine days later, more than 3 million people marched in the streets in more than 230 cities, demanding Dilma's removal from office and an end to corruption. It was the largest political protest in Brazilian history, surpassing the *diretas já* demonstrations of 1984 and the June 2013 protests. Many protestors carried signs praising Judge Sérgio Moro, the federal magistrate in the charge of the Operation Car Wash investigation.[29] Although the PT accused Moro of bias, he sought to maintain a nonpartisan stance.

In April, the Chamber of Deputies voted articles of impeachment against Dilma, alleging financial improprieties. The Senate formally accepted the charges. As a result, Vice President Temer took over as interim president while Dilma awaited judgment by the Senate. Aloysio was a member of the Senate committee in charge of examining the evidence against the president. Senate staffers found no evidence of illegal fiscal maneuvers, but they affirmed that Dilma had spent funds without the necessary authorization of Congress.[30] For Aloysio, this constituted an impeachable offense.[31] He and a majority of the members of the evidence committee recommended charges to the full Senate.[32] On August 26, the Polícia Federal recommended corruption and money-laundering charges against Lula and his wife. Three days later, Brazil's tax-collecting agency fined the Lula Institute millions of *reals* for financial irregularities—including a payment to the business of one of Lula's sons. (Paulo Vannuchi was not implicated in any of Lula's alleged misdeeds.)

On August 31, the 2016 Olympics were in full swing in Rio. This was to have been a crowning moment for Lula, Dilma, and the PT. Instead, they faced a tragedy. In Brasília, after Aloysio and other opposition senators gave passionate speeches calling for Dilma's removal, the Senate voted her out permanently. The conviction had less to do with any malfeasance than it did with the pressure from the populace, the sagging economy, and her record unpopularity. With the permission of the president of the Supreme Court, who oversaw the trial, the Senate ignored the Constitution and retained Dilma's right to run for public office; many politicians were under investigation and feared that, if convicted and removed from office, they, too, might be barred from future office. Temer immediately took the oath of office as the new president. However, his administration was far from clean. Several of his cabinet members, and eventually Temer himself, would come under investigation. Aloysio became the Temer administration's leader in the Senate. In the end, he maintained, Brazilian democracy had functioned properly,[33] but he sharply disagreed with his colleagues' decision to preserve Dilma's officeholding rights. In March 2017, Aloysio became Temer's minister of foreign relations. That same month, he came under investigation for allegedly having received illegal donations to his 2010 Senate campaign. Aloysio denied the allegations. In October 2018, by a vote of 3 to 2, a group of Supreme Court judges reviewing the allegations ordered an end to the investigation.

On July 12, 2017, Judge Moro found ex-president Lula guilty of corruption and money-laundering charges in connection with the illicit acquisition of the seaside apartment, which Lula had denied owning. He was sentenced to nine years and six months in prison, but allowed to remain free as he awaited his appeal. On January 24, 2018, the appeals court panel unanimously confirmed the conviction, augmenting the sentence to twelve years and one month. On April 7, Lula started serving his sentence in a jail cell at the Polícia Federal regional headquarters in Curitiba. Yet Lula remained popular. Many opinion polls showed him as virtually unbeatable in the 2018 presidential election. However, with his conviction, Brazil's election laws prevented him from running. A plaque on the Polícia Federal facility commemorates its inauguration by the Lula government in 2007. Lula had thus become engulfed in the combat of corruption that his own administration had helped to unleash. Paulo's warning to Lula in 2002 had proven prescient: "Look, any wrongdoing in the party, the PT is going to pay triple the political price of anybody else." Although there were some pro-Lula protests and a further political polarization of Brazilian society after his jailing, all players, as Aloysio indicated, respected the legal decisions.

In the October 2018 elections, Aloysio did not run for reelection to the Senate. Adriano failed in an attempt to return to the São Paulo State Assembly. Márcio, who came under consideration as a vice presidential running mate for Ciro Gomes in the presidential election, sought to run for governor of Minas Gerais but had his candidacy blocked by the PSB because of its alliance with the PT. In a deposition at the Polícia Federal resulting from the Car Wash probe, he rebutted the allegation of the use of illegal campaign contributions in his mayoral campaigns, noting that he used his own money to pay off campaign debts. Minas Gerais voters rejected Dilma in her bid to join the Senate; in a race with five candidates and the top two winning seats, she finished fourth. In the presidential contest, Lula led in the polls, but only as a hypothetical candidate; the courts rejected appeals to gain his release from prison and secure him a place in the race.

Jair Bolsonaro's long-shot candidacy defied the odds, as did Donald Trump's in the 2016 U.S. election. He ran on the ticket of the Social Liberal Party, a small, inconsequential party with a small number of elected officials. In a stunning development, on September 6, a mentally ill man stabbed Bolsonaro during a campaign rally, nearly killing him. Bolsonaro was hospitalized for weeks but gained vast exposure in the media. In the first round on October 7, Bolsonaro garnered 46 percent of the vote versus 29 percent by the PT candidate, Fernando Haddad, put officially into place by the party just a few weeks before the election. Haddad had served as minister of education under Lula and Dilma (2005–12) and mayor of São Paulo (2013–17). Running on the PDT ticket, Ciro Gomes finished third with only 12 percent of the vote, followed by ten other candidates with smaller percentages. On October, 28, Bolsonaro defeated Haddad in the second round with 55.13 percent of the vote.

Many referred to the outspoken Bolsonaro as a "Brazilian Trump." The seven-term, ultraright-wing congressman and former army captain made public statements against women, gays, and Afro-Brazilians. He regularly praised the dictatorship and approved of torture. During the 2016 impeachment proceedings, he dedicated his vote against Dilma to DOI-CODI torturer Ustra. In a 1999 interview, he stated that, instead of elections, Brazil needed a civil war in which the military should kill 30,000 leftists. During the second round of the 2018 campaign, he vowed to exile or imprison his political opponents.[34] Rather than Trump, some observers compared Bolsonaro to Philippine president Rodrigo Duterte, who condoned extrajudicial killings of alleged drug traffickers and users. Thus, Bolsonaro appeared to threaten the painstaking gains Brazil had made in the promotion of human rights and democracy. As Dilma's impeachment presented a stress test of Brazilian democracy, so perhaps did Bolsonaro's election. A central question was this: Would Bolsonaro lead Brazil down an authoritarian path?

Bolsonaro's election was both astounding and enigmatic. With his polarizing style, his arrival in the presidency seemed to represent more of a rejection of the PT and corruption than an embrace of his intolerance. What remained to be seen was whether, in contrast with Trump, Bolsonaro could moderate his tone and engage in a political dialogue. Perhaps a ray of hope lay in the fact that he chose Judge Moro as his minister of justice, a position that Bolsonaro planned to expand to include public safety and the combat of organized crime. The selection of the popular Moro seemed politically astute. It signaled respect for the Constitution and the rule of law and, perhaps, human rights.

THE ALN REVOLUTIONARIES had fought to transform Brazil. After the defeat of the revolution, they succeeded in inserting themselves into a highly flawed democratic and state-capitalist system. As rulers, they wanted to maintain their values and implement policies reflecting them. They helped define an era of Brazilian history. With Dilma's ouster, that era came to an end.[35] Bolsonaro's election confirmed this. And, in an echo of Paulo's concerns at the start of the mensalão crisis, the left-wing front nurtured by the PT over decades had perhaps disintegrated. Nevertheless, Brazil had changed profoundly, becoming a more inclusive nation socially and economically. Under Fernando Henrique and especially Lula, a nation of have-nots started to become a nation of haves. Despite its political system's tragic drawbacks, Brazil, by world standards, was one of the best-functioning democracies. From 1989 to 2014, it had seven routine elections with peaceful transitions of power. A full generation of Brazilians had experienced strengthened institutions.[36] Most Brazilians ultimately weren't interested in ideological debates. They wanted to thrive economically. Once their economic situation improved, they also wanted competent, ethical leaders to rescue them from the bane of corruption and keep alive the dream of a better life: reliable and respectful police, good health care, efficient transportation, and effective schools.[37] And, as Adriano observed, they wanted to move out of favelas. These desires Bolsonaro's election did *not* change.

In seeking social justice and the overthrow of a repressive dictatorship, the nine militants had joined an organization whose founder saw certain terrorist acts as a legitimate way to combat the military. Manoel and the other militants categorically rejected the label of "terrorists," but the kidnapping of Ambassador Elbrick, the attempt to hijack a jetliner, and other actions clearly could be classified as terrorism. As stated in the prologue, "terrorism" is a relative term. As a form of resistance against tyranny and torture, many of the ALN's actions might be seen as "good terrorism," the combating of obvious social injustice. At the same time, other forms of violence employed by the ALN—such as the execution of fellow ALN comrade Márcio Leite by Carlos Eugênio and three other guerrillas—proved an example of revolutionary excess. Ultimately, the ALN failed miserably as a military outfit. After its defeat by the security forces, it also disintegrated as a political organization. Its raison d'être—violence—was futile in the Brazil of the late 1960s and early 1970s.

However, surviving ALN militants continued to resist the dictatorship by rethinking their ideas and adopting *nonviolent, political* strategies. At the memorial Mass for Alexandre in 1973, supporters of the ALN within the USP joined with religious leaders and the political opposition to foment the first massive public antiregime protest of the 1970s. In the prisons, ostensibly powerless ALN prisoners organized themselves, smuggling in books and other crucial items, pressuring for the proper treatment of abused common criminals, protecting themselves from prison gangs, engaging in hunger strikes, acquiring recognition from the regime as prisoners of conscience, and obtaining transfer to political prisons. Allies outside the prisons revealed their plight to society and the international press.

Astute, ambitious, and creative, Márcio won early release from prison and started two telecommunications firms. He collaborated with a faction of nationalistic officers in carrying out the military government's goal of expanding the telephone system, a key example of how state-led capitalism worked, at least in the short run. In exile in France, Aloysio and Carlos Eugênio left the ALN to join the PCB's peaceful, democratic opposition. Spending time in Moscow and observing how Soviet censorship skewed people's view of politics, Aloysio rejected the lack of freedom in the Communist system. He returned from exile committed to democracy and individual freedom. In São Paulo, Adriano, Arlete, and Paulo discovered the power of grassroots opposition and political organizing in the *movimento popular*.

After the 1979 Amnesty Law, and especially with the return to civilian rule in 1985, the former ALN members ran for election and/or worked to govern a capitalist democracy. In the 1990s and later, they took on leadership positions at different levels of Brazilian society. They still pursued social justice, but they all worked for it by entering into, or at the very least accommodating to, the social and political mainstream. This allowed them to earn a living, but also the opportunity to reform the system. Had they rejected politics or joined the Left's remaining ultraradical fringe, they would have stood little chance of attaining power and wielding influence.

In their role as rulers, the former revolutionaries helped fortify both Brazil's capitalist system and its quest for social democracy. They defended human, civil, and labor rights; worked to protect the environment; sought to make public institutions more efficient and responsive to the public, including the rooting out of corruption; aimed to make democracy more inclusive; supported economic reforms; created jobs; and, in general, aimed to build a more equal and just society.

None of the former revolutionaries had any illusions about Brazil's many remaining hurdles. Just as the ALN guerrillas in 1969 failed to draw the common people into armed struggle, as leaders they encountered resistance, for example, in transforming cultural attitudes about public service. Except for Márcio and Aloysio, none came under investigation for corruption. Falsely accused in the mensalão scandal, Márcio was cleared. He rebutted new allegations against him in 2018. Aloysio was never charged. Each of the former militants struggled to make sense of these demoralizing scandals. Even though prosecution of the wrongdoers represented a historic step for Brazil, ongoing corruption threatened Brazil's aspirations to become a developed nation. In the search for power, led by Lula, Dirceu, and the PT, the Brazilian Left got caught up in the darker side of Brazilian political culture and political pragmatism.

At the same time, continuing Fernando Henrique's emphasis on accountability, Lula and Dilma had reinforced the institutions that combated corruption. This produced a political atmosphere in which even they as an ex-president and sitting president could not escape prosecution. From this perspective, Brazilians could be proud that their institutions were functioning, perhaps pointing to a potentially less corrupt system in the future. Applying justice to the political elite perhaps was the shock Brazil needed to start making government more responsive. If so, it could instill in Brazilians confidence that institutions and the rule of law could serve—and not victimize—them.

ACKNOWLEDGMENTS

I spent nearly a quarter century researching and writing this book. I am profoundly grateful to the many individuals and institutions who have made it possible. First, the work would not have been possible without the generous time provided by the nine main interviewees of this work: Adriano, Aloysio, Arlete, Carlos Eugênio, Colombo, Jessie, Manoel, Márcio, and Paulo. Just as generous and helpful were the other former revolutionaries and activists who shared their stories with me in depth: Alberto Alonso Lázaro, Amparo Araújo, Dulce Chaves Pandolfi, Enzo Nico Júnior, Guiomar Silva Lopes, Hamilton Pereira da Silva (Pedro Tierra), Itoby Alves Corrêa Jr., Lisete Lídio de Sílvio, Maria Cristina Vannucchi Leme, Maurice Politi, Neide Richopo, Ruy de Goes Leite de Barros, and Takao Amano. I had other key interviews and/or conversations with Ricardo Apgaua, Carlos Alberto Lobão Cunha, César Augusto Teles, Concepción Martín Pérez, Frei Betto (Carlos Alberto Libânio Christo), Geraldo Siqueira, Gilney Amorim Viana, Janaína de Almeida Teles, Luiz Antonio Alves de Souza, Maria Amélia de Almeida Teles (Amelinha), Percival Maricato, and Vera Maria Tude de Souza. Marival Chaves provided a valuable interview on the inner workings of the DOI-CODI. I also thank the former militants who completed a biographical survey: Alcides Yukimitsu Mamizuka, Ana de Cerqueira César Corbisier, André Tsutomu Ota, Antenor Meyer, Antonio Ribeiro Penna, Carlos Lichtsztejn, Cloves de Castro, Conceição Imaculada de Oliveira, Domingos Fernandes, Efigênia Maria de Oliveira, Eliane Toscano Zamikhowsky, José Carlos Vidal, Jun Nakabayashi, Ligia Aparecida Cardieri Mendonça, Luiz Alberto Ravaglio, Luiz Oswaldo Carneiro Rodrigues, Nair Benedicto, Paulo de Tarso Venceslau, Rafael de Falco Netto, Regina Elza Solitrenick, Reinaldo Guarany, Robêni Baptista da Costa, Rogério de Campos Teixeira, Vinicius Medeiros Caldevilla, Walderês Nunes Loureiro, Wilimar da Rocha, and Yves do Amaral Lesbaupin.

In Brazil I received invaluable assistance from friends and fellow scholars Marco Aurélio Vannucchi Leme de Mattos and Regiane Mattos. They kindly opened their home in São Paulo on numerous occasions, providing a wonderful base from which to work. Marco's research on and knowledge of the dictatorship and the revolutionary Left helped shape my understanding of the period and its aftermath. In 2008, Marco also provided important research assistance in São Paulo, as did Maria Fernando Magalhães Scelza and Carolina de Campos Carvalho in Rio. Also in Rio, Carolina, Aline Pinto Marques, Andreia Cesar dos Santos, Bárbara de Souza Fontes, Clara Faulhaber do Vale, Jessica Ausier da Costa, Katarina Wolter, Leonardo Jorge A. Ramos, Louise Cazelgrandi Ramos, and Sue Ellen Souza performed the challenging task of transcribing the recorded interviews.

In 2007, I had the privilege of spending three months as a visiting scholar at one of the leading centers for oral history and the study of contemporary Brazil, the Centro de Pesquisa e Documentação de História Contemporânea do Brasil of the Fundação Getúlio Vargas in Rio. Director and friend Celso Castro provided an amenable work environment, connections, and intellectual stimulation. Maria Celina D'Araujo also provided valuable input.

Edileuza Pimenta de Lima furnished contacts, data, and historical perspective on the ALN. As usual, Marcelo Ridenti provided a helpful sociological perspective on my work as well as conversations and much e-mail correspondence about the dictatorship and the revolutionary Left. Friend and scholar Heitor Frúgoli deepened my understanding of São Paulo as an urban space. David Fleischer kept me informed on key trends in the Brazilian political economy and pointed out news on former militants. Friend and activist Magali Godoi provided unique insight into the revolutionary Left and the struggle for human rights in Brazil. Friend and fellow Brazilianist Ralph Della Cava once again acted as a mentor and generous landlord for the many months of lodging in his Rio apartment. Marcelo Ulisses Machado generously volunteered his photographic expertise to provide a number of the images. Vladimir Sacchetta did the kind of superb photo research for which he is famed in Brazil. Caio Túlio Costa generously shared documents and exchanged ideas about the resistance in São Paulo. Carlos Fico furnished copies of important American documents and afforded intellectual and moral support. Mário Magal-

documents and afforded intellectual and moral support. Mário Magalhães also shared important documents, provided tips and contacts, and
discussed his impressions of the ALN and the status of its former militants. In Brazil, additional ideas and assistance also came from Adler do
Couto Andrade, Ana Flávia Pescuma, Angelo del Vecchio, Beatriz Kusch-
nir, Cecília Coimbra, Cecília Mariz, Célia Tavares, Clara Schainer, Denise
Rollemberg, Jaime Ginzburg, João Roberto Martins Filho, Jorge Zaveru-
cha, Kelly Santos, Lucas Souza, Luiz Maklouf Carvalho, Paulo Botelho,
Thomaz Gollop, and Vanilda Paiva. As always, Nelly Boonen was an important contact and friend in São Paulo. Cita Melo provided valuable
support and friendship in Recife.

Carlos Eduardo Lins da Silva did yeoman's work in reading a much
longer, earlier version of the manuscript, suggesting important corrections
and additions. He also sent news items on former militants. At the start
of the project, Elio Gaspari provided valuable suggestions and insight. Old
friend and comrade in writing Norman Oder provided a thorough edit of,
and effective commentary on, the manuscript. James Green advised on
several stages of the project and also read the manuscript, providing per-
spicacious comments and challenging me to strengthen key aspects of the
analysis. Jim's friendship and moral support helped inspire me to complete
this book. I also received encouragement and valuable assistance from
Bryan McCann (who read part of the manuscript), and also Christopher
Dunn, Timothy Power, Anthony Pereira, Rafael Ioris, Joel Wolfe, Marshall Eakin, Margaret Keck, Daryle Williams, Seth Garfield, Victoria
Langland, Judy Bieber, Jerry Dávila, Natan Zeichner, Barbara Weinstein,
Amy Chazkel, Dain Borges, William C. Smith, and Jeffrey Lesser. Paul
Drake and Eric Van Young contributed with ideas and support.

I am also grateful for the helpful comments from the anonymous re-
viewer at University of Notre Dame Press. Notre Dame editors Stephen
Little and Eli Bortz masterfully guided the book to publication, patiently
waiting through delays as I worked to include a more in-depth look at the
Dilma Rousseff government and the 2016 impeachment. Scott Barker did
a brilliant and thorough copy edit, and Wendy McMillen, Matthew Dowd,
and Susan Berger did wonderful work on various aspects of the final product. Literary agent Carol Mann provided encouragement and insightful
feedback on the project.

This project got an intellectual boost and took on a broader scope
thanks to my participation in the workshop Constructive Transformation:

Studying Cases of Political Incorporation at the Maxwell School's Moyni-han Institute of Global Affairs and Program on the Analysis and Resolu-tion of Conflicts, Syracuse University, October 4–7, 2007. That led to the publication of my article "Mainstreaming the Revolutionaries" in *Conflict Transformation and Peacebuilding: Moving from Violence to Sustainable Peace*, edited by Bruce Dayton and Louis Kriesberg, of the Syracuse fac-ulty. I learned of the workshop from fellow Brazilianist, friend, and Syra-cuse faculty member John Burdick. John also provided ideas and intellec-tual support for the project. I received helpful feedback on papers presented at the American Historical Association/Conference on Latin American History (2005 and 2010), the international seminar on the fortieth anni-versary of the social upheaval of 1968 at the Universidade Federal do Rio de Janeiro (2008), and the Brazilian Studies Association (2008).

Financial support was indispensable. I received a National Endow-ment for the Humanities Summer Stipend (summer 2001), a Fulbright–Hays Faculty Research Abroad award for research in Brazil and the crucial transcription of the interviews (June–August 2007), and the American Council of Learned Societies Fellowship Program award for a sabbatical year of research and writing (September 2007–May 2008.) At the Univer-sity of San Diego (USD), I received ongoing travel and research support for the project from the College of Arts and Sciences Faculty Research Grant program, the International Center's International Opportunity Grants program, Department of History travel funds, the Academic Stra-tegic Priorities Fund, the University Professorship awards program, and other grants from the College of Arts and Sciences and Provost's Office. For the support at USD, I am grateful to provosts Frank Lazarus, Julie Sullivan, and Gail Baker; deans Patrick Drinan, Nicholas Healy, Mary Boyd, and Noelle Norton; History chairs James Gump, Molly McClain, Colin Fisher, and Yi Sun; and Denise Dimon, the director of the Inter-national Center. In the Department of History, executive assistants Mau-reen Byrnes and Holly Smith provided important administrative support. USD student Bridget Evans efficiently converted many hours of cassette tape interviews into digital files. I am especially grateful to my other His-tory colleagues for their intellectual stimulation and encouragement: Ryan Abrecht, Ali Gheissari, Cecily Heisser, Channon Miller, Clara Oberle, David Miller, Kathryn Statler, Michael Gonzalez, Thomas Barton, and T. J. Tallie. I also had helpful conversations about the work with USD col-leagues Alejandro Meter, Ami Carpenter, Daniel Sheehan, and Topher McDougal.

I am forever indebted to my personal friends and extended family in Brazil: Eloi Melo and Henriette LaRovere and their clan; Fernando Ferreira and his clan; Maryse Bacellar (my Brazilian mom) and her clan; my brothers-in-law Ricardo Alves de Barros and Rogério Alves de Barros and their families; and my mother-in-law, Maria de Lourdes Alves Barros. I am also ever grateful for the friendship and intellectual support of Luiz Alberto Gómez de Souza and Lucia Ribeiro. Thanks also to dear friends Raquel Michelson and Terry Vincent McIntyre.

In San Diego, Allan and Jane Rappoport have provided love and inspiration, and, with their strong desire to see this book in print, kept me aware of the need to not turn it into an unending academic enterprise. And a special shout-out to Eric Watkins and Teresa Elston, friends and fellow followers of the international arena, and to old Yale friends Adam Glick, Stephen Downing, Gary Whitman, Stephen Prothero, David Chappell, Lisa Valkenier, Paul and Carole Bass, and Bill Glaser.

I also thank the global Huntington's disease community—including advocates in Brazil—for its dedication and solidarity. The Brazilian revolutionaries and antidictatorial militants have inspired me to become a better Huntington's advocate.

My parents, Paul and Carol Serbin, are deceased but forever in mind. Carol lost her battle with Huntington's in 2006. Paul, her "HD warrior" caregiver, left us in 2009. Without them, none of this would have been possible. Thank you, Mom and Dad, for raising me so well and fighting the good fight!

Above all, I am most deeply grateful to my lovely wife, Regina, and lovely daughter, Bianca. I traveled to Brazil and sat at the computer far too many times in seeking to complete this project. I thank them for continuing to love me throughout these absences. Regina, a native of Minas Gerais, has been a true companion throughout our twenty-seven years of marriage and a sagacious interpreter of Brazilian culture and history. She helped with many of the more difficult translations of the militants' words into English. Bianca became a bright teenager and then started college as this book went to press. I'll forever associate its completion with her far more important transition into adulthood. I am very proud of her as she seeks to leave her own mark on the world and make it a better place.

Naturally, despite the immense assistance I have received, all responsibility for this work is mine.

NOTES

Prologue

1. Kenneth P. Serbin, *Needs of the Heart* (Notre Dame, IN: University of Notre Dame Press, 2006).

2. Kenneth P. Serbin, *Secret Dialogues* (Pittsburgh: University of Pittsburgh Press, 2000).

3. For reflections on Brazil as the country of the future, see Marshall C. Eakin, *Brazil: The Once and Future Country* (New York: St. Martin's Press, 1997). On world power status, see Carlos Fico, *Reinventando o otimismo* (Rio de Janeiro: Editora Fundação Getúlio Vargas, 1997).

4. On development in the 1950s and 1960s, see Rafael R. Ioris, *Transforming Brazil* (New York: Routledge, 2014); on the rise of the auto industry, see Joel Wolfe, *Autos and Progress* (New York: Cambridge University Press, 2010).

5. Throughout I refer to most main figures by their first names, as they are customarily known in Brazil (see the list under Key Historical Figures). If people are known by nicknames or last names, I refer to them as such.

6. "Depoimento de Paulo Vannuchi," in *1964: Do golpe à democracia*, ed. Angela Alonso and Miriam Dolhnikoff, 359–80 (São Paulo: Hedra, 2015), 359.

7. On deaths, see Mário Magalhães, *Marighella* (São Paulo: Compania das Letras, 2012), 313.

8. "Depoimento de Paulo Vannuchi," 359–60.

9. Carlos Fico, *O grande irmão* (Rio de Janeiro: Civilização Brasileira, 2008), 72.

10. James N. Green, *We Cannot Remain Silent* (Durham, NC: Duke University Press, 2010), 3–4, 19–36, 37 (quotation), 38–48; see also Fico, *O grande irmão*.

11. Author's interview with Paulo de Tarso Vannuchi, São Paulo, July 23, 2001.

12. On executions, see Elio Gaspari, *As ilusões armadas: A ditadura escancarada* (São Paulo: Companhia das Letras, 2002), 2:377–90.

13. Rubens Valente and Gustavo Uribe, "Chefe da CIA disse que Geisel assumiu controle sobre execuções sumárias na ditadura," *Folha de S. Paulo*, May 11, 2018.

14. Paulo's branch of the family spells the last name as "Vannuchi," while others use "Vannucchi."

15. Serbin, *Secret Dialogues*, chap. 10.

16. Caio Túlio Costa, *Cale-se* (São Paulo: A Girafa, 2003).

17. Author's interview with Jessie Jane Vieira de Souza, Rio de Janeiro, August 3, 2002. Unless otherwise noted, all translations from Portuguese to English are mine.

18. Robert Service, *Stalin* (Cambridge, MA: Belknap Press, 2005); Maurice Meisner, *Mao Zedong* (Malden, MA: Polity, 2007).

19. Magalhães, *Marighella*, 89, 106, 124–26, 137, 165, 222–23; on democracy and parties, see Thomas E. Skidmore, *Politics in Brazil* (New York: Oxford University Press, 1967).

20. Magalhães, *Marighella*, 154–60, 168, 208–10, 227–37, 246–47, 267, 273; see also Marcelo Ridenti, *Brasilidade revolucionária* (São Paulo: Editora UNESP, 2010), 57–83.

21. Ridenti, *Brasilidade revolucionária*, 10, 12–13, 64.

22. Jacob Gorender, *Combate*, 5th rev. and augmented ed. (São Paulo: Ática, 1998), 289; for an overview of the extensive polemic on the character of the armed resistance, see Lucileide Costa Cardoso, "Revolução e resistência," *História: Revista da Faculdade de Letras da Universidade do Porto* 4 (2014): 33–49.

23. On the number of dead revolutionaries in Brazil, see Secretaria Especial dos Direitos Humanos, *Direito à memória e à verdade* (Brasília: Secretaria Especial dos Direitos Humanos da Presidência da República, 2007), 17; on the countryside, see Movimento dos Trabalhadores Rurais Sem Terra, *Assassinatos no campo* (São Paulo: Global, 1987); on the number of the guerrillas' victims, see Carlos Alberto Brilhante Ustra, *Rompendo o silêncio* (Brasília: Editerra, 1987), 181–93.

24. Author's interview with Paulo de Tarso Vannuchi, São Paulo, July 3, 2003.

25. Charles Marsh, *Strange Glory* (New York: Vintage, 2014), Kindle ed., chap. 13 (quotation).

26. Gérard Chaliand and Arnaud Blin, eds., *The History of Terrorism* (Berkeley: University of California Press, 2007).

27. Bruce Hoffman, "Defining Terrorism," *Social Science Record* 24, no. 1 (1986): 6–7.

28. David S. Reynolds, *John Brown, Abolitionist* (New York: Vintage, 2009), Kindle ed., chap. 2 (bloodthirsty), chap. 7 (good terrorism, social injustice); Doris Lessing, *The Good Terrorist* (London: Jonathan Cape, 1985).

29. Walter Laqueur, *The Age of Terrorism* (Boston: Little, Brown and Company, 1987), 181.

30. For a critique of the heroic perspective, see James N. Green, *Exile within Exiles* (Durham, NC: Duke University Press, 2018); for the classic example of the military view of the Left as villain, see Carlos Alberto Brilhante Ustra, *A verdade sufocada* (Brasília: Editora Ser, 2006).

31. Seth G. Jones, *How Terrorist Groups End* (Santa Monica, CA: Rand, 2008); Bruce W. Dayton and Louis Kriesberg, eds., *Conflict Transformation and Peacebuilding* (London: Routledge, 2009); Martha Crenshaw, ed. *Terrorism in Context* (University Park: Pennsylvania State University Press, 1995).

32. Tom Lodge, "Revolution Deferred: From Armed Struggle to Liberal Democracy," in *Conflict Transformation and Peacebuilding: Moving from Violence to Sustainable Peace*, ed. Bruce W. Dayton and Louis Kriesberg (London: Routledge, 2009), 156–71.

33. Zuenir Ventura, *1968: O que fizemos de nós* (São Paulo: Editora Planeta do Brasil, 2008).

34. Antonio Delfim Netto, "O capitalismo não é uma coisa," *CartaCapital*, October 20, 2015.

35. Joseph L. Love, "The Lula Government in Historical Perspective," in *Brazil under Lula: Economy, Politics, and Society under the Worker-President*, ed. Joseph L. Love and Werner Baer (New York: Palgrave MacMillan, 2009), 307.

36. Aldo Musacchio and Sergio G. Lazzarini, "The Reinvention of State Capitalism in Brazil," in *New Order and Progress: Development and Democracy in Brazil*, ed. Ben Ross Schneider (New York: Oxford University Press, 2016), 107.

37. Lincoln Secco, *História do PT*, 4th ed. (Cotia: Ateliê Editorial, 2015), 260.

38. Timothy J. Power, "Centering Democracy? Ideological Cleavages and Convergence in the Brazilian Political Class," in *Democratic Brazil Revisited*, ed. Peter Kingstone and Timothy J. Power (Pittsburgh: University of Pittsburgh Press, 2008), 81–106.

39. Ibid., 105.

40. Timothy J. Power, "The Reduction of Poverty and Inequality in Brazil: Political Causes, Political Consequences," in *New Order and Progress: Development and Democracy in Brazil*, ed. Ben Ross Schneider (New York: Oxford University Press, 2016), 212.

41. Kenneth P. Serbin, "A classe média na pior," *O Estado de S. Paulo*, December 27, 2015.

42. On social democracy, see Luiz Carlos Bresser-Pereira, *A construção política do Brasil*, 2nd ed. (São Paulo: Editora 34, 2015), 370–71, chap. 23, and the book's conclusion; Leonardo Avritzer, *Impasses da democracia* (Rio de Janeiro: Civilização Brasileira, 2016), 20.

43. Ryan Holmes, "The Future of Social Media? Forget About the U.S., Look to Brazil," *Forbes*, September 12, 2013.

44. Author's interview with Carlos Eugênio Sarmento Coêlho da Paz, Rio de Janeiro, June 28, 2001.

45. Kenneth P. Serbin, "Mainstreaming the Revolutionaries," in *Conflict Transformation and Peacebuilding: Moving from Violence to Sustainable Peace*, ed. Bruce W. Dayton and Louis Kriesberg, 204–19 (London: Routledge, 2009).

46. Quoted in author's interview with Colombo Vieira de Souza, Niterói, June 17, 2004.

47. Anthony W. Pereira, "Is the Brazilian State 'Patrimonial'?," *Latin American Perspectives* 43, no. 2 (2016): 135–52.

48. Marcus André Melo, "Political Malaise and the New Politics of Accountability: Representation, Taxation, and the Social Contract," in B. Schneider, *New Order and Progress*, 268–97.

49. Barbara Nunberg and Regina Silvia Pacheco, "Public Management Incongruity in 21st Century Brazil," in B. Schneider, *New Order and Progress*, 136–38.

50. On diverse political choices, see Takao Amano, *Assalto ao céu* (São Paulo: COM-ARTE, 2014), 115.

51. Author's interview with Manoel Cyrillo de Oliveira Netto, Gonçalves, Minas Gerais, July 14, 2015.

52. Cardoso, "Revolução e resistência."

53. Serbin, "Mainstreaming the Revolutionaries," 217.

54. Cardoso, "Revolução e resistência."

55. Serbin, "Mainstreaming the Revolutionaries," 217.

56. Author's interview with Jessie Jane Vieira de Souza, Niterói, June 17, 2004.

57. Author's interview with Manoel Cyrillo de Oliveira Netto, Gonçalves, Minas Gerais, July 14, 2015.

58. Author's interview with Paulo de Tarso Vannuchi, São Paulo, July 13, 2015.

59. Ellis Krauss posits that people often do not necessarily act according to their political beliefs; see Ellis S. Krauss, *Japanese Radicals Revisited* (Berkeley: University of California Press, 1974), 167–68; for a different but somewhat complementary view and a detailed study of political identity in Chile, see Katherine Hite, *When the Romance Ended* (New York: Columbia University Press, 2000).

60. Serbin, *Secret Dialogues*, 11–12.

61. Author's interview with Adriano Diogo, São Paulo, June 9, 2005.

62. Ben Ross Schneider, introduction to *New Order and Progress*, 12, 15.

CHAPTER ONE   The Surprise of the Century

1. Police report: Secretaria de Estado dos Negócios da Segurança Pública, Polícia Civil de São Paulo, Divisão de Informações, "Manoel Ciryllo [*sic*] de Oliveira Netto," Departamento Estadual de Ordem Política e Social, Arquivo do Estado de São Paulo (hereafter AESP, DEOPS-SP), document 52-Z-029362. Accuracy of police report confirmed in author's interview with Manoel Cyrillo de Oliveira Netto, Rio de Janeiro, June 20, 2006. Additional information from author's interview with Manoel, Rio de Janeiro, May 9, 2008.

2. Author's interview with Manoel Cyrillo de Oliveira Netto, Rio de Janeiro, June 20, 2006; author's interview with Takao Amano, São Paulo, June 2, 2006.

3. Author's interview with Manoel Cyrillo de Oliveira Netto, Rio de Janeiro, June 20, 2006.

4. Interview with Manoel Cyrillo de Oliveira Netto, Rio de Janeiro, June 19, 2006. For a detailed narrative of the Elbrick kidnapping, see Alberto Berquó, *O seqüestro dia a dia* (Rio de Janeiro: Nova Fronteira, 1997); on the Mein assassination, see "Telegram from the Embassy in Guatemala to the Department of State" (1968), in *Foreign Relations of the United States, 1964–1968*, ed. Under Secretary for Public Diplomacy and Public Affairs, U.S. Department of State, Bureau of Public Affairs (Washington, DC: U.S. Department of State, 2004); *History of the Bureau of Diplomatic Security* (Washington, DC: United States Department of State, Bureau of Diplomatic Security, 2011), 202; on the kidnapping, see also A. J. Langguth, *Hidden Terrors* (New York: Pantheon, 1978). Elbrick's statement to the Brazilian authorities is available in "Aviso No. 041/SI-Gab," Carlos Alberto da Fontoura, head of the Brazilian Serviço Nacional de Informações (SNI, or National Information Service), to Mário Gibson Barboza, Brasília, February 13, 1970, including appendix "Informação No. 05/SNI/GAB/7C (Embaixador CHARLES BURKE ELBRICK)" and other documents, Arquivo Nacional/Coreg. Fundo SNI/CSNCGI, ACE 45000/72, pp. 22–35. I thank Carlos Fico for providing me with a copy of these documents.

5. Interview with Manoel Cyrillo de Oliveira Netto, Rio de Janeiro, June 19, 2006.

6. Fernando Gabeira, *O que é isso, companheiro?*, 2nd rev. ed. (São Paulo: Companhia das Letras, 1996), 122.

7. Berquó, *O seqüestro dia a dia*, 88–95.

8. "Nixon acompanha a evolução dos acontecimentos," *O Globo*, September 5, 1969.

9. Joseph Novitski, "Gunmen Kidnap U.S. Envoy in Brazil," *New York Times*, September 5, 1969; "Terror in Brazil," *New York Times*, September 6, 1969; "Text of Manifesto from Kidnappers of U.S. Ambassador to Brazil," *New York Times*, September 6, 1969; on international coverage, see also "Seqüestro foi manchete em todo o mundo," *O Globo*, September 8, 1969.

10. Telephone interview with Valerie Elbrick (Paris), San Diego, November 18, 2008. On the historic nature of the Elbrick kidnapping, see also Langguth, *Hidden Terrors*, 181.

11. *History of the Bureau of Diplomatic Security*, 203, 205–6.

12. Telephone interview with Valerie Elbrick (Paris), San Diego, November 18, 2008. For a list of career ambassadors, see https://history.state.gov /departmenthistory/people/principalofficers/career-ambassador. For background on Elbrick, see also "A Sturdy Ambassador: Charles Burke Elbrick," *New York Times*, September 7, 1969.

13. Magalhães, *Marighella*, 350, 51 (quotation).

14. See ibid. for an overview of Marighella's life and the ALN; see also Frei Betto, *Batismo de sangue*, 14th rev. ed. (Rio de Janeiro: Rocco, 2006); Cristiane Nova and Jorge Nóvoa, eds., *Marighella: O homem por trás do mito* (São Paulo: Editora UNESP, 1999); Emiliano José, *Carlos Marighella: O inimigo número um da ditadura militar* (São Paulo: Sol & Chuva, 1997); Denise Rollemberg, "Carlos Marighella e Carlos Lamarca: Memórias de dois revolucionários," in *Revolução e democracia (1964– . . .)*, ed. Jorge Ferreira and Daniel Aarão Reis, 73–97 (Rio de Janeiro: Civilização Brasileira, 2007); on Marighella as a mulatto, see also Jeffrey Lesser, *A Discontented Diaspora* (Durham, NC: Duke University Press, 2007), 85.

15. This point suggested by Magalhães, *Marighella*, 511–12.

16. On the number of fighters, see Elio Gaspari, *As ilusões armadas: A ditadura envergonada* (São Paulo: Companhia das Letras, 2002), 1:352n23; on collaborators and contacts, see Magalhães, *Marighella*, 361.

17. Marcelo Ridenti, "Esquerdas armadas urbanas, 1964–1974," in *História do marxismo no Brasil: Partidos e movimentos após os anos 1960*, ed. Marcelo Ridenti and Danial Aarão Reis (Campinas, São Paulo: Editora da Unicamp, 2007), 106–7, and notes 5 and 6.

18. Magalhães, *Marighella*, 392–97; Betto, *Batismo de sangue*.

19. On the origins of these phrases, see Ridenti, "Esquerdas armadas urbanas, 1964–1974," 110.

20. Magalhães, *Marighella*, 362–63.

21. Author's interviews with Carlos Eugênio Sarmento Coêlho da Paz, Rio de Janeiro, July 14, 2001, and July 21, 2001. Author's interview with Paulo de Tarso Vannuchi, São Paulo, July 3, 2003.

22. Magalhães, *Marighella*, 377.

23. On 1968 protests in a global context, including a study of the Mexican incident, see Elaine Carey, ed., *Protests in the Streets* (Indianapolis, IN: Hackett, 2016).

24. Amano, *Assalto ao céu*, 49.

25. Magalhães, *Marighella*, 412.

26. CIA, Directorate of Intelligence, "Intelligence Memorandum. Brazil: The Road to Dictatorship," December 23, 1968, declassified CIA document, *Opening the Archives Project*, http://library.brown.edu/openingthearchives/.

27. U.S. Embassy, Rio de Janeiro, to Secretary of State, Washington, DC, Telegram No.14337, December 15, 1968, declassified State Department document, *Opening the Archives Project*.

28. Green, *We Cannot Remain Silent*, 102.

29. Fico, *O grande irmão*.

30. On this point, see also Green, *Exile within Exiles*.

31. Magalhães, *Marighella*, 416 (Del Roio, Marighella), 422 (Marighella), 452–53, 488.

32. Ibid., 487.

33. Ibid., 487, 495–96.

34. Elbrick quotation from Joseph Novitski, "Brazil Preparing New Restrictions," *New York Times*, September 9, 1969.

35. Gabeira, *O que é isso, companheiro?*, 124.

36. Telephone interview with Valerie Elbrick (Paris), San Diego, November 18, 2008.

37. Green, *We Cannot Remain Silent*, 160 (quotation), 161, 164.

38. Author's interview with Manoel Cyrillo de Oliveira Netto, Rio de Janeiro, June 19, 2006. On Elbrick's positions, see also Helena Salem, "Ficção é julgada sob as lentes da história," in *Versões e ficções: O seqüestro da história*, ed. Daniel Aarão Reis Filho et al. (São Paulo: Editora Fundação Perseu Abramo, 1997), 89.

39. Author's telephone interview with Valerie Elbrick (Paris), San Diego, November 18, 2008.

40. First quotation from Langguth, *Hidden Terrors*, 184. Second quotation and data on Elbrick's opposition to the dictatorship from "Aviso No. 041/ SI-Gab," Carlos Alberto da Fontoura, Serviço Nacional de Informações, to Mário Gibson Barboza, Brasília, February 13, 1970, including appendix "Informação No. 05/SNI/GAB/7C (Embaixador CHARLES BURKE ELBRICK)"

and other documents, Arquivo Nacional/Coreg. Fundo SNI/CSNCGI, ACE 45000/72.

41. Interviews with Manoel Cyrillo de Oliveira Netto, Rio de Janeiro, June 19 and 20, 2006. "Aviso No. 041/SI-Gab," Carlos Alberto da Fontoura, Serviço Nacional de Informações, to Mário Gibson Barboza, Brasília, February 13, 1970, including appendix "Informação No. 05/SNI/GAB/7C (Embaixador CHARLES BURKE ELBRICK)" and other documents, Arquivo Nacional/Coreg. Fundo SNI/CSNCGI, ACE 45000/72. According to Elbrick's statement in this document, the U.S. government "was in favor of Dom Hélder Câmara, because he . . . was a socialist and had the means necessary to bring together the diverse sectors of the Brazilian populace, especially those who were inclined to join the armed struggled." Details of the Rádio Nacional incident in Magalhães, *Marighella*, 454–59.

42. "Itamarati: Seqüestro é ato terrorista contra o Brasil," *O Globo*, September 5, 1969, 8.

43. Valerie Elbrick Hanlon, "'They've Got Your Father,'" *Washingtonian Magazine*, April 1998, 70 (quotations). Telephone interview with Valerie Elbrick (Paris), San Diego, November 18, 2008; telephone interview with Eliane Gurgel Valente (Paris), San Diego, December 2, 2008. *New York Times* coverage cited only ambassadorial personnel in Rio but nothing about the reaction of President Nixon or his cabinet. Nixon's spokesperson's brief statement of concern, and later his thanks to the Brazilian government, received coverage in the Brazilian press.

44. There are no writings on popular perceptions of the Elbrick kidnapping or, for that matter, of the guerrillas in general. A very brief reference to people's conversations about the incident is in Paulo Moreira Leite, "O que foi aquilo, companheiro," in *Versões e ficções*, 52; see also Langguth, *Hidden Terrors*, 185.

45. Details on the outcome of the kidnapping from Berquó, *O seqüestro dia a dia*; Gaspari, *As ilusões armadas*, 2:87–104; Gorender, *Combate*, chap. 23.

46. Quoted in Leslie Bethell and Celso Castro, "Politics in Brazil under Military Rule, 1964–1985," in *Brazil since 1930*, ed. Leslie Bethell, Cambridge History of Latin America (Cambridge: Cambridge University Press, 2008), 9:188. On the influence of the *Minimanual*, see Ariel Merari, "Terrorism as a Strategy," in *The History of Terrorism: From Antiquity to Al Qaeda*, ed. Gérard Chalian and Arnaud Blin (Berkeley: University of California Press, 2007), 35.

47. Magalhães, *Marighella*, 485, 501–6.

48. U.S. Department of State, "Memorandum of Conversation. Subject: Discussion of Brazilian Urban Terror Manual with Soviet Embassy Officer," May 11, 1970, declassified State Department document, *Opening the Archives Project*.

49. Magalhães, *Marighella*, 506.

50. Gorender, *Combate*, 106.

51. William Tosta, "'Em 3 décadas, 1 milhão de homicídios,'" *O Estado de S. Paulo*, January 20, 2008.

52. Https://ucr.fbi.gov/crime-in-the-u.s.

53. Author's nterview with Manoel Cyrillo de Oliveira Netto, Rio de Janeiro, May 9, 2008.

54. For an overview of this question, see Ridenti, "Esquerdas armadas urbanas, 1964–1974," 133–34n32.

55. Author's interview with Manoel Cyrillo de Oliveira Netto, Rio de Janeiro, June 21, 2006.

56. Magalhães, *Marighella*, 274, 332, 350–51.

57. Interview with Manoel Cyrillo de Oliveira Netto, Rio de Janeiro, June 21, 2006.

58. Edson Teixeira da Silva Jr., "Um combate ao silêncio" (Ph.D. diss., Universidade Federal Fluminense, 2005), chap. 4.

59. Gaspari, *As ilusões armadas*, 2:90.

60. Silvio Da-Rin, ed., *Hércules 56* (Rio de Janeiro: Jorge Zahar Editor, 2007), 291.

61. Author's interview with Manoel Cyrillo de Oliveira Netto, Rio de Janeiro, June 19, 2006.

62. Ibid.

63. Ibid.

64. Gaspari, *As ilusões armadas*, 1:326.

65. Gorender, *Combate*, 144.

66. Gaspari, *As ilusões armadas*, 1:326–27, including n54; ibid., 2:304; Magalhães, *Marighella*, 381–83. Historian James Green found no declassified documentation on Chandler in his study of U.S. State Department files on the Brazilian dictatorship (personal communication to author from James Green, October 6, 2008). I found nothing to substantiate the revolutionary Left's suspicions about Chandler in the several documents that I accessed in reference to the incident in declassified U.S. government documents in the *Opening the Archives Project*.

67. Interview with Manoel Cyrillo de Oliveira Netto, Rio de Janeiro, July 26, 2007.

68. Author's interview with Manoel Cyrillo de Oliveira Netto, Rio de Janeiro, May 9, 2008. On U.S. involvement in repression in Latin America, see, for example, Martha K. Huggins, *Political Policing* (Durham, NC: Duke University Press, 1998); John Dinges, *The Condor Years* (New York: The New Press, 2005).

69. Author's interview with Manoel Cyrillo de Oliveira Netto, Rio de Janeiro, July 26, 2007.

70. Author's interviews with Manoel Cyrillo de Oliveira Netto, Rio de Janeiro, July 26, 2007, and May 9, 2008 (slanderous, nobody was a terrorist).

71. Laqueur, *The Age of Terrorism*, 181.

72. Gaspari, *As ilusões armadas*, 1:285–307; Gorender, *Combate*, 164–65. José A. Argolo, Kátia Ribeiro, and Luiz Alberto M. Fortunato, *A direita explosiva* (Rio de Janeiro: Mauad, 1996). On the Burnier incident, see also Hélio Silva, *A vez e a voz dos vencidos* (Petrópolis: Vozes, 1988).

73. Salem, "Ficção é julgada sob as lentes da história," 75–76. The estimate of several hundred political prisoners is based on figures of arrests and number of individuals tortured in Gaspari, *As ilusões armadas*, 2:159–60. Langguth stated that even before Elbrick was let go the kidnappers wondered about demanding more prisoner releases (*Hidden Terrors*, 187).

74. On Brazil and the domino theory, see Green, *We Cannot Remain Silent*, chap. 1.

75. Author's interviews with Manoel Cyrillo de Oliveira Netto, Rio de Janeiro, June 19, 2006, and July 26, 2007.

CHAPTER TWO   The Wrath of the Dictators

1. On the kidnapping as a failed tactic, see Gaspari, *As ilusões armadas*, 2:98.

2. On the context of the increased repression after the kidnapping, see Silva Jr., "Um combate ao silêncio," chap. 4.

3. Maria Helena Moreira Alves, *Estado e oposição*, trans. Clóvis Marques (Petrópolis, Rio de Janeiro: Vozes, 1984), 157.

4. Berquó, *O seqüestro dia a dia*, 128–29.

5. Gorender, *Combate*, 184.

6. Gaspari, *As ilusões armadas*, 2:90–91.

7. Author's interview with Manoel Cyrillo de Oliveira Netto, Rio de Janeiro, June 19, 2006.

8. Gorender, *Combate*, 185–86.

9. Author's interview with Manoel Cyrillo de Oliveira Netto, Rio de Janeiro, June 19, 2006.

10. Gorender, *Combate*, 186.

11. Magalhães, *Marighella*, 497–98.

12. Author's interview with Manoel Cyrillo de Oliveira Netto, Rio de Janeiro, June 20, 2006. Information on this operation also in Gorender, *Combate*, 190; Gaspari, *As ilusões armadas*, 2:102.

13. Interview with Manoel Cyrillo de Oliveira Netto, Rio de Janeiro, June 20, 2006. Number of police officers from "Frente a frente a polícia e o terror: O que vai acontecer?" *Jornal da Tarde*, September 25, 1969, 34.

14. Secretaria Especial dos Direitos Humanos, *Direito à memória e à verdade*, 104.

15. This and the next two paragraphs are based on author's interview with Manoel Cyrillo de Oliveira Netto, Rio de Janeiro, June 20, 2006. Maria Helena de Souza identified in "Maria Helena está contando sua aventura com o terror," *Jornal da Tarde*, September 26, 1969; on the gun battles, see also "Autoridades prendem mais 8 terroristas," *Folha de S. Paulo*, September 26, 1969, 8; "Frente a frente a polícia e o terror: O que vai acontecer?," *Jornal da Tarde*, September 25, 1969; "Dops prende 6 em tiroteio," *O Estado de S. Paulo*, September 25, 1969, 21; "O sequestro já foi esclarecido," *O Estado de S. Paulo*, September 26, 1969, 12; "Artista de TV raptada por terroristas em SP," *Notícias Populares*, September 26, 1969, 10.

16. Author's interview with Manoel Cyrillo de Oliveira Netto, Rio de Janeiro, May 9, 2008.

17. Secretaria Especial dos Direitos Humanos, *Direito à memória e à verdade*, 104.

18. Author's interview with Manoel Cyrillo de Oliveira Netto, Rio de Janeiro, May 9, 2008.

19. Author's interview with Manoel Cyrillo de Oliveira Netto, Rio de Janeiro, June 20, 2006.

20. Gaspari, *As ilusões armadas*, 2:103. See also Gorender, *Combate*, 180.

21. DOI-CODI stood for Destacamento de Operações de Informações do Centro de Operações de Defesa Interna (Intelligence Operations Detachment of the Center for Internal Defense Operations).

22. Gaspari, *As ilusões armadas*, 2, 103–4. See also Elio Gaspari, "*O que é isso, companheiro?*: O operário se deu mal," in Reis Filho and Ridenti, *Versões e ficções*, 114–15.

23. Author's interview with Manoel Cyrillo de Oliveira Netto, Rio de Janeiro, June 20, 2006.

24. On Jonas's demise, see Gaspari, *As ilusões armadas*, 2:103–4. See also Gaspari, "*O que é isso, companheiro?*," 114–15. Details of torture from Franklin Martins, "As duas mortes de Jonas," in *Versões e ficções: O seqüestro da história*, ed. Daniel Aarão Reis Filho et al. (São Paulo: Editora Fundação Perseu Abramo, 1997), 118; details on death also in Edileuza Pimenta and Edson Teixeira, *Virgílio Gomes da Silva* (São Paulo: Plena Editorial, 2009), chap. 5; Magalhães, *Marighella*, 521–23.

25. Secretaria Especial dos Direitos Humanos, *Direito à memória e à verdade*, 104–5. See also Murilo Fiuza de Melo, "Primeiro desaparecido foi morto

sob tortura," *Folha de S. Paulo*, June 25, 2004. Manoel Cyrillo de Oliveira Netto provided me with a copy of the coroner's report and the photograph.

26. Pimenta and Teixeira, *Virgílio Gomes da Silva*, 105–6.

27. This and the next three paragraphs from author's interview with Manoel Cyrillo de Oliveira Netto, Rio de Janeiro, June 20, 2006.

28. "Resumo das declarações prestadas por Manoel Cyrillo de Oliveira à equipe de interrogação preliminar A-2 das 0900 às 1400 horas do dia 07 de outubro de 1969," AESP, DEOPS-SP, documents 50-Z-9-10050, 50-Z-9-10050-A, 50-Z-9-10051, and 50-Z-9-10052.

29. On Marighella's thinking on torture, see Magalhães, *Marighella*, 96, 536–37, 552. Both harsh criticism of and compassion for those who "broke" under torture were frequent themes in the interviews conducted for this book, as well as in the numerous memoirs by ex-revolutionaries. On machismo and torture, see, for example, James N. Green, "'Who Is the Macho Who Wants to Kill Me?,'" *Hispanic American Historical Review* 92, no. 3 (2012): 437–69.

30. Author's interview with Manoel Cyrillo de Oliveira Netto, Rio de Janeiro, June 20, 2006.

31. Magalhães, *Marighella*, 526.

CHAPTER THREE   Decapitating the Revolutionary Leadership

1. Silva Jr., "Um combate ao silêncio," chap. 4.

2. On the relationship between the ALN and the Dominicans, see Betto, *Batismo de sangue*.

3. The precise circumstances of Marighella's death have been the subject of great controversy in Brazil. The most recent and thorough investigation is by Marighella's biographer; see Magalhães, *Marighella*, chaps. 41–43; see also Gorender, *Combate*, chap. 25; Betto, *Batismo de sangue*; Silva Jr., "Um combate ao silêncio," chap. 4; Gaspari, *As ilusões armadas*, 2:141–57; Percival de Souza, *Autópsia do medo* (São Paulo: Editora Globo, 2000), 213–35.

4. Paris from author's interview with Itoby Alves Corrêa Junior, São Paulo, August 3, 2001.

5. On the origins of the program, see The Association for Diplomatic Studies and Training Foreign Affairs Oral History Project, "Ambassador A. Lincoln Gordon," interviewed by Charles Stuart Kennedy, September 30, 1987, p. 37, http://www.adst.org/OH TOCs/Gordon, Lincoln.1987.toc.pdf. On funding, see Timothy Naftali, ed., *John F. Kennedy: The Great Crises*, The Presidential Recordings (New York: W. W. Norton, 2001), 1:13. Photos of the Kennedy meeting with students available at John F. Kennedy Presidential Library

and Museum, Digital Identifier JFKWHP-1962-07-31-B; search for them at http://www.jfklibrary.org.

6. Antonio Pedroso Júnior, *Márcio, o guerrilheiro* (Rio de Janeiro: Papel Virtual, 2003), 29.

7. Author's interview with Aloysio Nunes Ferreira Filho, Brasília, July 6, 2015.

8. Ibid.

9. Author's interview with Aloysio Nunes Ferreira Filho, São Paulo, July 20, 2003. Perception of Aloysio's importance and role of pregnancy also confirmed in author's interview with Vera Maria Tude de Souza, São Paulo, June 17, 2003. Information on Aloysio's ALN activities also from Magalhães, *Marighella*, 377, 384–91.

10. Author's interviews with Manoel Cyrillo de Oliveira Netto, Rio de Janeiro, June 21, 2006, and July 26, 2007.

11. Betto, *Batismo de sangue*; Gorender, *Combate*, chap. 25.

12. Author's interviews with Manoel Cyrillo de Oliveira Netto, Rio de Janeiro, June 21, 2006, and July 26, 2007.

13. Gorender, *Combate*, 210, 217.

14. Luiz Maklouf Carvalho, *Mulheres que foram à luta armada* (São Paulo: Editora Globo, 1998), 320, 322, 324, 326–27, 328 (quotation); Gorender, *Combate*, 217. Background on Jessie's family's Communist background from author's interview with Jessie Jane Vieira de Souza, Rio de Janeiro, August 3, 2002.

15. Carvalho, *Mulheres que foram à luta armada*, 326, 328 (quotation).

16. Ibid., 325–26, 329–30.

17. Secretaria Especial dos Direitos Humanos, *Direito à memória e à verdade*, 131; see also the documentary by Lúcia Murat, *Que Bom Te Ver Viva* (1989).

18. Carvalho, *Mulheres que foram à luta armada*, 334.

19. Murat, *Que Bom Te Ver Viva*.

20. Quoted in Carvalho, *Mulheres que foram à luta armada*, 332.

21. Gorender, *Combate*, 217–18.

22. Details on this incident from author's interviews with Manoel Cyrillo de Oliveira Netto, Rio de Janeiro, June 19, 2006, and May 9, 2008. Manoel kept a copy of the statement and sent a typed copy to me in an e-mail communication on June 16, 2008.

23. Carvalho, *Mulheres que foram à luta armada*, 334. Information on solitary confinement also from author's interview with Jessie Jane Vieira de Souza, Rio de Janeiro, August 3, 2002.

24. Gorender, *Combate*, 218. See also Renato Martinelli, *Um grito de coragem* (São Paulo: COM-ARTE, 2006); details on Toledo's death also in Secretaria Especial dos Direitos Humanos, *Direito à memória e à verdade*, 134–36.

25. Gorender, *Combate*, 220–21. On the release of Silva, see Carvalho, *Mulheres que foram à luta armada*, 335.

26. Interview with Manoel Cyrillo de Oliveira Netto, Rio de Janeiro, June 20, 2006.

27. Berquó, *O seqüestro dia a dia*, 133–35.

CHAPTER FOUR   The Guerrilla's Lamentation

1. Ridenti, "Esquerdas armadas urbanas, 1964–1974," 109.

2. On dependence on violence, see Gaspari, *As ilusões armadas*, 1:352–54; Gorender, *Combate*, 168–69, 172–73, 207–14. For an example of the demand for a balance between violence and politics, see José Luiz Del Roio, *Zarattini* (São Paulo: Ícone Editora, 2006), chaps. 10–11.

3. Magalhães, *Marighella*, 362.

4. Author's interviews with Paulo de Tarso Vannuchi, São Paulo, July 23, 2001, and July 26, 2001 (quotation).

5. Magalhães, *Marighella*, 448.

6. Author's interviews with Manoel Cyrillo de Oliveira Netto, Rio de Janeiro, June 20, 2006, and July 26, 2007 (whoever carries a gun).

7. Martha Crenshaw, "How Terrorism Declines," *Terrorism and Political Violence* 3, no. 1 (1991): 83.

8. Maria Cláudia Badan Ribeiro, "Memória, história e sociedade" (Master's thesis, Universidade Estadual de Campinas, 2005), 129–30.

9. Denise Rollemberg, "Clemente," in *Perfis cruzados: Trajetórias e militância política no Brasil*, ed. Beatriz Kushnir (Rio de Janeiro: Imago, 2002), 82–83.

10. Pedroso Júnior, *Márcio, o guerrilheiro*, 159.

11. Ribeiro, "Memória, história e sociedade," 5.

12. Magalhães, *Marighella*, 467.

13. Ribeiro, "Memória, história e sociedade," 16.

14. Author's interview with Marival Chaves, Vila Velha, Espírito Santo, January 20, 1999. On Chaves's initial revelations, see Expedito Filho, "Autópsia da sombra," *Veja*, November 18, 1992, 20–32.

15. Carlos Eugênio Sarmento Coêlho da Paz, *Viagem à luta armada: Memórias romanceadas* (Rio de Janeiro: Civilização Brasileira, 1996).

16. Ribeiro, "Memória, história e sociedade," 252.

17. Carlos Eugênio's excellent memory also noted in Gorender, *Combate*, 279.

18. Author's interview with Carlos Eugênio Sarmento Coêlho da Paz, Rio de Janeiro, July 14, 2001.

19. Author's interview with Carlos Eugênio Sarmento Coêlho da Paz, Rio de Janeiro, August 27, 2007.

20. Author's interview with Marival Chaves, Vila Velha, Espírito Santo, January 20, 1999.

21. Rollemberg, "Clemente," 74.

22. Author's interview with Carlos Eugênio Sarmento Coêlho da Paz, Rio de Janeiro, July 14, 2001.

23. Rollemberg, "Clemente," 75.

24. Carlos Eugênio Sarmento Coêlho da Paz, *Nas trilhas da ALN* (Rio de Janeiro: Bertrand Brasil, 1997), 132.

25. Rollemberg, "Clemente," 77.

26. Ribeiro, "Memória, história e sociedade," 102–3, 119–25.

27. Ibid., 129–30, 133.

28. Author's interview with Carlos Eugênio Sarmento Coêlho da Paz, Rio de Janeiro, July 14, 2001.

29. Ribeiro, "Memória, história e sociedade," 119.

30. Paz, *Nas trilhas*, 150.

31. Paz, *Viagem*, 50.

32. Ibid., 104.

33. Ibid., 112–13.

34. Ibid., 105.

35. Author's interview with Carlos Eugênio Sarmento Coêlho da Paz, Rio de Janeiro, July 21, 2001.

36. Paz, *Viagem*, 125–26 (quotation).

37. Ribeiro, "Memória, história e sociedade," 103, 14 (quotations). I thank James Green for the observation about masculinity.

38. Paz, *Viagem*, 135 (you're crazy), 57 (those who opposed), 132 (honor), 176 (excesses), 20 (revolutionary).

39. Paz, *Nas trilhas*, 35.

40. Paz, *Viagem*, 171 (quotation), 180.

41. Paz, *Nas trilhas*, 62.

42. Paz, *Viagem*, 205.

43. Pedroso Júnior, *Márcio, o guerrilheiro*, 29.

44. Martinelli, *Um grito de coragem*.

45. Author's interview with Ricardo Apgaua, Belo Horizonte, July 5, 2001; Pedroso Júnior, *Márcio, o guerrilheiro*, 73–79.

46. Martinelli, *Um grito de coragem.*

47. Pedroso Júnior, *Márcio, o guerrilheiro*, 111–13, 121–30.

48. Ribeiro, "Memória, história e sociedade," 207.

49. Luiz Henrique de Castro Silva, "O revolucionário da convicção" (Master's thesis, Universidade Federal do Rio de Janeiro, 2008), 340–61. Martinelli, *Um grito de coragem*, 86–94. On execution, see Paz, *Viagem*, 181.

50. Ribeiro, "Memória, história e sociedade," 9.

51. Martinelli, *Um grito de coragem*, 22. Information on the number of days disappeared from author's interview with Carlos Eugênio Sarmento Coêlho da Paz, Rio de Janeiro, July 21, 2001.

52. Paz, *Viagem*, 204.

53. Ribeiro, "Memória, história e sociedade," 177, 212–13.

54. Pedroso Júnior, *Márcio, o guerrilheiro*, 105.

55. Martinelli, *Um grito de coragem*, 22.

56. Expedito Filho, "Memória do terror," *Veja*, July 31, 1996, 7–8.

57. Paz, *Viagem*, 204–5.

58. Martinelli, *Um grito de coragem*, 134–35.

59. Ibid., 26, 128 (quotation). For defense of the face, see Luís Mir, *A revolução impossível* (São Paulo: Editora Best Seller, 1994), 587.

60. Gorender, *Combate*, 278–82.

61. Author's interview with Ricardo Apgaua, Belo Horizonte, July 5, 2001.

62. Gorender, *Combate*, 279–80; see also Carvalho, *Mulheres que foram à luta armada*, 248–49.

63. Pedroso Júnior, *Márcio, o guerrilheiro*, 196, 204–7.

64. Ibid., 167–68, 178–79; see also Carvalho, *Mulheres que foram à luta armada*, 248–49. A similar sentiment expressed in author's interview with Ricardo Apgaua, Belo Horizonte, July 5, 2001.

65. Ribeiro, "Memória, história e sociedade," 7–8, 206, 207 (quotation).

66. Pedroso Júnior, *Márcio, o guerrilheiro*, 196, 201–2; see also Mir, *A revolução impossível*, 587.

67. Martinelli, *Um grito de coragem*, 23; see also Del Roio, *Zarattini*, 154. A similar sentiment expressed in author's interview with Ricardo Apgaua, Belo Horizonte, July 5, 2001.

68. Author's interview with Carlos Eugênio Sarmento Coêlho da Paz, Rio de Janeiro, July 21, 2001.

69. Expedito Filho, "Memória do terror," 8.

70. Ribeiro, "Memória, história e sociedade," 213.

71. Author's interview with Carlos Eugênio Sarmento Coêlho da Paz, Rio de Janeiro, July 14, 2001.

72. Paz, *Nas trilhas*, 89–98.

73. Author's interview with Carlos Eugênio Sarmento Coêlho da Paz, Rio de Janeiro, July 14, 2001.

74. Ibid.

75. Paz, *Viagem*, 203.

76. Ibid., 205.

77. Ibid., 205–6.

78. Ibid., 203, 222.

79. Ibid., 211–12, 213 (quotation). Terrorismo Nunca Mais, http://www .ternuma.com.br/index.php/noticias/2106-a-historia-do-terrorismo-no-brasil. See also the film by Chaim Litkewski, *Cidadão Boilesen* (Brazil, 2009). The Tiradentes Revolutionary Movement was unrelated to the Tiradentes prison.

80. Paz, *Viagem*, 33 (super-guerrilla), 199 (first wife), 80 (learned).

81. Secretaria Especial dos Direitos Humanos, *Direito à memória e à verdade*, 300–303.

82. Paz, *Viagem*, 79.

83. Ibid., 173.

84. Paz, *Nas trilhas*, 30.

85. Paz, *Viagem*.

86. Ribeiro, "Memória, história e sociedade," 190–91.

87. Paz, *Viagem*.

CHAPTER FIVE   The Resistance Becomes Nonviolent

1. Paz, *Nas trilhas*, 36–37, 101; Secretaria Especial dos Direitos Humanos, *Direito à memória e à verdade*, 300; see also Gorender, *Combate*, 272.

2. Gorender, *Combate*, 272; for the organizations involved, see Gaspari, *As ilusões armadas*, 2:397n85.

3. Secretaria Especial dos Direitos Humanos, *Direito à memória e à verdade*, 335–37.

4. Kenneth P. Serbin, *Diálogos na sombra*, trans. Carlos Eduardo Lins da Silva and Maria Cecília de Sá Porto (São Paulo: Companhia das Letras, 2001), 385–88.

5. Aldo Vannucchi, *Alexandre Vannucchi Leme* (São Paulo: Contexto, 2014), 16.

6. Ibid., 22.

7. Marcelo de Paiva Abreu, "The Brazilian Economy, 1930–1980," in *Brazil since 1930*, Vol. 9 of *The Cambridge History of Latin America*, Vol. 9, ed. Leslie Bethell (Cambridge: Cambridge University Press, 2008), 378, 380.

8. Robert Walker, Stephen Perz, Eugenio Arima, and Cynthia Simmons, "Engineering Earth," in *Engineering Earth: The Impacts of Megaengineering Projects*, ed. Stanley D. Brunn (Dordrecht: Springer, 2011), 576–81.

9. Costa, *Cale-se*, 44, 170–72; on Boal's ALN link, see Magalhães, *Marighella*, 366–67, 509. Late 1970 date of News Theater from author's interview with Alberto Alonso Lázaro, São Paulo, July 24, 2001.

10. Author's interview with Adriano Diogo, São Paulo, July 2, 2003. On Kahn, see Greg Grandin, *Fordlandia* (New York: Metropolitan Books, 2009), 117.

11. Serbin, *Diálogos na sombra*, 384–86. Confirmation of Alexandre's status as ALN political coordinator in author's interviews with USP geology graduates Enzo Luís Nico Júnior, São Paulo (July 29, 1999), Antônio Carlos Bertachini and Fernando Antonio Rodrigues de Oliveira, Belo Horizonte (July 5, 2001), and Luiz Antonio Bongiovanni, São Paulo (July 22, 2001). Confirmation as recruiter in author's interview with Geraldo Augusto de Siqueira Filho, São Paulo, March 15, 1998.

12. Vannucchi, *Alexandre Vannucchi Leme*, 35–36.

13. Author's interview with Carlos Eugênio Sarmento Coêlho da Paz, Rio de Janeiro, January 30, 1997.

14. Author's interview with Adriano Diogo, São Paulo, May 19, 1997. On Centros Acadêmicos and Central Student Directorates, see Victoria Langland, *Speaking of Flowers* (Durham, NC: Duke University Press, 2013), 93–94. Information on Centros Acadêmicos at the USP from author's interviews with Luiz Antônio Alves de Souza, São Paulo (March 17, 1998) and Aloysio Nunes Ferreira Filho, São Paulo (July 20, 2003).

15. Vannucchi, *Alexandre Vannucchi Leme*, 23.

16. Costa, *Cale-se*, 23.

17. Author's interview with Fernando Antonio Rodrigues de Oliveira, Belo Horizonte, July 5, 2001.

18. Serbin, *Diálogos na sombra*, 389.

19. Author's interview with Paulo de Tarso Vannuchi, São Paulo, July 23, 2001.

20. Ibid.

21. Ibid. Background on strike also from author's interview with Manoel Cyrillo de Oliveira Netto, Rio de Janeiro, June 21, 2006. For an overview of the strike, see Maurice Politi, *Resistência atrás das grades* (São Paulo: Plena Editorial, 2009).

22. Author's interview with Paulo de Tarso Vannuchi, São Paulo, July 23, 2001. Confirmation of Ustra as a practitioner of torture from author's interview with Marival Chaves, Vila Velha, Espírito Santo, January 20, 1999. On

Ustra's refusal of an interview for this author's research, see Serbin, *Diálogos na sombra*, 388.

23. Author's interview with Manoel Cyrillo de Oliveira Netto, Rio de Janeiro, June 21, 2006.

24. Author's interview with Paulo de Tarso Vannuchi, São Paulo, July 23, 2001.

25. Vannucchi, *Alexandre Vannucchi Leme*, 19.

26. Author's interview with Concepción Martín Pérez, São Paulo, March 15, 1998.

27. Number of women from author's interview with Arlete Diogo, São Paulo, June 16, 2003. Screams from author's interview with Neide Richopo, São Paulo, January 14, 1999.

28. Costa, *Cale-se*, 24.

29. Description of cell from ibid., 45–46.

30. Author's interview with Adriano Diogo, São Paulo, May 19, 1997.

31. Author's interview with Neide Richopo, São Paulo, January 14, 1999.

32. Serbin, *Diálogos na sombra*, 389.

33. Ibid., 388; for the time of day, see Secretaria Especial dos Direitos Humanos, *Direito à memória e à verdade*, 338.

34. Author's interview with Marival Chaves, Vila Velha, Espírito Santo, January 20, 1999.

35. Author's interviews with Paulo de Tarso Vannuchi, São Paulo, September 11, 1996 (like a brother), and July 23, 2001 (quotation).

36. Author's interview with José Oliveira Leme, Sorocaba, São Paulo, March 16, 1998.

37. Serbin, *Diálogos na sombra*, 390.

38. Author's interview with Neide Richopo, São Paulo, January 14, 1999.

39. Author's interview with José Oliveira Leme, Sorocaba, São Paulo, March 16, 1998. See also Costa, *Cale-se*, 60–61.

40. Author's interview with Adriano Diogo, São Paulo, May 19, 1997.

41. Costa, *Cale-se*, 44–48.

42. Author's interview with Adriano Diogo, São Paulo, May 19, 1997.

43. Costa, *Cale-se*, 47.

44. Author's interview with Adriano Diogo, São Paulo, May 19, 1997.

45. Costa, *Cale-se*, 48.

46. Author's interview with Arlete Diogo, São Paulo, June 16, 2003.

47. Author's interview with Adriano Diogo, São Paulo, May 19, 1997.

48. Author's interview with Arlete Diogo, São Paulo, June 16, 2003.

49. Author's interview with Arlete Diogo, São Paulo, June 14, 2006.

50. Author's interview with João Carlos Moreira Gomes, Belo Horizonte, July 5, 2001.

51. Author's interview with Geraldo Augusto de Siqueira Filho, São Paulo, March 15, 1998.

52. Serbin, *Diálogos na sombra*, 395. Primary participation of students noted in author's interview with Ruy de Goes Leite de Barros, São Paulo, July 18, 2001.

53. Author's interview with João Carlos Moreira Gomes, Belo Horizonte, July 5, 2001. João Carlos read from Letter to the Hebrews 11:1, 33–40, and 12:1.

54. Costa, *Cale-se*, 98–102; for an overview of the significance of 1968 and student protests, see Langland, *Speaking of Flowers*.

55. Serbin, *Diálogos na sombra*, 395.

56. Costa, *Cale-se*, 102–4.

57. Serbin, *Diálogos na sombra*, 397.

58. Author's interview with Arlete Diogo, São Paulo, June 16, 2003.

59. Serbin, *Diálogos na sombra*, 398–99; Costa, *Cale-se*, 103–4.

60. Costa, *Cale-se*, 76–77.

61. Author's interview with Arlete Diogo, São Paulo, May 19, 1997.

62. Author's interview with Adriano Diogo, São Paulo, May 19, 1997.

63. Ibid. Herzog was tortured to death at the São Paulo DOI-CODI in 1975. With echoes of the Mass for Alexandre, a memorial service for Herzog at the São Paulo cathedral attracted thousands of people. Labor leader Santo Dias was shot to death by police in São Paulo in 1979. Internationally recognized environmentalist Chico Mendes was murdered in the Amazon in 1988.

64. Langland, *Speaking of Flowers*, 210.

65. Author's interview with Adriano Diogo, São Paulo, May 19, 1997.

66. Serbin, *Diálogos na sombra*, 398 (quotation), 399–403.

67. Author's interview with Antônio Carlos Bertachini, Belo Horizonte, July 5, 2001.

68. Author's interview with Luiz Antonio Bongiovanni, São Paulo, July 22, 2001. Significance of assemblies also indicated in author's interview with Agamenon Dantas, São Paulo, January 15, 1999. See also Costa, *Cale-se*, 88–89.

69. Author's interview with Fernando Antonio Rodrigues de Oliveira, Belo Horizonte, July 5, 2001.

70. Author's interview with Luiz Antonio Bongiovanni, São Paulo, July 22, 2001.

71. Ibid. Queiroz's phrase and lack of enthusiasm also recalled in author's interview with Ruy de Goes Leite de Barros, São Paulo, July 18, 2001.

72. Ridenti, "Esquerdas armadas urbanas, 1964–1974," 107, and nn5 and 6; Gaspari, *As ilusões armadas*, 1:352, and n23.

73. Costa, *Cale-se*, chaps. 6–12; on Queiroz's death, see also Secretaria Especial dos Direitos Humanos, *Direito à memória e à verdade*, 340–41.

74. Author's interview with Arlete Diogo, São Paulo, June 16, 2003.

75. Ibid.

76. Author's interview with Adriano Diogo, São Paulo, May 19, 1997.

77. Costa, *Cale-se*, 275.

78. Author's interview with Adriano Diogo, São Paulo, May 19, 1997.

79. Secretaria Especial dos Direitos Humanos, *Direito à memória e à verdade*, 355–56.

80. Gaspari, *As ilusões armadas*, 2:399–464.

81. Secretaria Especial dos Direitos Humanos, *Direito à memória e à verdade*, 363–66.

82. Ibid., 382–83; see also Carvalho, *Mulheres que foram à luta armada*, 431–38.

83. Ribeiro, "Memória, história e sociedade," 234–36, 255.

84. Information on armed actions from e-mail from Cloves de Castro to author's research assistant, October 16, 2008. Demobilization of the ALN also noted in author's interview with Amparo Araújo, Recife, July 16, 2003.

85. Author's interview with Alberto Alonso Lázaro, São Paulo, July 24, 2001.

86. Author's interviews with Antônio Carlos Bertachini, João Carlos Moreira Gomes, and Fernando Antonio Rodrigues de Oliveira, Belo Horizonte, July 5, 2001.

87. Gaspari, *As ilusões armadas*, 2:407.

88. Secretaria Especial dos Direitos Humanos, *Direito à memória e à verdade*.

89. Elio Gaspari, *O sacerdote e o feiticeiro: A ditadura derrotada* (São Paulo: Companhia das Letras, 2003), 3:459.

90. Author's interview with Arlete Diogo, São Paulo, July 25, 2001.

91. Ronald M. Schneider, *"Order and Progress": A Political History of Brazil* (Boulder, CO: Westview, 1991), 272; see also Gaspari, *O sacerdote e o feiticeiro*, 3:469–81.

CHAPTER SIX   Political Prisoners

1. Author's interview with Manoel Cyrillo de Oliveira Netto, Rio de Janeiro, June 20, 2006.

2. Frei Betto, *Against Principalities and Powers*, trans. John Drury (Maryknoll, NY: Orbis, 1977).

3. Frei Betto later combined the two books into one annotated edition; see *Cartas da prisão, 1969–1973* (Rio de Janeiro: Agir, 2008).

4. Author's interview with Manoel Cyrillo de Oliveira Netto, Rio de Janeiro, June 20, 2006.

5. Author's interviews with Manoel Cyrillo de Oliveira Netto, Rio de Janeiro, June 21, 2006, and May 9, 2008.

6. The precise circumstances of João's death remain unknown; see Secretaria Especial dos Direitos Humanos, *Direito à memória e à verdade*, 316–17.

7. Author's interview with Manoel Cyrillo de Oliveira Netto, Rio de Janeiro, June 21, 2006.

8. This and the next five paragraphs based on author's interview with Manoel Cyrillo de Oliveira Netto, Rio de Janeiro, June 21, 2006.

9. Author's interview with Manoel Cyrillo de Oliveira Netto, Rio de Janeiro, May 9, 2008.

10. Magalhães, *Marighella*, chaps. 9 and 10.

11. "Conjunto de documentos sobre a situação dos presos políticos em Ilha Grande," http://arquivosdaditadura.com.br/documento/galeria/conjunto-documentos-sobre-situacao-presos.

12. Author's interview with Colombo Vieira de Souza, Rio de Janeiro, August 3, 2002.

13. *Filho* means "junior" in English.

14. Ruy Castro, *O anjo pornográfico* (São Paulo: Companhia das Letras, 1992), 389–93. Reason for code name from author's interview with Colombo Vieira de Souza, Rio de Janeiro, August 3, 2002.

15. Author's interview with Colombo Vieira de Souza, Rio de Janeiro, August 3, 2002.

16. Ottoni Fernandes Júnior, *O baú do guerrilheiro* (Rio de Janeiro: Record, 2004), 198.

17. Author's interview with Colombo Vieira de Souza, Rio de Janeiro, August 3, 2002.

18. André Torres, *Exílio na Ilha Grande* (Petrópolis: Vozes, 1978); Fernandes Júnior, *O baú do guerrilheiro*, 198.

19. Author's interview with Colombo Vieira de Souza, Rio de Janeiro, August 3, 2002.

20. Fernandes Júnior, *O baú do guerrilheiro*, 198–99.

21. Author's interview with Colombo Vieira de Souza, Rio de Janeiro, August 3, 2002.

22. Fernandes Júnior, *O baú do guerrilheiro*, 199–200.

23. "Conjunto de documentos sobre a situação dos presos políticos em Ilha Grande."

24. Ibid.

25. Fernandes Júnior, *O baú do guerrilheiro*, 278.

26. Elio Gaspari, *O sacerdote e o feiticeiro: A ditadura encurralada* (São Paulo: Companhia das Letras, 2004), 4:84, 86 (quotation).

27. Author's interview with Colombo Vieira de Souza, Rio de Janeiro, August 3, 2002.

28. Fernandes Júnior, *O baú do guerrilheiro*, 281.

29. On Frei Caneca the historical figure, see Serbin, *Needs of the Heart*, 44–45; on political prisoners in the complex, including forms of resistance, see Fernandes Júnior, *O baú do guerrilheiro*, 173; on the history of the prison complex, see Carlos Eduardo Moreira de Araújo, "Da casa de correção da corte ao Complexo Penitenciário da Frei Caneca: Um breve histórico do sistema prisional no Rio de Janeiro, 1834–2006," *Cidade Nova Revista*, no. 1 (2007): 147–61.

30. Fernandes Júnior, *O baú do guerrilheiro*, 281.

31. Author's interview with Jessie Jane Vieira de Souza, Rio de Janeiro, August 3, 2002.

32. Ibid.

33. Anthony W. Pereira, "'Persecution and Farce': The Origins and Transformation of Brazil's Political Trials, 1964–1979," *Latin American Research Review* 33, no. 1 (1998): 43–66; Anthony W. Pereira, "The Dialectics of the Brazilian Military Regime's Political Trials," *Luso-Brazilian Review* 41, no. 2 (2005): 162–83.

34. Gaspari, *As ilusões armadas*, 2:228; for an example of a civilian judge's actions, see Serbin, *Diálogos na sombra*, chap. 9.

35. Author's interview with Paulo de Tarso Vannuchi, São Paulo, July 23, 2001.

36. Felipe Werneck, "Juiz reconhece que havia tortura de presos políticos," *Exame.com*, July 31, 2014, https://exame.abril.com.br/brasil/juiz-reconhece -que-havia-tortura-de-presos-politicos/.

37. Author's interview with Paulo de Tarso Vannuchi, São Paulo, July 23, 2001.

38. Ibid.

39. Ibid.

CHAPTER SEVEN   Moderation in Exile

1. Denise Rollemberg, *Exílio* (Rio de Janeiro: Record, 1999), 53.

2 Author's interview with Aloysio Nunes Ferreira Filho, São Paulo, July 20, 2003. On the Leninist Tendency, see Del Roio, *Zarattini*, chaps. 9–11, appendix 3.

3. Author's interview with Aloysio Nunes Ferreira Filho, São Paulo, July 20, 2003. For the date of the return to the PCB, e-mail from Aloysio to

the author, January 18, 2015. Confirmation of Aloysio's work in author's telephone interview with Frei Oswaldo Rezende (Belo Horizonte), Rio de Janeiro, August 18, 2002.

4. Author's interview with Aloysio Nunes Ferreira Filho, São Paulo, July 20, 2003. Information on time at Besançon University from Aloysio's e-mail to the author, January 18, 2015. Information on Vera's family's contribution and housing situation from author's interview with Vera Maria Tude de Souza, São Paulo, June 17, 2003. On the Institut de Recherche et de Formation en vue du Développement Harmonisé, see Michelly Ramos de Angelo, "O IRFED e a formação de profissionais brasileiros em *Desenvolvimento do Território*," in *Anais do XI seminário de história da cidade e do urbanismo* (Vitória, Espírito Santo: UFES, 2010), online resource.

5. Author's interviews with Aloysio Nunes Ferreira Filho, São Paulo, July 20, 2003, and Brasília, June 22, 2004 (access to Italian Communist newspaper).

6. Author's interview with Aloysio Nunes Ferreira Filho, Brasília, June 22, 2004.

7. Ibid. Confirmation of Aloysio's transformation in author's telephone interview with Frei Oswaldo Rezende (Belo Horizonte), Rio de Janeiro, August 18, 2002.

8. Rollemberg, *Exílio*, 141–43.

9. Rollemberg, "Debate no exílio: Em busca da renovação," in *História do marxismo no Brasil: Partidos e movimentos após os anos 1969*, ed. Marcelo Ridenti and Daniel Aarão Reis (Campinas, São Paulo: Editora da Unicamp, 2007), 291, 294, 308–16, 318–19.

10. Author's interview with Aloysio Nunes Ferreira Filho, São Paulo, July 20, 2003.

11. Author's interview with Vera Maria Tude de Souza, São Paulo, June 17, 2003.

12. Author's interview with Carlos Eugênio Sarmento Coêlho da Paz, Rio de Janeiro, July 14, 2001.

13. Author's interview with Carlos Eugênio Sarmento Coêlho da Paz, Rio de Janeiro, June 28, 2001.

14. Paz, *Viagem*, 15–16.

15. Author's interview with Carlos Eugênio Sarmento Coêlho da Paz, Rio de Janeiro, July 14, 2001.

16. Interview with Carlos Eugênio Sarmento Coêlho da Paz conducted by Denise Rollemberg, Rio de Janeiro, July 31, 2000.

17. Author's interview with Carlos Eugênio Sarmento Coêlho da Paz, Rio de Janeiro, July 14, 2001.

18. Ibid.

19. Interview with Carlos Eugênio Sarmento Coêlho da Paz conducted by Denise Rollemberg, Rio de Janeiro, July 31, 2000.

20. Author's interviews with Carlos Eugênio Sarmento Coêlho da Paz, Rio de Janeiro, July 14, 2001, and June 21, 2006 (convinced several).

21. Ribeiro, "Memória, história e sociedade," 250.

22. Rollemberg, "Debate no exílio," 298–304.

23. Alves, *Estado e oposição*, 187–89.

24. Del Roio, *Zarattini*, 194–95.

25. Author's interview with Paulo de Tarso Vannuchi, São Paulo, July 23, 2001.

26. Rollemberg, "Debate no exílio," 294.

27. Author's interview with Carlos Eugênio Sarmento Coêlho da Paz, Rio de Janeiro, June 21, 2006.

28. Author's interview with Carlos Eugênio Sarmento Coêlho da Paz, Rio de Janeiro, July 14, 2001. Respect and aloofness from Ribeiro, "Memória, história e sociedade," 248–49.

29. This and the next two paragraphs based on author's interview with Carlos Eugênio Sarmento Coêlho da Paz, Rio de Janeiro, July 14, 2001.

CHAPTER EIGHT   Power to the People, Brazilian-Style

1. Author's interview with Arlete Diogo, São Paulo, May 19, 1997.

2. Author's interviews with Adriano Diogo, São Paulo, May 19, 1997, and July 25, 2001 (every church).

3. Author's interview with Arlete Diogo, São Paulo, July 25, 2001.

4. Lúcio Kowarick and Clara Ant, "Cortiço: Cem anos de promiscuidade," *Novos Estudos Cebrap* 1, no. 2 (1982): 59–64.

5. Author's interview with Adriano Diogo, São Paulo, July 25, 2001.

6. Kowarick and Ant, "Cortiço."

7. Author's interview with Adriano Diogo, São Paulo, July 25, 2001.

8. Ibid.

9. Ibid.

10. Author's interview with Arlete Diogo, São Paulo, July 25, 2001.

11. Ibid.

12. Author's interview with Adriano Diogo, São Paulo, July 25, 2001.

13. Giuseppina De Grazia, "O movimento operário e as Associações de Trabalhadores em São Paulo," *Lutas Sociais*, no. 25-26 (2010-2011): 140–41.

14. Author's interview with Adriano Diogo, São Paulo, July 25, 2001.

15. Author's interviews with Arlete Diogo, São Paulo, July 25, 2001, and June 16, 2003 (union representative).

16. Author's interview with Adriano Diogo, São Paulo, July 25, 2001.

17. See, for example, Marcelo Ridenti, *Em busca do povo brasileiro* (Rio de Janeiro: Record, 2000), esp. chaps. 1–3.

18. Serbin, "Mainstreaming the Revolutionaries," 209–10; see also Ana Maria Doimo, "Igreja e movimentos sociais pós-70 no Brasil," in *Catolicismo: Cotidiano e movimentos*, ed. Pierre Sanchis, 275–308, Catolicismo no Brasil atual (São Paulo: Edições Loyola, 1992); Kathryn Hochstetler, "Democratizing Pressures from Below? Social Movements in the New Brazilian Democracy," in *Democratic Brazil: Actors, Institutions, and Processes*, ed. Peter Kingstone and Timothy J. Power (Pittsburgh: University of Pittsburgh Press, 2000), 162.

19. Author's interview with Adriano Diogo, São Paulo, July 25, 2001.

20. Author's interview with Paulo de Tarso Vannuchi, São Paulo, July 26, 2001.

21. Paulo Freire, *Pedagogy of the Oppressed*, trans. Myra Bergman Ramos (New York: Herder and Herder, 1970); for a critical view of Freire, see Vanilda Paiva, *Paulo Freire e o nacionalismo desenvolvimentista*, 2nd ed. (São Paulo: Graal, 2000).

22. Author's interview with Paulo de Tarso Vannuchi, São Paulo, July 26, 2001.

23. Maria Rita Kehl and Paulo Vannuchi, "Madre Cristina," in *Rememória: Entrevistas sobre o Brasil do século XX*, ed. Ricardo de Azevedo and Flamrion Maués, 153–71 (São Paulo: Editora Fundação Perseu Abramo, 1997).

24. Author's interview with Paulo Vannuchi, São Paulo, July 23, 2001.

25. Denise Paraná, *Lula* (São Paulo: Editora Fundação Perseu Abramo, 2002), 26–27.

26. Alves, *Estado e oposição*, 246–53.

27. Paraná, *Lula*, 144.

28. Brigitte Hersant Leoni, *Fernando Henrique Cardoso*, trans. Dora Rocha (Rio de Janeiro: Nova Fronteira, 1997).

29. Author's interview with Aloysio Nunes Ferreira Filho, São Paulo, July 20, 2003.

30. Leoni, *Fernando Henrique Cardoso*.

31. Brazil today has twenty-six states, plus the Federal District, the location of Brasília.

32. Alves, *Estado e oposição*, 253–61; see also Paraná, *Lula*, 28; John D. French, "Lula, the 'New Unionism,' and the PT: How Factory Workers Came to Change the World, or At Least Brazil," *Latin American Politics and Society* 51, no. 4 (2009): 157–69.

33. Glenda Mezarobba, "Um acerto de contas" (master's thesis, Universidade de São Paulo, 2003).

34. Carlos Fico, *Como eles agiam* (Rio de Janeiro: Record, 2001), esp. chap. 6.

35. Author's interview with Adriano Diogo, São Paulo, July 25, 2001.

CHAPTER NINE   The Entrepreneurs

1. Author's interview with Márcio Araújo de Lacerda, Brumadinho, June 21, 2003.

2. Ibid.

3. Lt. Col. Manoel Alfredo Camarão de Albuquerque, "Relatório," Belo Horizonte, June 9, 1969, 9–10; ibid., May 22, 1969, pp. 9–10, 12, 35–37, 53; "Relatório," investigation regarding attempted robbery at Casa Tucano, Belo Horizonte, 1969, esp. p. 6. Each document from the collection Departamento de Ordem Política e Social de Minas Gerais, Arquivo Público Mineiro, Belo Horizonte.

4. Author's interview with Márcio Araújo de Lacerda, Brumadinho, June 4, 2005.

5. Author's interview with Márcio Araújo de Lacerda, Brumadinho, June 21, 2003.

6. Author's interview with Márcio Araújo de Lacerda, Brumadinho, June 4, 2005.

7. This paragraph and the next based on author's interview with Márcio Araújo de Lacerda, Brumadinho, June 21, 2003.

8. Recording by Márcio Araújo de Lacerda, Brumadinho, July 15, 2007, as complement to interviews with author.

9. Ibid. For background on the prison and conditions, see Daniela Arbex, *Cova 312* (São Paulo: Geração Editorial, 2015).

10. Author's interview with Marcello Guilherme Abi-Saber, Belo Horizonte, June 23, 2003.

11. Author's interview with Márcio Araújo de Lacerda, Brumadinho, June 21, 2003.

12. Ibid. On TV via satellite, see Lia Ribeiro Dias and Patrícia Cornils, *Alencastro* (São Paulo: Plano Editorial, 2004), 66.

13. Author's interview with Márcio Araújo de Lacerda, Brumadinho, June 21, 2003. And see Arbex, *Cova 312*, 227–32.

14. Author's interview with Márcio Araújo de Lacerda, Brumadinho, June 21, 2003.

15. Author's interview with Ricardo Apgaua, Belo Horizonte, July 5, 2001.

16. Author's interview with Márcio Araújo de Lacerda, Belo Horizonte, July 8, 2015.

17. Author's interview with Márcio Araújo de Lacerda, Brumadinho, June 22, 2003.

18. Alexei Barrionuevo, "Fearful Brazilians," *New York Times*, May 4, 2009, https://www.nytimes.com/2009/05/04/world/americas/04brazil.html.

19. José Antônio de Alencastro e Silva, *Telecomunicações* (São Josê dos Pinhais: Editel, 1990).

20. Dias and Cornils, *Alencastro*, 66–67.

21. Milton Santos and María Laura Silveira, "Do meio natural ao meio técnico-científico-informacional," in *O Brasil: Território e sociedade no início do século XXI*, ed. Milton Santos and María Laura Silveira (Rio de Janeiro: Record, 2001), 49; Santos and Silveira, "A constituição do meio técnico-científico-informacional e a renovação da materialidade no território," in *O Brasil*, 77, 79, 81.

22. Alencastro e Silva, *Telecomunicações*, 8, 31, 54, 57–61.

23. Musacchio and Lazzarini, "The Reinvention of State Capitalism in Brazil," 113–14.

24. Dias and Cornils, *Alencastro*, 71.

25. Santos and Silveira, "A constituição do meio técnico-científico-informacional," in *O Brasil*, 81; on Embratel, Telebrás, and the military's overall role in telecommunications, see also Alencastro e Silva, *Telecomunicações*.

26. Dias and Cornils, *Alencastro*, 72, 75.

27. Cilene Gomes, "Telecomunicações, informática e informação e a remodelação do território brasileiro," in *O Brasil*, 345–46, 48–49.

28. Abreu, "The Brazilian Economy, 1930–1980," 377–78; on specific measures to control foreign participation, see Dias and Cornils, *Alencastro*, 92–97.

29. Lynn Krieger Mytelka, "The Telecommunications Equipment Industry in Brazil and Korea," in *Competition, Innovation and Competitiveness in Developing Countries*, ed. Lynn Krieger Mytelka (Paris: Development Centre, Organisation for Economic Co-operation and Development, 1999), 120.

30. Author's interviews with Márcio Araújo de Lacerda, Brumadinho, June 21, 2003, and June 22, 2003.

31. Author's interview with Márcio Araújo de Lacerda, Brumadinho, June 22, 2003.

32. Author's interviews with Márcio Araújo de Lacerda, Brumadinho, June 21, 2003, and June 4, 2005 (I didn't want).

33. Author's interview with Márcio Araújo de Lacerda, Brumadinho, June 22, 2003.

34. Author's interviews with Márcio Araújo de Lacerda, Brumadinho, June 21, 2003 (in mid-1975), and June 22, 2003.

35. Author's interview with Márcio Araújo de Lacerda, Brumadinho, June 21, 2003.

36. Author's interview with Márcio Araújo de Lacerda, Brumadinho, June 22, 2003.

37. Recording by Márcio Araújo de Lacerda, Brumadinho, July 15, 2007, as complement to interviews with author.

38. Author's interview with Márcio Araújo de Lacerda, Brumadinho, June 22, 2003.

39. Ibid.

40. Ibid.

41. Author's interview with José Antônio de Alencastro e Silva, Brasília, July 7, 2003.

42. Author's interview with Márcio Araújo de Lacerda, Brumadinho, June 22, 2003.

43. Author's interview with Marcello Guilherme Abi-Saber, Belo Horizonte, June 23, 2003.

44. Elvira Lobato, "Grupo mineiro vence licitação no Chile," *Folha de S. Paulo*, March 20, 1997.

45. Author's interview with Márcio Araújo de Lacerda, Brumadinho, June 22, 2003.

46. Ibid.

47. Author's interview with Marcello Guilherme Abi-Saber, Belo Horizonte, June 23, 2003.

48. Author's interview with Márcio Araújo de Lacerda, Brumadinho, June 22, 2003. Information on profit-sharing from author's interview with Marcello Guilherme Abi-Saber, Belo Horizonte, June 23, 2003. See also Beth Koike, "Se todas fossem como você," *CartaCapital*, May 24, 2000, 56. On Construtel's striving for ethical business practices, see Ricardo Rievers, "Ética reforça atendimento," *Gazeta Mercantil*, March 2, 1999.

49. Ben Ross Schneider, *Business Politics and the State* (Cambridge: Cambridge University Press, 2004), 107–13; see also Bolívar Lamounier and Isabel Vericat, "Empresarios, partidos y democratización en Brasil (1974–1990)," *Revista Mexicana de Sociología* 54, no. 1 (1992): 77–97.

50. Author's interview with Márcio Araújo de Lacerda, Brumadinho, June 22, 2003.

51. Dias and Cornils, *Alencastro*, 88; Mytelka, "The Telecommunications Equipment Industry in Brazil and Korea," 115–16.

52. Dias and Cornils, *Alencastro*, 90–98, 100–110; Mytelka, "The Telecommunications Equipment Industry in Brazil and Korea," 122–30.

53. Dias and Cornils, *Alencastro*, 107–8.

54. Author's interview with Márcio Araújo de Lacerda, Brumadinho, June 22, 2003.

55. Ibid.

56. Author's interview with Marcello Guilherme Abi-Saber, Belo Horizonte, June 23, 2003.

57. Author's interview with Márcio Araújo de Lacerda, Brumadinho, June 22, 2003.

58. Author's interview with Marcello Guilherme Abi-Saber, Belo Horizonte, June 23, 2003.

59. Author's interview with Márcio Araújo de Lacerda, Brumadinho, June 22, 2003.

60. Author's interview with Percival Menon Maricato, São Paulo, August 20, 2007.

61. Author's interview with Maurice Politi, São Paulo, August 9, 2008.

62. Daniel Politi, "Uncomfortable Truths," *New York Times*, September 28, 2012.

63. Author's interview with Manoel Cyrillo de Oliveira Netto, Rio de Janeiro, June 21, 2006.

64. Gomes, "Telecomunicações, informática e informação e a remodelação do território brasileiro," in *O Brasil*, 352, 354.

65. Alencastro e Silva, *Telecomunicações*, 33–34.

66. B. Schneider, *Business Politics and the State*.

67. Musacchio and Lazzarini, "The Reinvention of State Capitalism in Brazil," 115–16.

CHAPTER TEN   From Bullets to Ballots

1. Leslie Bethell and Celso Castro, "Politics in Brazil under Military Rule, 1964–1985," 213.

2. Alves, *Estado e oposição*, 259–66; Flamarion Maués and Zilah Wendel Abramo, eds., *Pela democracia, contra o arbítrio* (São Paulo: Editora Fundação Perseu Abramo, 2006), chap. 5.

3. R. Schneider, *"Order and Progress,"* 288–89, 295–97.

4. Marcelo de Paiva Abreu, "The Brazilian Economy, 1980–1994," in Bethell, *Brazil since 1930*, 397–403.

5. Alves, *Estado e oposição*, 300–305.

6. Dias and Cornils, *Alencastro*, 78–79, 136–39.

7. Bethell and Castro, "Politics in Brazil under Military Rule, 1964–1985," 216–17; on Riocentro, see also Júlio de Sá Bierrenbach, *Riocentro* (Rio de Janeiro: Domínio Público, 1996); Argolo, Kátia Ribeiro, and Fortunato, *A direita explosiva*, 263–68.

8. Author's interview with Aloysio Nunes Ferreira Filho, São Paulo, July 20, 2003.

9. Ibid.

10. Author's interview with Aloysio Nunes Ferreira Filho, São Paulo, June 7, 2004; emphasis on "wide-ranging" by Aloysio.

11. Ibid.

12. Auro Augusto Caliman, ed. *Legislativo paulista* (São Paulo: Imprensa Oficial: 1998), 154.

13. Author's interview with Aloysio Nunes Ferreira Filho, São Paulo, June 7, 2004.

14. Author's interview with Aloysio Nunes Ferreira Filho, São Paulo, July 20, 2003.

15. Author's interview with Aloysio Nunes Ferreira Filho, São Paulo, June 7, 2004.

16. Paulo Henrique Martinez, "O Partido dos Trabalhadores e a conquista do estado, 1980–2005," in *História do marxismo no Brasil: Partidos e movimentos após os anos 1960*, ed. Marcelo Ridenti and Danial Aarão Reis (Campinas, São Paulo: Editora da UNICAMP, 2007), 239–47, 248 (quotation).

17. Daniel Aarão Reis, "O Partido dos Trabalhadores: Trajetória, meta-morfoses, perspectivas," in *Revolução e democracia (1964–...)*, ed. Jorge Ferreira and Daniel Aarão Reis, *As esquerdas no Brasil* (Rio de Janeiro: Civilização Brasileira, 2007), 507.

18. Francisco Carlos Palomanes Martinho, "A armadilha do novo: Luiz Inácio Lula da Silva e uma esquerda que se imaginou diferente," in Ferreira and Reis, *Revolução e democracia (1964–...)*, 541–62.

19. Author's interview with Paulo de Tarso Vannuchi, São Paulo, July 26, 2001.

20. Martinho, "A armadilha do novo," 544–45, 547, 549–50; see also Margaret Keck, *The Workers' Party* (New Haven, CT: Yale University Press, 1992), 95–97; on the oppressiveness of Brazilian labor law, see John D. French, *Drowning in Laws* (Chapel Hill: University of North Carolina Press, 2004).

21. Reis, "O Partido dos Trabalhadores," 509–10; Martinho, "A armadilha do novo," 546; Keck, *The Workers' Party*, 245–46.

22. Keck, *The Workers' Party*, 238–40, 242, 245.

23. Author's interview with Adriano Diogo, São Paulo, July 25, 2001.

24. Background on Dirceu in Maués and Abramo, *Pela democracia, contra o arbítrio*, 55–56, 243–44, 267–69, 403–6; Ventura, *1968: O que fizemos de nós*; see also Otávio Cabral, *Dirceu* (Rio de Janeiro: Record, 2013); for an extensive critique of Cabral's book, see Mario Sergio Conti, "Chutes para todo lado," *Piauí*, August 2013.

25. Author's interview with Adriano Diogo, São Paulo, July 25, 2001.

26. Ibid. For background on Erundina, see José Nêumanne, *Erundina* (Rio de Janeiro: Espaço e Tempo, 1989).

27. Author's interview with Adriano Diogo, São Paulo, July 25, 2001.

28. Author's interview with Arlete Diogo, São Paulo, July 25, 2001.

29. Author's interview with Adriano Diogo, São Paulo, July 25, 2001.

30. Author's interview with Adriano Diogo, São Paulo, July 1, 2003.

31. Author's interview with Arlete Diogo, São Paulo, June 16, 2003.

32. Lawrence Weschler, *A Miracle, a Universe*, 2nd ed. (Chicago: University of Chicago Press, 1998), chap. 1; Lucas Figueiredo, *Olho por olho* (Rio de Janeiro: Record, 2009).

33. Zuenir Ventura, "'Thriller' dos anos negros," *Jornal do Brasil*, August 25, 1990, 6–8.

34. Ibid.

35. Author's interview with Paulo de Tarso Vannuchi, São Paulo, July 26, 2001.

36. Ibid. See also the March 2007 recorded interview with Paulo de Tarso Vannuchi at http://www.tvmpf.mpf.mp.br/videos/69/retrieve/?format=480p.

37. Author's interview with Paulo de Tarso Vannuchi, São Paulo, July 26, 2001.

38. Author's interviews with Jessie Jane Vieira de Souza and Colombo Vieira de Souza, Rio de Janeiro, August 3, 2002.

39. Author's interview with Jessie Jane Vieira de Souza, Rio de Janeiro, August 3, 2002.

40. Author's interviews with Colombo Vieira de Souza, Rio de Janeiro, August 3, 2002, and Niterói, June 17, 2004.

41. Reis, "O Partido dos Trabalhadores," 508.

42. Author's interviews with Colombo Vieira de Souza, Rio de Janeiro, August 3, 2002, and June 24, 2003. On Juarez's prominence, see Sérgio Martins Pereira, "CUT e Força Sindical em Volta Redonda: Modelos de sindicalismo ou trajetórias de lideranças?," *Enfoques* 5, no. 2 (2006): 103–19; Celia Maria Leite Costa, Dulce Chaves Pandolfi, and Kenneth Serbin, eds., *O bispo de Volta Redonda* (Rio de Janeiro: Editora FGV, 2001), 161.

43. Author's interview with Jessie Jane Vieira de Souza, Rio de Janeiro, June 24, 2003.

44. Author's interview with Colombo Vieira de Souza, Rio de Janeiro, June 24, 2003. See also Márcia de Paula Leite, "As aventuras de Juarez," *Lua Nova* 1, no. 3 (1984): 22–23.

45. Author's interview with Colombo Vieira de Souza, Rio de Janeiro, June 24, 2003.

46. Costa, Pandolfi, and Serbin, *O bispo de Volta Redonda*, 153.

47. Author's interview with Colombo Vieira de Souza, Rio de Janeiro, June 24, 2003. For details of the strike, see Sandra Mayrink Veiga and Isaque Fonseca, *Volta Redonda* (Petrópolis: Vozes, 1990), 54–58; Edson Teixeira da

Silva Jr. et al., "'A greve continua!': Algumas considerações historiográficas sobre os movimentos grevistas de Volta Redonda," *Cadernos UniFOA*, no. 7 (2008): 31–32; see also the documentary by Pablo Marins Bedê, *A greve de 1984* (2013).

48. Author's interview with Jessie Jane Vieira de Souza, Rio de Janeiro, June 24, 2003.

49. Author's interview with Colombo Vieira de Souza, Rio de Janeiro, June 24, 2003.

50. Author's interview with Colombo Vieira de Souza, Rio de Janeiro, August 3, 2002.

51. Author's interview with Jessie Jane Vieira de Souza, Rio de Janeiro, June 24, 2003.

52. Author's interview with Manoel Cyrillo de Oliveira Netto, Rio de Janeiro, June 21, 2006.

53. Ibid.

54. Author's interview with Carlos Eugênio Sarmento Coêlho da Paz, Rio de Janeiro, January 30, 1997.

55. Author's interview with Carlos Eugênio Sarmento Coêlho da Paz, via Facebook, March 27, 2015.

56. Author's interview with Carlos Eugênio Sarmento Coêlho da Paz, Rio de Janeiro, August 27, 2007.

57. Author's interview with Carlos Eugênio Sarmento Coêlho da Paz, via Facebook, March 27, 2015.

58. "O porão iluminado," *Veja*, July 24, 1985, 110.

59. Weschler, *A Miracle, a Universe*, 71–78.

60. Archdiocese of São Paulo, *Brasil: Nunca mais* (Petrópolis: Vozes, 1985), 26.

CHAPTER ELEVEN   A Proletarian versus a Free-Marketer for President

1. R. Schneider, *"Order and Progress,"* 310.

2. Leslie Bethell and Jairo Nicolau, "Politics in Brazil, 1985–2002," in Bethell, *Brazil since 1930*, 234–35.

3. On everyday Brazilians' involvement in the Sarney plan, see Charleston José de Sousa Assis, "Fiscais do Sarney? Algumas considerações sobre a participação popular no Plano Cruzado," in *Não foi tempo perdido: Os anos 80 em debate*, ed. Samantha Viz Quadrat, 337–61 (Rio de Janeiro: 7 Letras, 2014); on illiterates and the vote, see Bethell and Nicolau, "Politics in Brazil, 1985–2002," 234, 237. Details and effect of the cruzado program also from my observations while conducting research in Brazil from June to September 1986.

4. R. Schneider, *"Order and Progress,"* 320–27.

5. Bethell and Nicolau, "Politics in Brazil, 1985–2002," 234, 237.

6. Abreu, "The Brazilian Economy, 1980–1994," in Bethell, *Brazil since 1930*, 406–18; R. Schneider, *"Order and Progress,"* 330–32, 344–45; on use of term hyperinflation, see Hugo Passarelli, "Inflação: Um problema que não pode ser esquecido," *O Estado de S. Paulo*, September 7, 2011. Details on effect of inflation also from my observations while conducting research in Brazil from June to September 1987 and from June 1988 to November 1991.

7. Bethell and Nicolau, "Politics in Brazil, 1985–2002," 240–44.

8. Ibid., 242, 244 (quotation).

9. Martinho, "A armadilha do novo," 551–52.

10. Author's interview with Aloysio Nunes Ferreira Filho, Brasília, June 22, 2004.

11. Author's interview with Aloysio Nunes Ferreira Filho, São Paulo, June 7, 2004.

12. For the number of votes, see Pereira, "CUT e Força Sindical em Volta redonda," 107. Rank in voting from author's interview with Colombo Vieira de Souza, Rio de Janeiro, June 24, 2003.

13. Author's interview with Colombo Vieira de Souza, Rio de Janeiro, June 24, 2003.

14. Author's interview with Jessie Jane Vieira de Souza, Rio de Janeiro, June 24, 2003.

15. Author's interview with Colombo Vieira de Souza, Rio de Janeiro, June 24, 2003.

16. Ibid.

17. French, *Drowning in Laws*, 7, 9, 151.

18. Author's interview with Colombo Vieira de Souza, Rio de Janeiro, June 24, 2003.

19. Author's interview with Jessie Jane Vieira de Souza, Rio de Janeiro, June 24, 2003.

20. Ibid.

21. Silva Jr. et al., "'A greve continua!'" 32–34; for tanks and other armaments and painted faces, see Costa, Pandolfi, and Serbin, *O bispo de Volta Redonda*, 154, 156.

22. Costa, Pandolfi, and Serbin, *O bispo de Volta Redonda*, 154–55.

23. Silva Jr. et al., "'A greve continua!'" 34–35; Veiga and Fonseca, *Volta Redonda*; Costa, Pandolfi, and Serbin, *O bispo de Volta Redonda*, chap. 10.

24. Kenneth P. Serbin, "Woman's Election Still Shocks Brazilian Politics," *National Catholic Reporter*, April 7, 1989.

25. Author's interview with Arlete Diogo, São Paulo, June 16, 2003.

26. Costa, Pandolfi, and Serbin, *O bispo de Volta Redonda*, 157–58. I witnessed the Mass; see Kenneth P. Serbin, "Elites Were Winners in Brazil, but Workers Are Poised to Pounce," *National Catholic Reporter*, December 28, 1989, 5–6.

27. Author's interview with Colombo Vieira de Souza, Rio de Janeiro, June 24, 2003.

28. Author's interview with Jessie Jane Vieira de Souza, Rio de Janeiro, June 24, 2003.

29. Costa, Pandolfi, and Serbin, *O bispo de Volta Redonda*, 161–62; Kenneth P. Serbin, "Brazilian Bishop Who Backed Strikers Gets Death Threats," *National Catholic Reporter*, December 30, 1988.

30. Veiga and Fonseca, *Volta Redonda*, 219–20, 221 (quotation).

31. Costa, Pandolfi, and Serbin, *O bispo de Volta Redonda*, 162–63; see also the documentary by Pablo Marins Bedê, *Acidente e morte de Juarez Antunes* (2013).

32. Author's interview with Jessie Jane Vieira de Souza, Rio de Janeiro, June 24, 2003.

33. Costa, Pandolfi, and Serbin, *O bispo de Volta Redonda*, 159–61.

34. Author's interview with Colombo Vieira de Souza, Rio de Janeiro, June 24, 2003.

35. Author's interview with Jessie Jane Vieira de Souza, Rio de Janeiro, June 24, 2003.

36. Abreu, "The Brazilian Economy, 1980–1994," 416.

37. Bethell and Nicolau, "Politics in Brazil, 1985–2002," 246.

38. On the perception of Gabeira on the Brazilian Left, see Green, "'Who Is the Macho Who Wants to Kill Me?,'" 467; on Gabeira and the 1989 campaign, see André Naddeo, "Candidatura de 1989 foi de 'sacrifício,' diz Gabeira, que quase foi vice de Lula," *UOL Notícias*, November 14, 2009, https://noticias.uol.com.br/especiais/eleicoes-1989/ultnot/2009/11/14/ult9005u11.jhtm.

39. Bethell and Nicolau, "Politics in Brazil, 1985–2002," 246–47.

40. "A guerra ao turbante," *Veja*, March 23, 1988.

41. Abreu, "The Brazilian Economy, 1980–1994," 418.

42. For first-round vote tallies, see Bethell and Nicolau, "Politics in Brazil, 1985–2002," 247–48. For an initial, contemporary interpretation of the crisis of the Left in Latin America, see Jorge G. Castañeda, *Utopia Unarmed* (New York: Knopf, 1993).

43. I conducted research in Brazil throughout most of 1989. For an example of impressions of the campaign, see Serbin, "Elites Were Winners in Brazil, but Workers Are Poised to Pounce."

44. Author's interview with Paulo de Tarso Vannuchi, São Paulo, July 26, 2001.

45. Author's interviews with Paulo de Tarso Vannuchi, São Paulo, July 26, 2001, and July 3, 2003.

46. Author's interview with Paulo de Tarso Vannuchi, São Paulo, July 26, 2001.

47. Ibid.

48. Bethell and Nicolau, "Politics in Brazil, 1985–2002," 249.

49. Author's interview with Paulo de Tarso Vannuchi, São Paulo, July 26, 2001.

50. Ibid.

51. Keck, *The Workers' Party*, 250; William R. Nylen, "The Making of a Loyal Opposition: The Workers' Party (PT) and the Consolidation of Democracy in Brazil," in *Democractic Brazil: Actors, Institutions and Processes*, ed. Peter R. Kingstone and Timothy J. Power, 126–43 (Pittsburgh: University of Pittsburgh Press, 2000).

52. A similar discussion is in Bethell and Nicolau, "Politics in Brazil, 1985–2002," 249.

CHAPTER TWELVE   Revolutionaries in Suits and Ties

1. On the politics of the Collor era, see Bethell and Nicolau, "Politics in Brazil, 1985–2002," 250–55; for an early, on-the-ground assessment of the impeachment, see Kenneth P. Serbin, "Collor's Impeachment and the Struggle for Change," *North-South Focus* 2, no. 2 (1993); on the corruption scandals and the impeachment, see also Mario Sergio Conti, *Notícias do Planalto* (São Paulo: Companhia das Letras, 1999); Brasilio Sallum Jr., *O impeachment de Fernando Collor* (São Paulo: Editora 34, 2015); on the economy under Collor, see Abreu, "The Brazilian Economy, 1980–1994," 418–25; on the Collor plan's effect on the populace, see, for example, Marina Schmidt, "Traumas do confisco da poupança ainda permanecem," *Jornal do Comércio*, March 17, 2015; on lawsuits, see Vinicius Albuquerque, "Plano Collor, que confiscou poupança, completa 20 anos," *R7*, March 16, 2010, http://noticias.r7.com/economia/noticias/plano -collor-que-confiscou-a-poupanca-completa-20-anos-20100316.html. Details and effect of Collor's economic program also from my observations while conducting research in Brazil from October 1988 to November 1991.

2. Abreu, "The Brazilian Economy, 1980–1994," 418, 420, 424–25; for an overview and analysis of privatization, see Musacchio and Lazzarini, "The Reinvention of State Capitalism in Brazil."

3. Musacchio and Lazzarini, "The Reinvention of State Capitalism in Brazil," 108, 116–18, 122–30.

4. Peter R. Kingstone, "Muddling through Gridlock: Economic Policy Performance, Business Responses, and Democratic Sustainability," in *Democratic Brazil: Actors, Institutions, and Processes*, ed. Peter R. and Timothy J. Power Kingstone (Pittsburgh: University of Pittsburgh Press, 2000), 190–94. Peter R. Kingstone and Aldo F. Ponce, "From Cardoso to Lula: The Triumph of Pragmatism in Brazil," in *Leftist Governments in Latin America: Successes and Shortcomings*, ed. Kurt Weyland, Raúl L. Madrid, and Wendy Hunter (Cambridge: Cambridge University Press, 2010), 102.

5. Guiomar Namo de Mello et al., "Pelo futuro de São Paulo"; copy of document furnished to author by Itoby Alves Corrêa Jr.

6. Ibid. On the manifesto's pro-Maluf inclinations, see "Maluf forma equipe 'apartidária,'" *Jornal do Brasil*, November 20, 1992.

7. Carlos Eduardo Alves and Mário Cesar Carvalho, "Manifesto de ex-comunistas sofre críticas," *Folha de S. Paulo*, October 30, 1992; Juca Kfouri, "Sobre o manifesto," *O Estado de S. Paulo*, November 4, 1992; Rodolfo Konder, "O PT colhe a tempestade," *O Estado de S. Paulo*, November 6, 1992.

8. Konder, "O PT colhe a tempestade."

9. "Maluf forma equipe 'apartidária.'"

10. Author's interview with Itoby Alves Corrêa Jr., São Paulo, August 3, 2001. Assessment of Itoby's importance in ALN from author's interview with Carlos Eugênio Sarmento Coêlho da Paz, Rio de Janeiro, June 28, 2001.

11. Author's interview with Carlos Eugênio Sarmento Coêlho da Paz, Rio de Janeiro, June 28, 2001.

12. Author's interviews with Itoby Alves Corrêa Jr., São Paulo, August 3, 2001 (quotations), São Paulo, June 17, 2005, and Rio de Janeiro, June 23, 2005.

13. Author's interviews with Manoel Cyrillo de Oliveira Netto, Rio de Janeiro, July 26, 2007, and May 9, 2008. Explanation of film's name from e-mail from Manoel Cyrillo de Oliveira Netto to author, June 12, 2008.

14. Carlos Eduardo Lins da Silva, "EUA negarão visto para Gabeira ir à ONU," *Folha de S. Paulo*, December 3, 1998; "Gabeira ainda tenta visto para os EUA," *Folha de S. Paulo*, November 30, 1998.

15. Author's interview with Manoel Cyrillo de Oliveira Netto, Gonçalves (Minas Gerais), July 14, 2015.

16. Author's interview with Manoel Cyrillo de Oliveira Netto, Rio de Janeiro, July 26, 2007.

17. Bethell and Nicolau, "Politics in Brazil, 1985–2002," in Bethell, *Brazil since 1930*, 255.

18. Author's interview with Aloysio Nunes Ferreira Filho, São Paulo, July 20, 2003.

19. Fernando Henrique Cardoso, *Accidental President* (New York: Public Affairs, 2006), 174–75 (nightmares), 183, 185.

20. Abreu, "The Brazilian Economy, 1980–1994," 425–27.

21. Kingstone, "Muddling through Gridlock," 194–99.

22. Marcelo de Paiva Abreu and Rogério L. F. Werneck, "The Brazilian Economy, 1994–2004: An Interim Assessment," in Bethell, *Brazil since 1930*, 431–49; Augusto Gazir, "Iogurte é a nova bandeira do Real," *Folha de S. Paulo*, December 20, 1996.

23. Matias Spektor, *18 dias* (Rio de Janeiro: Objetiva, 2014), 56–57.

24. Bethell and Nicolau, "Politics in Brazil, 1985–2002," 260–74; on human rights, see also Spektor, *18 dias*, 78–79; Cardoso, *Accidental President*, 204–5.

25. Spektor, *18 dias*, 57–58, 100–101.

26. Bethell and Nicolau, "Politics in Brazil, 1985–2002," 260–61; see also Abreu and Werneck, "The Brazilian Economy, 1994–2004," 449–50; Tyler Priest, "Petrobras in the History of Offshore Oil," in *New Order and Progress: Development and Democracy in Brazil*, ed. Ben Ross Schneider (New York: Oxford University Press, 2016), 68.

27. Priest, "Petrobras in the History of Offshore Oil," 69; Aldo Musacchio and Sergio G. Lazzarini, "The Reinvention of State Capitalism in Brazil," 120–22.

28. Kingstone and Ponce, "From Cardoso to Lula," 103; Peter Kingstone, *Political Economy of Latin America* (New York: Routledge, 2011), 126.

29. Spektor, *18 dias*, 58. On college graduates in the civil service, see Nunberg and Pacheco, "Public Management Incongruity in 21st Century Brazil," 144–45; on Bolsa Escola, see also Celia W. Dugger, "To Help Poor Be Pupils, Not Wage Earners, Brazil Pays Parents," *New York Times*, January 3, 2004.

30. Larry Rohter, *Brazil on the Rise* (New York: Palgrave Macmillan, 2010), 254.

31. Bryan McCann, *The Throes of Democracy* (London: Zed Books, 2008), 30, 32–33.

32. José Serra, "The Political Economy of the Brazilian Struggle Against AIDS," in *Institute for Advanced Study Friends Forum, Paper No. 17* (Princeton, NJ: Princeton University Press, 2004); A. Nunn, E. Da Fonseca, and S. Gruskin, "Changing Global Essential Medicines Norms to Improve Access to AIDS Treatment: Lessons from Brazil," *Global Public Health* 4, no. 2 (2009): 53–77.

33. Spektor, *18 dias*, 58.

34. Abreu and Werneck, "The Brazilian Economy, 1994–2004," 436–44; on the Clinton–Fernando Henrique connection, see Spektor, *18 dias*, 68–70, 100–106.

35. Kingstone and Ponce, "From Cardoso to Lula," 103–4.

36. Gisele Gouget, Lorenzo Aldé, and Adrianna Setemy, "Quércia, Orestes," in *Dicionário Histórico-Biográfico Brasileiro* (Rio de Janeiro: Centro de Pesquisa e de Documentação de História Contemporânea do Brasil, 2010).

37. Author's interview with Aloysio Nunes Ferreira Filho, São Paulo, June 7, 2004.

38. Antônio Flávio Pierucci and Marcelo Coutinho de Lima, "São Paulo 92, a vitória da direita," *Novos Estudos CEBRAP*, no. 35 (1993): 94–99.

39. Author's interview with Aloysio Nunes Ferreira Filho, São Paulo, June 7, 2004.

40. Author's interview with Aloysio Nunes Ferreira Filho, São Paulo, July 20, 2003.

41. My observations and conversations in the São José do Rio Preto region, August 7–9, 2002. Quotations from author's interview with Aloysio Nunes Ferreira Filho, São Paulo, July 20, 2003.

42. For a critical view of development in Ribeirão Preto, see Maria Esther Fernandes, ed., *A cidade e seus limites* (São Paulo and Ribeirão Preto: Annablume; FAPESP; Unaerp, 2004).

43. Quotations from author's recording of speech by Aloysio Nunes Ferreira Filho, Catanduva, August 8, 2002.

44. Author's interview with Aloysio Nunes Ferreira Filho, São Paulo, June 7, 2004.

45. Author's interview with Aloysio Nunes Ferreira Filho, Brasília, June 22, 2004.

46. Ibid. Fernando Henrique praised Aloysio's political abilities in several diary entries; see Fernando Henrique Cardoso, *Diários da presidência, 1995–1996* (São Paulo: Companhia das Letras, 2015), 227–29, 323, 326, 369 (quotation).

47. Author's interview with Aloysio Nunes Ferreira Filho, Brasília, June 22, 2004.

48. Author's interview with Aloysio Nunes Ferreira Filho, São Paulo, June 7, 2004.

49. Cardoso, *Accidental President*, 233. On the benefits of the Telebrás privatization, and a critique of other privatizations, see also McCann, *The Throes of Democracy*, 34–37.

50. Rohter, *Brazil on the Rise*, 144.

51. Author's interview with Aloysio Nunes Ferreira Filho, Brasília, June 22, 2004. For a discussion of neoliberalism and the Washington Consensus, see McCann, *The Throes of Democracy*, 3–6.

52. Author's interview with Aloysio Nunes Ferreira Filho, São Paulo, July 20, 2003.

53. This paragraph and the next two based on author's interview with Aloysio Nunes Ferreira Filho, Brasília, June 22, 2004.

54. Ibid.

55. Leonencio Nossa, "Celso Daniel e Toninho, os pesadelos do PT," *O Estado de S. Paulo*, October 12, 2013; Romeu Tuma Júnior, *Assassinato de reputações* (Rio de Janeiro: Topbooks, 2013).

56. Author's interview with Aloysio Nunes Ferreira Filho, São Paulo, July 7, 2004.

57. Author's interview with Aloysio Nunes Ferreira Filho, Brasília, June 22, 2004.

58. Ibid.

59. Bethell and Nicolau, "Politics in Brazil, 1985–2002," 260–61; Cardoso, *Accidental President*, 232–33.

60. Author's interview with Marcello Guilherme Abi-Saber, Belo Horizonte, June 23, 2003. On profit sharing, see also Koike, "Se todas fossem como você."

61. Author's interview with Márcio Araújo de Lacerda, Brumadinho, June 22, 2003. Figure on donations from June 4, 2005 interview.

62. Author's interview with Márcio Araújo de Lacerda, Brumadinho, June 22, 2003.

63. Author's interview with Marcello Guilherme Abi-Saber, Belo Horizonte, June 23, 2003.

64. Author's interview with Márcio Araújo de Lacerda, Brumadinho, June 22, 2003.

65. Ibid.

66. Author's interview with Márcio Araújo de Lacerda, Brumadinho, June 4, 2005.

67. Author's interview with Márcio Araújo de Lacerda, Belo Horizonte, July 8, 2015.

68. Author's interview with Márcio Araújo de Lacerda, Brumadinho, June 22, 2003.

69. Ibid.

70. Author's interviews with Paulo de Tarso Vannuchi, São Paulo, July 26, 2001, July 3, 2003, and June 7, 2005 (quotation).

71. Author's interview with Paulo de Tarso Vannuchi, São Paulo, July 26, 2001.

72. Paulo Vannuchi, "Democracia, liberalismo, socialismo e a contribuição de Norberto Bobbio" (master's thesis, Universidade de São Paulo, 2001), 8 (big problem), 10 (champions).

73. Ibid., 310.

74. Secco, *História do PT*, 162–64.

75. Ibid., 145 (Dirceu quotation), 146–98. Adriano's comments from author's interview with Adriano Diogo, São Paulo, June 12, 2006.

76. Secco, *História do PT*, 162.

77. For a detailed study of factions, see ibid. Author's interview with Adriano Diogo, São Paulo, July 25, 2001. Author's interview with Arlete Diogo, São Paulo, June 16, 2003.

78. Author's interview with Adriano Diogo, São Paulo, August 4, 2001, and visit with Adriano to the East Zone, same date. Rap song recorded during visit. Additional perspective from author's interview with Adriano Diogo, São Paulo, July 2, 2003. Author's interview with Valdênia Aparecida Paulino, São Paulo, August 4, 2001. On Valdênia, see Eleonora de Lucena, "De catadora a ouvidora," *Folha de S. Paulo*, October 8, 2012.

79. Author's interview with Adriano Diogo, São Paulo, July 25, 2001.

80. Author's interview with Adriano Diogo, São Paulo, July 1, 2003.

81. Ibid. On Paulipetro, see Silvana de Freitas, "STJ pode responsibilizar Maluf no caso Paulipetro," *Folha de S. Paulo*, August 2, 1997; for background on Maluf, see Bryan Pitts, "The Audacity to Strong-Arm the Generals: Paulo Maluf and the 1978 São Paulo Gubernatorial Contest," *Histpanic American Historical Review* 92, no. 3 (2012): 471–505.

82. Author's interview with Adriano Diogo, São Paulo, July 1, 2003. For details of the conflict, see Marco Antônio C. Teixeira, "Diagnóstico de conflitos sócio-ambientais na cidade de São Paulo," *Cadernos Cedec* (São Paulo: Cedec, 1995), 12–25.

83. Author's interviews with Adriano Diogo, São Paulo, July 25, 2001, July 1, 2003, and July 2, 2003.

84. Author's interview with Adriano Diogo, São Paulo, July 1, 2003.

85. Myryam Athie, "CPI-2001-PAS" (São Paulo: Câmara Municipal de São Paulo, 2001) (the final report of the city council investigation [CPI]). On corruption in the Maluf and Pitta administrations, see Rogério Bastos Arantes, "O Ministério Público e a corrupção política em São Paulo," in *Justiça e cidadania no Brasil*, ed. Maria Tereza Sadek (Rio de Janeiro: Centro Edelstein de Pesquisas Sociais, 2009), 15–61.

86. Author's interview with Adriano Diogo, São Paulo, August 4, 2001.

87. Bruno Tavares and Marcelo Godoy, "Esquema que tirou R$ 100 mi da saúde tem 5 suspeitos presos," *O Estado de S. Paulo*, October 31, 2008.

88. Author's interview with Arlete Diogo, São Paulo, June 16, 2003.

89. Author's interview with Jessie Jane Vieira de Souza, Niterói, June 17, 2004.

90. Author's interview with Colombo Vieira de Souza, Niterói, June 17, 2004. On the murder of the priest, see also Maurílio Mendonça, "Julgamento do assassinato de padre Gabriel é anulado," *A Gazeta*, September 14, 2011.

91. Author's interview with Colombo Vieira de Souza, Niterói, June 17, 2004. For background on Vasco Alves, see "Alves, Vasco," in *Dicionário Histórico-Biográfico Brasileiro*, ed. Christiane Jalles de Paula and Lattman-Weltman (Rio de Janeiro: Centro de Pesquisa e de Documentação de História Contemporânea do Brasil, 2010).

92. Author's interview with Colombo Vieira de Souza, Niterói, June 17, 2004.

93. Ibid.

94. Ibid.

95. Author's interview with Jessie Jane Vieira de Souza, Niterói, June 17, 2004.

96. Author's interview with Colombo Vieira de Souza, Niterói, June 17, 2004.

97. Author's interview with Jessie Jane Vieira de Souza, Niterói, June 17, 2004.

98. Author's interview with Colombo Vieira de Souza, Niterói, June 17, 2004.

99. Author's interview with Carlos Eugênio Sarmento Coêlho da Paz, via Facebook, March 27, 2015.

100. Author's interviews with Carlos Eugênio Sarmento Coêlho da Paz, Rio de Janeiro, June 28, 2001, and July 21, 2001 (quotation).

101. Author's interviews with Carlos Eugênio Sarmento Coêlho da Paz, Rio de Janeiro, June 28, 2001, and August 5, 2002.

102. Author's interview with Carlos Eugênio Sarmento Coêlho da Paz, Rio de Janeiro, August 5, 2002.

103. Author's interview with Carlos Eugênio Sarmento Coêlho da Paz, Rio de Janeiro, June 28, 2001.

104. Author's interview with Carlos Eugênio Sarmento Coêlho da Paz, Rio de Janeiro, August 5, 2002.

105. Author's interview with Carlos Eugênio Sarmento Coêlho da Paz, Rio de Janeiro, June 28, 2001.

CHAPTER THIRTEEN   The "American Dream" in Power

1. Secco, *História do PT*, 200.

2. For an overview of the 2002 election, see Bethell and Nicolau, "Politics in Brazil, 1985–2002," in Bethell, *Brazil since 1930*, 274–79. Impressions of the campaign also from my observations in Brazil.

3. Author's interview with Paulo de Tarso Vannuchi, São Paulo, June 18, 2003.

4. André Singer, *Os sentidos do Lulismo* (São Paulo: Companhia das Letras, 2012), 100.

5. On instability, see Abreu and Werneck, "The Brazilian Economy, 1994–2004," 444–46.

6. Andrés Oppenheimer, *Saving the Americas*, trans. Tanya Huntington (Mexico City: Random House Mondadori, 2007), 235, 236 (quotation); Marcio Aith, "Lula representa o sonho norte-americano, mas não a realidade," *Folha de S. Paulo*, June 6, 2002.

7. Spektor, *18 dias*, 41.

8. Bethell and Nicolau, "Politics in Brazil, 1985–2002," 276; Abreu and Werneck, "The Brazilian Economy, 1994–2004," 448–49.

9. Bresser-Pereira, *A construção política do Brasil*, 350.

10. Abreu and Werneck, "The Brazilian Economy, 1994–2004," 446.

11. Author's interview with Aloysio Nunes Ferreira Filho, Brasília, June 22, 2004.

12. Author's interviews with Paulo de Tarso Vannuchi, São Paulo, June 18, 2003, and July 3, 2003. João Carlos Silva, "Jesse Jackson compara Lula a Luther King e Nelson Mandela," *Folha de S. Paulo*, September 29, 2002; see also the documentary by João Moreira Salles, *Atos: A campanha pública de Lula* (2006).

13. Author's interview with Paulo Vannuchi, São Paulo, July 13, 2015.

14. Florência Costa, "Capitalismo de resultados," *IstoÉ*, August 9, 2002.

15. Author's interview with Paulo de Tarso Vannuchi, São Paulo, July 3, 2003.

16. A similar observation is in Secco, *História do PT*, 265.

17. Author's interview with Gilberto Carvalho, São Paulo, August 10, 2002. On seminarians and radical Catholicism, see Serbin, *Needs of the Heart*.

18. Author's interview with Gilberto Carvalho, São Paulo, August 10, 2002.

19. "Lula elogia governo Médici," *Folha de S. Paulo*, August 30, 2002.

20. Elio Gaspari, "Lula 2002 toma Romanée-Conti 1997," *Folha de S. Paulo*, October 9, 2002.

21. Bethell and Nicolau, "Politics in Brazil, 1985–2002," 275, 277, 279; on the election, see also the documentary by João Moreira Salles, *Entreatos: Lula a 30 dias do poder* (2004); Paulo Vannuchi, "Brasil 2002: Como se construiu a vitória do PT," unpublished paper, 2002.

22. Martinho, "A armadilha do novo," 557; among many other analyses of Lula's rise to power, see Singer, *Os sentidos do Lulismo*; McCann, *The Throes of Democracy*, chap. 1; Wendy Hunter, *Transformation of The Workers' Party* (New York: Cambridge University Press, 2010); Kingstone and Ponce, "From Cardoso to Lula"; Love, "The Lula Government in Historical Perspective"; Richard Bourne, *Lula of Brazil* (Berkeley: University of California Press, 2008).

380 Notes to Pages 257–261

23. Author's interview with Paulo Vannuchi, São Paulo, July 3, 2003. "PT monta 'superestrutura' para Lula," *Folha de S. Paulo*, October 28, 2002.

24. Martinho, "A armadilha do novo," 557.

25. Bresser-Pereira, *A construção política do Brasil*, 344–46.

26. Ben Ross Schneider, introduction to *New Order and Progress*, ed. Schneider, 2, 13–14; on ministries and employees, see Barbara Nunberg and Regina Silvia Pacheco, "Public Management Incongruity in 21st Century Brazil," in *New Order and Progress*, 138–41, 143.

27. Aldo Musacchio and Sergio G. Lazzarini, "The Reinvention of State Capitalism in Brazil," in *New Order and Progress*, 118–20, 122–30.

28. Kingstone and Ponce, "From Cardoso to Lula," 115, 121–22.

29. McCann, *The Throes of Democracy*, 39–40.

30. Stefan Schmalz, "The Brazilian Economy: From the Crisis of Import Substitution to the Programa de Aceleração do Crescimento," in *The Political System of Brazil*, ed. Dana de la Fontaine and Thomas Stehnken (Berlin: Springer, 2016), 275–77; Eduardo Cucolo, "Brasil se torna 4° maior credor dos EUA," *Folha de S. Paulo*, November 19, 2009.

31. Rohter, *Brazil on the Rise*, 3, 148–49, 157–59, 163–65, 167; on acquisitions of American companies, see also Cristiane Correa, *Sonho grande* (Rio de Janeiro: Primeira Pessoa, 2013).

32. Bresser-Pereira, *A construção política do Brasil*, 345.

33. B. Schneider, introduction to *New Order and Progress*.

34. Kingstone and Ponce, "From Cardoso to Lula," 105, 111, 115.

35. Singer, *Os sentidos do Lulismo*, 165–66; Gustavo Gantois and Mariana Londres, "Era Lula cria mais empregos que governos FHC, Itamar, Collor e Sarney juntos," *R7*, November 18, 2010; "Governo Lula criou 2,464 milhões de empregos em 4 anos," *O Estado de S. Paulo*, December 24, 2006.

36. Melo, "Political Malaise and the New Politics of Accountability: Representation, Taxation, and the Social Contract," 294n27.

37. Sérgio Costa, Barbara Fritz, and Martina Sproll, "Dilma 2.0: From Economic Growth with Distribution to Stagnation and Increasing Inequalities?," *Latin American Research Review* 46, no. 3 (2015): 22.

38. Rohter, *Brazil on the Rise*, 176; for historical background on the development of Petrobras's exploration capacity, see Priest, "Petrobras in the History of Offshore Oil."

39. Ricardo Batista Amaral, *A vida quer é coragem* (Rio de Janeiro: Sextante, 2011), 171.

40. Rohter, *Brazil on the Rise*, 176–82.

41. Amaral, *A vida quer é coragem*, 173.

42. Priest, "Petrobras in the History of Offshore Oil," 53.

43. Author's interviews with Manoel Cyrillo de Oliveira Netto, Rio de Janeiro, June 21, 2006 (blew up), and July 26, 2007 (self-destruction).

44. Author's interview with Manoel Cyrillo de Oliveira Netto, Gonçalves, July 14, 2015. On Maria Augusta, see Luiza Villaméa, "Companheiras de armas," *IstoÉ*, June 29, 2005.

45. Author's interview with Manoel Cyrillo de Oliveira Netto, Gonçalves, July 14, 2015.

46. Reis, "O Partido dos Trabalhadores: Trajetória, metamorfoses, perspectivas," 524, 526; on consumer credit, see also Singer, *Os sentidos do Lulismo*, 67–68.

47. Singer, *Os sentidos do Lulismo*, 68.

48. Secco, *História do PT*, 206, 43; Kingstone and Ponce, "From Cardoso to Lula," 102–3, 116–17; on public housing, see also Amaral, *A vida quer é coragem*, 198–99.

49. Camila Vital Nunes Pereira, "The Alleviation of Poverty by the Bolsa Família Program, Brazil" (Ph.D. diss., Howard University, 2014), 138.

50. Singer, *Os sentidos do Lulismo*, 69–70, 167; on lack of manipulation, see also Wendy Hunter and Timothy J. Power, "Rewarding Lula: Executive Power, Social Policy, and the Brazilian Elections of 2006," *Latin American Politics and Society* 49, no. 1 (2007): 18.

51. Bresser-Pereira, *A construção política do Brasil*, 346–48.

52. Power, "The Reduction of Poverty and Inequality in Brazil: Political Causes, Political Consequences," 212 (quotation), 213–14, 216, 221–22.

53. B. Schneider, introduction to *New Order and Progress*, 11; see also Costa, Fritz, and Sproll, "Dilma 2.0," 22.

54. Martinho, "A armadilha do novo," 558.

55. Singer, *Os sentidos do Lulismo*; Hunter and Power, "Rewarding Lula."

56. Avritzer, *Impasses da democracia*, 21–22, 28.

57. Singer, *Os sentidos do Lulismo*, passim; Hunter and Power, "Rewarding Lula"; Power, "The Reduction of Poverty and Inequality in Brazil," 227–29.

58. Author's interview with Paulo de Tarso Vannuchi, São Paulo, July 3, 2003.

59. Author's interview with Paulo de Tarso Vannuchi, São Paulo, June 18, 2003.

60. Ibid.

61. Author's interview with Paulo de Tarso Vannuchi, São Paulo, June 18, 2003.

62. Author's interview with Paulo de Tarso Vannuchi, São Paulo, June 7, 2005.

63. Author's interview with Paulo de Tarso Vannuchi, São Paulo, June 18, 2003.

64. Heber Silveira Rocha, "Juventude e políticas públicas: Formação de agenda, elaboração de alternativas e embates no Governo Lula," Master's thesis (Fundação Getúlio Vargas, São Paulo, 2012), 71–74, 79, 120, 129–30; Instituto Cidadania, ed., "Projeto Juventude: Documento de conclusão" (São Paulo: Instituto Cidadania, 2004).

65. "Projeto Juventude: Resumo das intervenções—13/6/2003" (Instituto Cidadania, 2003). I attended the meeting as an observer.

66. Rocha, "Juventude e políticas públicas," 74–75, 78 (juvenile delinquency), 128, 135.

67. Author's interview with Paulo de Tarso Vannuchi, São Paulo, June 7, 2005.

68. Ibid.

69. Costa, Fritz, and Sproll, "Dilma 2.0," 22.

70. Author's interview with Paulo de Tarso Vannuchi, São Paulo, June 7, 2005.

71. Rocha, "Juventude e políticas públicas," 87, 110, 125, 128.

72. Author's interview with Paulo de Tarso Vannuchi, São Paulo, June 7, 2005.

73. Rocha, "Juventude e políticas públicas," 135.

74. "10.06.2010—Projovem assegura inclusão de milhares de jovens em todo o Brasil," http://www.secretariadegoverno.gov.br/noticias/2010/06/10-06-2010-projovem-assegura-inclusao-de-milhares-de-jovens-em-todo-o-brasil.

75. Tufi Machado Soares, Maria Eugénia Ferrão, and Cláudio de Albuquerque Marques, "Análise da evasão no ProJovem Urbano: Uma abordagem através do Modelo de Regressão Logística Multinível," *Ensaio: Avaliação e Políticas Públicas em Educação* 19, no. 73 (2011): 841–60.

76. Amaral, *A vida quer é coragem*, 168–70, 174–75.

77. Maria Celina D'Araujo, *Governo Lula* (Rio de Janeiro: Centro de Pesquisa e Documentação de História Contemporânea do Brasil/Fundação Getúlio Vargas, 2007), 56.

78. Secco, *História do PT*, 206–7.

79. B. Schneider, introduction to *New Order and Progress*, 12.

80. Kingstone and Ponce, "From Cardoso to Lula," 98, 102, 119–21.

81. Idelber Avelar, "The June 2013 Uprisings and the Waning of Lulismo in Brazil: Of Antagonism, Contradiction, and Oxymoron," *Luso-Brazilian Review* 54, no. 1 (2017): 16, 17 (quotation).

82. Miguel Carter, "Epilogue. Broken Promise: The Land Reform Debacle under the PT Governments," in *Challenging Social Inequality: The Landless Rural Workers Movement and Agrarian Reform in Brazil*, ed. Miguel Carter

(Durham: Duke University Press, 2015), 413–28; Sue Branford, "Working with Governments: The MST's Experience with the Cardoso and Lula Administrations," in *Challenging Social Inequality*, 331–50.

83. Love, "The Lula Government in Historical Perspective," 306.

84. Schmalz, "The Brazilian Economy," 273.

85. Bresser-Pereira, *A construção política do Brasil*, 384; Rohter, *Brazil on the Rise*, 152–56, 164–65.

86. Frei Betto, *Calendário do poder* (Rio de Janeiro: Rocco, 2007), 524, 526–27; on the limitations of Bolsa Família, see also Pereira, "The Alleviation of Poverty by the Bolsa Família Program, Brazil," 141–42, 146–48, 150–52.

87. For political analysis of the mensalão, see Kingstone and Ponce, "From Cardoso to Lula," 120–21.

88. Nunberg and Pacheco, "Public Management Incongruity in 21st Century Brazil," 138–41.

89. Author's interview with Paulo de Tarso Vannuchi, São Paulo, June 7, 2005.

90. Author's interviews with Paulo de Tarso Vannuchi, São Paulo, July 3, 2003, and June 7, 2005 (quotation, corruption).

91. Luiz Inácio Lula da Silva, "Apresentação," in *Reforma política e cidadania*, ed. Maria Victoria Benevides, Paulo Vannuchi, and Fábio Kerche (São Paulo: Editora Fundação Perseu Abramo, 2003), 11.

92. David Samuels, "Financiamento de campanha e eleições no Brasil: O que podemos aprender com o 'caixa um' e propostas de reforma," in *Reforma política e cidadania*, 385; for an overview of corruption and the political system, see Avritzer, *Impasses da democracia*.

93. Author's interview with Paulo de Tarso Vannuchi, São Paulo, June 7, 2005.

94. "Lula exime governo e cobra PT por erros," *Folha de S. Paulo*, July 18, 2005.

95. Secco, *História do PT*, 227–33.

96. Frei Betto, "Obrigado, Lula," http://www.vermelho.org.br/noticia .php?id_noticia=143550; Amaral, *A vida quer é coragem*, 259–60; Avritzer, *Impasses da democracia*, 17–18.

97. Melo, "Political Malaise and the New Politics of Accountability," 279.

98. "Ex-preso político assumirá ministério," *Folha de S. Paulo*, December 14, 2005. Author's interview with Paulo de Tarso Vannuchi, São Paulo, June 5, 2006.

99. Author's interview with Paulo de Tarso Vannuchi, São Paulo, June 5, 2006.

100. Ibid.

101. Ibid.

102. Author's interview with Paulo de Tarso Vannuchi, São Paulo, July 3, 2003.

103. Author's interview with Paulo de Tarso Vannuchi, São Paulo, June 5, 2006.

104. "Depoimento de Paulo Vannuchi," in Alonso and Dolhnikoff, eds., *1964: Do golpe à democracia*, 375–76.

105. Author's interview with Paulo de Tarso Vannuchi, São Paulo, June 5, 2006.

106. Ibid. Nina Schneider, "Breaking the 'Silence' of the Military Regime: New Politics of Memory in Brazil," *Bulletin of Latin American Research* 30, no. 2 (2011): 198–212.

107. Author's interview with Paulo de Tarso Vannuchi, São Paulo, June 5, 2006.

108. Secretaria Especial dos Direitos Humanos, *Direito à memória e à verdade*.

109. Frederico Vasconcelos, "Governo desiste de recorrer de decisão sobre o Araguaia," *Folha de S. Paulo*, September 23, 2007.

110. Marco Weissheimer, "'Esquerda errou ao virar as costas para questão dos mortos e desaparecidos,'" *Sul21*, May 23, 2016, https://www.sul21.com.br/entrevistas-2/2016/05/esquerda-errou-ao-virar-as-costas-para-questao-dos-mortos-e-desaparecidos/; "PNDH-3: Verdade, justiça e reparação. Entrevista especial com Jair Krischke," *IHU On-Line*, January 9, 2010, http://www.ihu.unisinos.br/entrevistas/28780-pndh-3-verdade-justica-e-reparacao-entrevista-especial-com-jair-krischke.

111. Vannildo Mendes and Tânia Monteiro, "Lula: 'Desaparecidos são ferida aberta,'" *O Estado de S. Paulo*, August 30, 2007; Eliane Cantanhêde, "Vários mundos, dois governos," *Folha de S. Paulo*, August 30, 2007; Weissheimer, "'Esquerda errou ao virar as costas para questão dos mortos e desaparecidos.'"

112. Author's interview with Paulo de Tarso Vannuchi, São Paulo, June 5, 2006.

113. N. Schneider, "Breaking the 'Silence' of the Military Regime," 198.

114. Caio Quero, "Entenda a polêmica sobre a Comissão Nacional da Verdade," *BBC*, January 13, 2010, https://www.bbc.com/portuguese/noticias/2010/01/100112_comissao_qanda_cq.

115. Paulo Vannuchi, "Direitos humanos e o fim do esquecimento," in *10 anos de governos pós-neoliberais no Brasil: Lula e Dilma*, ed. Emir Sader, 337–59 (São Paulo and Rio de Janeiro: Boitempo and FLACSO Brasil, 2013), 343 (ideological attack), 356–57, 358 (lynching), 359.

116. N. Schneider, "Breaking the 'Silence' of the Military Regime," 198–99.

117. Pedro Widmar, "The Truth Commission," *The Rio Times*, January 19, 2010, https://riotimesonline.com/brazil-news/rio-politics/the-pndh-3-and-the-truth-commission/.

118. "PNDH-3: Verdade, justiça e reparação. Entrevista especial com Jair Krischke."

119. Glenda Mezarobba, "Justiça de transição e a comissão da verdade," in *1964: Do golpe à democracia*, 353.

120. Quero, "Entenda a polêmica sobre a Comissão Nacional da Verdade."

121. N. Schneider, "Breaking the 'Silence' of the Military Regime," 201.

122. Bernardo Mello Franco, "Corte condena Brasil por 62 mortes no Araguaia," *Folha de S. Paulo*, December 15, 2010; Aton Fon Filho and Suzana Figueiredo, "Revistando a Anistia—Os fantasmas do passado, os temores do presente, as sombras sobre o futuro," in *Direitos Humanos no Brasil 2011: Relatório da Rede Social de Justiça e Direitos Humanos*, ed. Tatiana Merlino and Maria Luisa Mendonça (São Paulo: Rede Social de Justiça e Direitos Humanos, 2011), 135–41.

123. "Depoimento de Paulo Vannuchi," 376.

124. Author's interview with Paulo de Tarso Vannuchi, São Paulo, June 5, 2006. Vannuchi, "Direitos humanos e o fim do esquecimento."

125. Author's interview with Paulo de Tarso Vannuchi, São Paulo, July 13, 2015; Secretaria Especial dos Direitos Humanos, *Brasil direitos humanos, 2008* (Brasília: SEDH, 2008).

126. Author's interview with Paulo de Tarso Vannuchi, São Paulo, June 5, 2006.

127. Ibid.

128. Author's interview with Paulo de Tarso Vannuchi, São Paulo, June 5, 2006. Paulo Vannuchi, "Avanços nos direitos humanos," *Folha de S. Paulo*, May 14, 2006; for an example of bipartisan collaboration, see Paulo Vannuchi and Paulo Sérgio Pinheiro, "Não esquecer Corumbiara," *Folha de S. Paulo*, August 13, 2006; on continuity between Fernando Henrique and Lula, see Paulo Sérgio Pinheiro, preface to *Relatório Nacional sobre os Direitos Humanos no Brasil* (São Paulo: Núcleo de Estudos da Violência, University of São Paulo, 2010), 9–10; Andréa Barros, "'Não existem direitos humanos à brasileira,'" *O Estado de S. Paulo*, June 4, 2006 (honest broker); on China, see Denise Chrispim Marin, "Diálogo com China vai driblar direitos humanos," *Folha de S. Paulo*, November 21, 2006.

129. Author's interview with Paulo de Tarso Vannuchi, São Paulo, June 5, 2006. U.S. Department of State, "Brazil," http://www.state.gov/j/drl/rls/hrrpt/2005/61718.htm.

130. *Relatório Nacional sobre os Direitos Humanos no Brasil* (São Paulo: Núcleo de Estudos da Violência, University of São Paulo, 2010), 9 (quotation),

11–12, 17–18. For 2016, see Thiago Amâncio, "Mortes violentas crescem e atingem maior número, já registrado no país," *Folha de S. Paulo*, October 30, 2017. For 2017, see Shasta Darlington, "A Year of Violence Sees Brazil's Murder Rate Hit Record High," *New York Times*, August 10, 2018, https://www.nytimes.com/2018/08/10/world/americas/brazil-murder-rate-record.html.

131. McCann, *The Throes of Democracy*, chap. 2; Maria Helena Moreira Alves and Philip Evanson, *Living in the Crossfire* (Philadelphia: Temple University Press, 2011).

132. Luciana Constantino, "Chacinas podem levar à aparição de novos PCCs," *Folha de S. Paulo*, May 22, 2006 (outlaws); Márcio Sampaio de Castro, "Maltratados direitos fundamentais" *Valor Econômico*, January 19, 2007.

133. Vannuchi and Pinheiro, "Não esquecer Corumbiara."

134. Author's interview with Márcio Araújo de Lacerda, Brumadinho, June 22, 2003. Author's interview with Ciro Gomes, Brasília, July 8, 2003.

135. Author's interview with Tânia Bacelar, Brasília, July 8, 2003.

136. Author's interview with Márcio Araújo de Lacerda, Brumadinho, June 22, 2003.

137. Author's interviews with Márcio Araújo de Lacerda, Brumadinho, June 22, 2003 (quotations), and June 4, 2005.

138. Author's conversation with Márcio Araújo de Lacerda, Brasília, June 23, 2004.

139. Author's interviews with Márcio Araújo de Lacerda, Brumadinho, June 22, 2003, and June 4, 2005.

140. Author's interview with Márcio Araújo de Lacerda, Brumadinho, June 4, 2005.

141. Bruno Peres, "Dilma e Lula irão juntos à conclusão da transposição do São Francisco," *Valor Econômico*, August 21, 2015; Tereza Cruvinel, "Dilma inaugura a obra mais importante para o Nordeste," *Brasil 247*, August 17, 2015, https://www.brasil247.com/pt/blog/terezacruvinel/193206/Dilma-inaugura-a-obra-mais-importante-para-o-Nordeste.htm; Augusto Nunes, "Lula usou o São Francisco para inventar a obra que vira ruína sem ter existido," *Veja.com*, December 11, 2015, https://veja.abril.com.br/blog/augusto-nunes/lula-usou-o-sao-francisco-para-inventar-a-obra-que-vira-ruina-sem-ter-existido/.

142. Author's interview with Márcio Araújo de Lacerda, Brumadinho, June 22, 2003.

143. "Lista relaciona 31 beneficiários de R$ 56 mi," *Folha de S. Paulo*, August 2, 2005; Marta Salomon and Rubens Valente, "Saque de R$ 457 mil derruba assessor de Ciro," *Folha de S. Paulo*, August 3, 2005.

144. Author's interview with Márcio Araújo de Lacerda, São Paulo, June 2, 2006. Eduardo Scolese, "Fora do governo, Ciro ataca PT e Palocci," *Folha de S. Paulo*, April 1, 2006.

145. Author's interview with Márcio Araújo de Lacerda, Belo Horizonte, July 8, 2015.

146. Leonel Rocha, "Os problemas do amigo de Dilma," *Época*, February 26, 2010.

147. Author's interview with Márcio Araújo de Lacerda, Brumadinho, June 22, 2003; recording by Márcio Araújo de Lacerda, Brumadinho, January 22, 2007, as complement to interviews with author.

148. Author's interview with Márcio Araújo de Lacerda, Belo Horizonte, July 8, 2015. On the 2008 election, see, for example, Paulo Peixoto and Fernanda Odilla, "Lacerda supera revés de campanha, vence 2º turno e dá fôlego para Aécio," *Folha de S. Paulo*, October 27, 2008.

149. *Plano estratégico de Belo Horizonte 2030: A cidade que queremos* (Belo Horizonte: Prefeitura de Belo Horizonte, 2010).

150. Leonardo Augusto and Alice Maciel, "Prefeito de BH emprega 11 antigos funcionários em cargos de confiança," *O Estado de Minas*, May 25, 2012.

151. Author's interview with Márcio Araújo de Lacerda, Belo Horizonte, July 8, 2015.

152. "Márcio Lacerda, de Belo Horizonte lidera ranking dos prefeitos de 8 capitais," Datafolha, http://datafolha.folha.uol.com.br/opiniaopublica/2010 /12 /1223779-marcio-lacerda-de-belo-horizonte-lidera-ranking-dos-prefeitos -de-8-capitais.shtml.

153. Author's interview with Adriano Diogo, São Paulo, July 1, 2003.

154. Rohter, *Brazil on the Rise*, 150.

155. Authors interviews with Adriano Diogo, São Paulo, June 15, 2003, June 29, 2003, July 1, 2003, and June 9, 2005.

156. Authors interviews with Adriano Diogo, São Paulo, June 15, 2003, June 29, 2003 (quotation), July 1, 2003, and June 9, 2005.

157. Authors interviews with Adriano Diogo, São Paulo, June 15, 2003, June 29, 2003, July 1, 2003, June 9, 2005 (quotations), and June 10, 2005. My observations at Parque do Ibirapuera, June 29, 2003.

158. Author's interview with Adriano Diogo, June 9, 2005.

159. Author's interview with Aloysio Nunes Ferreira Filho, São Paulo, June 7, 2004.

160. Author's interview with Aloysio Nunes Ferreira Filho, Brasília, June 22, 2004.

161. Author's interview with Aloysio Nunes Ferreira Filho, São Paulo, June 14, 2006.

162. Author's interviews with Arlete Diogo, São Paulo, June 16, 2003, June 15, 2005, and June 14, 2006 (quotations).

163. Author's interview with Colombo Vieira de Souza, Niterói, June 17, 2004.

164. Author's interview with Jessie Jane Vieira de Souza, Niterói, June 17, 2004.

165. Author's interview with Jessie Jane Vieira de Souza, Niterói, July 16, 2015.

166. Author's interviews with Carlos Eugênio Sarmento Coêlho da Paz, São Paulo, June 30, 2003, Rio de Janeiro, July 11, 2003 (rupture), Rio de Janeiro, June 22, 2005, Rio de Janeiro, June 21, 2006, and Rio de Janeiro, August 27, 2007 (domesticated, troubled, glamorous). On domesticated democracy, see Luis Felipe Miguel, "A democracia domesticada: Bases antidemocráticas do pensamento democrático contemporâneo," *DADOS* 45, no. 3 (2002): 483–511; on household water, see Kingstone and Ponce, "From Cardoso to Lula," 117–18.

167. Secco, *História do PT*, 241; Bresser-Pereira, *A construção política do Brasil*, 344.

168. Author's interview with Paulo de Tarso Vannuchi, São Paulo, June 7, 2005.

169. Kingstone and Ponce, "From Cardoso to Lula," 99.

170. Ibid., 102.

171. Nunberg and Pacheco, "Public Management Incongruity in 21st Century Brazil," 146–55.

172. Bresser-Pereira, *A construção política do Brasil*, 345–46, 348–51, 384.

173. Kingstone and Ponce, "From Cardoso to Lula," 123.

174. B. Schneider, introduction to *New Order and Progress*, 11, 13–14.

175. José Dirceu, "Só repressão não resolve," *Jornal do Brasil*, July 12, 2007.

176. Avelar, "The June 2013 Uprisings and the Waning of Lulismo in Brazil," 18; emphasis in original.

177. Reis, "O Partido dos Trabalhadores," 523–24.

178. B. Schneider, introduction to *New Order and Progress*, 11–12.

179. Singer, *Os sentidos do Lulismo*, 129–30.

180. Power, "The Reduction of Poverty and Inequality in Brazil," 216.

CHAPTER FOURTEEN   An Ex-Revolutionary at the Helm
Encounters Turbulence and Hostility

1. Background on Dilma from the biography by Amaral, *A vida quer é coragem*; see also Luiz Maklouf Carvalho, "As armas e os varões: a educação política e sentimental de Dilma Rousseff," *Piauí*, April 2009, 22–31; on Dilma's revolutionary past and the foundation of VAR-Palmares, see also Green, *Exile within Exiles*.

2. Author's interview with Adriano Diogo, São Paulo, July 2, 2015.

3. Background on Dilma and the 2010 election from Amaral, *A vida quer é coragem*, generally, 301 (quotations).

4. Author's interviews with Arlete Diogo, São Paulo, July 12, 2015; Jessie Jane Vieira de Souza, Niterói, July 16, 2015; Colombo Vieira de Souza, Niterói, July 16, 2015; Manoel Cyrillo de Oliveira Netto, Gonçalves, Minas Gerais, July 14, 2015; Márcio Araújo de Lacerda, Belo Horizonte, July 8, 2015; and Adriano Diogo, São Paulo, July 2, 2015.

5. Author's interview with Paulo de Tarso Vannuchi, São Paulo, July 13, 2015.

6. Wendy Hunter, "The 2010 Elections in Brazil," *Electoral Studies*, no. 31 (2012): 225–28.

7. Ricardo Setti, "Com 11 milhões de votos, Aloysio Nunes (PSDB) é o senador mais votado da história," *Veja Online*, October 3, 2010. Author's interview with Aloysio Nunes Ferreira Filho, Brasília, July 6, 2015.

8. Author's interview with Aloysio Nunes Ferreira Filho, Brasília, July 6, 2015.

9. Ibid.

10. Juliana Bertazzo, "An Initial Survey of the Dilma Rousseff Administration in Brazil," *Critical Sociology* 38, no. 6 (2012): 890.

11. Power, "The Reduction of Poverty and Inequality in Brazil," 214.

12. Bresser-Pereira, *A construção política do Brasil*, 354–59, 368, 387, 389–92; on deindustrialization, see also Secco, *História do PT*, 269; Costa, Fritz, and Sproll, "Dilma 2.0," 21.

13. Rafael Fagundes Cagnin et al., "A gestão macroeconômica do governo Dilma (2011 e 2012)," *Novos Estudos Cebrap*, no. 97 (2013): 169–85.

14. Timothy J. Power, "Continuity in a Changing Brazil: The Transition from Lula to Dilma," in *Brazil under The Workers' Party: Continuity and Change from Lula to Dilma*, ed. Fábio Castro, Kees Koonings, and Marianne Wiesebron (New York: Palgrave Macmillan, 2014), 31–32.

15. Ibid. On combatting corruption, see also Manuel Balán, "Surviving Corruption in Brazil: Lula's and Dilma's Success Despite Corruption Allegations, and Its Consequences," *Journal of Politics in Latin America* 6, no. 3 (2014): 80–84.

16. Balán, "Surviving Corruption in Brazil," 82.

17. John D. French and Alexandre Fortes, "Nurturing Hope, Deepening Democracy, and Combating Inequalities in Brazil: Lula, the Workers' Party, and Dilma Rousseff's 2010 Election as President," *Labor: Studies in Working-Class History of the Americas* 9, no. 1 (2012): 18–19.

18. Avritzer, *Impasses da democracia*, 120; on urban relocations and other problems related to the 2016 Olympics, see also the documentary *The Lords of the Rings*, in *Real Sports with Bryant Gumbel* (HBO, 2016).

19. Power, "Continuity in a Changing Brazil," 30.

20. Secco, *História do PT*, 280–81.

21. Musacchio and Lazzarini, "The Reinvention of State Capitalism in Brazil," 130.

22. Bresser-Pereira, *A construção política do Brasil*, 359–61; on the economy in 2013, see also Ney Figueiredo, "Os empresários e os movimentos de rua," in *Junho de 2013: A sociedade enfrenta o estado*, ed. Rubens Figueiredo (São Paulo: Summus Editorial, 2014), 61.

23. Cláudia Izique, "Não foi só pelos 20 centavos," in Figueiredo, *Junho de 2013*, 15.

24. Rubens Figueiredo, "Apresentação," in Figueiredo, *Junho de 2013*, 7; Izique, "Não foi só pelos 20 centavos," in ibid.; on the uniqueness of the Brazilian protests, see Melo, "Political Malaise and the New Politics of Accountability: Representation, Taxation, and the Social Contract," in B. Schneider, *New Order and Progress*, 275; on higher estimates of numbers of protestors, see Avelar, "The June 2013 Uprisings and the Waning of Lulismo in Brazil," 19.

25. Luiz Eduardo Soares, *Rio de Janeiro* (São Paulo: Companhia das Letras, 2015), 192–93, 211–13, 215.

26. Izique, "Não foi só pelos 20 centavos," 18–19.

27. Soares, *Rio de Janeiro*, 197–98 (quotations), 201, 208–10; for an overview of the protests, see Figueiredo, *Junho de 2013*; Maria Borba, Natasha Felizi, and João Paulo Reys, eds., *Brasil em movimento* (Rio de Janeiro: Rocco, 2014); Flavio Morgenstern, *Por trás da máscara* (Rio de Janeiro: Record, 2015); Avritzer, *Impasses da democracia*; on polyphony of demands, see also Avelar, "The June 2013 Uprisings and the Waning of Lulismo in Brazil."

28. For rejection of violence, see Roberto Macedo, "Uma visão econômica e política dos protestos juninos," in Figueiredo, *Junho de 2013*, 59.

29. Ney Figueiredo, "Os empresários e os movimentos de rua," 61–63.

30. Avelar, "The June 2013 Uprisings and the Waning of Lulismo in Brazil," 21.

31. Rubens Figueiredo, "Apresentação," in Figueiredo, *Junho de 2013*, 8.

32. Rubens Figueiredo, "A 'espiral do silêncio' e a escalada da insatisfação," in ibid., 23.

33. Bernardo Sorj, "Entre o local e o global," in Figueiredo, *Junho de 2013*, 92.

34. Similar observation in Soares, *Rio de Janeiro*, 194.

35. Secco, *História do PT*, 271, 76 (suppress), 77, 78 (confrontation), n28. Author's interview with Adriano Diogo, São Paulo, September 21, 2013.

36. Denis Rosenfeld, "Entre a libertação e a usurpação," in Figueiredo, *Junho de 2013*, 138.

37. Izique, "Não foi só pelos 20 centavos," 19 (quotation), 20.

38. Rosenfeld, "Entre a libertação e a usurpação," in Figueiredo, *Junho de 2013*, 138, 44.

39. Secco, *História do PT*, 272–73; Rosenfeld, "Entre a libertação e a usurpação," 139, 141–44; Avelar, "The June 2013 Uprisings and the Waning of Lulismo in Brazil," 21–22.

40. Author's interview with Paulo de Tarso Vannuchi, São Paulo, July 13, 2015.

41. Izique, "Não foi só pelos 20 centavos," 19.

42. Author's interview with Márcio de Araújo Lacerda, Belo Horizonte, July 8, 2015. Fernanda Brescia, "Filho do prefeito de BH anuncia desligamento do Comitê da Copa," *G1*, October 27, 2011, http://g1.globo.com/minas-gerais /noticia/2011/10/filho-do-prefeito-de-bh-anuncia-desligamento-do-comite -da-copa.html.

43. Author's interview with Márcio de Araújo Lacerda, Belo Horizonte, July 8, 2015.

44. Power, "The Reduction of Poverty and Inequality in Brazil," 230–31.

45. Melo, "Political Malaise and the New Politics of Accountability," 269–70, 279–91.

46. Figueiredo, "A 'espiral do silêncio' e a escalada da insatisfação," 24, 28, 33–37; on federal publicity spending, see also Macedo, "Uma visão econômica e política dos protestos juninos," 50; on nonpartisan and middle-class status of protestors, see also Bernardo Sorj, "Entre o local e o global," 93, 97; Tulio Kahn, "A segurança pública e as manifestações de junho de 2013," in ibid., 118–19, 122; on detachment from the PT and Maluf, and also on private health insurance, see Melo, "Political Malaise and the New Politics of Accountability," 276, 278, 281, 293, n17; on social diversity in the protests, see Soares, *Rio de Janeiro*, 196–97, 201–2, 204; on poor quality of public transport, see also José Nêumanne Pinto, "A multidão poderosa virou plebe ignara e tudo ficou como dantes na República de Abrantes," in Figueiredo, *Junho de 2013*, 105; on government ineffectiveness and distrust of politicians, see Roberto Pires, "The Midlife of Participatory Institutions in Brazil," *Latin American Research Review* 46, no. 3 (2015): 28–30; Nunberg and Pacheco, "Public Management Incongruity in 21st Century Brazil"; on government ineffectiveness as a cause of the protests, see Rodrigo Rodrigues-Silveira, "Intergovernmental Relations and State Capacity in Brazil: Challenges for Dilma's Second Term and Beyond," *Latin American Research Review* 46, no. 3 (2015): 31–33; Fábio de Castro and Renata Motta, "Environmental Politics under Dilma: Changing Relations between the Civil Society and the State," *Latin American Research Review* 46, no. 3 (2015): 25–27. Information on middle-class nature of protests (in São Paulo) from author's interview with Adriano Diogo, São Paulo, September 21, 2013.

47. Figueiredo, "A 'espiral do silêncio' e a escalada da insatisfação," 33.

48. Tulio Kahn, "A segurança pública e as manifestações de junho de 2013," 125.

49. Soares, *Rio de Janeiro*, 202, 213.

50. Macedo, "Uma visão econômica e política dos protestos juninos," 58.

51. Secco, *História do PT*, 270.

52. Marcelo S. Tognozzi, "A força das redes sociais," in Figueiredo, *Junho de 2013*; on bypassing of leaders and declining institutions, see also Bernardo Sorj, "Entre o local e o global," 89–90.

53. Balán, "Surviving Corruption in Brazil," 83, 85; Melo, "Political Malaise and the New Politics of Accountability," 272.

54. Bresser-Pereira, *A construção política do Brasil*, 359–61; Rosenfeld, "Entre a libertação e a usurpação," 134; Avritzer, *Impasses da democracia*, 16.

55. Bresser-Pereira, *A construção política do Brasil*, 361–62.

56. B. Schneider, introduction to *New Order and Progress*, 2, 10.

57. Marco Antonio Villa, *Uma país partido* (São Paulo: LeYa, 2014), 24, 38; Mihir Zaveri, Susan Carroll, and Ben Tavener, "Brazilian scandal centers on purchase of Pasadena refinery," *Houston Chronicle*, November 8, 2015.

58. Villa, *Uma país partido*, 68, 72–73.

59. Avritzer, *Impasses da democracia*, 12, 17, 19, 135, n28.

60. Ministério Público Federal, "Caso Lava Jato: entenda o caso," http://lavajato.mpf.mp.br/entenda-o-caso.

61. Elio Gaspari, "Há dez anos, o juiz Moro disse tudo," *Folha de S. Paulo*, December 21, 2014; Edmondo Berselli, "The Crisis and Transformation of Italian Politics," *Daedalus* 130, no. 3 (2001): 1–24.

62. Tom Schoenberg, Jessica Brice, and Erik Larson, "Brazil 'Carwash' Probe Yields Largest-Ever Corruption Penalty," *Bloomberg*, December 21, 2016, https://www.bloomberg.com/news/articles/2016-12-21/odebrecht-braskem -agree-to-carwash-penalty-of-3-5-billion.

63. B. Schneider, introduction to *New Order and Progress*, 10; Tyler Priest, "Petrobras in the History of Offshore Oil," 56, 70–72.

64. Marianne Braig, Timothy J. Power, and Lucio Rennó, "Brazil 2015 and Beyond: The Aftermath of the 2014 Elections and Implications for Dilma's Second Term," *Latin American Research Review* 46, no. 3 (2015): 15–17; Villa, *Uma país partido*.

65. Author's interview with Aloysio Nunes Ferreira Filho, Brasília, July 6, 2015.

66. Villa, *Uma país partido*, 142–43, 156.

67. Author's interview with Aloysio Nunes Ferreira Filho, Brasília, July 6, 2015.

68. Author's interviews with Adriano Diogo, São Paulo, September 21, 2013, and July 2, 2015. I participated in and observed the work of the São Paulo commission on September 20, 2013.

69. Glenda Mezarobba, "Lies Engraved on Marble and Truths Lost Forever," *Sur Journal* 12, no. 21 (2015): 97–104; Glenda Mezarobba, "Justiça de transição e a comissão da verdade," in Alonso and Dolhnikoff, *1964: Do golpe à democracia*, 352–56.

70. Author's interview with Márcio de Araújo Lacerda, Belo Horizonte, July 8, 2015.

71. Kenneth P. Serbin, "Desarmando o extremismo," *O Estado de S. Paulo*, November 9, 2014; on the audit request, see Andreza Matais, Vera Rosa, and Beatriz Bulla, "PSDB de Aécio Neves pede auditoria na votação," *O Estado de S. Paulo*, October 30, 2014.

72. Braig, Power, and Rennó, "Brazil 2015 and Beyond," 16; see also Avritzer, *Impasses da democracia*, 44–45, 126.

73. Bresser-Pereira, *A construção política do Brasil*, 361–62.

74. "Multidão vai às ruas contra Dilma e assusta o governo," *Folha de S. Paulo*, March 16, 2015; "Manifestantes protestam contra Dilma em todos os estados, DF e exterior," *G1*, March 15, 2015, http://g1.globo.com/politica /noticia/2015/03/manifestantes-protestam-contra-dilma-em-estados-no-df-e -no-exterio.html.

75. Avritzer, *Impasses da democracia*, 118.

76. Braig, Power, and Rennó, "Brazil 2015 and Beyond," 16–17.

CHAPTER FIFTEEN   Brazil Five Decades after the Kidnapping

1. Unless otherwise noted, all quotations of Manoel in this chapter from author's interview with Manoel Cyrillo de Oliveira Netto, Gonçalves, Minas Gerais, July 14, 2015.

2. On this point, see "21st Century Golpismo: A NACLA Roundtable," *NACLA Report on the Americas* 48, no. 4 (2016): 328.

3. For an overview of this problem, see Timothy J. Power, *The Political Right in Postauthoritarian Brazil* (University Park: Pennsylvania State University Press, 2000).

4. Author's interviews with Manoel Cyrillo de Oliveira Netto, Rio de Janeiro, June 19, 2006, June 20, 2006 (semidemocracy), July 26, 2007, and August 1, 2007.

5. Author's interview with Adriano Diogo, São Paulo, July 2, 2015. Adriano quoted in Elaine Patrícia Cruz, "CPI das universidades sugere que trote

seja considerado crime de tortura," *Agência Brasil,* March 10, 2015; Ulysses Tassinari, "Comissão Parlamentar de Inquérito constituída pelo Ato nº 56, de 2014, com a finalidade de investigar as violações dos direitos humanos e demais ilegalidades ocorridas no âmbito das Universidades do Estado de São Paulo ocorridas nos chamados 'trotes,' festas e no seu cotidiano acadêmico. Relatório Final" (São Paulo: Assembleia Legislativa do Estado de São Paulo, 2015).

6. Author's interview with Adriano Diogo, São Paulo, July 2, 2015.

7. Ibid. On coalition management, see Melo, "Political Malaise and the New Politics of Accountability," 276.

8. Author's interview with Adriano Diogo, São Paulo, July 2, 2015.

9. Author's interview with Arlete Diogo, São Paulo, July 12, 2015.

10. Ibid. For description and investigation of the sticker, see "Governo pede punição para quem fez adesivo de Dilma com pernas abertas," *VR14,* July 2, 2015, https://www.tribunapr.com.br/noticias/politica/governo-cobra -punicao-para-quem-fez-adesivo-de-dilma-com-as-pernas-abertas/; on the new conservatism, a phenomenon especially involving the traditional middle class and including attitudes of intolerance and support for free-market and anticorruption measures, see Avritzer, *Impasses da democracia,* 115, 128, 131.

11. All quotations of Jessie and Colombo in this chapter from author's interviews with Jessie Jane Vieira de Souza and Colombo Vieira de Souza, Niterói, July 16, 2015.

12. Unless otherwise noted, all quotations of Márcio in this chapter from author's interview with Márcio Araújo de Lacerda, Belo Horizonte, July 8, 2015.

13. Author's interview with Josué Costa Valadão, Belo Horizonte, July 8, 2015.

14. Author's interview with Márcio Araújo de Lacerda, Belo Horizonte, July 8, 2015.

15. Information on emphasis on preschools also from author's interview with Beatriz de Oliveira Góes, Belo Horizonte, July 8, 2015. Information on preschools also from Prefeitura Municipal de Belo Horizonte, "Informe: In-auguração da UMEI Mantiqueira e da Escola Municipal Jardim Leblon; almoço no Restaurante Popular I e visita às obras na regional noroeste" (2015).

16. Author's interview with Márcio Araújo de Lacerda, Belo Horizonte, July 8, 2015.

17. Information on adaptation to a political role also from author's inter-views with Régis Augusto Souto, Belo Horizonte, July 8, 2015, and Pier Gior-gio Senesi Filho, Belo Horizonte, July 8, 2015.

18. On the National Mayors' Conference see, for example, "Presidente da FNP se reúne com parlamentares," *Frente Nacional de Prefeitos. Informativo 79*

(2015). Author's interview with Márcio Araújo de Lacerda, Belo Horizonte, July 8, 2015.

19. Prefeitura Municipal de Belo Horizonte, "Políticas públicas de BH são apresentadas no Vaticano," news release, 2015, http://portalpbh.pbh.gov.br /pbh/contents.do?evento=conteudo&idConteudo=203661&chPlc=203661; "Vatican to Host Meetings on Climate Change, Human Trafficking," *Vatican Radio*, July 15, 2015, https://www.crsdop.org/Vatican-to-host-meetings-on -Climate-Change-Human-Trafficking?lang=fr.

20. For background on MOVE, see "Transporte Rápido por Ônibus, o BRT, de Belo Horizonte vai se chamar Move," *Hoje em Dia*, August 11, 2013, https://www.hojeemdia.com.br/horizontes/transporte-r%C3%A1pido-por-% C3%B4nibus-o-brt-de-belo-horizonte-vai-se-chamar-move-1.185010; Empresa de Transportes e Trânsito de Belo Horizonte, "MOVE: Perguntas Frequentes," http://www.bhtrans.pbh.gov.br/portal/page/portal/portalpublico /Temas/Onibus/MOVE/perguntas-frequentes-MOVE.

21. Author's notes from talk by Leonardo Boff, São Paulo, July 13, 2015.

22. All quotations of Paulo in this chapter from author's interview with Paulo de Tarso Vannuchi, São Paulo, July 13, 2015.

23. Unless otherwise noted, all quotations of Aloysio in this chapter from author's interview with Aloysio Nunes Ferreira Filho, Brasília, July 6, 2015. On the Fiscal Responsibility Law, see chapter 12.

24. Speech by Aloysio Nunes Ferreira Filho, Federal Senate, Brasília, July 6, 2015.

25. On compromise and details of the bills, see "Votação da maioridade penal na Câmara pode levar à retomada do debate no Senado," *Veja*, online edition, April 4, 2015.

26. Carla Gullo and Maria Laura Neves, "A mulher do presidente," *Marie Claire*, April 2009.

27. Avelar, "The June 2013 Uprisings and the Waning of Lulismo in Brazil," 11.

28. Melo, "Political Malaise and the New Politics of Accountability," 280.

29. "Maior manifestação da história do País aumenta pressão por saída de Dilma," *O Estado de S. Paulo*, March 13, 2016; "Juiz Sergio Moro, da Lava Jato, é exaltado como herói em protestos," *Folha de S. Paulo*, March 13, 2016.

30. "Perícia vê ação de Dilma em decretos, mas não identifica nas pedaladas," *G1*, June 27, 2016, http://g1.globo.com/politica/noticia/2016/06/pericia -ve-acao-de-dilma-em-decretos-mas-nao-identifica-nas-pedaladas.html.

31. Aloysio Nunes Ferreira Filho, "A farsa do golpe," *Folha de S. Paulo*, August 31, 2016.

32. I observed the proceedings of this committee on April 28, 2016.

33. Ferreira Filho, "A farsa do golpe."

34. Mariana Simões, "Brazil's New President, Jair Bolsonaro, in His Own Words," *New York Times*, October 28, 2018, https://www.nytimes.com/2018/10/28/world/americas/brazil-president-jair-bolsonaro-quotes.html.

35. On the end of an era, see also Avritzer, *Impasses da democracia*, 109.

36. B. Schneider, introduction to *New Order and Progress*, 1.

37. On the shifting balance between prosperity and tolerance of malfeasance, see Melo, "Political Malaise and the New Politics of Accountability," 280.

REFERENCES

"21st Century Golpismo: A NACLA Roundtable." *NACLA Report on the Americas* 48, no. 4 (2016): 322–33.

Abreu, Marcelo de Paiva. "The Brazilian Economy, 1930–1980." In Bethell, *Brazil since 1930*, 283–393.

———. "The Brazilian Economy, 1980–1994." In Bethell, *Brazil since 1930*, 395–429.

Abreu, Marcelo de Paiva, and Rogério L. F. Werneck. "The Brazilian Economy, 1994–2004: An Interim Assessment." In Bethell, *Brazil since 1930*, 431–54.

"A guerra ao turbante." *Veja*, March 23, 1988, 38–44.

Alencastro e Silva, José Antônio de. *Telecomunicações: Histórias para a história*. São Josê dos Pinhais: Editel, 1990.

Alves, Maria Helena Moreira. *Estado e oposição no Brasil (1964–1984)*. Translated by Clóvis Marques. Petrópolis, Rio de Janeiro: Vozes, 1984.

Alves, Maria Helena Moreira, and Philip Evanson. *Living in the Crossfire: Favela Residents, Drug Dealers, and Police Violence in Rio de Janeiro*. Philadelphia: Temple University Press, 2011.

Amano, Takao. *Assalto ao céu*. São Paulo: COM-ARTE, 2014.

Amaral, Ricardo Batista. *A vida quer é coragem: A trajetória de Dilma Rousseff, a primeira presidenta do Brasil*. Rio de Janeiro: Sextante, 2011.

Angelo, Michelly Ramos de. "O IRFED e a formação de profissionais brasileiros em *Desenvolvimento do Território*." In *Anais do XI seminário de história da cidade e do urbanismo*. Vitória, Espírito Santo: UFES, 2010.

Arantes, Rogério Bastos. "O Ministério Público e a corrupção política em São Paulo." In *Justiça e cidadania no Brasil*, edited by Maria Tereza Sadek, 15–61. Rio de Janeiro: Centro Edelstein de Pesquisas Sociais, 2009.

Araújo, Carlos Eduardo Moreira de. "Da casa de correção da corte ao Complexo Penitenciário da Frei Caneca: Um breve histórico do sistema prisional no Rio de Janeiro, 1834–2006." *Cidade Nova Revista*, no. 1 (2007): 147–61.

Arbex, Daniela. *Cova 312*. São Paulo: Geração Editorial, 2015.

Archdiocese of São Paulo. *Brasil: Nunca mais*. Petrópolis: Vozes, 1985.

Argolo, José A., Kátia Ribeiro, and Luiz Alberto M. Fortunato. *A direita explosiva no Brasil*. Rio de Janeiro: Mauad, 1996.

Assis, Charleston José de Sousa. "Fiscais do Sarney? Algumas considerações sobre a participação popular no Plano Cruzado." In *Não foi tempo perdido: Os anos 80 em debate*, edited by Samantha Viz Quadrat, 337–61. Rio de Janeiro: 7 Letras, 2014.

Athie, Myryam. "CPI-2001-PAS." São Paulo: Câmara Municipal de São Paulo, 2001.

Avelar, Idelber. "The June 2013 Uprisings and the Waning of Lulismo in Brazil: Of Antagonism, Contradiction, and Oxymoron." *Luso-Brazilian Review* 54, no. 1 (2017): 9–27.

Avritzer, Leonardo. *Impasses da democracia no Brasil*. Rio de Janeiro: Civilização Brasileira, 2016.

Balán, Manuel. "Surviving Corruption in Brazil: Lula's and Dilma's Success Despite Corruption Allegations, and Its Consequences." *Journal of Politics in Latin America* 6, no. 3 (2014): 67–93.

Bedê, Pablo Marins. *Acidente e morte de Juarez Antunes*. Documentary. 2013. https://www.youtube.com/watch?reload=9&v=WA2noWagkHo.

———. *A greve de 1984*. Documentary. 2013.

Berquó, Alberto. *O seqüestro dia a dia*. Rio de Janeiro: Nova Fronteira, 1997.

Berselli, Edmondo. "The Crisis and Transformation of Italian Politics." *Daedalus* 130, no. 3 (2001): 1–24.

Bertazzo, Juliana. "An Initial Survey of the Dilma Rousseff Administration in Brazil." *Critical Sociology* 38, no. 6 (2012): 889–92.

Bethell, Leslie, ed. *Brazil since 1930*. Vol. 9 of *The Cambridge History of Latin America*. Cambridge: Cambridge University Press, 2008.

Bethell, Leslie, and Celso Castro. "Politics in Brazil Under Military Rule, 1964–1985." In Bethell, *Brazil since 1930*, 165–230.

Bethell, Leslie, and Jairo Nicolau. "Politics in Brazil, 1985–2002." In Bethell, *Brazil since 1930*, 231–79.

Betto, Frei. *Against Principalities and Powers: Letters from a Brazilian Jail*. Translated by John Drury. Maryknoll, NY: Orbis Books, 1977.

———. *Batismo de sangue: Guerrilha e morte de Carlos Marighella*. 14th rev. and augmented ed. Rio de Janeiro: Rocco, 2006.

———. *Calendário do poder*. Rio de Janeiro: Rocco, 2007.

———. *Cartas da prisão, 1969–1973*. Rio de Janeiro: Agir, 2008.

———. "Obrigado, Lula." http://www.vermelho.org.br/noticia.php?id_noticia =143550.

Bierrenbach, Júlio de Sá. *Riocentro: Quais os responsáveis pela impunidade?* Rio de Janeiro: Domínio Público, 1996.

Borba, Maria, Natasha Felizi, and João Paulo Reys, eds. *Brasil em movimento: Reflexões a partir dos protestos de junho.* Rio de Janeiro: Rocco, 2014.

Bourne, Richard. *Lula of Brazil: The Story So Far.* Berkeley: University of California Press, 2008.

Braig, Marianne, Timothy J. Power, and Lucio Rennó. "Brazil 2015 and Beyond: The Aftermath of the 2014 Elections and Implications for Dilma's Second Term." *Latin American Research Review* 46, no. 3 (2015): 15–17.

Branford, Sue. "Working with Governments: The MST's Experience with the Cardoso and Lula Administrations." In *Challenging Social Inequality: The Landless Rural Workers Movement and Agrarian Reform in Brazil,* edited by Miguel Carter, 331–50. Durham, NC: Duke University Press, 2015.

Bresser-Pereira, Luiz Carlos. *A construção política do Brasil: Sociedade, economia e Estado desde a Independência.* 2nd ed. São Paulo: Editora 34, 2015.

Cabral, Otávio. *Dirceu: a biografia: Do movimento estudantil a Cuba, da guerrilha à clandestinidade, do PT ao poder, do palácio ao mensalão.* Rio de Janeiro: Record, 2013.

Cagnin, Rafael Fagundes, Daniela Magalhães Prates, Maria Cristina P. de Freitas, and Luís Fernando Novais. "A gestão macroeconômica do governo Dilma (2011 e 2012)." *Novos Estudos Cebrap,* no. 97 (November 2013): 169–85.

Caliman, Auro Augusto, ed. *Legislativo paulista: Parlamentares, 1835–2003.* São Paulo: Imprensa Oficial, 1998.

Cardoso, Fernando Henrique. *Accidental President of Brazil: A Memoir.* New York: Public Affairs, 2006.

———. *Diários da presidência, 1995–1996.* São Paulo: Companhia das Letras, 2015.

Cardoso, Lucileide Costa. "Revolução e resistência: Historiografia e luta armada no Brasil." *História: Revista da Faculdade de Letras da Universidade do Porto* 4 (2014): 33–49.

Carey, Elaine, ed. *Protests in the Streets: 1968 Across the Globe.* Indianapolis, IN: Hackett, 2016.

Carter, Miguel. "Epilogue. Broken Promise: The Land Reform Debacle under the PT Governments." In *Challenging Social Inequality: The Landless Rural Workers Movement and Agrarian Reform in Brazil,* 413–28. Durham: Duke University Press, 2015.

Carvalho, Luiz Maklouf. "As armas e os varões: A educação política e sentimental de Dilma Rousseff." *Piauí,* April 2009, 22–31.

———. *Mulheres que foram à luta armada.* São Paulo: Editora Globo, 1998.

Castañeda, Jorge G. *Utopia Unarmed: The Latin American Left after the Cold War.* New York: Knopf, 1993.

Castro, Fábio de, and Renata Motta. "Environmental Politics under Dilma: Changing Relations between the Civil Society and the State." *Latin American Research Review* 46, no. 3 (2015): 25–27.

Castro, Márcio Sampaio de. "Maltratados direitos fundamentais" *Valor Econômico*, January 19, 2007.

Castro, Ruy. *O anjo pornográfico: A vida de Nelson Rodrigues.* São Paulo: Companhia das Letras, 1992.

Chaliand, Gérard, and Arnaud Blin, eds. *The History of Terrorism: From Antiquity to al Qaeda.* Berkeley: University of California Press, 2007.

"Conjunto de documentos sobre a situação dos presos políticos em Ilha Grande." http://arquivosdaditadura.com.br/documento/galeria/conjunto -documentos-sobre-situacao-presos.

Conti, Mario Sergio. "Chutes para todo lado." *Piauí*, August 2013.

———. *Notícias do Planalto: A imprensa e Fernando Collor.* São Paulo: Companhia das Letras, 1999.

Correa, Cristiane. *Sonho grande: Como Jorge Paulo Lemann, Marcel Telles e Beto Sicupira revolucionaram o capitalismo brasileiro e conquistaram o mundo.* Rio de Janeiro: Primeira Pessoa, 2013.

Costa, Caio Túlio. *Cale-se.* São Paulo: A Girafa, 2003.

Costa, Celia Maria Leite, Dulce Chaves Pandolfi, and Kenneth Serbin, eds. *O bispo de Volta Redonda: Memórias de Dom Waldyr Calheiros.* Rio de Janeiro: Editora FGV, 2001.

Costa, Florência. "Capitalismo de resultados." *IstoÉ*, August 9, 2002.

Costa, Sérgio, Barbara Fritz, and Martina Sproll. "Dilma 2.0: From Economic Growth with Distribution to Stagnation and Increasing Inequalities?" *Latin American Research Review* 46, no. 3 (2015): 21–24.

Crenshaw, Martha. "How Terrorism Declines." *Terrorism and Political Violence* 3, no. 1 (1991): 69–87.

———, ed. *Terrorism in Context.* University Park: Pennsylvania State University Press, 1995.

D'Araujo, Maria Celina. *Governo Lula: Contornos sociais e políticos da elite do poder.* Rio de Janeiro: Centro de Pesquisa e Documentação de História Contemporânea do Brasil/Fundação Getúlio Vargas, 2007.

Da-Rin, Silvio, ed. *Hércules 56: O seqüestro do embaixador americano em 1969.* Rio de Janeiro: Jorge Zahar Editor, 2007.

Dayton, Bruce W., and Louis Kriesberg, eds. *Conflict Transformation and Peacebuilding: Moving from Violence to Sustainable Peace.* London: Routledge, 2009.

De Grazia, Giuseppina. "O movimento operário e as Associações de Trabalhadores em São Paulo." *Lutas Sociais*, no. 25-26 (2010-2011): 133–47.

Delfim Netto, Antonio. "O capitalismo não é uma coisa." *CartaCapital*, October 20, 2015.

Del Roio, José Luiz. *Zarattini: A paixão revolucionária*. São Paulo: Ícone Editora, 2006.

"Depoimento de Paulo Vannuchi." In *1964: Do golpe à democracia*, edited by Angela Alonso and Miriam Dolhnikoff, 359–80. São Paulo: Hedra, 2015.

Dias, Lia Ribeiro, and Patrícia Cornils. *Alencastro: O general das telecomunicações*. São Paulo: Plano Editorial, 2004.

Dinges, John. *The Condor Years: How Pinochet and His Alles Brought Terrorism to Three Continents*. New York: The New Press, 2005.

Doimo, Ana Maria. "Igreja e movimentos sociais pós-70 no Brasil." In *Catolicismo: Cotidiano e movimentos*, edited by Pierre Sanchis, 275–308. São Paulo: Edições Loyola, 1992.

Eakin, Marshall C. *Brazil: The Once and Future Country*. New York: St. Martin's Press, 1997.

Expedito Filho. "Autópsia da sombra." *Veja*, November 18, 1992, 20–32.

———. "Memória do terror." *Veja*, July 31, 1996, 7–8, 10.

Fernandes Júnior, Ottoni. *O baú do guerrilheiro: Memórias da luta armada urbana no Brasil*. Rio de Janeiro: Record, 2004.

Fernandes, Maria Esther, ed. *A cidade e seus limites: As contradições do urbano na "Califórnia Brasileira."* São Paulo and Ribeirão Preto: Annablume; FAPESP; Unaerp, 2004.

Ferreira, Jorge, and Daniel Aarão Reis, eds. *Revolução e democracia (1964– . . .)*. Rio de Janeiro: Civilização Brasileira, 2007.

Fico, Carlos. *Como eles agiam: Os subterrâneos da ditadura militar: espionagem e polícia política*. Rio de Janeiro: Record, 2001.

———. *O grande irmão: O governo dos Estados Unidos e a ditadura militar brasileira, da Operação Brother Sam aos anos de chumbo*. Rio de Janeiro: Civilização Brasileira, 2008.

———. *Reinventando o otimismo: Ditadura, propaganda e imaginário social no Brasil*. Rio de Janeiro: Editora Fundação Getúlio Vargas, 1997.

Figueiredo, Lucas. *Olho por olho: Os livros secretos da ditadura*. Rio de Janeiro: Record, 2009.

Figueiredo, Ney. "Os empresários e os movimentos de rua." In *Junho de 2013: A sociedade enfrenta o estado*, edited by Rubens Figueiredo, 61–72. São Paulo: Summus Editorial, 2014.

Figueiredo, Rubens. "Apresentação." In Figueiredo, *Junho de 2013*, 7–13.

———. "A 'espiral do silêncio' e a escalada da insatisfação." In Figueiredo, *Junho de 2013*, 23–38.

———, ed. *Junho de 2013: A sociedade enfrenta o estado*. São Paulo: Summus Editorial, 2014.

Fon Filho, Aton, and Suzana Figueiredo. "Revistando a Anistia—Os fantasmas do passado, os temores do presente, as sombras sobre o futuro." In *Direitos Humanos no Brasil 2011: Relatório da Rede Social de Justiça e Direitos Humanos*, edited by Tatiana Merlino and Maria Luisa Mendonça, 135–41. São Paulo: Rede Social de Justiça e Direitos Humanos, 2011.

Freire, Paulo. *Pedagogy of the Oppressed*. Translated by Myra Bergman Ramos. New York: Herder and Herder, 1970.

French, John D. *Drowning in Laws: Labor Law and Brazilian Political Culture*. Chapel Hill: University of North Carolina Press, 2004.

———. "Lula, the 'New Unionism,' and the PT: How Factory Workers Came to Change the World, or At Least Brazil." *Latin American Politics and Society* 51, no. 4 (2009): 157–69.

French, John D., and Alexandre Fortes. "Nurturing Hope, Deepening Democracy, and Combating Inequalities in Brazil: Lula, the Workers' Party, and Dilma Rousseff's 2010 Election as President." *Labor: Studies in Working-Class History of the Americas* 9, no. 1 (2012): 7–28.

Gabeira, Fernando. *O que é isso, companheiro?* 2nd rev. ed. São Paulo: Companhia das Letras, 1996.

Gantois, Gustavo, and Mariana Londres. "Era Lula cria mais empregos que governos FHC, Itamar, Collor e Sarney juntos." *R7*, November 18, 2010.

Gaspari, Elio. *As ilusões armadas*. Vol. 1, *A ditadura envergonhada*; Vol. 2, *A ditadura escancarada*. São Paulo: Companhia das Letras, 2002.

———. "*O que é isso, companheiro?* O operário se deu mal." In Reis Filho and Ridenti, *Versões e ficções*, 111–15.

———. *O sacerdote e o feiticeiro*. Vol. 3, *A ditadura derrotada*; Vol. 4, *A ditadura encurralada*. São Paulo: Companhia das Letras, 2003, 2004.

Gomes, Cilene. "Telecomunicações, informática e informação e a remodelação do território brasileiro." In *O Brasil: Território e sociedade no início do século XXI*, edited by Milton Santos and María Laura Silveira, 345–56. Rio de Janeiro: Record, 2001.

Gorender, Jacob. *Combate nas trevas: A esquerda brasileira, das ilusões perdidas à luta armada*. 5th rev. and augmented ed. São Paulo: Ática, 1998.

Gouget, Gisele, Lorenzo Aldé, and Adrianna Setemy. "Quércia, Orestes." In *Dicionário Histórico-Biográfico Brasileiro*. Rio de Janeiro: Centro de Pesquisa e de Documentação de História Contemporânea do Brasil, 2010.

"Governo Lula criou 2,464 milhões de empregos em 4 anos." *O Estado de S. Paulo*, December 24, 2006.

Grandin, Greg. *Fordlandia: The Rise and Fall of Henry Ford's Forgotten Jungle City*. New York: Metropolitan Books, 2009.

Green, James N. *Exile within Exiles: Herbert Daniel, Gay Brazilian Revolutionary.* Durham, NC: Duke University Press, 2018.

———. *We Cannot Remain Silent: Opposition to the Brazilian Military Dictatorship in the United States.* Durham, NC: Duke University Press, 2010.

———. "'Who Is the Macho Who Wants to Kill Me?' Male Homosexuality, Revolutionary Maculinity, and the Brazilian Armed Struggle of the 1960s and 1970s." *Hispanic American Historical Review* 92, no. 3 (2012): 437–69.

Gullo, Carla, and Maria Laura Neves. "A mulher do presidente." *Marie Claire*, April 2009.

Hanlon, Valerie Elbrick. "'They've Got Your Father.'" *Washingtonian Magazine*, April 1998, 70.

History of the Bureau of Diplomatic Security of the United States Department of State. Washington, DC: United States Department of State, Bureau of Diplomatic Security, 2011.

Hite, Katherine. *When the Romance Ended: Leaders of the Chilean Left, 1968–1998.* New York: Columbia University Press, 2000.

Hochstetler, Kathryn. "Democratizing Pressures from Below? Social Movements in the New Brazilian Democracy." In *Democratic Brazil: Actors, Institutions, and Processes,* edited by Peter Kingstone and Timothy J. Power, 162–82. Pittsburgh: University of Pittsburgh Press, 2000.

Hoffman, Bruce. "Defining Terrorism." *Social Science Record* 24, no. 1 (1986): 6–7.

Holmes, Ryan. "The Future of Social Media? Forget About the U.S., Look to Brazil." *Forbes*, September 12, 2013.

Huggins, Martha K. *Political Policing: The United States and Latin America.* Durham, NC: Duke University Press, 1998.

Hunter, Wendy. "The 2010 Elections in Brazil." *Electoral Studies*, no. 31 (2012): 225–28.

———. *The Transformation of The Workers' Party in Brazil, 1989–2009.* New York: Cambridge University Press, 2010.

Hunter, Wendy, and Timothy J. Power. "Rewarding Lula: Executive Power, Social Policy, and the Brazilian Elections of 2006." *Latin American Politics and Society* 49, no. 1 (2007): 1–30.

Ioris, Rafael R. *Transforming Brazil: A History of National Development in the Postwar Era.* New York: Routledge, 2014.

Instituto Cidadania, ed., "Projeto Juventude: Documento de conclusão." São Paulo: Instituto Cidadania, 2004.

Izique, Cláudia. "Não foi só pelos 20 centavos." In Figueiredo, *Junho de 2013,* 15–22.

Jones, Seth G. *How Terrorist Groups End: Lessons for Countering Al Qa'ida.* Santa Monica, CA: Rand, 2008.

José, Emiliano. *Carlos Marighella: O inimigo número um da ditadura militar.* São Paulo: Sol & Chuva, 1997.

Kahn, Tulio. "A segurança pública e as manifestações de junho de 2013." In Figueiredo, *Junho de 2013*, 115–31.

Keck, Margaret. *The Workers' Party and Democratization in Brazil.* New Haven, CT: Yale University Press, 1992.

Kehl, Maria Rita, and Paulo Vannuchi. "Madre Cristina." In *Rememória: Entrevistas sobre o Brasil do século XX*, edited by Ricardo de Azevedo and Flamrion Maués, 153–71. São Paulo: Editora Fundação Perseu Abramo, 1997.

Kingstone, Peter. *The Political Economy of Latin America: Reflections on Neoliberalism and Development.* New York: Routledge, 2011.

Kingstone, Peter R. "Muddling Through Gridlock: Economic Policy Performance, Business Responses, and Democratic Sustainability." In *Democratic Brazil: Actors, Institutions, and Processes*, edited by Peter R. Kingstone and Timothy J. Power, 185–203. Pittsburgh: University of Pittsburgh Press, 2000.

Kingstone, Peter R., and Aldo F. Ponce. "From Cardoso to Lula: The Triumph of Pragmatism in Brazil." In *Leftist Governments in Latin America: Successes and Shortcomings*, edited by Kurt Weyland, Raúl L. Madrid and Wendy Hunter, 98–123. Cambridge: Cambridge University Press, 2010.

Koike, Beth. "Se todas fossem como você." *CartaCapital*, May 24, 2000, 56.

Kowarick, Lúcio, and Clara Ant. "Cortiço: Cem anos de promiscuidade." *Novos Estudos Cebrap* 1, no. 2 (1982): 59–64.

Krauss, Ellis S. *Japanese Radicals Revisited: Student Protest in Postwar Japan.* Berkeley: University of California Press, 1974.

Lamounier, Bolívar, and Isabel Vericat. "Empresarios, partidos y democratización en Brasil (1974–1990)." *Revista Mexicana de Sociología* 54, no. 1 (1992): 77–97.

Langguth, A. J. *Hidden Terrors: The Truth About U.S. Police Operations in Latin America.* New York: Pantheon, 1978.

Langland, Victoria. *Speaking of Flowers: Student Movements and the Making and Remembering of 1968 in Military Brazil.* Durham, NC: Duke University Press, 2013.

Laqueur, Walter. *The Age of Terrorism.* Boston: Little, Brown and Company, 1987.

Leite, Márcia de Paula. "As aventuras de Juarez." *Lua Nova* 1, no. 3 (1984): 22–23.

Leite, Paulo Moreira. "O que foi aquilo, companheiro." In Reis Filho and Ridenti, *Versões e ficções*, 51–60.

Leoni, Brigitte Hersant. *Fernando Henrique Cardoso: O Brasil do possível.* Translated by Dora Rocha. Rio de Janeiro: Nova Fronteira, 1997.

Lesser, Jeffrey. *A Discontented Diaspora: Japanese Brazilians and the Meanings of Ethnic Militancy, 1960–1980.* Durham, NC: Duke University Press, 2007.

Lessing, Doris. *The Good Terrorist.* London: Jonathan Cape, 1985.

Litkewski, Chaim. *Cidadão Boilesen.* Documentary. Brazil, 2009. https://www.youtube.com/watch?v=UP7CYhmK-hs.

Lodge, Tom. "Revolution Deferred: From Armed Struggle to Liberal Democracy." In *Conflict Transformation and Peacebuilding: Moving from Violence to Sustainable Peace*, edited by Bruce W. Dayton and Louis Kriesberg, 156–71. London: Routledge, 2009.

The Lords of the Rings. In *Real Sports with Bryant Gumbel*, documentary. HBO, 2016.

Love, Joseph L. "The Lula Government in Historical Perspective." In *Brazil under Lula: Economy, Politics, and Society under the Worker-President*, edited by Joseph L. Love and Werner Baer, 305–15. New York: Palgrave Macmillan, 2009.

Macedo, Roberto. "Uma visão econômica e política dos protestos juninos." In Figueiredo, *Junho de 2013*, 39–60.

Magalhães, Mário. *Marighella: O guerrilheiro que incendiou o mundo.* São Paulo: Compania das Letras, 2012.

Marsh, Charles. *Strange Glory: A Life of Dietrich Bonhoeffer.* New York: Vintage, Kindle ed., 2014.

Martinelli, Renato. *Um grito de coragem: Memórias da luta armada.* São Paulo: COM-ARTE, 2006.

Martinez, Paulo Henrique. "O Partido dos Trabalhadores e a conquista do estado, 1980–2005." In *História do marxismo no Brasil: Partidos e movimentos após os anos 1960*, edited by Marcelo Ridenti and Danial Aarão Reis, 239–88. Campinas, São Paulo: Editora da UNICAMP, 2007.

Martinho, Francisco Carlos Palomanes. "A armadilha do novo: Luiz Inácio Lula da Silva e uma esquerda que se imaginou diferente." In Ferreira and Reis, *Revolução e democracia (1964– . . .)*, 541–62.

Martins, Franklin. "As duas mortes de Jonas." In Reis Filho and Ridenti, *Versões e ficções*, 117–24.

Maués, Flamarion, and Zilah Wendel Abramo, eds. *Pela democracia, contra o arbítrio: A oposição democrática, do golpe de 1964 à campanha das Diretas Já.* São Paulo: Editora Fundação Perseu Abramo, 2006.

McCann, Bryan. *The Throes of Democracy: Brazil since 1989.* London: Zed Books, 2008.

Meisner, Maurice. *Mao Zedong.* Malden, MA: Polity, 2007.

Melo, Marcus André. "Political Malaise and the New Politics of Accountability: Representation, Taxation, and the Social Contract." In Schneider, *New Order and Progress*, 268–97.

Merari, Ariel. "Terrorism as a Strategy of Insurgency." In *The History of Terrorism: From Antiquity to Al Qaeda*, edited by Gérard Chalian and Arnaud Blin, 12–51. Berkeley: University of California Press, 2007.

Mezarobba, Glenda. "Justiça de transição e a comissão da verdade." In *1964: Do golpe à democracia*, edited by Angela Alonso and Miriam Dolhnikoff, 343–58. São Paulo: Hedra, 2015.

———. "Lies Engraved on Marble and Truths Lost Forever." *Sur Journal* 12, no. 21 (2015): 97–104.

———. "Um acerto de contas com o futuro: A anistia e suas conseqüências— um estudo do caso brasileiro." Master's thesis, Universidade de São Paulo, 2003.

Miguel, Luis Felipe. "A democracia domesticada: Bases antidemocráticas do pensamento democrático contemporâneo." *DADOS* 45, no. 3 (2002): 483–511.

Mir, Luís. *A revolução impossível: A esquerda e a luta armada no Brasil*. São Paulo: Editora Best Seller, 1994.

Morgenstern, Flavio. *Por trás da máscara*. Rio de Janeiro: Record, 2015.

Movimento dos Trabalhadores Rurais Sem Terra. *Assassinatos no campo: Crime e impunidade, 1964–1985*. São Paulo: Global, 1987.

Murat, Lúcia. *Que Bom Te Ver Viva*. Documentary. 1989.

Musacchio, Aldo, and Sergio G. Lazzarini. "The Reinvention of State Capitalism in Brazil." In Schneider, *New Order and Progress*, 107–33.

Mytelka, Lynn Krieger. "The Telecommunications Equipment Industrty in Brazil and Korea." In *Competition, Innovation and Competitiveness in Developing Countries*, edited by Lynn Krieger Mytelka, 115–61. Paris: Development Centre, Organisation for Economic Co-operation and Development, 1999.

Naftali, Timothy, ed. *John F. Kennedy: The Great Crises*. Edited by Philip Zelikow and Ernest May. 3 vols. The Presidential Recordings. New York: W. W. Norton, 2001.

Nêumanne, José. *Erundina: A mulher que veio com a chuva*. Rio de Janeiro: Espaço e Tempo, 1989.

Nova, Cristiane, and Jorge Nóvoa, eds. *Marighella: O homem por trás do mito*. São Paulo: Editora UNESP, 1999.

Nunberg, Barbara, and Regina Silvia Pacheco. "Public Management Incongruity in 21st Century Brazil." In Schneider, *New Order and Progress*, 134–61.

Nunn, A., E. Da Fonseca, and S. Gruskin. "Changing Global Essential Medicines Norms to Improve Access to AIDS Treatment: Lessons from Brazil." *Global Public Health* 4, no. 2 (2009): 131–49.

Nylen, William R. "The Making of a Loyal Opposition: The Workers' Party (PT) and the Consolidation of Democracy in Brazil." In *Democractic Brazil: Actors, Institutions and Processes*, edited by Peter R. Kingstone and Timothy J. Power, 126–43. Pittsburgh: University of Pittsburgh Press, 2000.

"O porão iluminado." *Veja*, July 24, 1985, 108–10.

Oppenheimer, Andrés. *Saving the Americas*. Translated by Tanya Huntington. Mexico City: Random House Mondadori, 2007.

Paiva, Vanilda. *Paulo Freire e o nacionalismo desenvolvimentista*. 2nd ed. São Paulo: Graal, 2000.

Paraná, Denise. *Lula, o filho do Brasil*. São Paulo: Editora Fundação Perseu Abramo, 2002.

Paulo, Archdiocese of São. *Brasil: Nunca mais*. Petrópolis: Vozes, 1985.

Paz, Carlos Eugênio Sarmento Coêlho da. *Nas trilhas da ALN: Memórias romanceadas*. Rio de Janeiro: Bertrand Brasil, 1997.

———. *Viagem à luta armada: Memórias romanceadas*. Rio de Janeiro: Civilização Brasileira, 1996.

Pedroso Júnior, Antonio. *Márcio, o guerrilheiro: Vida e morte de um jovem preparado para vencer*. Rio de Janeiro: Papel Virtual, 2003.

Pereira, Anthony W. "The Dialectics of the Brazilian Military Regime's Political Trials." *Luso-Brazilian Review* 41, no. 2 (2005): 162–83.

———. "Is the Brazilian State 'Patrimonial'?" *Latin American Perspectives* 43, no. 2 (2016): 135–52.

———. "'Persecution and Farce': The Origins and Transformation of Brazil's Political Trials, 1964–1979." *Latin American Research Review* 33, no. 1 (1998): 43–66.

Pereira, Camila Vital Nunes. "The Alleviation of Poverty by the Bolsa Família Program, Brazil." Ph.D. diss., Howard University, 2014.

Pereira, Sérgio Martins. "CUT e Força Sindical em Volta redonda: Modelos de sindicalismo ou trajetórias de lideranças?" *Enfoques* 5, no. 2 (2006): 103–19.

Pierucci, Antônio Flávio, and Marcelo Coutinho de Lima. "São Paulo 92, a vitória da direita." *Novos Estudos CEBRAP*, no. 35 (1993): 94–99.

Pimenta, Edileuza, and Edson Teixeira. *Virgílio Gomes da Silva: De retirante a guerrilheiro*. São Paulo: Plena Editorial, 2009.

Pinheiro, Paulo Sérgio. Preface to *Relatório Nacional sobre os Direitos Humanos no Brasil*, 9–13. São Paulo: Núcleo de Estudos da Violência, University of São Paulo, 2010.

Pinto, José Nêumanne. "A multidão poderosa virou plebe ignara e tudo ficou como dantes na República de Abrantes." In Figueiredo, *Junho de 2013*, 99–114.

Pires, Roberto. "The Midlife of Participatory Institutions in Brazil." *Latin American Research Review* 46, no. 3 (2015): 28–30.

Pitts, Bryan. "The Audacity to Strong-Arm the Generals: Paulo Maluf and the 1978 São Paulo Gubernatorial Contest." *Histpanic American Historical Review* 92, no. 3 (2012): 471–505.

Plano estratégico de Belo Horizonte 2030: A cidade que queremos. Belo Horizonte: Prefeitura de Belo Horizonte, 2010.

Politi, Maurice. *Resistência atrás das grades.* São Paulo: Plena Editorial, 2009.

Power, Timothy J. "Centering Democracy? Ideological Cleavages and Convergence in the Brazilian Political Class." In *Democratic Brazil Revisited*, edited by Peter Kingstone and Timothy J. Power, 81–106. Pittsburgh: University of Pittsburgh Press, 2008.

———. "Continuity in a Changing Brazil: The Transition from Lula to Dilma." In *Brazil under The Workers' Party: Continuity and Change from Lula to Dilma*, edited by Fábio Castro, Kees Koonings, and Marianne Wiesebron, 10–35. New York: Palgrave Macmillan, 2014.

———. *The Political Right in Postauthoritarian Brazil: Elites, Institutions, and Democratization.* University Park: Pennsylvania State University Press, 2000.

———. "The Reduction of Poverty and Inequality in Brazil: Political Causes, Political Consequences." In Schneider, *New Order and Progress*, 212–37.

Priest, Tyler. "Petrobras in the History of Offshore Oil." In Schneider, *New Order and Progress*, 53–77.

"Projeto Juventude: Resumo das intervenções—13/6/2003." Instituto Cidadania, 2003.

Reis, Daniel Aarão. "O Partido dos Trabalhadores: Trajetória, metamorfoses, perspectivas." In Ferreira and Reis, *Revolução e democracia (1964– . . .)*, 503–40.

Reis Filho, Daniel Aarão, and Marcelo Ridenti, eds. *Versões e ficções: O seqüestro da história.* São Paulo: Editora Fundação Perseu Abramo, 1997.

Relatório Nacional sobre os Direitos Humanos no Brasil. São Paulo: Núcleo de Estudos da Violência, University of São Paulo, 2010.

Reynolds, David S. *John Brown, Abolitionist: The Man Who Killed Slavery, Sparked the Civil War, and Seeded Civil Rights.* New York: Vintage, Kindle ed., 2009.

Ribeiro, Maria Cláudia Badan. "Memória, história e sociedade: a contribuição da narrativa de Carlos Eugênio Paz." Master's thesis, Universidade Estadual de Campinas, 2005.

Ridenti, Marcelo. *Brasilidade revolucionária*. São Paulo: Editora UNESP, 2010.

———. *Em busca do povo brasileiro: Artistas da revolução: do CPC à era da TV.* Rio de Janeiro: Record, 2000.

———. "Esquerdas armadas urbanas, 1964–1974." In *História do marxismo no Brasil: Partidos e movimentos após os anos 1960*, edited by Marcelo Ridenti and Danial Aarão Reis, 105–51. Campinas, São Paulo: Editora da Unicamp, 2007.

Rocha, Heber Silveira. "Juventude e políticas públicas: Formação de agenda, elaboração de alternativas e embates no Governo Lula." Master's thesis, Fundação Getúlio Vargas, São Paulo, 2012.

Rocha, Leonel. "Os problemas do amigo de Dilma." *Época*, February 26, 2010.

Rodrigues-Silveira, Rodrigo. "Intergovernmental Relations and State Capacity in Brazil: Challenges for Dilma's Second Term and Beyond." *Latin American Research Review* 46, no. 3 (2015): 31–33.

Rohter, Larry. *Brazil on the Rise: The Story of a Country Transformed.* New York: Palgrave Macmillan, 2010.

Rollemberg, Denise. "Carlos Marighella e Carlos Lamarca: memórias de dois revolucionários." In Ferreira and Reis, *Revolução e democracia (1964– . . .)*, 73–97.

———. "Clemente." In *Perfis cruzados: Trajetórias e militância política no Brasil*, edited by Beatriz Kushnir, 73–84. Rio de Janeiro: Imago, 2002.

———. "Debate no exílio: em busca da renovação." In *História do marxismo no Brasil: Partidos e movimentos após os anos 1969*, edited by Marcelo Ridenti, and Daniel Aarão Reis, 291–339. Campinas, São Paulo: Editora da Unicamp, 2007.

———. *Exílio: Entre raízes e radares.* Rio de Janeiro: Record, 1999.

Rosenfeld, Denis. "Entre a libertação e a usurpação." In Figueiredo, *Junho de 2013*, 133–44.

Salem, Helena. "Ficção é julgada sob as lentes da história." In Reis Filho and Ridenti, *Versões e ficções*, 71–92.

Salles, João Moreira. *Atos: A campanha pública de Lula.* Documentary. 2006.

———. *Entreatos: Lula a 30 dias do poder.* Documentary. 2004.

Sallum, Brasilio, Jr. *O impeachment de Fernando Collor: Sociologia de uma crise.* São Paulo: Editora 34, 2015.

Samuels, David. "Financiamento de campanha e eleições no Brasil: O que podemos aprender com o 'caixa um' e propostas de reforma." In *Reforma política e cidadania*, edited by Maria Victoria Benevides, Paulo Vannuchi, and Fábio Kerche, 364–91. São Paulo: Editora Fundação Perseu Abramo, 2003.

Santos, Milton, and María Laura Silveira. "A constituição do meio técnico-científico-informacional e a renovação da materialidade no território." In Santos and Silveira, *O Brasil*, 55–92.

———. "Do meio natural ao meio técnico-científico-informacional." In Santos and Silveira, *O Brasil*, 23–53.

———, eds. *O Brasil: Território e sociedade no início do século XXI.* Rio de Janeiro: Record, 2001.

Schmalz, Stefan. "The Brazilian Economy: From the Crisis of Import Substitution to the Programa de Aceleração do Crescimento." In *The Political System of Brazil*, edited by Dana de la Fontaine and Thomas Stehnken, 265–81. Berlin: Springer, 2016.

Schneider, Ben Ross. *Business Politics and the State in Twentieth-Century Latin America.* Cambridge: Cambridge University Press, 2004.

———. Introduction to *New Order and Progress*, 1–23.

———, ed. *New Order and Progress: Development and Democracy in Brazil.* New York: Oxford University Press, 2016.

Schneider, Nina. "Breaking the 'Silence' of the Military Regime: New Politics of Memory in Brazil." *Bulletin of Latin American Research* 30, no. 2 (2011): 198–212.

Schneider, Ronald M. *"Order and Progress": A Political History of Brazil.* Boulder, CO: Westview, 1991.

Secco, Lincoln. *História do PT.* 4th ed. Cotia: Ateliê Editorial, 2015.

Secretaria Especial dos Direitos Humanos. *Brasil direitos humanos, 2008: A realidade do país aos 60 anos da Declaração Universal.* Brasília: SEDH, 2008.

———. *Direito à memória e à verdade: Comissão Especial sobre Mortos e Desaparecidos Políticos.* Brasília: Secretaria Especial dos Direitos Humanos da Presidência da República, 2007.

Serbin, Kenneth P. "Collor's Impeachment and the Struggle for Change." *North-South Focus* 2, no. 2 (1993).

———. *Diálogos na sombra: Bispos e militares, tortura e justiça social na ditadura.* Translated by Carlos Eduardo Lins da Silva and Maria Cecília de Sá Porto. São Paulo: Companhia das Letras, 2001.

———. "Mainstreaming the Revolutionaries: National Liberating Action and the Shift from Resistance to Democracy in Brazil, 1964–Present." In *Conflict Transformation and Peacebuilding: Moving from Violence to Sustainable Peace*, edited by Bruce W. Dayton and Louis Kriesberg, 204–19. London: Routledge, 2009.

———. *Needs of the Heart: A Cultural and Social History of Brazil's Clergy and Seminaries.* Notre Dame, IN: University of Notre Dame Press, 2006.

———. *Secret Dialogues: Church–State Relations, Torture, and Social Justice in Authoritarian Brazil.* Pittsburgh: University of Pittsburgh Press, 2000.

Serra, José. "The Political Economy of the Brazilian Struggle against AIDS." In *Institute for Advanced Study Friends Forum, Paper No. 17*. Princeton, NJ: Princeton University, 2004.

Service, Robert. *Stalin: A Biography*. Cambridge, MA: Belknap, 2005.

Setti, Ricardo. "Com 11 milhões de votos, Aloysio Nunes (PSDB) é o senador mais votado da história." *Veja Online*, October 3, 2010.

Silva, Hélio. *A vez e a voz dos vencidos*. Petrópolis: Vozes, 1988.

Silva, Edson Teixeira da, Jr. "Um combate ao silêncio: A Ação Libertadora Nacional (ALN) e a repressão política." Ph.D. diss., Universidade Federal Fluminense, 2005.

Silva, Edson Teixeira da, Jr., Ivanilde de Sousa e Silva, Luis Carlos Castilho, Priscila Silveira, and Roosevelt Bruno de Souza Chrisóstimo. "'A greve continua!': Algumas considerações historiográficas sobre os movimentos grevistas de Volta Redonda." *Cadernos UniFOA*, no. 7 (2008): 24–38.

Silva, Luiz Henrique de Castro. "O revolucionário da convicção: Joaquim Câmara Ferreira, o Velho Zinho." Master's thesis, Universidade Federal do Rio de Janeiro, 2008.

Silva, Luiz Inácio Lula da. "Apresentação." In *Reforma política e cidadania*, edited by Maria Victoria Benevides, Paulo Vannuchi, and Fábio Kerche, 9–12. São Paulo: Editora Fundação Perseu Abramo, 2003.

Singer, André. *Os sentidos do Lulismo: Reforma gradual e pacto conservador*. São Paulo: Companhia das Letras, 2012.

Skidmore, Thomas E. *Politics in Brazil, 1930–1964: An Experiment in Democracy*. New York: Oxford University Press, 1967.

Soares, Luiz Eduardo. *Rio de Janeiro: Histórias de vida e morte*. São Paulo: Companhia das Letras, 2015.

Soares, Tufi Machado, Maria Eugénia Ferrão, and Cláudio de Albuquerque Marques. "Análise da evasão no ProJovem Urbano: Uma abordagem através do Modelo de Regressão Logística Multinível." *Ensaio: Avaliação e Políticas Públicas em Educação* 19, no. 73 (2011): 841–60.

Sorj, Bernardo. "Entre o local e o global." In Figueiredo, *Junho de 2013*, 87–98.

Souza, Percival de. *Autópsia do medo: Vida e morte do delegado Sérgio Paranhos Fleury*. São Paulo: Editora Globo, 2000.

Spektor, Matias. *18 dias: Quando Lula e FHC se uniram para conquistar o apoio de Bush*. Rio de Janeiro: Objetiva, 2014.

Tassinari, Ulysses. "Comissão Parlamentar de Inquérito constituída pelo Ato nº 56, de 2014, com a finalidade de investigar as violações dos direitos humanos e demais ilegalidades ocorridas no âmbito das Universidades do Estado de São Paulo ocorridas nos chamados 'trotes,' festas e no seu cotidiano acadêmico. Relatório Final." São Paulo: Assembleia Legislativa do Estado de São Paulo, 2015.

Teixeira, Marco Antônio C. "Diagnóstico de conflitos sócio-ambientais na cidade de São Paulo." In *Cadernos Cedec* 45. São Paulo: Cedec, 1995.

"Telegram from the Embassy in Guatemala to the Department of State." In *Foreign Relations of the United States, 1964–1968*, edited by Under Secretary for Public Diplomacy and Public Affairs U.S. Department of State, Bureau of Public Affairs, Document 114. Washington, DC: U.S. Department of State, 2004.

Tognozzi, Marcelo S. "A força das redes sociais." In Figueiredo, *Junho de 2013*, 73–86.

Torres, André. *Exílio na Ilha Grande*. Petrópolis: Vozes, 1978.

Tuma Júnior, Romeu. *Assassinato de reputações: Um crime de estado*. Rio de Janeiro: Topbooks, 2013.

Ustra, Carlos Alberto Brilhante. *A verdade sufocada: A história que a esquerda não quer que o Brasil conheça*. Brasília: Editora Ser, 2006.

———. *Rompendo o silêncio*. Brasília: Editerra, 1987.

U.S. Department of State. "Brazil." http://www.state.gov/j/drl/rls/hrrpt/2005 /61718.htm.

Vannucchi, Aldo. *Alexandre Vannucchi Leme: Jovem, estudante, morto pela ditadura*. São Paulo: Contexto, 2014.

Vannuchi, Paulo. "Brasil 2002: Como se construiu a vitória do PT." Unpublished paper, 2002.

———. "Democracia, liberalismo, socialismo e a contribuição de Norberto Bobbio." Master's thesis, Universidade de São Paulo, 2001.

———. "Direitos humanos e o fim do esquecimento." In *10 anos de governos pós-neoliberais no Brasil: Lula e Dilma*, edited by Emir Sader, 337–59. São Paulo and Rio de Janeiro: Boitempo and FLACSO Brasil, 2013.

Veiga, Sandra Mayrink, and Isaque Fonseca. *Volta Redonda, entre aço e as armas*. Petrópolis: Vozes, 1990.

Ventura, Zuenir. *1968: O que fizemos de nós*. São Paulo: Editora Planeta do Brasil, 2008.

Villa, Marco Antonio. *Uma país partido: 2014—a eleição mais suja da história*. São Paulo: LeYa, 2014.

Villaméa, Luiza. "Companheiras de armas." *IstoÉ*, June 29, 2005.

"Votação da maioridade penal na Câmara pode levar à retomada do debate no Senado." *Veja*, online edition, April 4, 2015.

Walker, Robert, Stephen Perz, Eugenio Arima, and Cynthia Simmons. "The Transamazon Highway: Past, Present, Future." In *Engineering Earth: The Impacts of Megaengineering Projects*, edited by Stanley D. Brunn, 569–99. Dordrecht: Springer, 2011.

Werneck, Felipe. "Juiz reconhece que havia tortura de presos políticos." *Exame
    .com*, July 31, 2014. https://exame.abril.com.br/brasil/juiz-reconhece-que
    -havia-tortura-de-presos-politicos/.
Weschler, Lawrence. *A Miracle, a Universe: Settling Accounts with Torturers.* 2nd
    ed. Chicago: University of Chicago Press, 1998.
Wolfe, Joel. *Autos and Progress: The Brazilian Search for Modernity.* New York:
    Cambridge University Press, 2010.

INDEX

Page numbers followed by *f* indicate figures.

KENNETH P. SERBIN is professor of history at the University of San Diego and author of *Needs of the Heart: A Social and Cultural History of Brazil's Clergy and Seminaries* (University of Notre Dame Press, 2006) and *Secret Dialogues: Church-State Relations, Torture, and Social Justice in Authoritarian Brazil*.

Lightning Source UK Ltd.
Milton Keynes UK
UKHW022038120719
346008UK00003B/47/P